FINE WINE
EDITIONS

THE FINEST WINES OF
BORDEAUX

A Regional Guide to the Best Châteaux
and Their Wines

JAMES LAWTHER MW

Foreword by Hugh Johnson | Photography by Jon Wyand

UNIVERSITY OF CALIFORNIA PRESS
Berkeley | Los Angeles

University of California Press,
one of the most distinguished university presses in the United States,
enriches lives around the world by advancing scholarship
in the humanities, social sciences, and natural sciences.
Its activities are supported by the UC Press Foundation and by
philanthropic contributions from individuals and institutions.
For more information, visit www.ucpress.edu

First published in
North America by
University of California Press
Berkeley and Los Angeles, California

Fine Wine Editions
Publisher Sara Morley
General Editor Neil Beckett
Editor David Williams
Subeditor David Tombesi-Walton
Editorial Assistant Clare Belbin
Map Editor Jeremy Wilkinson
Maps Tom Coulson, Encompass Graphics, Hove, UK
Indexer Ann Marangos
Americanizer Christine Heilman
Production Nikki Ingram

Library of Congress Control Number : 2010921498

ISBN 978-0-520-26657-5 (paper : alk. paper)

Manufactured in China

10 9 8 7 6 5 4 3 2 1
16 15 14 13 12 11 10

Contents

Foreword

by Hugh Johnson

Fine wines detach themselves from the rest not by their pretensions but by their conversation—the conversation, that is, that they provoke and stimulate, even, I sometimes think, by joining in themselves.

Is this too surreal a thought? Don't you exchange ideas with a truly original, authentic, coherent wine? You are just putting the decanter down for the second time. You have admired its colour, remarked on a note of new oak now in decline and a ripe blackcurrant smell growing by the minute, when a tang of iodine interrupts you, the voice of the sea as clear as if you had just parked your car on the beach and opened the door. Picture the Gironde, the wine is saying. You know the slope with its pale stones and its long gray view. I am Latour. Keep me on your tongue and I will explain everything: my grapes, the sun I missed in August, and the baking September days up to harvest. Is my strength draining away? Then I am old, but all the more eloquent; you see my weak points now, but my character is clearer than ever.

He who has ears to hear, let him hear. The vast majority of the world's wines are like French cartoons, *sans paroles*. Fine wines are thoroughbreds with form and mettle, even on their off days or when they are outrun. If a seemingly disproportionate number of words and, naturally, money are lavished on them, it is because they set the pace. What do you aspire to without a model? And far from being futile, aspiration has given us, and continues to give us, more thoroughbreds, more conversation, and more seductive voices to beguile us.

Just 20 or 30 years ago, the wine world was a plain with isolated peaks. It had crevasses, not to mention abysses, too, but we did our best to avoid them. The collision of continents thrust up new mountain ranges, while erosion turned barren new rock into fertile soil. Do I need to mention the clambering explorers, the pioneers who planted at high altitudes with aspirations that seemed presumptuous at the time? If they started by making wine with little to say, those who persevered found a new grammar and a new vocabulary, to add its voice to conversations that will soon, it seems, be worldwide.

Even among the most established there is continual change, as their language produces its own literature, and its literature new masterpieces. Far from being regions where everything has been discovered and every decision taken, the classic regions of the wine world are where the finest tuning takes place—where it is financially rewarding to go to the greatest efforts and explore in the greatest depth every elusive nuance that soils and techniques can offer.

Bordeaux is the prototype—indeed, the epitome. The arrival of each vintage sends ripples around the fine-wine world, even setting the reputation of the vintage for other regions. Such is fame.

But Bordeaux is also misunderstood. To the distant or unfocused observer it seems set in stone—creamy freestone with wrought-iron balconies. In fact, almost every aspect bar the gravel and limestone has passed through multiple mutations: of culture, technology, grape varieties, and above all, ownership.

Its 1855 Classification was a PR masterstroke, like Rolls-Royce's ticking clock. The problem with such memorable stories is that they become impossible to dislodge. The story of who is making the finest wines today, in what districts and what châteaux, and with what philosophy and technology, needs telling and retelling, with constant revisions.

Preface
by James Lawther

A book on Bordeaux invariably throws the spotlight on the locomotives of the region, and this one is no exception to the rule. History and that very Gallic word "terroir" (roughly translated as "the concept of place") dictate, but so, too, does the pursuit of perfection and the means necessary to achieve this eventual goal.

As outlined in the introductory chapters "History" and "Climate, Soil, and Grape Varieties," Bordeaux's emergence as a fine-wine region owes as much to geography, history, and human intervention as it does to climate and soil. The latter two elements undeniably dictate style and a "qualitative hierarchy" in terms of the potential to make great wine. But thereafter, it has been wealth, consistency, and dedication that have pushed the major estates to the fore.

The choice of the finest châteaux, therefore, underlines, in many cases, not only the influence of site but also the advantage of a lifeblood of investment down through the ages. In the 21st century, the clearest visual evidence of this is manifest in the state-of-the-art cellars and cutting-edge technology. But as underlined in the chapter on viticulture, it has been primarily the resources, often human, devoted to the vineyard that have made the difference in recent years.

A great number of the properties selected will, I am sure, be considered predestined for this book, while others will court a little more controversy. This is inevitable where the choice is subjective and where only a microcosm of Bordeaux is under scrutiny. Remember that at the last count (2008 figures), Bordeaux had a total of 293,800 acres (118,900 hectares) of vineyards and 9,100 wine growers, producing a total of 4.8 million hectoliters, or 640 million bottles (and that was down on previous years).

The opening chapters and the regional introductions provide a slightly more broad-brush interpretation of Bordeaux. Thereafter, the portraits represent the finest châteaux, though occasionally on a varying scale in order to take into account the size and diversity of the region. The level of investment (and return) in the "minor" appellations is usually of a different order from those with a more privileged name. The criteria for selection, however, remain the same: the influence of terroir and investment, and the search for identity and perfection.

I have visited all the châteaux represented in the book, some on several occasions, and all during the year of writing (2009). In most instances I've been lucky enough to taste a range of both younger and older wines. Those noted under "Finest Wines" are, in keeping with the definition used for this series, those that I think are most worth writing about—be it for their absolute quality, for some other intrinsic interest, or for their sound value. Wines tasted recently, the majority in 2009, have been highlighted, with the vintage date shown in bold script; vintages tasted at an earlier date appear in normal script, with the year and venue usually specified.

James Lawther

Blue Blood, New Blood, and Money

Bordeaux, arguably the greatest and certainly the most famous of the world's fine-wine regions, is also its most unfairly caricatured. When we think of Bordeaux, we may think with admiration of the great châteaux and the transcendent wines they produce. Such wines, after all, are among the highest peaks of Western—let alone vinous—culture, and they are envied and imitated wherever wine is produced. But for all that names such as Latour, Pétrus, and Yquem may have acquired a totemic significance among the world's wine drinkers and collectors, the region

itself can come across as stubbornly unlovable. Too often it presents itself, and is presented, as a stuffily bourgeois, conservative kind of place, an uninviting mix of the insular and the hidebound.

And yet the history of Bordeaux is of a region that is very far from parochial. It is often forgotten, for example, or at least overlooked, that the city of Bordeaux was once a thriving port, France's most important, and second only to London in the world in the 17th century. At that time, it was a hugely important hub for transatlantic trade and traffic with northern Europe. Wine and other

Above: Claude Joseph Vernet's portrayal of the port of Bordeaux in 1759, the Dutch flag reflecting the role of foreign merchants

commodities—such as cloth, spices, sugar, coffee, cereals, and whale oil—were sold, encouraging the presence of a melting pot of brokers and merchants. Northern Europeans, led by the English and Dutch, mixed freely with the Portuguese and Spanish, many of whom were fleeing religious persecution in their own countries. Bordeaux was an open, market-oriented city with a decidedly liberal creed.

Indeed, commerce has always been Bordeaux's raison d'être and is implicit in the story of its viticultural evolution. A conduit to the Atlantic Ocean provided the platform for trade, with wine being one of the key exports. Vineyards became a source of investment, with an ever-widening circle of ownership. As the reputations of individual châteaux grew, so did the desire for possession, with proprietorship moving from an agricultural base to bureaucrats and nobility, then to merchants, bankers, captains of industry, foreign investors, and eventually corporations. The advantage has been cycles of new investment, often for ailing crus—a boon for Bordeaux that continues today.

And how! Sales of prestigious Bordeaux properties were brisk in the opening years of the new millennium. Among the châteaux to change hands since 2000 have been the Médoc classed growths Montrose, Pichon Comtesse de Lalande, and Marquis d'Alesme Becker. In St-Emilion, the classified estates of Soutard and the renamed Belair-Monange also went under new ownership. Paris-based business tycoons, a Champagne house, an insurance company... these were the profiles of some of the buyers. New blood and new money—but hasn't this always been the way in Bordeaux?

Medieval beginnings

The early history of the region recounts the founding of the city of Burdigala or Bordeaux by the Bituriges Vivisques in the 3rd century BC. This Celtic tribe appears to have cultivated the vine, in particular the Biturica grape variety once thought to be the forerunner of Cabernet. The Romans extended vineyard plantings in the 1st century BC, but it was several centuries later, during the Middle Ages, that Bordeaux's nascent economy first took shape. And then it was an Anglo-French marriage alliance that sparked the beginnings of commercial trade.

That union took place in 1152, when the future Henry II of England married Eleanor of Aquitaine, placing the extended region of Gascony and the ports of Bordeaux, Bayonne, and later Libourne (founded in 1270) in English hands. A cross-Channel trade in wine and cloth developed, nurtured by exemption from certain taxes and other privileges for the Bordelais. Commerce developed slowly, but by the early 14th century, annual exports already averaged some 83,000 tonneaux (roughly 750,000hl) of wine.

Bordeaux itself was still a minor player in terms of production. The vineyards were around the city center in what is now Pessac-Léognan; on the marshy *palus* close to the river; at Bourg and Blaye on the other side of the Gironde estuary; and in the Entre-Deux-Mers. The slack was taken up by wines from the "Haut-Pays"—Bergerac, Cahors, and Gaillac—their movement controlled by officials in Bordeaux who prioritized the local production. Light in color and structure, less red than rosé or *clairet* (hence the English "claret"), the wines of Bordeaux at this juncture had to be consumed rapidly before they had time to spoil.

The English monopoly of the market ended in 1453, with the loss of Bordeaux following the defeat of the English army lead by John Talbot, Earl of Shrewsbury, at the hands of the French King Charles VII at Castillon la Bataille. The Bordelais maintained their privileges, but trade with England dwindled as English merchants moved to newer, friendlier pastures in Spain and Portugal. Hope was placed on an influx of Dutch, Flemish, Hanseatic, and Scottish traders as exports to England fell to 10,000 tonneaux (90,000hl) a year in the 16th century.

Below: The effigies of Henry II of England and Eleanor of Aquitaine, whose marriage left Bordeaux in English hands for 300 years

Dutch indulgence and the birth of the château

While the English took a temporary back seat, the Dutch exerted a growing influence in the region through the 16th and 17th centuries. Their thirst for bulk white wine for distillation led to the expansion of vineyards in the Charente, Blaye, and Entre-Deux-Mers. Sweet white wine was also at a premium, leading to increased demand for wines from Bergerac and Sauternes.

A number of Dutch merchants installed themselves in Bordeaux. The oldest house still in existence today, Beyerman opened an office at 45 Quai des Chartrons in 1620 to ensure the purchase of wine. The early years were typical of the era. The Beyerman fleet, operating out of Rotterdam, alternated between whale hunting, the spice trade, and wine, replacing barrels of whale oil with those of wine for sale in Holland, Belgium, Germany, and Scandinavia.

Vineyards for the production of red wine were still tightly bound to the *palus* and the stony soils of the Graves around the city of Bordeaux. Records from this time confirm the tentative creation of individual domaines. Jean de Pontac established the estate of Haut-Brion in 1533, while his brother-in-law Arnaut de Lestonnac, a prosperous merchant, founded La Mission Haut-Brion with the acquisition of a parcel of vines known as Arrejedhuys in 1540. At roughly the same time, the de Ferron family increased the family holdings near Léognan, Jean-Charles de Ferron taking the title of Seigneur de Carbonnieux. The vineyard of Pape Clément, in the hands of the Church since the early 14th century, was mentioned under this name for the first time in 1561.

A century later, Jean de Pontac's descendant Arnaud III de Pontac, a wealthy and politically powerful figure (he was appointed first president of the Bordeaux parliament in 1653), became the first producer in Bordeaux to market a wine under the name of the place where it was made. The 1660

Above: Arnaud III de Pontac, who gave the name of his estate, Haut-Brion, to his wine and opened a London tavern to sell it

cellar ledger of King Charles II of England (held today in the national archives in London) bears witness to this, as do the famous words penned by the diarist Samuel Pepys in 1663, following a visit to a London tavern: "I drank a sort of French wine, called Ho Bryan [sic], that hath a good and most particular taste that I ever met with."

Haut-Brion was to be the template for the château system we know today. It also launched a different style of Bordeaux. New French Claret, as it came to be known, gained a following in the expanding English market of the 18th century, its quality obtaining a higher premium than that for other wines. Using some of the latest winemaking techniques, such as racking, sulfuring, and the topping-off of barrels, as well as working with more care in the vineyard, Haut-Brion was deeper-colored, fuller-bodied, and didn't perish overnight. There is no specific evidence of the grape varieties used, but it seems probable that Cabernet, Merlot, and Malbec, among others, would have contributed to the blend.

The Médoc as an area of production was late on the scene—marshy and inhospitable, with access principally by boat via the estuary. It wasn't until Dutch engineers drained the land in the 17th century that the planting of vineyards got seriously under way. Reference is made to the acquisition of land around the gravelly outcrop of La Mothe de Margaux, the future Château Margaux, by Pierre de Lestonnac in the 1570s, the other great estates of Latour and Lafite being founded a little later, but all three were more recognizable in their present guise by the mid-17th century.

The 1700s—*le siècle des lumières*
The 18th century was an immensely prosperous era for Bordeaux. Trade launched in the late 17th century with French colonies in the West Indies (principally the Dominican Republic and Haiti of today) flourished. Sugar, coffee, and wine were the main staples, along with slaves, Bordeaux becoming the second most important port after Nantes for the French slave trade, with expeditions via Africa a regular occurrence. The wine trade, too, remained of critical importance, particularly that with northern Europe (Germany, Scandinavia) and the ports of Brittany, Normandy, and northern France.

In the Médoc, planting continued apace, while individual estates established their names as grands crus, part of the wave of New French Claret. The owners were, in the main, the *noblesse de la robe*—lawyers and local politicians of noble or quasi-noble strain—people like Nicolas-Alexandre, Marquis de Ségur, who in the first half of the 18th century owned Latour, Lafite, Mouton, and Calon-Ségur. The English part of the market had now declined to about 5 percent of the total volume of wine Bordeaux exported, but London was the key market for the grands crus.

Until the 18th century, the city of Bordeaux had maintained a walled-in, medieval appearance, but the huge influx of wealth changed all this.

The majority of the city's principal buildings, parks, and monuments were constructed during this period, including the Grand Théâtre, Place de la Bourse, waterfront or *quais*, Palais Rohan, Jardin Public, and Place de la Victoire, all of which can still be seen today.

Foreign wine merchants were obliged to ply their trade outside the old city, so they drifted to a waterfront area downstream from the Château Trompette (now the Esplanade des Quinconces). As the wine trade flourished in the 18th century, so the Quartier des Chartrons, named after the Carthusian priory established in the 14th century, grew and expanded. The Quai des Chartrons became the principal address for négociants and *courtiers*, with Dutch, English, Scottish, Irish, German, and Scandinavian names. Houses, cellars, and warehouses were built, and a small army of people was employed to carry out the tasks of making, maturing, and shipping the wine. Today, the architecture is a reminder of this glorious past, as are family names such as Beyerman, Schÿler, Barton, and Johnston, all still associated with the Bordeaux wine trade. One can quite understand how the négociant Emile Castéja came to the conclusion that "Bordeaux is a club where only strangers are admitted."

Post-Revolutionary change and the Golden Age
Following the French Revolution, the Church, nobility, and political elite were stripped of their land, and the estates were auctioned off as *biens nationaux*. A new type of owner appeared in Bordeaux—the financiers, businessmen, and merchants who had profited from Bordeaux's commercial prosperity. Of course, the foreign wine merchants who had come to Bordeaux to make their fortunes were particularly well placed for investing in châteaux. It wasn't simply a matter of money, though they certainly had enough of that. They also had the inside knowledge that comes

Above: The resplendent Place de la Bourse, one of Bordeaux's many landmarks dating from the prosperous 18th century

from running the trade, and so, when they took the plunge, it was usually at the top end.

A typical example of the post-Revolution proprietor was Charles Peixotto, a Jewish banker of Portuguese extraction who in 1791 acquired Château Pape Clément. But there were many other representatives of the new breed, among them the Dutch company of Beyerman, which purchased Château Haut-Brion in 1825 (only to resell to a Parisian banker, the Marquis de las Marismas, in 1836); Maison Nathaniel Johnston, of Scottish descent, which became part owners of Château Latour in 1840 and owners of châteaux Ducru-Beaucaillou and Dauzac in 1865; and the Irish

Barton family, who purchased Château Langoa in 1821 and a portion of the Léoville estate in 1826, both of which remain in their hands to this day.

The Golden Age of Bordeaux, which lasted from the mid- to late 19th century, saw the arrival of wealth from farther afield, confirming the desirability of the great estates, particularly those of the Médoc, as prestigious acquisitions. The 1855 Classification validated this perception. The Peréire brothers Isaac and Emile, bankers and financiers whose grandfather had fled Portugal in 1741, purchased Château Palmer in 1853, the same year Baron Nathaniel de Rothschild from the English

Above: Bonnat's portrait of the banker Isaac Peréire, who, with his brother Emile, purchased Château Palmer in 1853

branch of the family acquired Château Brane-Mouton, now Mouton Rothschild. Later, in 1868, his French cousin Baron James de Rothschild bought Château Lafite. A pattern of investment in Bordeaux by wealthy businessmen and financiers was established and has never really changed. Bordeaux remains a *vignoble de marchands*, the opposite of Burgundy's *vignoble de paysans*.

Despite the problems of oidium, mildew, and phylloxera, the latter arriving in Bordeaux around 1865, the market remained buoyant and the region maintained a relatively high level of prosperity. The traditional trade with northern Europe continued to be strong, while the United States and South America (particularly Argentina) grew in importance. New money continued to pour in, and prominent estates continued to attract new buyers such as Alcide Bellot des Minières, who, having made his fortune from plantations in the United States, purchased Château Haut-Bailly in 1872, and the banking Achille-Fould family, who acquired Château Beychevelle in 1890.

So far, little reference has been made to St-Emilion or Pomerol, but both regions remained peripheral, in terms of both commercial activity and attracting outside investment, at least until the late 19th century. Before the Revolution, much of the land in the area had been owned by the Church. Post-Revolution, it was sold off piecemeal. Properties were therefore small, and the area was culturally as well as geographically distant, separated from the business hub of the city of Bordeaux by two major rivers (the first bridge across the Garonne, the Pont de Pierre, was completed only in 1821). There was not even a local Chamber of Commerce to defend interests until 1910. It was for these reasons that St-Emilion and Pomerol were absent from the 1855 Classification. Trade outside the region, however, did exist, mainly with Belgium and northern France, traditionally the home for these wines until the late 20th century.

The gray years

Being a market-driven economy—and one of international dimension—Bordeaux has always been subject to cyclical change. "Boom and bust" is an epithet that can be readily applied, but few were prepared for the duration of the recession that started in the early part of the 20th century.

Phylloxera had already reduced the vineyard area and extracted a heavy toll on resources. Thereafter, a sequence of local, international, political, and viticultural events made matters worse.

A run of poor vintages—stretching up to 1945, with a handful of exceptions—provided the backdrop. There was also the small matter of two world wars, the economic depression of the 1930s, Prohibition in the United States, revolution in Russia, and a crisis of confidence in the authenticity and provenance of wine (which would lead to the creation of the *appellation contrôlée* system in 1935). This was, to put it mildly, a debilitated market. There was precious little money for investment; owners were often tied to long-term contracts with négociants to weather the storm; and although many properties were for sale, there were few purchasers with the cash or the will to buy them. One of the few exceptions was Château Haut-Brion, which was acquired by the American Dillon family (more bankers) in 1934.

The situation improved marginally after World War II, but it was a halting progress. The number of quality vintages improved but money was still tight, and in 1974 the market crashed when oil prices soared, leaving négociants holding stocks of the overpriced and unwanted vintages of 1972 and 1973. The crisis was exacerbated by what was known as the Cruse scandal, where red table wine was fraudulently sold as AOC Bordeaux, and several négociants, including Cruse, were often unwittingly implicated in the scam.

In terms of property, the 1950s and 1960s saw a handful of isolated groups taking advantage of the depressed market. Négociants such as Jean-Pierre Moueix started purchasing in Pomerol and St-Emilion. French colonists (known as *pieds-noirs*) arrived from the war in Algeria to seek a replacement for their annexed properties overseas—the Perrin family, for example, acquired Château Carbonnieux, and the Tari family bought Château Giscours. The British Pearson Group took over a very run-down Château Latour, while local residents André and Lucien Lurton resurrected a number of estates in the Médoc and Graves. It was all balm for Bordeaux, but financing for radical improvement was still limited, and there was the added dilemma of a severe frost in 1956 that, on the Right Bank in particular, destroyed a high proportion of the vineyard.

1982 and all that

Much has already been written about the celebrated 1982 vintage, but it really was a watershed year in many ways. It was the first truly great vintage since 1970—a success throughout Bordeaux (saving Sauternes) and one of plethoric volume. It ushered in a richer, riper, more modern style of Bordeaux. It satisfied consumers qualitatively and financially. It stimulated the wine press, launching the career of American critic Robert Parker and the 100-point system of scoring wines. Above all, it pushed Bordeaux back into the international arena, providing much-needed cash for reform and renovation in the vineyards and wineries. The machine was up and running again, the momentum maintained by a spate of good to excellent vintages that followed (1983, 1985, 1986, 1988, 1989, 1990) and by advances in viticultural and winemaking technology.

With Bordeaux flourishing, the investors returned in droves, in a way that parallels the Golden Age of the 19th century. A massive turnover of prestige properties started in the late 1980s and has only begun to abate with the world economic crisis triggered in 2008. Steadily rising land prices contributed to the frenetic movement in the grand cru market. Inheritance tax based on land values is a heavy burden, but a still greater problem, due to Napoleonic law, is the shared ownership that increases with every generation. Family conflicts fanned by rising land values and marginal returns

for multiple shareholders are more often than not the main reason for property sales. With a new, single owner, the buck stops there, and in the long term there's often a handsome return.

For this reason, the market has been partly driven by institutional investment for the first time. Insurance companies like AXA Millésimes (châteaux Pichon-Longueville, Suduiraut, and Petit Village), GMF (châteaux Beychevelle and Beaumont), and La Mondiale (châteaux Soutard and Larmande) have been significant players, but the profile of investors also stretches to banks (Crédit Agricole Grands Crus at châteaux Grand-Puy Ducasse, Meyney, and de Rayne Vigneau), pension funds (Colony Capital at Château Lascombes), and other large international corporations (Suntory at Château Lagrange).

There has been no shortage, either, of wealthy businessmen eager to add a top-flight grand cru to their portfolios. The prime examples are French magnates and rivals François Pinault and Bernard Arnault—the former acquiring Château Latour in 1993; the latter (with partner Baron Albert Frère), Château Cheval Blanc in 1998. Foreign businessmen have also been in the mix, as demonstrated by Dutch entrepreneur Eric Albada Jelgersma at châteaux Giscours (1990s) and du Tertre (1997) and the Wertheimers of Chanel (French nationals but based in the United States) at châteaux Rauzan-Ségla (1994) and Canon (1996).

Other examples are many and have often resulted in what appears to be overnight change. One has only to think of the arrival of Gérard Perse in St-Emilion (châteaux Monbousquet, Pavie, and Pavie Decesse); Daniel and Florence Cathiard (Château Smith Haut Lafitte); and Alfred-Alexandre Bonnie (Château Malartic Lagravière) in Pessac-Léognan to see what can be achieved in a relatively short space of time. Where there is

Left: Artistry and elegance may be the classic image of Bordeaux châteaux, but noble rot and revelry also have a place

good terroir, motivation, and a considerable war chest for improvements ($20 million at Malartic Lagravière), progress can be strikingly rapid.

Still a viticultural El Dorado

The latter part of the 20th century and early years of the 21st have constituted another golden era for Bordeaux. The good vintages have continued (1995, 1996, 1998, 2000, 2001, 2003, 2005, 2009), ensuring a buoyant market, with interest from Asia adding another dimension to trade. Grand cru châteaux have improved their vineyards and wineries, taking full advantage of their gains. Another analogy can be found in the city of Bordeaux itself. As in the 18th and 19th centuries, when commerce was also thriving, Bordeaux has had a makeover. Buildings have been renovated, a new tram system has been put in place, and the waterfront has been restored as the focal point of the city.

Will it last? Vintages since 2005 have done little to excite consumers or trade (though at the time of writing, 2009 presages extremely well). In 2009, exchange rates were discouraging, a global recession was in full swing, and business on the *Place de Bordeaux* was at an ebb. Distribution in the United States was also in turmoil following the exit from the market in fine Bordeaux of Château & Estate and Southern Wine & Spirits. The only good news was the buoyancy of trade in China and Hong Kong. Only time will tell whether Bordeaux has again hit troubled waters.

What is clear is that Bordeaux remains a viticultural El Dorado for men and women of wealth. A primal desire for land; the honor of owning a distinguished piece of French culture and great bottles for posterity; the need to satisfy a business plan—the attractions of Bordeaux are many and various. The pendulum may swing again, but customers for the great châteaux will always be around. They are the guaranteed lifeblood of Bordeaux.

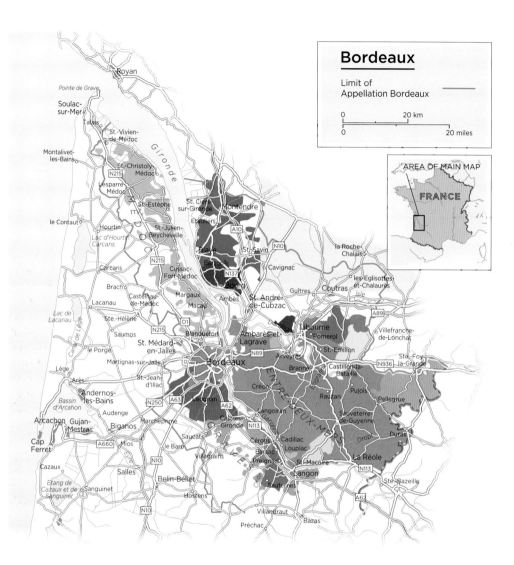

Appellations/ Sub-regions

	Haut-Médoc		Côtes de Francs		Pessac-Léognan
	St-Emilion		Blayes, Côtes de Blaye, and Premières Côtes de Blaye		Graves
	Pomerol		Bourg, Côtes de Bourg, and Bourgeois		Cérons
	St-Emilion Satellites		Premières Côtes de Bordeaux		Sauternes and Barsac
	Fronsac and Canon-Fronsac		Graves de Vayres		Loupiac
	Côtes de Castillon		Ste-Foy-Bordeaux		Ste-Croix-du-Mont
	Lalande-de-Pomerol		Côtes de Bordeaux-St-Macaire		Entre-Deux-Mers

Bordelais DNA

If one were basing one's decision on climate and soil alone, it is fair to say that one would probably not settle on Bordeaux as a place for making fine wine. As respected academic, Professor Gérard Seguin, formerly of the Faculté d'Oenologie in Bordeaux, explains in his treatise on the subject, *Les Terroirs des Grands Crus de Bordeaux*, the development of Bordeaux as a fine-wine region owes more to geography, history, and human intervention than to terroir: "On the face of it, the climatic conditions of Bordeaux appear not to have predestined the region for the production of high-quality wines."

And so it seems when one studies the data. Temperatures are mild—the yearly average is 55.5°F (13°C)—though they are sufficiently high in July and August, at 68°F (20°C). Sunlight hours are moderate due to cloud cover (1,360 hours from April to September); and the level of humidity (76 percent) combined with spring and summer temperatures is propitious for fungal diseases. Average annual rainfall hovers around 33.5in (850mm), a significant amount falling in the summer months, with an average 4.5in (110mm) in the six-week ripening period in September and October.

The conditions on paper are far from ideal, then. Yet this marginal climate—labeled maritime, oceanic, or temperate—clearly puts a stamp on the character and style of Bordeaux wine. The moderate temperature is the defining factor. It helps growers avoid *surmaturité*, yet it is sufficient for the slow ripening of the grape varieties cultivated in the region. The result for red Bordeaux is, broadly speaking, adequate color, a balanced degree of alcohol, and an acidity that offers freshness on the palate. Aromatically, the nuance is of red fruits, the riper notes of prune and jam linked to climatically extreme vintages like 2003, or to the practice of late harvesting and long hang-times. Generally, it's a climate that allows balance and finesse.

Vintage variation

The variability of Bordeaux's climate from one year to the next causes a change in vine behavior that, naturally enough, leads to great variation in the quality and style of vintages. It is often assumed that heat is the main factor here, but given the levels of humidity and rainfall in Bordeaux, a more persuasive thesis is that "water-deficit stress" is more influential—in other words, the drier the year, the better the quality of the wine. The idea was put to the test recently in a study by Kees van Leeuwen, a professor of viticulture at Bordeaux University (ENITA), and consultant to Château Cheval Blanc. In assessing the "water uptake" conditions for 32 Bordeaux vintages (1974–2005) via a water-deficit stress index (veraison to ripeness), van Leeuwen showed that water stress was the unconditional factor in the quality of the vintage. Dry years were without exception very good to great (1990, 1995, 1998, 2000, 2001, and 2005—the driest vintage ever), while wet years were inevitably poor (1992, 1997, 2002). Warm years could be outstanding (1989, 1990, 2005) but they could also be average to poor (1994, 1997, 1999), and some of the cooler vintages were excellent (1985, 1988, 1996). The one year to defy the conclusion was 1982, which was a relatively wet vintage.

Another explanation of vintage quality is supplied by Bordeaux University's Faculté d'Oenologie via an assessment of the 2008 vintage. The report notes that for the "perfect red vintage," five successive factors are necessary in the growth cycle of the vine: an early and rapid flowering (for even maturity and yield); a little water stress at berry set (to limit berry size); the cessation of vine growth before veraison; an adequate leaf canopy to ensure complete ripeness of the berries; and clement conditions during the harvest to bring maturity to the later-ripening parcels and varieties.

Once again, water balance seems to be the critical element. The first two of the Faculté's factors require a relatively warm, dry spring. The third (and most decisive) factor calls for a dry July; the fourth, moderate heat in August accompanied by just enough rain to assist photosynthesis; and the last factor, an anticyclone in September and October to stave off autumnal depressions. Based on this assessment, the report declares 2005 "perfect," since all five factors were satisfied. By comparison, 2006 was "very good," since the first three factors were fulfilled, and 2007 merely "honorable," since only the fifth condition (which saved it) applied. 2008 satisfied factors three (the essential), four (at least partially), and five, so the report declares it a "good" rather than an "exceptional" year.

The effects of climate change

This is a subject of some concern, as climatologists predict an average temperature rise of 5.5–7.2°F (3–4°C) in Bordeaux this century. The worry is that Bordeaux will lose its *typicité* of balance and finesse, the hallmarks of a grand vin, the grapes ripening sooner, with a higher sugar content, and the wines consequently becoming more *méridional* in style.

There's already evidence that the greenhouse effect has had some bearing on the style of the region's wines. It's important to remember that, as little as 40 years ago, Bordeaux's red varieties were considered almost too late-ripening for the prevailing climatic conditions. Since the 1980s, however, maturity has been less of a problem, and although improved vineyard husbandry has no doubt played a part in this development, climate is the overriding factor. Today, the average alcohol content is closer to 13% naturally, rather than 12% with the aid of chaptalization (the addition of sugar to the unfermented grape must), as was common in the past. The later-ripening varieties—Cabernet Sauvignon and Cabernet Franc—have certainly benefited from the change.

But what if things go too far? The first victim will be the early-ripening Merlot, now 63 percent

of total red plantings in Bordeaux. Viticultural practices will need to be adapted to delay ripening, through particular rootstocks and clones, less leaf removal, and possibly lower trellising. A greater proportion of Cabernet Sauvignon may be desirable. The establishment of a mature vineyard is a lifetime's occupation, so action will need to be taken now.

Climatic hazards

Frost and hail are among the climatic hazards that afflict Bordeaux. Winter temperatures rarely dip to the extremes where vines are destroyed (1956 was the last great winter frost when vineyards, particularly on the Right Bank, were razed). But spring frosts cause damage from time to time. The last major spring frost was in 1991, though some regions were hit in 1994 and 1997. Wind machines have been installed in zones that are particularly prone to frost (the parcels of white varieties at Domaine de Chevalier in Pessac-Léognan, for example), but their use is not widespread.

Hail is even more haphazard and unpredictable than frost, but the consequences in terms of quantity and quality can be every bit as damaging. A localized occurrence, hail usually creates a band of destruction, with vines only inches outside its path escaping unscathed. The timing is random. In 1999, hail struck 1,350 acres (550ha) of St-Emilion in early September, while in May 2009 Bordeaux was hit by two hailstorms in the same week. The first cut a swath through the southern Médoc and Margaux, then Bourg and Blaye, while the second started in the Graves and worked its way across the Entre-Deux-Mers, St-Emilion, and Côtes de Castillon. The storms were sudden and violent, with hailstones the size of golf balls, and some 29,500 acres (12,000ha) of vineyard were damaged, some properties losing their entire crop.

Right: Bordeaux still has gray and misty days, as here at Château Margaux, but climate change is already apparent

Bodies of water

Unlike Burgundy, Bordeaux is relatively flat. The highest point in St-Emilion is just over 330ft (100m) above sea level; in the Médoc, 145ft (44m) at Listrac. Altitude, exposure, and slope are all, therefore, much less dramatic. There are other geographic features, though, that have a localized bearing on climate—most notably the presence of bodies of water. In the Médoc, temperatures are influenced by the proximity of the Gironde estuary, with minimum temperatures being higher close to the river and maximum temperatures slightly lower. This results in an earlier ripening cycle, and vineyards closer to the estuary tend to reach maturity a week ahead of those 6 miles (10km) away. The thermal effect also provides protection against frost. In Sauternes, the proximity of the rivers Garonne and Ciron (smaller and cooler) explains the regular occurrence of mists that in the fall help precipitate the onset of botrytis.

Soil

Bordeaux has a great variety of soils; clay, gravel, limestone, silt, and sand can all be found in different mixes and from varying geological eras. Such is the diversity that soil alone cannot define the style of Bordeaux's wine. It does, however, support two important conclusions. "Certain soils have a bigger potential to make great wine, so a qualitative hierarchy can be applied," says van Leeuwen. "We also know by tasting assessment that different soils produce a variation in the tenor of the wine."

In experiments conducted over three years (1992–1994) by Yves Glories, the former doyen of Bordeaux's Faculté d'Oenologie, grapes from Merlot vines of identical age but from different soils in St-Emilion were vinified apart but with the same protocol and the resulting wines tasted.

Right: The old adage that the best châteaux see the river is eloquent testimony to the beneficial influence of the Gironde

Above: Whether clay, gravel, or limestone, the most crucial aspect of a soil is its ability to regulate the supply of water to the vine

"All were stunningly different," says van Leeuwen. The conclusion was that clay soils produced deep-colored, tannic wines but with the tannins fleshed out, giving the impression of opulence or roundness on the palate. Gravelly soils, by contrast, provided a richness of fruit, aromatic complexity, and length on the palate but tannins that were more abrasive in youth. Limestone soils offered finesse in the wine, with less aggressive tannins, greater acidity (and therefore freshness), and less weight but considerable complexity with age.

The qualitative feature of Bordeaux's better soils is the ability to restrict the vine's water supply, thus reducing vine vigor and berry size and concentrating color pigments and tannins. Soil and climate go hand in hand in this respect—hence the vintage variation in Bordeaux's humid regime. The lower the reserves of water in the soil during the growing season, the better the wine.

Three soils of disparate composition top the pyramid in terms of regulating water supply: gravel (mixed with silt, sand, and clay), dense clay, and *calcaire à astéries* (starfish limestone). The first,

clearly associated with the Médoc, is free-draining due to the stony content but allows deep rooting to permit water uptake when necessary. The dense clay soils are typical of the Pomerol plateau. The clay has the ability to retain a high water content, expanding and crushing the tiny roots, or *radicelles*, when there's heavy rain (as well as creating a compact runoff), thus limiting water uptake but allowing the rooting system to develop via fissures for sustenance in dry periods. St-Emilion's limestone plateau is the classic example of *calcaire à astéries*. The topsoil is thin, the roots of the vine descending to the bedrock, where the porous limestone rations the uptake of water, absorbing the excess volume in times of heavy rain and distributing moisture by capillarity in dry periods.

When discussing terroir in Bordeaux, it is important not to overlook human intervention. The identification of the best soils, choice of grape varieties, and use of appropriate land management are critical factors in a climatically demanding environment. The motivation also remains very human: commerce and trade.

Grape varieties

Along with climate and soil, the vine completes the triumvirate that interacts to create a wine's identity. The vine's grape variety clearly has a bearing on flavor and form, soil adding a further nuance. In Bordeaux, the *typicité* of a cru is generally transmitted through a varying blend of grape varieties rather than through any one. Those permitted and planted in the region are: for red, Merlot, Cabernet Sauvignon, Cabernet Franc, Petit Verdot, and Malbec; and for white, Semillon, Sauvignon Blanc, and Muscadelle.

Until the 18th century, precise information on grape varieties cultivated in Bordeaux was scarce. Clearly there were many (more than 60), including Vidure or Bidure (synonyms for Cabernet Sauvignon), which was believed at the time to be the descendant of Biturica, a vine cultivated by the Bituriges Vivisques in the 3rd century BC.

Several classifications were published in the 19th century, including those of Paguierre (1829), Comte Odart in his *Ampélographie Universelle* (1841), Petit-Lafitte (1850), and Féret (1874). The latter's report at the time of the outbreak of phylloxera lists the following red varieties as *cépages de fond*: Malbec, Cabernets (Cabernet Franc, Cabernet Sauvignon, Carmenère), Merlot, Petit Verdot, and Syrah. The publication also gives the proportion of the blend according to region:
• Haut-Médoc and grands crus des Graves: half to three-quarters of Cabernets according to the canton and commune, the rest Merlot and Malbec;
• Libournais (St-Emilion, Pomerol, Fronsac, Castillon, Lussac): one-third Cabernet, one-third Merlot, one-third Malbec.

After phylloxera, the viticultural landscape changed dramatically as growers adapted to new grafting and rootstocks, as well as to new commercial realities. Some varieties disappeared altogether (Syrah, Pinot Noir), others were radically reduced (Malbec, Petit Verdot), while Carmenère

became incidental. Merlot developed significantly, replacing Malbec in most regions, with Cabernet Sauvignon reinforcing its presence, particularly in the Médoc.

The progress of Merlot has continued in the modern era, but perhaps the greatest change has been the move from white to red varieties. Until the 1970s, the Bordeaux vineyard was evenly split between red and white, whereas today red varieties account for 89 percent of plantings. Merlot currently represents 63 percent of total red plantings, while Cabernet Sauvignon accounts for 25 percent, Cabernet Franc 11 percent, and other red varieties 1 percent. For whites, Semillon is the largest with 53 percent, followed by Sauvignon Blanc with 38 percent, Muscadelle 6 percent, and other white varieties 3 percent.

Red varieties

Merlot The most widely planted variety in Bordeaux, Merlot has become the viticultural panacea of the region. It has an earlier ripening cycle than Cabernet (though it is susceptible to spring frost and *coulure*, due to early budding and flowering), and it is adaptable to a variety of soils, producing a smooth and generous style of wine that is accessible early on. Sugar, and therefore alcohol, levels tend to be higher than for Cabernet, which is why there is some disquiet about how the variety will perform should climate change continue. Vigorous and productive on fertile soils, Merlot achieves its finest expression (rich and powerful, with deep color and expressive fruit) on soils with a high clay content or on fissured limestone (both cool and damp), most notably in St-Emilion and Pomerol (Pétrus and Le Pin are pure unblended versions). The Libournais as a whole remains the cradle for the variety, with 75 percent of plantings, but considerable headway has also been made in the Médoc and Graves, where Merlot accounts respectively for 41 and 53 percent of plantings. The harvest date is particularly important for Merlot, because the window of opportunity is shorter than for Cabernet, and there is a high risk of rot and low acidity if picking is delayed too long.

Cabernet Sauvignon The classic variety of the Médoc and, to a certain extent, of the Graves, Cabernet Sauvignon at its best provides all the attributes required of a *grand vin de Bordeaux*: color, tannic structure, freshness, and an aromatic complexity that increases with age. The Médoc first growths—Lafite, Latour, Margaux, and Mouton—use up to 90 percent in the blend. Small-berried and thick-skinned, with a high seed-to-pulp ratio, it has an impressive phenolic content but is susceptible to fungal diseases such as esca, eutypiose, and oidium. As a late-ripening variety, it is best suited to warm, dry, free-draining soils and, in Bordeaux's temperate climate, requires favorable late-season conditions. In youth the aroma is that of black currant and dark fruit, but this can turn to vegetal and green-pepper notes if the grapes are underripe.

Cabernet Franc Also known as Bouchet in the Libournais, Cabernet Franc can be as remarkable as it can be disappointing. Its distinguished admirers in St-Emilion and Pomerol (such as Ausone, Angélus, Cheval Blanc, Le Dôme, Figeac, Lafleur, and Vieux Château Certan) observe color, elegance, finesse, and structure, so they use a high proportion in the blend. In the Médoc, where it can be dilute and lacking in structure, success is more relative, and the variety is used more sparingly.

Ripening after Merlot but before Cabernet Sauvignon, Cabernet Franc has specific requirements for successful cultivation: low yields (40hl/ha), good vine age, and a proportion of clay in the soil or subsoil. The raw material is also important. Whereas commercial clones of Cabernet Sauvignon and Merlot are considered

Merlot

satisfactory, many experts in the region claim that those for Cabernet Franc are poor. The successful châteaux often use their own selections.

Petit Verdot A traditional Bordeaux grape once heavily planted on the alluvial riverbank soils of the *palus*, Petit Verdot is now a marginal variety found primarily in the Médoc. Late-ripening, sensitive to water stress, and difficult to cultivate, it is used when fully ripe in tiny proportions (up to about 10 percent) in a blend with Cabernet Sauvignon and Merlot. Its attributes include color, tannin, acidity, and spicy aromas. Very occasionally it is produced as an unblended cuvée (at châteaux Moutte Blanc and Mirambeau Papin).

Malbec Before phylloxera, Malbec (known as Pressac in the Libournais and as Cot in Cahors) was probably the most planted red variety in Bordeaux—the Merlot of its day. It's now rarely used in grands vins and is found mainly in Bourg and Blaye, with odd parcels in St-Emilion and Pomerol. Best cultivated in clay-limestone soils, Malbec is an early-ripening variety with large berries, susceptible to mildew, *coulure*, and rot.

White varieties

Semillon Once the most-planted grape variety in Bordeaux, Semillon remains the region's principal white. If yields are contained, its golden berries have the ability to make high-quality dry and sweet white wines that are full, rich, round, and delicately aromatic, with good acidity and the potential to age. The constitution of its berries makes Semillon susceptible to botrytis, or noble rot (and gray rot if overcropped), so it's the grape of predilection for the sweet wines of Sauternes, Barsac, and other *vins liquoreux*. It can be the unique variety (Château Climens) but is often blended with the livelier Sauvignon Blanc. The finest dry styles are found in the Graves and Pessac-Léognan, usually in a blend, the most *typé* being Château Laville Haut-Brion with 80 percent.

Sauvignon Blanc Cultivated in the Entre-Deux-Mers for its zesty, aromatic (boxwood to passion fruit), easy-drinking character, Sauvignon Blanc also makes serious ageworthy wines—witness Domaine de Chevalier and châteaux Couhins-Lurton and Smith Haut Lafitte in Pessac-Léognan. Winemaking techniques (barrel fermentation and maturation) play a part, but quality is distinctly linked to the maturity of the grapes. Like Semillon, it ripens before red varieties for the production of dry styles but can be picked late for Sauternes. It is susceptible to fungal diseases and gray rot.

Sauvignon Gris Possibly a mutation of Sauvignon Blanc, Sauvignon Gris existed in the early 20th

Sauvignon Blanc

century (as confirmed in the 1910 ampelography of Viala and Vermorel) but was then virtually wiped out. An example was located in the southern Graves in 1973, and from this a commercial clone was produced by Bordeaux's Chambre d'Agriculture toward the end of the 1980s. Being earlier-ripening and fuller-bodied, with higher sugar levels and a less marked aromatic character, it is now used as a complement to Sauvignon Blanc in dry white wines throughout the region, notably in Pessac-Léognan and the Graves.

Muscadelle Coveted for its musky aroma, Muscadelle is a prolific and difficult variety to cultivate (due to its susceptibility to fungal diseases and gray rot) and is therefore grown sparingly in Bordeaux. It is used mainly for sweet white wines but rarely in top Sauternes.

Returning to Roots

As a subject that evades colorful prose, viticulture tends to play second fiddle in a discourse on the wines of Bordeaux. It is far more graphic to attribute change to a fashionable consultant or new oak barrels than to all those unglamorous man-hours spent pruning, trellising, or deleafing. Yet it is an indisputable fact that progress in Bordeaux since the 1990s is primarily due to improvements in the vineyard.

The transformation started in the 1980s, with a few forward-thinking individuals cutting back on fertilizers and introducing green-harvesting to reduce yields. Hubert de Boüard at Angélus and Christian Moueix at Pétrus are two who come to mind. It accelerated in the 1990s, spurred on by the garagistes' adoption of precision viticulture allied to tailor-made winemaking. If it was producers on the Right Bank who led the way, the Left Bank soon caught on, the resources of the major estates enabling them to advance in strides.

The focus now is clearly on the vineyard as the origin of great wine. Many of the practices are simply a throwback to the past (such as deleafing and plowing), but high-level research has helped determine methods of cultivation, too. Cost is always a factor, and a number of the techniques discussed in this chapter will apply only to the grands crus. It's also important to remember that it's a chain of work rather than any single link that will eventually enhance the quality of the harvest.

Clones and clonal research

Most of the work on commercial clones for Bordeaux's principal grape varieties was carried out in the 1960s (by the Chambre d'Agriculture and Institut National de la Recherche Agronomique in Bordeaux), with official approval (the *agrément*) given in the 1970s. Those in use today (clones 169, 191, or 337 for Cabernet Sauvignon, and 181 for Merlot) date from this period and have not been bettered since.

Whereas Cabernet Sauvignon, Merlot, and Sauvignon Blanc clones are considered to be of good quality, those for Cabernet Franc and Semillon are now deemed poor. A new clone for Cabernet Franc, however, is under way, the project of Marie-Catherine Dufour of Bordeaux's Chambre d'Agriculture. The program started in 1999, and the hope is that the clone will be available commercially by 2013 or 2014.

A number of châteaux already have their own selections, more often than not propagated from vines within the estate. This is particularly the case for Cabernet Franc at Château Cheval Blanc, as well as at châteaux Ausone, Angélus, Canon-la-Gaffelière, and Pavie Macquin, while at Château Trottevieille a parcel of ungrafted Cabernet Franc planted between 1890 and 1895 has been used for a special bottling since 2004.

Probably the most exhaustive program of clonal selection on an independent basis has been that conducted at Château Haut-Brion. Research started in the 1970s at the instigation of Jean-Bernard Delmas, first with clones approved by INRA (Institut National de la Recherche Agronomique) then with selections from the estate. Cabernet Sauvignon, Merlot, and Cabernet Franc were evaluated by microvinification for yield, sugar level, acidity, color, and tannin, and by the 1980s it was possible to draw several interesting conclusions.

It was confirmed that 10 percent of the clones from a given variety performed consistently at Haut-Brion; 80 percent varied according to the vintage; and 10 percent were consistently unsatisfactory. It was decided that a mix of clones generally gave better results. So when a parcel is replanted, the following formula applies: one-third is planted using the 10 percent of clones that had been shown to perform consistently well; one-third

Right: Pontet-Canet has gone even further than other properties in its return to more natural methods of cultivation

is made up of the 80 percent of clones that were deemed to have a variable performance; and one-third receives the officially approved commercial clones. About 40 percent of the Haut-Brion vineyard is now planted with its own massal selection, and the vineyard of La Mission Haut-Brion is arriving at the same proportion.

Rootstocks

There's some evidence to suggest that a Bordeaux grower called Leo Laliman was the first to advise grafting European vines on to American rootstocks to combat phylloxera in 1869. The majority of the 30 rootstocks now officially allowed in France were then developed toward the end of the 19th century, with only two recent additions established by INRA in Bordeaux in the 1970s.

In reality, only 13 rootstocks are used in Bordeaux, the figure diminishing further when quality considerations enter the equation. When deciding on a rootstock, growers have to take into account a variety of factors, including the grape variety that will be grafted on to the rootstock, the rootstock's ability to adapt to the specific soil of the vineyard, and the rootstock's ability to promote low or high vigor and late or early ripening. Quality means a low-vigor rootstock—hence the gradual abandonment of the vigorous SO4, widely used in Bordeaux in the 1960s, when high yield was the motif. The same applies to 5BB.

Favored low-vigor rootstocks now include Riparia Gloire de Montpellier, 420A, and 101–14. The latter works well with Cabernet Sauvignon but is sensitive to dry conditions. 420A adapts well to Merlot and is late-ripening, while Riparia is early-ripening. It has been used at Château Cheval Blanc since the early 1990s, but the later ripening 420A is now being used in response to climate change. The choice for any grower is critical, because once the decision is made, the rootstock is likely to be there for at least a generation.

Above: Books on viticulture from the 19th century reflect the fundamental importance of innovations made at the time

Vine densities

Unlike their counterparts in the New World, French growers, including those in Bordeaux, are obliged to abide by the decrees of the relevant AOC when deciding on the precise density of their plantings. A minimum 5,000 vines/ha is required in St-Emilion, for example, and 6,500–10,000 vines/ha in the Médoc communes.

A large body of research has proved that an increase in the density of planting helps improve grape quality and, within limits, reduce yield. Quality is improved by optimizing photosynthesis with a greater leaf surface or canopy to receive the sun's rays, while vigor is reduced through better transpiration and controlled watering.

The only argument against high-density planting is the greater cost of production, since vineyards planted at higher densities require more labor and machinery to work them. Figures presented by Kees van Leeuwen and Jean-Philippe Roby in 2008 show that a parcel planted at 3,333 vines/ha will cost $5,600/ha to run, whereas one planted at 5,000 vines/ha will cost $8,400/ha. This, of course, has to be balanced against the selling price of the wine.

Historically, the grands crus of the Médoc have planted at a high density of 8,000–10,000 vines/ha (3ft 3in [1m] between the vines and up to 4ft [1.2m] between the rows). The soils are poor (on fertile soils, the vine is too vigorous for this level of density), and with the increase in the leaf canopy, per-hectare yields can be higher (50hl/ha easily attainable) without any noticeable impact on quality. Viticulturally, it's an interesting equation given the retail price of the wines.

Traditionally, densities have always been lower in St-Emilion, though 5,000 vines/ha is considered adequate for quality wines. Where finances and replanting permit, this figure is being increased. Château Cheval Blanc has been planting at 7,700 vines/ha since 2000, while at Château Ausone, proprietor Alain Vauthier has planted just under a hectare at a density of 12,600 vines/ha: "In terms of quality and production, it's in my interest to increase the density at Ausone. Whether that's the case at Château Simard, where I've also planted at high density, will ultimately depend on the returns."

Training and pruning

An alternative or complementary means of increasing the vine-leaf spread is to raise the height of the trellising. There's a correlation between the height of the canopy and the width of the rows that maximizes sunlight. Below an index of 0.6 (height of canopy divided by width of row), the canopy is insufficient for photosynthesis.

Above: An old vine pruned according to the *taille Bordelaise* in a densely planted vineyard of the northern Médoc

Above an index of one, the canopy may be higher but there's then the risk of shadow falling on neighboring rows. In other words, nothing is ordained, and it's up to the grower to find the best compromise. In general, though, higher trellising has been in vogue in Bordeaux, with the leaf canopy moving to around 4ft (1.2m) in height.

The form of pruning is also governed by AOC rules. In the Médoc and Graves, producers have traditionally pruned to two fruiting canes, one at right angles on either side of the vine, each with three to five buds. The form resembles Guyot *double*, without the additional tiny spur (or *cot*) stipulated in the Guyot method. This system is known locally as the *taille Bordelaise* and is now practiced on the Right Bank as well. The advantages are an even spread of grape bunches and leaves, as well as an easier system for workers tackling green-harvesting or deleafing.

Guyot *simple* or Guyot *double* are otherwise the methods used for quality-minded producers. It's rare to find spur-pruned or cordon-trained vines at grand cru level, but there are exceptions to the rule. François Mitjavile has adopted this system at Château Tertre Roteboeuf in St-Emilion with positive results. The vine with the mature branch is pruned low to the ground, approximately 8–12in (20–30cm) in height, to benefit from the heat of the soil, and the trellising is raised a further 4ft 3in (1.3m) for an adequate leaf canopy and better photosynthesis. The density of plantation is a reasonably traditional 5,555 vines/ha.

Soil management

Soil analysis or mapping is one solution for determining a cultivation regimen. A detailed plan of soil types and their properties allows the application of parcel-by-parcel management. Decisions on such matters as drainage, rootstock, grape variety, pruning method, grass cover, and compost can then be defined. Most reports are obtained by digging pits to obtain soil samples that are then laboratory tested, but in 2006 Château Cos d'Estournel applied an innovative system borrowed from mining exploration called "measurement of soil resistivity" (linked to GPS) to map its 220-acre (89ha) vineyard in St-Estèphe.

The advent of soil analysis has made the use of fertilizers more coherent. If a parcel needs adjustment in terms of mineral content, the report will advise, and action can be taken; if not, the soil is left alone. At a number of properties, organic compost has now replaced chemical fertilizers.

There's also been a steady return to plowing in order to limit the use of chemical weedkillers, aerate the soil, and force the rooting system

deeper. This usually takes the form of a deep plowing in the fall and in March/April to bank up then liberate earth around the vines, followed by a lighter plowing in the late spring and summer. Again, cost is a factor, as is access to the right equipment. Several systems for under-vine plowing have been developed, including a locally manufactured pneumatic hoeing machine that automatically regulates depth (the winner of the Trophée d'Or for innovation at Bordeaux's Vinitech exposition in 2008).

Grass cover between rows is a regular occurrence these days, particularly on the Right Bank. It has two specific benefits, in that it helps halt erosion on sloping vineyards and curbs vigor in the vine. It does this by competing with the vine for water (in particular, absorbing late summer rain) and by reducing nitrogen status. The natural grass can be left to grow or be cut short, even eliminated, in particularly dry years. The usual practice, as demonstrated at Château Canon-la-Gaffelière on St-Emilion's *pied de côtes*, is to have grass cover every other row, the rows alternating each year. Studies have been made on seeding grass and other crops, but as far as François Mitjavile at Tertre Roteboeuf is concerned, they've proved inconclusive. "Until the benefits are proven, I'll stay with natural grass cover as I have for the past 30 years," he declares.

Green work

The *travail en vert* is pretty well a year-round occupation and has done much to add precision to viticulture at top estates in Bordeaux. It may be classed as canopy management but is actually about defining yield and ripeness, as well as helping to prevent disease. The operation starts with the skilled task of pruning (December to March). Some Bordeaux estates now allot the

Right: At the onset of veraison, some of the less ripe grapes are green-harvested, now a common way of reducing yields

same parcels for pruning to the same personnel on a yearly basis, so the work can be followed and familiarity helps ensure a more efficient job. The next foray into the vineyard is in May and June, when water sprouts on the trunk and arms of the vine are removed (*épamprage*). They have no active part in the ripening process and end up giving too much shade. Excess buds or double buds may also be eliminated (*ébourgeonnage*).

Green-harvesting, or the removal of grape bunches to limit yield, started in Bordeaux in the 1980s and is now a fairly systematic process, certainly at grand cru level. It takes place in July, after flowering and just before veraison. A second *éclaircissage* may be contemplated in late August, depending on the size of the grape bunches. The occasional estate, such as Château Sociando-Mallet, eschews the operation, relying instead on pruning to dictate yield.

Deleafing around the grape clusters is another operation that takes place in July to permit ventilation and allow sunshine to penetrate, thus improving conditions for ripening and helping to prevent disease. The leaves are usually plucked "sunrise side," though occasionally the other side is also plucked in August or September if climatic conditions dictate. The torrid 2003 vintage was a reminder that deleafing is not obligatory every year and may even, as then, be counterproductive.

By definition, the work in the vineyards is labor-intensive, so human resources have to be available and the cost of that resource merited by the price of the wine. A permanent team of 45 staff works year-round in the 282-acre (114ha) vineyard of Château Lafite Rothschild, where evidently the price of the resulting wine makes it worthwhile. They are supplemented by a further 40 casual workers to help with the green-harvesting and deleafing in the summer months.

Left: Ever-greater efforts are being made in the vineyards, from sexual confusion (bottom middle) to hand-harvesting

Organics and disease

Bordeaux's humid climate makes it susceptible to cryptogamic or fungal diseases. Oidium (powdery mildew) and mildew (downy mildew) are regular blights, the latter prevalent during the growing season in 2007 and 2008. Producers in the region are well rehearsed in combating this, though, the problems being preventable with sulfur (for oidium), copper-based solutions (for mildew), and other antifungal sprays. Local weather stations assist with the timing of the spraying.

Botrytis is another bane. In certain conditions it can turn to noble rot, a state required for the production of Sauternes. In others, it becomes the undesirable gray rot, which affects the quality and volume of the harvest. The "green" work assists in prevention, but most producers employ anti-botrytis sprays with a treatment just after flowering and another at veraison.

Diseases of the wood are also prevalent, with esca now taking over from eutypiose as the more virulent in the region. Cabernet Sauvignon and Sauvignon Blanc are the two varieties particularly affected. There are treatments but no sure remedy, so the problem is both economic (thanks to loss of yield and the necessity to replant) and qualitative (the reduction in the age of the vines).

The conditions make it difficult to consider organic viticulture in Bordeaux, the commercial risk often too extreme to contemplate. Just over 4,950 acres (2,000ha) of the region's 296,500 acres (120,000ha) are officially registered as organic, which is only 2 percent of the vineyard. A few have embraced biodynamics, but they are mainly small estates (in terms of area) on the Right Bank. The exception to the rule is Château Pontet-Canet in Pauillac, which started biodynamic conversion in 2004. The level of commitment is admirable, because a virulent attack of mildew in 2007 necessitated conventional treatment, requiring the process of conversion to be started all over again.

Many leading estates, however, have parcels where organic or biodynamic viticulture is being tested, and most producers are already embracing sustainable viticulture (*lutte raisonnée*). This usually takes the form of less frequent spraying (aided by weather reports) with less aggressive products. It can also include the abandonment of weedkillers, use of organic compost, and other efforts to improve the ecosystem. One such is the use of tiny vials of female pheromone in the vineyard to disrupt the reproductive cycle of the grape-berry moth, rather than resorting to insecticides. The method, known as *confusion sexuelle*, was developed by INRA at Château Couhins in Pessac-Léognan and gained official approval in 1995.

The harvest: when and how

At harvest time, the objective, it goes without saying, is to pick grapes at optimum ripeness. In the past, sugar and acidity levels (along with pH) helped gauge picking dates, and this is still the case to some extent, but phenolic, or physiological, ripeness (the maturity of anthocyanins and tannins) has now become the main criterion. The quantity of phenolics can be measured scientifically, and one of the newer figures to be handed out proudly at en primeur tastings, alongside the alcohol level, is the score on the *indice des polyphénols totaux* (IPT, or total phenolics index). Statistics are one thing, but tasting the fruit, seeds, and skins provides a gustatory analysis that sometimes has the final say.

The pursuit of phenolic ripeness has meant leaving bunches hanging longer on the vine— hence the importance of the green work, preparing the vineyard either to cope with the eventuality of rain or to exploit the benefits of an Indian summer as the harvest approaches. The theoretical date is usually calculated as 110 days from the midpoint of flowering. This was pushed out to a record 135 days in 2008 as producers sought to make the best of the late-season sunshine after an indifferent year. Stylistically, too, there are producers who push to the limits of overripeness. According to climatic conditions, harvest dates for red varieties can vary by up to three weeks, starting in early to mid-September and running to the end of October. Alcohol levels have increased partly as a result of the longer hang-time, and 1999 was the last vintage when chaptalization was employed on any scale.

The period of harvest has also lengthened as producers wait for ripeness in the different grape varieties and parcels. It's now more of a stop–start affair, since parcels of vines are picked according to maturity, sometimes with two- to three-day gaps between plots. The Haut-Brion team can take two weeks to pick the 12 acres (5ha) of white varieties that produce white Haut-Brion and Laville Haut-Brion. Alternatively, picking can be done quickly. François Mitjavile issues a day's notice to his 70-odd pickers when he feels the time is right, and they harvest the 12 acres (5ha) of Merlot at Tertre Roteboeuf in a day. This is rather more difficult at large estates like châteaux Lafite and Mouton Rothschild, where the organization of 300 to 400 pickers (mostly bused in from the city of Bordeaux) has all the makings of a military maneuver.

Machine-harvesting is another credible option, but the assumption is that, at grand cru level, most if not all the picking will be done by hand. The emphasis on work practices in the vineyard has meant that gentle handling of the fruit has become something of an obsession. At some top estates, grapes are picked into shallow plastic crates, or *cagettes*, to avoid bruising or crushing. Large tractors pulling trailers with a mass of oozing fruit are a thing of the past at this level. Sorting can be done at the vine or on sorting tables in the vineyard.

Right: Smaller containers than in the past are now widely used by conscientious producers to protect their fruit

Translating Terroir

It is now widely accepted that great wine is made in the vineyard and that the quality of the fruit is paramount. But the raw product still has to be transformed into wine. Bordeaux, blessed with a university containing a Faculté d'Oenologie and dedicated research institutes (including the Institut des Sciences de la Vigne et du Vin, opened in 2009), has always been at the cutting edge of winemaking technology, and this is reflected in the expertise and hardware found at grand cru châteaux today. There is choice in, and control over, the winemaking process, and the level of attention to detail in the cellar often makes the difference between a good wine and an exceptional one. "We can't rely on terroir alone," says Thomas Duroux, managing director of Château Palmer and formerly the winemaker at Tenuta dell'Ornellaia in Italy. "Technology has a part to play in the production of a great wine."

Sorting and handling: the gentle touch

The emphasis placed on the quality of the grapes in the vineyard has now stretched to how they are handled in the winery. Gentle handling is the order of the day, and with it a scrupulous process of sorting and selection to weed out any unwanted matter (leaves, stalks, damaged or unripe berries, and so on). Sorting tables (some that vibrate), peristaltic pumps, conveyor belts, less aggressive destemmers—all are part of the armory for the reception and processing of red grapes. At Château Palmer, for instance, the sorting system was changed in 2005 and now includes a perforated vibrating table (to drain moisture and eliminate small *millerandés* berries), a conveyor-belt-system sorting table (with eight people sorting), a destemmer (new generation, 2009), a second vibrating table, and a second sorting table (with 14 people sorting).

Left: There is now greater control over the winemaking process than ever before as technology enhances tradition

The advance in technology has not stopped there. Borrowing ideas from the agriculture industry, several machines have been invented to provide greater precision in the sorting and to reduce the personnel required. Château Angélus introduced the Mistral into the chain of sorting in 2006. Originally invented for selecting peas, the Mistral table funnels the berries into channels and eliminates lighter material by a jet of air.

The Tribaie is a machine that works by specific gravity and sugar concentration in the fruit. A rotating adhesive drum first takes out leaves and stalks, then allows the grapes to flow into a grape must of known density, where they are separated and streamed, the ripe grapes sinking and filing in one direction, the less ripe grapes floating in another. The system was invented by Philippe Bardet, a grower in St-Emilion, and is used by André Lurton at Château Rochemorin. More recently (2008), it has been in use at Château Valandraud. "The Tribaie removes the equivalent of about 5–10 percent more grapes per vat that are not fully ripe, thus improving selection and quality," says Rémi Dalmasso, winemaker for the Jean-Luc Thunevin properties.

The latest machine on the market (or rather machines, because there are presently two versions from competing companies) is an optical grape-sorting system. The software provides artificial vision to recognize the shape and color of berries, unwanted fruit being removed by a jet of air. Château Smith Haut Lafitte trialed the system in 2008 and purchased one in 2009 (as did Château Léoville-Las-Cases and several other estates). "The machine detects the subtleties of color better than the human eye and is more consistent than teams of sorters that change throughout the day," explains Smith Haut Lafitte technical director Fabien Tietgen.

Gentle handling continues with the flow of grapes to the fermentation vats. Hand destemming is an old technique reinvented for some of the properties owned by Bernard Magrez, including Château Pape Clément, and was also tried at Château Angélus in 2009. Also at Angélus, conveyor belts take the grapes to the tanks over which they are lightly crushed before tumbling in. Crushing is generally lighter than in the past and, in some cases, shunned completely. Ideally, pumps are avoided and a system of gravity feeding used. This is the case at most of the newly constructed cellars such as those of Cos d'Estournel, Malartic Lagravière, and Faugères. In a modern design, the practice looks ingenious, but it's not a new idea, as the 19th-century museum at Château Lynch-Bages reveals. Financing again plays a huge part, and those who are unable or unwilling to incur the expense remain reliant on hoppers, pumps, and a thorough selection in the vineyard.

Fermentation techniques

Bordeaux winemakers have a range of techniques open to them when it comes to fermentation and extraction, the dictates being the quality of the vintage and the style of wine required. The initial decision is the choice of fermentation tank. With the trend toward parcel-by-parcel vineyard management, the tendency has been to reduce the size of vats. The first thing Duroux requested when he arrived at Château Palmer in 2004 was to have the 200hl stainless-steel tanks split into double 90hl versions. At about the same time, the number of tanks at Château Haut-Bailly was quadrupled to 30, for the 81.5-acre (33ha) vineyard.

Stainless steel, oak, and cement are all available in Bordeaux, sometimes all three at the same property. Temperature-control systems can be adapted to all, as can the truncated conical form preferred for extraction. Each has its positive and negative points, but stainless steel is the easiest to run from the point of view of hygiene and is, therefore, widespread. Cement is largely a Right

Bank tradition and efficient for maintaining a uniform temperature. Oak tanks are good for extraction, due to the natural oxygenation via the wood. When they are new, they add *sucrosité* and structure to a wine, but they are costly and difficult to maintain.

One option prior to alcoholic fermentation is a cold (46–54°F [8–12°C]) pre-fermentation soak, the must protected from oxidation by sulfur dioxide or dry ice. Protagonists feel the advantages of this technique are the extraction of color and aroma in the absence of alcohol. Antagonists have another view. "The fruit aromas are eventually eradicated by the oxidative process of aging the wine in barrel," says consultant Eric Boissenot, "and there's a loss of quality in the tannins, which appear more astringent."

Choices during the alcoholic fermentation include the decision to inoculate with yeast, the temperature (75–82.5°F [24–28°C] is the normal range), the extraction method (*remontage, pigeage,* or *délestage*), and the length of the maceration (generally 15–21 days). The final decisions are based on the amount of extraction required. Concentration can be obtained by bleeding the tanks (*saignée*) prior to fermentation or by the use of concentrators. At grand cru level several are in circulation (often based on reverse osmosis), but they are used sparingly according to the vintage and the vat, and producers are discreet about their existence, even though they are legally tolerated. Concentration is applied to the unfermented juice. Another common technique is microoxygenation. Carried out during fermentation *sous marc*, a homeopathic dose of oxygen helps disguise vegetal notes and stabilize tannins.

The finished wine is then run off and the *marc* pressed. Modern presses—some, contemporary versions of the traditional vertical press; others,

Right: Old oak fermentation vats are still widely used, as here at Léoville-Las-Cases, but they need an experienced hand

pneumatic—are gentler than previous versions and give a better quality of press wine, which can be an important component in the final blend. At Palmer, they have up to 200 barrels of press wine, which can be 10 percent of the final blend. Conversely, the press wine at Haut-Bailly is deemed too rustic and never used in the grand vin.

Barrel aging

At most progressive châteaux, and where volume permits, malolactic fermentation usually takes place in (new) oak barrels. There's a better integration of oak (possibly because the wine goes "hot" into the barrel) at an early stage, and the fruit expression is enhanced. Commercially, this is a valuable asset for young wines destined to be revealed at en primeur tastings in April, but researchers believe that in the long term there is little difference between completing malolactic fermentation in barrel or in tank. Experiments with delayed malolactic fermentation in June have proved beneficial, not least because the addition of sulfur dioxide can be avoided, but the commercial pressure of en primeur means this is unlikely to be adopted as a universal practice.

In terms of aging in barrel, the 225-liter *barrique Bordelaise* is still the classic recipient for grand cru wines. Winemakers will usually employ a blend of barriques from different cooperages and will also vary the proportion of new oak. Compared to the 1980s (indeed, up to 1995), the proportion of new oak barrels used by châteaux has generally diminished, and the toasting of the barrels has also been moderated. That said, 100 percent new oak is still the choice of the first growths and producers such as Jean-Luc Thunevin. "New barrels give more color, aroma, flesh, and *sucrosité*, provide added oak tannins, and are microbiologically safer," says Rémi Dalmasso,

Left: The periodic racking of barrels, as here at Château Margaux, is a laborious but necessary part of traditional *élevage*

Thunevin's winemaker. At around $800 a barrel (excluding tax), however, such a decision does not come cheaply.

The maturation of wine in barrel (*élevage*) involves moderate and sporadic contact with air, the oxygen helping to fix color and round out tannins. The process also assists with the clarification of the wine and imparts flavor. The traditional method of *élevage* in Bordeaux is to rack the wine from barrel to barrel, aerating and clarifying in the process, every three to four months, the total period of maturation these days anything from 16 to 22 months. Another more controversial method now in use is the aging of the wine on fine lees without racking but with microoxygenation (*cliquage*) instead. Simon Blanchard, an oenologist and associate of wine consultant Stéphane Derenoncourt explains: "The *bâtonnage* helps flesh out the wine, making it richer and rounder, with better oak integration, but the method can incite reduction, which we counterbalance with *cliquage*."

Derenoncourt is a strong advocate of this method, and a large number of his consultancies, including top growths, are matured this way. But other producers, including progressive thinkers like Hubert de Boüard at Château Angélus and Jean-Luc Thunevin of Château Valandraud, are wary of the technique and have stayed with the classic system of racking. "Racking is a gentle method if done correctly. It allows the barrels to be disinfected, which is good for hygiene, and it is less extreme than aging on lees with *bâtonnage*," says Eric Boissenot.

An additional approach practiced by some châteaux (and by consultants like Derenoncourt and Michel Rolland) is the aging of the wine on fine lees with minimal racking, perhaps only once in the first year. The objectives are again richness of flavor and texture, aided by a reduction in the levels of sulfur dioxide, but the process needs to be handled with care to avoid microbiological instability and the threat of volatile acidity and *Brettanomyces*.

Fining and/or filtration are the usual practices at the end of *élevage*. Fresh egg whites (four to six per barrel) for fining is still the practice at traditional Bordeaux châteaux, but powdered albumin and agents such as bentonite are also much in use. At grand cru level, any filtration is normally light, with a membrane filter for clarity.

Blending and selection

There are two schools of thought when it comes to blending young wines in Bordeaux. The traditional argument is that blending should be carried out early so that the components have time to knit. The different grape varieties from the various cuvées are tasted, a selection is made, and the blend is produced in February or March at the time of the first racking, with only the press-wine component to be added later. A second course of action, advocated by consultant oenologist Michel Rolland among others, is to keep the components separate for observation during maturation and to blend at the last minute, just before bottling. A convincing case can be made for either method, but the validity of en primeur samples with respect to the final wine is obviously open to question.

The creation of second and even third labels provides châteaux with a means of selection for the grand vin. Selections have undoubtedly become more severe since the mid-1990s. In 2008, only 40 percent of the production made it into Château Latour, 47 percent destined for Les Forts de Latour and 13 percent for the third wine, Pauillac. The same year at Château Beychevelle, 55 percent of the crop made the top wine, whereas in 1982 the figure was 96 percent. Even in outstanding vintages such as 2005 there has been no letting up on this draconian procedure. Château Haut-Brion selected 55 percent of the crop for the grand vin, and Château Léoville-Las-Cases just

37 percent. Quality is the objective, but commercial considerations and brand building play a part.

Dry white wines

Châteaux that aspire to making Bordeaux's finest dry white wines have taken a leaf out of the Sauternes producers' manual and now hand-harvest by successive passages (*tries*) through the vineyard to pick at optimum maturity. Machine-harvesting in the cool of the evening or early morning is the option for other producers. Excessive water stress in the summer months is less desirable for white varieties than for red, since aroma can be blunted and balance lost. Adequate moisture is required to maintain freshness, fruit, and harmony, so top dry white vintages do not always correspond to red—witness 2002 and 2007.

Oenologically, the main concern is protection against oxidation with inert gas, temperature control and sulfur dioxide being the relevant tools of the trade. The trend is usually to press whole grape bunches, but occasionally grapes are destemmed and lightly pressed, or pressed under controlled conditions to undergo skin contact for added aroma and body in the wine. The grapes (generally Sauvignon Blanc) have to be ripe and healthy to undergo this procedure.

Cold-settling (*débourbage à froid*) to remove unwanted solids (earth, damaged grapes, etc) precedes fermentation in barrel. The proportion of new oak is definitely in decline, with Professor Denis Dubourdieu, the father of modern white-wine making in Bordeaux, showing the way. Back in 1987, the Sauvignon Blanc from his own Clos Floridène, was fermented and aged in 50 percent new oak barrels. By 1996, the figure had dropped to 15 percent, and now it is zero. A wine like Domaine de Chevalier is fermented and matured in 35 percent new oak barrels. Added flavor and texture

Right: Wines need to be tasted from barrel, but a carefully placed pebble makes sure that the same one is not overused

are obtained by maturing the wines on fine lees, which are regularly put into suspension by stirring. Bottling generally takes place about ten months after the harvest.

Sauternes

The success of a vintage in Sauternes and other sweet wine appellations is due almost entirely to the apparition of noble rot and the quality of the fruit at harvest—hence the importance of precision in the picking. This can last three months or be over in 14 days. Fine-tuning in the cellar revolves around the quality of the pressed juice. The process of pressing (using pneumatic and vertical presses) is long and slow, with a gradual increase in pressure allowing the separation of three or four batches of juice. The final press is usually the most aromatic and richest in sugar but, to provide balance and harmony, needs to be blended with other lots. One of the details involves matching a particular batch of juice to the most suitable barrel. At properties such as châteaux Climens and Lafaurie-Peyraguey, 30 percent new oak barrels are used (the rest one and two years), and maturation lasts 16–18 months. Despite the minimal quantities produced, selection is still imposed at grand cru level via the use of a second label (sometimes 35–50 percent of the crop) or by selling on discarded lots to the négociants.

Consultants and taste

The role of the consultant in Bordeaux has taken on a wider dimension in recent years, with marketing subliminally added to the traditional brief of viticulture and winemaking. With the offer from Bordeaux as large as ever and markets harder to pierce, the Rolland or Derenoncourt trademark has become an effective selling tool. The name of the consultant also says something about the style of the wine. Emile Peynaud, an academic

from the Institut d'Oenologie, set the mold in the post–World War II years with his ability clearly to communicate basic winemaking principles (malolactic fermentation, hygiene, temperature control) to the cellar masters responsible for the wine. His approach was seen as modern but today would be interpreted as classic Bordeaux winemaking, with balance, finesse, length, and structure for bottle aging the cornerstones of his design. Jacques Boissenot, his assistant for many years, upholds the same principles today. Discreet by nature and inclination, he and his son Eric avoid extremes (ripe but not overripe grapes, gentle extraction, early blending, careful use of press wine), preferring subtlety in wine. Their portfolio reads like a who's who of the Médoc. Michel Rolland is a cheerful, outgoing character, which is reflected in the style of wine he prefers. He has always preached ripeness in the grapes and still believes that most Bordeaux producers pick too soon. It's perhaps a bit of a caricature, but his trademark is for dark, rich, supple wines that exude a certain power. This is easier to see among his consultancies in Pomerol and St-Emilion, but he's also active in the Médoc and Pessac-Léognan.

Unlike the Boissenots and Rolland, Stéphane Derenoncourt is not an oenologist but a self-taught winemaker. His knowledge stems from a close affinity with the vineyard, and he, like Rolland, leans toward later and riper harvesting. Techniques in the cellar such as *pigeage* and barrel aging on lees with *cliquage* tend to highlight the fruit aspect of the wine at an early stage. Most of his consultancies are on the Right Bank, but he, too, has now spread into the Médoc and Pessac-Léognan. Other important consultants include Denis Dubourdieu, renowned for his expertise on white wines but with an expanding portfolio of red-wine producers; Gilles Pauquet (retained by Cheval Blanc); and, of the younger generation, Olivier Dauga, Jean-Philippe Fort, and Christian Veyry.

Left: The first-year barrel cellar at Château Margaux, with rows of carefully regimented barriques from its own cooperage

Paris 1855 to Parker 100

Bordeaux operates a unique commercial system known as the *Place de Bordeaux*. Organizationally, it's akin to a virtual stock exchange (there's no physical structure) where négociants buy wine from châteaux and from each other before selling on to customers around the world. Because of the bias of interest on both sides, the reliance on trust rather than written contracts, as well as the sheer number of wines, a third party—the *courtier*—operates as an interface to arbitrate in transactions.

This three-tier system inevitably has its detractors, not least because it precludes the direct sale of wine to distributors and levers price to cover margins for the intermediaries. But it has proved a very effective way of getting a large volume of wine onto the market quickly, and has remained resilient despite cyclical fluctuations in the economy and trade, and despite predictions of its imminent demise.

Its existence owes much to the historical evolution and social structure of the region. As the vineyards in pre-Revolution Bordeaux expanded, particularly in the Graves and Médoc, so the social framework was reinforced. The vineyards (certainly the best of them) were owned by the men of power and wealth—the Church, the nobility, and politicians—while the trading was carried out by the merchant class, a disparate and often transient group of businessmen. Relations between the two were uneasy, so to facilitate commerce, the *courtier* soon found a place. A man of confidence for both sides, with experience on the ground, the *courtier* helped source wine, negotiate payment, and smooth transactions in return for a commission (traditionally set at 2 percent on each transaction).

Brokers were active when the English first arrived to purchase wine in the Middle Ages and later assisted the Dutch in their acquisition of bulk white and sturdy red *palus* wines. The role, though, grew in consequence and stature as pricing structures for wines from different regions and for different markets became established—and certainly from the mid-18th century, when the notion and value of individual crus became more defined. The *courtiers* became "guardians of the temple," the hub around which prices were negotiated and recorded, and successful businesses were passed on through the generations.

A classic example is the house of Tastet & Lawton, the oldest in the city today. Abraham Lawton arrived in Bordeaux from his home town of Cork in 1739 at age 23, setting up as a broker and purchaser of wines. His son Guillaume then took over the business; his grandson Edouard put up the brass plate of Tastet & Lawton at the present address of 60 Quai des Chartrons in the 1830s. This respected firm is still one of the four principal *courtiers* operating on the *Place de Bordeaux* and remains in family hands. In the company archives, a collection of old ledgers record in copperplate hand the number and price of tonneaux purchased from a particular château for a specified négociant as far back as 1806.

The 1855 Classification

It's within this context that the famous 1855 Classification of the wines of the Médoc (plus Château Haut-Brion) and Sauternes was set up. The best of the region's wines were solicited for the 1855 Universal Exposition of Paris, and to accompany them a classification was supplied by the Bordeaux brokers at the behest of the Bordeaux Chamber of Commerce. The red wines of the Médoc were ranked in five grades according to price, and the sweet white wines of Sauternes in two, with the exception of Château d'Yquem, which was given a class of its own: premier cru supérieur (*see Chapter 12, Classifications*).

The fact that the *courtiers* produced the Classification within two weeks of the Chamber

Above: The Palais d'Industrie at the Exposition Universelle of 1855, for which the Médoc classification of that year was prepared

of Commerce's request indicates that a hierarchy of properties already existed and that they merely provided a statement explaining this hierarchy. As already mentioned, prices for individual crus had been recorded from at least the mid-18th century, and this was by no means the first classification of its kind. A history had already been created, with price the measure of quality and market strength.

As it turns out, the 1855 Classification has since become cast in stone. The only changes have been the addition of Château Cantemerle as a fifth growth soon after the original list was compiled (deemed an oversight due to a monopoly of distribution by the Dutch) and the promotion of Château Mouton Rothschild from second to first growth in 1973, thanks to the price of the wines and the tenacity of Baron Philippe de Rothschild.

A roll of honor for the châteaux, the 1855 Classification has remained a driving force for the region, the value in publicity alone worth its weight in gold. And despite strong arguments for revision, it still provides the pricing structure found on the *Place de Bordeaux* today.

Subsequent classifications

Additional classifications have since been established to give a hierarchical account of other châteaux and regions in Bordeaux (*see Chapter 12*). The only exception among the major appellations is Pomerol, where there is no official classification.

Crus bourgeois The term cru bourgeois was originally coined at the end of the 15th century to denote properties owned by the well-to-do middle

WHAT'S IN A LABEL?

Bordeaux label terminology can be confusing. Some terms, such as *grand vin*, are not officially controlled, so do not necessarily reflect the quality of the wine; some *grands vins*, including those above, are indeed great, but others are not. Even when the terms are officially regulated, they are inconsistently applied. Some châteaux use legitimate variations, such as cru classé without the specific rank, while others eschew terms to which they are entitled. As always, the most important words are those of the château as the producer.
Top: Being outside the Médoc, Haut-Brion was the honorable exception in the 1855 classification, its price and reputation warranting premier grand cru classé status. While Margaux also displays this status, Lafite, the first of the firsts in 1855, does not.

Second row: Léoville Poyferré happily identifies itself as a second growth, while neighboring Léoville Barton (also a second growth) and Lynch Bages (a fifth growth) identify themselves merely as cru classé and grand cru classé.
Third row: Even the greatest Pomerols share the same appellation as the most humble, without any classification. In St-Emilion, Cheval Blanc, which could identify itself as premier grand cru classé A, does not, while Mondotte does not even apply for such status and depends on its brand name.
Bottom: Graves are classified but not further subdivided. Fourcas Hosten was proud to be a cru bourgeois supérieur, while Sociando-Mallet, which could have enjoyed a similar status, has relied on the name of the property and proprietor.

classes, as distinct from the aristocrats of the city. In the Médoc the list gradually became more democratic. A hierarchy was eventually formalized by the *courtiers* in 1932 as the Classification of the Crus Bourgeois of the Médoc.

It generously contained 444 châteaux ranked in three categories (crus bourgeois supérieurs exceptionnels, crus bourgeois supérieurs, and crus bourgeois) covering what are now the six communal and two regional appellations of the Médoc. It was instigated at a difficult economic juncture to give promotional support to châteaux not classified in 1855. Over the years, though, policing and standards declined, and the listing began to run out of control.

Finally, a new classification (valid for ten years) was inaugurated in 2003, formalized by a jury that took into account the management and standing of each property, as well as tasting a number of stipulated vintages from each. All told, 247 châteaux (from 490 potential candidates) were ranked in ascending order as crus bourgeois (151), crus bourgeois supérieurs (87), and crus bourgeois exceptionnels (9). It didn't go down well with everyone, though: the rejected properties were unhappy with both the organization and the procedure. They took legal action that led to the eventual abolition of the classification and the suppression of the cru bourgeois label from 2008.

In 2009, the growers' *syndicat*, the Alliance des Crus Bourgeois, was in the throes of establishing a new classification scheme. This will award the cru bourgeois certificate on a yearly basis, following a blind tasting by an independent panel. There will be no fixed hierarchy of châteaux, as in the 1932 or 2003 versions. If generally accepted and officially sanctioned, the first vintage under these conditions would be the 2008, which it was hoped would launch in 2010. Desperate times call for desperate measures, and for many châteaux, cru bourgeois status is an obligatory marketing aid.

Graves It is surprising that Bordeaux's oldest viticultural region, the Graves, did not have a classification until 1953. Graves wines traded below those of the Médoc in the run-up to the 1855 Classification—hence their absence, the only exception being Château Haut-Brion. A classification was finally established 100 years later by a commission of *courtiers* under the direction of INAO.

The *courtiers* took pricing into account but added that the concepts of "notoriety" and "quality adjudged by tasting" would also be taken into consideration. One designated grade was created, cru classé de Graves, the other major difference being that it was applicable to both red and dry white wines. Initially five white and 11 red wines from 12 châteaux were awarded the status. A revision then took place, made official in 1959, adding a further two reds and three whites to the original list. All told, 15 châteaux were included, a figure that increased to 16 when, in 1968, Château Couhins became two separate entities, Couhins and Couhins-Lurton.

In 2006, Château La Tour Haut-Brion was integrated into Château La Mission Haut-Brion, but otherwise the classification has remained the same. A little updating, however, wouldn't be out of order. The much-admired white wine of Château Smith Haut Lafitte, for example, was not included in 1959 because there was little or no production, and a property like Château Les Carmes Haut-Brion also has sufficient grounds for inclusion. There are two major obstacles. The crus classés de Graves are all located in the Pessac-Léognan appellation (created in 1987), but the classification is officially administered by the Graves *syndicat*, so politics play a strong part. Furthermore, the threat of a legal furor now hangs heavy in the event of any change, as a result of the problems surrounding the crus bourgeois and St-Emilion revisions.

St-Emilion The wines of St-Emilion failed to make the 1855 Classification because they were not embraced by the Bordeaux Chamber of Commerce or the city's *courtiers*. As with the Graves, it took another century to instigate a classification, the first endorsed in 1955. Four appellations were designated—St-Emilion, St-Emilion grand cru, St-Emilion grand cru classé, and St-Emilion premier grand cru classé, the latter two numbering 63 and 12 châteaux respectively. An important modern innovation was that the classification would be revised every ten years.

An amendment in 1958 upgraded châteaux Ausone and Cheval Blanc to premiers grands crus classés (A)—a status they have retained. The other ten properties were registered as premiers grands crus classés (B). A full revision occurred in 1969, leaving the premiers grands crus classés as before but increasing the grands crus classés to 72.

The third classification was postponed from 1979 until 1986 due to bureaucratic reform. St-Emilion premier grand cru classé and grand cru classé slipped from AOC status but were still officially recognized, the former reduced to 11 with the demotion of Château Beau-Séjour Bécot, and the latter to 63. Unlike the 1855 Classification of the Médoc, there's a stricter control in St-Emilion on new parcels of vines, and Beau-Séjour Bécot fell foul of this administrative rule.

The St-Emilion classification was now gaining impetus as a vehicle for change and promotion, the price and quality of the wines being among the determining factors that a professional jury took into consideration. The 1996 edition introduced further modification. Châteaux Angélus and Beau-Séjour Bécot were promoted to premiers grands crus classés, taking the tally to 13, while the grands crus classés were reduced to 55.

In 2006, the jury announced an even more radical revision. Two châteaux, Pavie Macquin and Troplong Mondot, were promoted to premiers grands crus classés, taking the total to 15, while among the grands crus classés there were 11 demotions and six newly promoted châteaux, leaving a total of 46 in this category.

The commercial sanctions (loss of value of land and wines) were too much for the demoted châteaux to stand, however, and several instituted legal action, accusing the jury of procedural irregularities. A stream of litigation and court rulings followed, and the St-Emilion classification itself was at risk. But in May 2009 an official compromise was found. The 1996 classification was reinstated, with the addition of the properties promoted in 2006 (both premiers grands crus classés and grands crus classés), taking the former to 15 and the latter to 57. This classification is binding up to and including the 2011 vintage; thereafter, a new classification with a revised set of rules will be introduced.

The actors and en primeur

The *Place de Bordeaux* operates as an internal market, with châteaux, négociants, and *courtiers* the principal actors. Archaic, even chaotic, as seen from outside, its strength is the collective ability to distribute a large volume of wine to markets around the world. "Supply and demand" is the economic model that applies.

The négociants, of which there are 300–400 in Bordeaux, handle 70 percent of the region's production (5.7 million hl in 2007), the rest sold directly by the producers. Around 100 négociants are involved in the grand cru sector, where there are two major activities: *vins livrables* (bottled wines) and en primeur. "The best formula for Bordeaux is to sell en primeur but keep vintages alive by having stocks to sell," says John Kolasa, who wears two hats as managing director of Château Rauzan-Ségla and of négociant Ulysse Cazabonne.

Right: St-Emilion producers can manage ceremonial shows of unity but have been divided over revisions to their classification

Above: Jacques Thienpont nosing a barrel sample at Le Pin, as fortunate press and trade do at the annual en primeur tastings

The *courtiers* are implicated in both activities and, as far as bottled wines are concerned, are in competition with each other. Finding châteaux to present, discovering quantities of classed growths or their second wines, and perhaps older vintages as well, requires a presence on the ground, knowing the needs of individual négociants and moving faster than the competition. Some 75 percent of the business handled by the négociants, as well as the entire en primeur grand cru market, passes through the *courtiers*. There are around 130 registered *courtiers* but no more than ten of significance when it comes to en primeur.

The futures, or en primeur, system is a paper transaction that permits the sale of wine up to two years before it is bottled. It provides cash flow for the châteaux and, in a perfect world, a decent margin for négociants (10–18 percent), as well as an attractive price for consumers. The youthful, unfinished wines are assessed by the trade and press in April following the vintage, then prices are released by the châteaux (and published by the *courtiers*) in May and June. The négociants buy at the opening price (*prix de sortie*) and must then respect a minimum price stipulated by most châteaux for selling on.

In bygone times, particularly in pre-château-bottling days, the négociants held the whip hand on price. The *courtiers* also held greater sway. Since 1982 it's been a seller's market, and the châteaux have called the tune. Further pressure is exerted by the allocation system. The top grands crus are released on a quota system, a château working with as many as 100 négociants to spread distribution. If a négociant decides to turn down his allocation in a difficult year, he risks losing it or having it reduced in a successful vintage. Procuring extra wine means a plea to the château or dealing with a fellow négociant—in which case, the price is likely to climb.

The market today

The number of châteaux that sell en primeur through the *Place* is tiny considering there are 9,500 growers in the region. In 2005, around 430 châteaux offered their wines en primeur, of which 230 were classed growths or equivalent. In 2008, the number fell to 332, of which 205 were classed-growth level. This does not, of course, mean that all the wines sold. In 2008, 75 percent of the wines offered on the *Place* were sold (to the négociants), whereas the figure for 2005 was 93 percent (according to Tastet & Lawton). The majority of négociants these days are wary of holding stock, preferring to buy a guaranteed brand then sell on quickly, even for a small margin, in order to safeguard allocations. That said, overstocking occurs when the market slows. The downturn in 2009 left merchants with an accumulation of 2006, 2007, and 2008 on their hands.

By nature, the Bordeaux market is speculative, and this aspect has escalated over the years. Several blue-chip châteaux have been identified as providing potentially substantial returns, and the *Place* has become more and more polarized toward buying and selling this select group of 50 or 60 châteaux, an unofficial club of first growths (the 1855 premiers crus plus Ausone and Cheval Blanc), and a select number of properties in the Médoc, Pessac-Léognan, St-Emilion, and Pomerol.

The economic model of supply and demand counts considerably in their case. Due to lower yields and greater selection, there's less grand vin from top estates than in the past. Ausone's current annual production of 1,250–1,600 cases is half what it was in the early 1980s, while that of Lafite Rothschild is down from 30,000 cases to an average 20,000. Demand, however, has grown, with wealthy new customers from Asia and South America joining the traditional markets of Belgium, Germany, Switzerland, the United Kingdom, and the United States.

In 2009, the London International Vintners Exchange, the fine-wine trading platform better known as Liv-ex, recalculated the 1855 Classification according to recent prices (*see Chapter 12*). The average case price for qualifying wines (Médoc and Pessac-Léognan châteaux with a minimum production of 2,000 cases) was computed for the vintages 2003–07 inclusive, and 60 wines were placed in five price bands as in 1855. First growths were wines that sold at £2,000 per case and above; second growths, £500–2,000; third growths, £300–500; fourth growths, £250–500; and fifth growths, £200–250.

The results are fascinating and help provide a more realistic view of the market today. There's plenty of movement up and down the scale, but of particular note were the accession of La Mission Haut-Brion to first-growth status, Lynch-Bages and Palmer to second growth, the integration of six other Pessac-Léognans, and the absence of ten of the original 1855 châteaux. Liv-ex added a postscript stating that a dozen second wines from top châteaux (Forts de Latour, Carruades de Lafite, etc) could have been included but were left out so as not to complicate matters.

Pricing is by no means dictated solely by the quality of the vintage; market conditions also play their part—hence the fickle nature of the system. The mediocre 1997 vintage was priced higher than the considerably better 1996 because of supposed demand from East Asia. The wines were bought by the négociants but heavily discounted later as the Asian economy declined, leaving customers who bought en primeur taking a loss. The same is likely to happen with the pleasant but average 2007. Having set a new high with prices for 2005, châteaux owners continued to be bullish with prices for 2006 and 2007. Then, with the economic downturn in 2009, they were obliged to reduce prices on the better 2008 vintage, devaluing the stock of 2006 and 2007.

Another factor in pricing is rivalry between châteaux. There's a good deal of jockeying for position on the market, and pricing is a declaration of the strength of the brand. A drop in price in relation to a comparable neighbor is not something the owner of a grand cru will contemplate lightly, since it may be taken as a sign of vulnerability. An upbeat policy on pricing is therefore a natural reaction in order to safeguard market position, even though it may defy the logic of the economic times or the vintage.

The secondary market has also had a considerable effect on pricing and the status of the brand. With age and scarcity, mature vintages of the blue-chip châteaux become an even more speculative commodity, the prices achieved increasing the value of the cru. Even with the economic downturn in 2009, the global auction market continued to be strong, with several sales in London, New York, and Hong Kong reaching totals in excess of their already high presale estimates. Asian buyers in particular were active in driving prices. At China's first fine-wine auction, held in Beijing in June 2009, two bottles of 1982 Lafite Rothschild fetched $10,700—four times their estimate.

In short, investment and speculation have become extreme for an elite group of châteaux, pushing price beyond the means of the regular wine lover into the realms of the super-rich or professional investor. The creation of wine funds since 2000 is a reflection of the situation. The *Place* stumbles on, with vintage variation and the prevailing economic climate providing the highs and lows but with a dwindling number of châteaux it can faithfully serve. At the same time, the Internet is making it possible to forge new links between merchants or producers and consumers, so perhaps this will be the long-term solution for châteaux and consumers who feel unloved by the *Place*.

The influence of critics

The global nature of the en primeur market since the 1980s has given rise to the heightened role of the wine critic. Previously, the pundit had a more parochial existence, offering comment to a limited audience in a specific country. Now critics have become more visible and voluble, the Internet and modern communications speeding their words around the globe. The result has been greater competition between châteaux, with ensuing improvements in quality as producers strive to reassure clients with positive news in the press.

Here, it's not only words that count. Ever since *Wine Spectator* and Robert Parker's *Wine Advocate* embraced the American college-based 100-point scoring system, numerical values have held sway. Wines may be given a lyrical description, but numbers transmit the basic message much more quickly and to an international audience. Consumer-led, the system has also suited many merchants, who use the scores as a marketing aid.

There are other internationally respected critics, including France's Michel Bettane and the UK's Jancis Robinson MW, but when it comes to having an impact on price and sales, American critic Robert Parker clearly leads the field. His scores have a bearing on en primeur prices and continue to influence the secondary market.

Much has been made of Parker's declining clout. It is certainly true that a high Parker score is no longer sufficient for garage wines to sell. And in the 2008 en primeur campaign, many châteaux announced prices before Parker published his scores. But the 2008 campaign also showed that his influence is still considerable. Despite the early release and the drop in prices, there was nonetheless a flurry of activity around his high-scoring wines, with a consequent rise in price. "Parker sells wine" is still the often-quoted line.

Right: Although the influence of critics is most important at the en primeur stage, it is also felt by merchants in the region

BORDEAUX

ST. EMILION

* POMEROL

* MEDOC

* ST. JULIEN

* ST. ESTEPHE

* PAUILLAC

* MARGAUX

* LISTRAC / MOULIS

* GRAVES

* SAUTERNES

* CADILLAC

* COTES DE CASTILLON

* COTES DE FRANCS ...

CAVE
CLIMATISEE

JCB
JCB CARD

AMERICAN
EXPRESS
Cartes et
American Express
Travelers Cheques

Diners Club
International

EN DEGUSTATION
FREE TASTING

The Médoc

The Médoc is the peninsula that runs north from the city of Bordeaux to the Pointe de Grave and, ultimately, the Atlantic Ocean. The vineyards hug the eastern flank, along the Gironde estuary—the nearest 1,650ft (500m) from the alluvial *palus* and water's edge; those farther inland, up to 8 miles (12km) away. To the west is pine forest and, eventually, sandy beaches. The land is flat, the high point, at Listrac, a mere 145ft (44m). Intermittent scrub and pasture break the landscape of vines, as do the drainage channels (*jalles*) laid by Dutch engineers in the 17th century. The prime land for viticulture is on the gravel *croupes* found predominantly in the communes of St-Estèphe, Pauillac, St-Julien, and Margaux, but also in Moulis, Listrac, and the subregional appellations of Médoc and Haut-Médoc. The gravel and climate, moderated by the estuary and bolstered by climate change, enable Cabernet Sauvignon to ripen here, making it the region's main variety, though Merlot has been on the rise. In the celebrated communes, the monotony of the countryside is broken by 18th- and 19th-century châteaux, many belonging to estates classified in 1855. Elsewhere, a host of properties has for many years found a common identity in the label "cru bourgeois." A classification of these in 2003 was annulled following litigation; but from 2008, a cru bourgeois certificate is to be reintroduced on a yearly basis.

St-Estèphe

St-Estèphe is the most northerly of the Médoc's four principal communal appellations. It has varied soils, with gravel *croupes* over to the east near the estuary, a bedrock of limestone (the *calcaire de St-Estèphe*) that outcrops in certain areas, and deposits of sand and clay, particularly in the west and north of the appellation. This influences the choice of grape variety and adds a varying nuance

Right: The typically flat Médocain landscape, the sea of vines broken only occasionally by pasture or scrub, as here in St-Julien

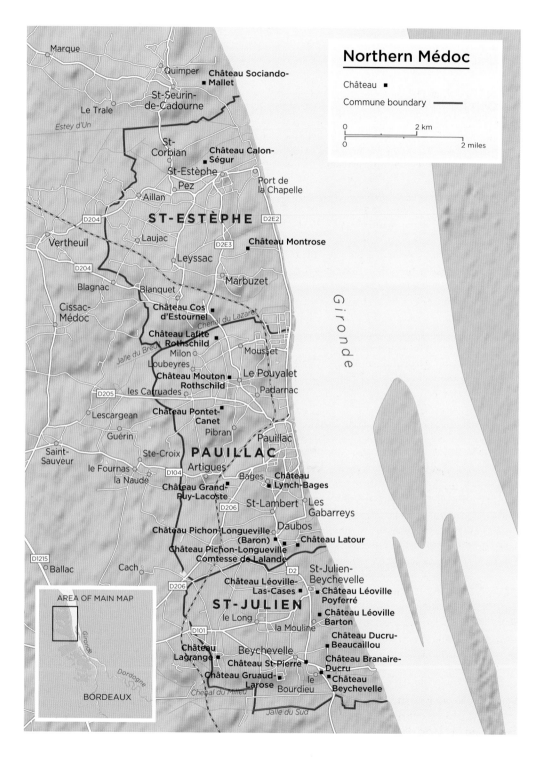

Northern Médoc

Château ■
Commune boundary ────

0   2 km
0   2 miles

Marque

Quimper

Château Sociando-Mallet ■

St-Seurin-de-Cadourne

Le Trale

Estey d'Un

St-Corbian

Château Calon-Ségur ■

St-Estèphe

Pez

Aillan

Port de la Chapelle

ST-ESTÈPHE

D204

D2E2

Laujac

Vertheuil

D2E3

Château Montrose ■

Leyssac

D204

Blagnac

Marbuzet

Blanquet

Cissac-Médoc

Château Cos d'Estournel ■

Chenal du Lazaret

Château Lafite Rothschild ■

Jalle du Breu

Milon

Loubeyres

Mousset

Château Mouton Rothschild ■

Le Pouyalet

les Carruades

Padarnac

Lescargean

Château Pontet-Canet ■

D205

Guérin

Pibran

Saint-Sauveur

Ste-Croix

PAUILLAC

Pauillac

le Fournas

Artigues

D104

la Naude

Bages

Château Grand-Puy-Lacoste ■

Château Lynch-Bages ■

St-Lambert

Les Gabarreys

D206

Daubos

Château Pichon-Longueville (Baron) ■

Château Latour ■

Château Pichon-Longueville Comtesse de Lalande ■

D1215

Ballac

Cach

St-Julien-Beychevelle

D2

Château Léoville-Las-Cases ■

Château Léoville-Poyferré ■

D206

AREA OF MAIN MAP

ST-JULIEN

le Long

Château Léoville-Barton ■

la Mouline

Gironde

D101

Château Ducru-Beaucaillou ■

Château Lagrange ■

Beychevelle

Château Branaire-Ducru ■

Dordogne

Château St-Pierre ■

Château Gruaud-Larose ■

le Bourdieu

Château Beychevelle ■

BORDEAUX

Chenal du Milieu

Jalle du Sud

Gironde

to the style of the wine. Cabernet Sauvignon is still the major variety, but with the preponderance of cooler soils, Merlot has become of greater consequence, representing 40 percent of the 3,000 acres (1,230ha) in production. There are only five classed growths, which produce 20 percent of the volume (8.7 million bottles yearly), while the lion's share of 54 percent is generated by the crus bourgeois and 17 percent by the cooperative. The increase in Merlot and modern winemaking techniques have smoothed St-Estèphe's once hard, austere edge, but the wines are still rich, full, and robust, for long aging.

Pauillac

Pauillac, for many, is the quintessential wine of the Médoc: powerful, concentrated, long-lived, with a pencil-lead mineral quality and distinct nuance of black currant, cedar, and cigar box. It perhaps comes as no surprise to find that three of the 1855 first growths—Lafite, Latour, and Mouton—as well as 15 other classified estates are located here. Bounded by St-Estèphe to the north and St-Julien to the south, Pauillac's 2,965 acres (1,200ha) of vineyard are divided into two zones. North of the town of Pauillac, the land is higher at 100ft (30m), the gravel soils deep and resting on a bed of sandy marl and limestone. Both Lafite and Mouton are here. South of Pauillac, the land is lower, the stony, gravel soils heavier, with more clay. The prime example is the Enclos of Latour. As in St-Julien, proximity to the estuary plays an essential part in ripening, the vineyards to the west of the appellation being later by two or three days. This is Cabernet Sauvignon country, the grape variety occasionally amounting to over 80 percent in the blends originating here.

St-Julien

One of St-Julien's great strengths is that 80 percent of the 2,220-acre (900ha) vineyard is owned by 11 highly motivated crus classés, including five second growths. Both individually and collectively, these have been investing in the region—witness the $5-million joint-investment water-purification plant built to serve the whole appellation in 2000. This compact region consists of two well-exposed and well-drained gravelly plateaux, bounded to the north by Pauillac and to the south and west by the Haut-Médoc. In the east, a ridge of deep gravel overlooks the Gironde estuary, while just south of this on the Beychevelle plateau, the limestone bedrock is higher and the gravel not quite so deep. Slightly inland there's more deep gravel but with a higher proportion of clay. Thereafter, as the vineyards run farther west, the gravel becomes thinner and the soil sandier. There can also be a difference of two or three days in maturity. Overall, this is a good ripening zone, but with natural variations according to vineyard location—hence the different nuances in the wines. Another variable is the grape variety. The gravel soils lean toward a dominance of Cabernet Sauvignon, but less so than in Pauillac. Good St-Julien is medium-bodied, dry but with mellow fruit, restrained, digestible, and long-lived.

Margaux

The most southerly and extensive of the communal appellations, Margaux has 3,680 acres (1,490ha) under production. These are spread through five communes, including Arsac, Labarde, Cantenac, Soussans, and Margaux itself. The gravelly soils are the poorest in the Médoc, with low clay content and scant fertility, ideal for the cultivation of little else but the vine, in particular Cabernet Sauvignon. They assist in providing a slightly earlier ripening date than appellations farther north, and in the production of wines of a more delicate weight and texture, with a firm-but-fine tannic structure. This distinguishing feature can be altered by winemaking techniques and by the fact that not all Margaux's soils are deep gravel. Limestone, sand, and clay are also part of the profile. Because most châteaux own parcels of land in various communes and have a variety of soils, the puzzle becomes more complicated. The boundaries of the appellation have been altered recently, with the upgrading of land that used to be Haut-Médoc and the rejection of parcels from the appellation. Overall, the surface area has been only marginally changed, but there could be litigation from producers who have lost their once-valuable Margaux land. The 21 Margaux châteaux classified in 1855 represent 70 percent of the production. Having long trailed in the wake of producers in St-Julien and Pauillac, Margaux has made considerable progress in recent years.

Moulis and Listrac

The tiny communal appellations of Moulis and Listrac, northwest of Margaux, are roughly the same size—1,570 and 1,655 acres (635 and 670ha) respectively—each producing 4 million bottles a year. The wines are fresh and clearly Médoc in style, though a little more rounded due to a higher proportion of Merlot. Listrac tends to be more austere than Moulis, which can be close to St-Julien in character, but much depends on the terroir and the level of ripeness reached. The farther west the vineyards, the later the ripening. The advantage in Moulis is that a large chunk of the vineyard in the east has deep, well-drained, Günzian gravel soils that are good for Cabernet Sauvignon. Elsewhere in the appellation, clay-limestone soils demand a higher proportion of Merlot. A pocket of Pyrenean gravel soils (lighter and sandier than the Günzian) exists in the far west corner of the appellation. The same soil types are found in Listrac but with a dominance of clay-limestone followed by Pyrenean gravel. Cabernet Sauvignon ripens only on the latter—hence the increase of Merlot to around 65 percent. The Pyrenean gravel flows in a strip along the N215 road. There are no classed growths in either appellation, and in Listrac the cooperative accounts for 25 percent of the production.

Haut-Médoc

In the southern half of the Médoc peninsula, the 11,400 acres (4,600ha) of viticultural land not in the six communal appellations are designated Haut-Médoc. The region follows the Gironde estuary from Blanquefort to St-Seurin de Cadourne 37 miles (60km) farther north. Due to the extent of the appellation, there's a varying nuance to the terroir and wines. On the flat land south of Margaux, the soils are mainly gravel and sand, leading to a naturally finer, delicate style. Heading north, the soils are heavier, with more quartzlike gravel and clay, so the wines can be sturdier and even acquire a St-Estèphe-like vigor where limestone-clay becomes predominant. Cabernet Sauvignon is still the prominent variety, but overall plantings have moved closer to 50/50 Cabernet Sauvignon and Merlot, with a little Cabernet Franc and Petit Verdot. Five châteaux in the Haut-Médoc were classified in 1855, but it is more closely associated with the crus bourgeois. An association of properties, Biturica, represents the most progressive in the region.

Médoc

The appellation Médoc, formerly Bas-Médoc, is situated beyond St-Estèphe in the northern third of the peninsula. The land is flat with marshy areas, pasture, and generally heavier, claylike gravel soils. Cabernet Sauvignon used to be the dominant grape variety but has been gradually overhauled by Merlot—a wise decision that has led to higher quality. Just under 600 growers, two-thirds members of the local cooperatives, cultivate 14,100 acres (5,700ha), producing an average of 38 million bottles of red wine a year. The wines are generally fruity and forward, but some producers are using modern techniques in the vineyard and winery to provide greater weight, fruit, and style.

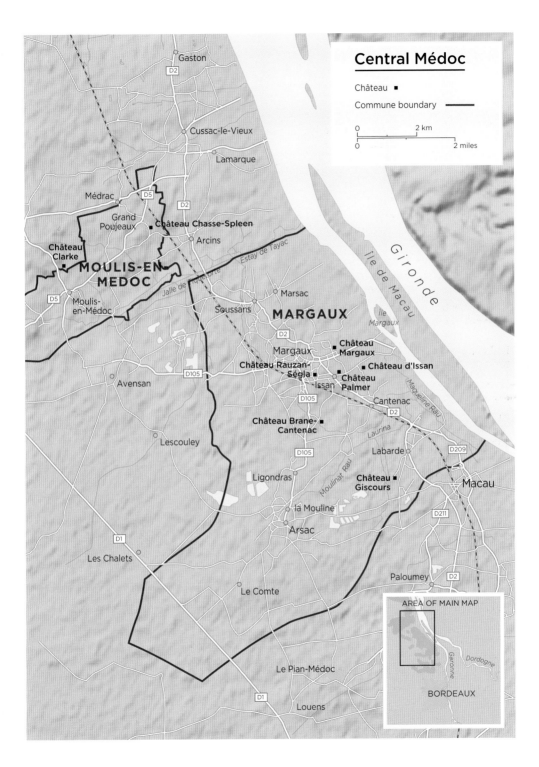

Central Médoc

- Château ■
- Commune boundary ▬▬▬

0　　　　　2 km
0　　　　　2 miles

Gaston
D2

Cussac-le-Vieux

Lamarque

Médrac

D5

Grand
Poujeaux

Château Chasse-Spleen

Arcins

Château
Clarke

MOULIS-EN-MEDOC

D5

Moulis-
en-Médoc

Estay de Tayac

Jalle de Tiquetorte

Marsac

Soussans

MARGAUX

D2

Île
Margaux

Île de Macau

Gironde

Margaux

Château
Margaux

Château Rauzan-
Ségla

Château d'Issan

Issan

Château
Palmer

Avensan

D105

Cantenac

D2

Maqueline Rau

Château Brane-
Cantenac

Laurina

Lescouley

Labarde

D209

Château
Giscours

Macau

Ligondras

Moulinat Rau

la Mouline

D105

Arsac

D211

D1

Le Comte

Paloumey

D2

Les Chalets

Le Pian-Médoc

D1

Louens

AREA OF MAIN MAP

Garonne

Dordogne

BORDEAUX

Cos d'Estournel

There is no château as such at Cos d'Estournel, but the building that houses the cellars is the most eye-catching edifice in the Médoc today. An extraordinary pagoda-like construction—complete with gargoyles and a carved door from Zanzibar—greets visitors. And behind that door is now a no-less-spectacular state-of-the-art *cuvier*, inaugurated in 2008.

The reputation of Cos has been riding high for some time, and part of that success is due to the constant reappraisal that goes on here. Certainly, the present regime of owner Michel Reybier and general manager Jean-Guillaume Prats continues to leave no stone unturned and to invest heavily to achieve the required results. "Cos has always been characterized by rigor, innovation, and the will to do something different," says Prats. Recent vintages have pushed Cos to within touching distance of the first growths.

Cos d'Estournel owes much to the vision of Louis Gaspard d'Estournel. It was he who discerned the quality of the terroir and who, from 1811, started to expand the vineyard and develop the property. It was also his insistence on quality and the construction of the oriental-looking *chai* in 1830 that transformed the estate's reputation and led to its eventual consecration as a second growth. His efforts took their toll, however. Crippling debts forced him to sell to London bankers Martyns in 1852, a year before his death.

The estate changed hands numerous times in the years after d'Estournel's death. The Basque Errazu family acquired the property in 1869 before selling it on to the Charmolües, owners of Château Montrose, who in turn sold it on to Fernand Ginestet in 1917. There followed a period of stability, the estate staying in the Ginestet family for most of the 20th century, and Ginestet's grandson, Bruno Prats, managing the estate from 1970 until it was sold to the Merlaut family and Argentinian investors in 1998. Prats's astute management, particularly of the vineyard, laid the foundations for the continuing success at Cos—a situation his son Jean-Guillaume inherited when he succeeded as general manager. In 2000, the property was acquired by the present owner, French food manufacturer Michel Reybier.

In the old Gascon tongue, *cos* means "hill of pebbles," and this describes the terroir quite nicely. A mound of Quaternary gravel deposited on St-Estèphe's limestone bedrock rises 66ft (20m) above the marshy lowland to the south, with a tiny stream, the Jalle de Breuil, separating Cos from Lafite Rothschild opposite. Clay is found at greater depth and more obviously on the lower slopes. There are other subtleties in the soil structure, as a recent survey revealed. The report indicated as many as 250 variations in soil type at Cos, including the recent extension of parcels close to Château Lilian Ladouys and the integration of the 7ha (17-acre) Château Marbuzet, both destined for the second wine, Pagodes de Cos.

This detailed study has had quite an impact on the delimitation and management of individual parcels. The result in 2008, and contrary to the general tendency in Bordeaux, was that the proportion of grand vin increased to 78 percent of production, whereas in 2007 and previous years it had been around 55 percent. "The reappraisal of cultivation methods, lower yields, and the adaptation of grape variety and rootstock enabled us to use parcels that previously went into the second wine," explains Jean-Guillaume Prats.

The new *cuvier*—with its 72 cone-shaped stainless-steel tanks, ranging from 19 to 115hl in size—enables the handling of individual parcels to be taken to its logical conclusion. There are other "bells and whistles" in the winery to admire. A cooling tunnel reduces the temperature of the grapes to 37°F (3°C), to prevent oxidation during destemming and, later, to carry out cold

Right: The spectacular pagoda-like facade at Cos was inspired by India, where it shipped much of its wine in the 19th century

pre-fermentation maceration. Gravity feeding is, of course, de rigueur, but the idea of gentle handling has been taken one step further with the use of four 100-liter "lift-tanks" that replace the traditional system of pumping with that of rack and return.

FINEST WINES

Château Cos d'Estournel

Since 1982, Château Cos d'Estournel hasn't really put a foot wrong. The 1999 was a little off-track, but apart from that, the wines have been among the best in the Médoc. They are generally full-bodied, their complexity and bearing providing a style that's closer to Pauillac than St-Estèphe, but with an enviable unctuousness that has always been associated with the high proportion of Merlot (40%) in the blend. Recent vintages have seen a change, with a higher proportion of Cabernet Sauvignon (85% in 2007 and 2008) and a style that's denser, spicier, and more masculine. "We're doing everything to favor the Cabernet Sauvignon, and from now on it will represent 75–85 percent of the wine," says Jean-Guillaume Prats. The majority of Merlot, therefore, now goes to the second wine,

Pagodes de Cos. The use and choice of barrels have always been a point of discussion at Cos. Bruno Prats used heavily toasted barrels in the 1980s but only 50 percent new oak. In the 1990s the toasting was more restrained, but the new oak occasionally reached 100 percent. In the new millennium, the benchmark appears to be 80 percent. The last time I had the chance to taste a vertical of older vintages was in 2003. Wines that impressed were the rich, generous 1982★; powerful, brooding 1986; fine, linear 1988; suave, exotic 1990★; and the rather sumptuous but structured 1995★. Since 2005, there's also been a white Cos d'Estournel, the fruit (80/20 SB/Semillon) coming from a vineyard in the north of the Médoc at Jau-Dignac and Loirac. **2005★** Enormous power and concentration. Dense, structured, oozing fruit, with a glow of alcohol on the finish. An immense, eminently ageworthy wine.

Château Cos d'Estournel
Total area: 366 acres (148ha)
Area under vine: 220 acres (89ha)
Production: grand vin 250,000–300,000 bottles; second wine 60,000–80,000 bottles
33180 St-Estèphe
Tel: +33 5 56 73 15 50
www.estournel.com

Montrose

It's all gone green at Château Montrose. Not the wine, I hasten to add, but the impressively forward-thinking approach to the environment. Since acquiring the property in 2006, construction magnates Martin and Olivier Bouyges have introduced a raft of changes, many of them environmentally inclined. They have restored buildings with better insulation, added solar panels, and installed a geothermal heat pump. As Jean-Bernard Delmas, the new but highly experienced managing director says, it's all part of the Bouyges' attempts "to set an example in sustainable development."

For all the changes, however, one thing that has remained unaltered is the terroir, which has always been a vital factor in Montrose's long-standing reputation. On a gravel ridge about half a mile (800m) from the estuary, the vineyard has a similar profile to the *enclos* of Latour and Léoville-Las-Cases. The gravel is deep and formed of large pebbles laced with ferrous sand and marly clay (12 percent). The gentle slope provides good drainage, while ripening conditions are influenced by the southeasterly exposure and proximity to the Gironde, which moderates temperatures.

Historically, Montrose was quick to prove its worth. The vineyard was planted only from 1815 onward, and the consecration of second growth given in 1855. The property used to be part of the Calon estate, owned initially by the Ségur family then bought in 1778 by Etienne Théodore Dumoulin. Thirty-seven years later, his son, also Etienne Théodore, realizing the potential of an area of gravelly scrub known as La Lande de l'Escargeon to the south of the property, started clearing the land and planting vines.

By 1825, some 15 acres (6ha) had been planted, a small château and cellars built, and the name Montrose clearly registered in the first official survey of St-Estèphe. The name *mont-rose* may derive from the pink hue of the flowering heather in those far-off days. In 1855 the estate comprised some 237 acres (96ha), of which 125 acres (50ha) were under vine. The vineyard was further expanded under the ownership of Mathieu Dollfus (1866–87) to its present size of 173 acres (70ha). He also built workers' cottages at the bottom of the hill and a rail line and landing stage for loading casks, but these have long since disappeared. Louis Victor Charmolüe then acquired the property in 1896, and it remained in the same family until Jean-Louis Charmolüe sold to the Bouyges in 2006.

Over the years, the vineyard has been well maintained, with missing vines replaced by complantation and the density maintained at 9,000 vines/ha. The new regime feels that some parcels need replanting, and a program has been put in place. Likewise, there's been a return to traditional methods of plowing and working the soil, as well as the total abolition of herbicides and insecticides. Cabernet Sauvignon represents 65 percent of the vineyard; Merlot, which is planted at the foot of the slope and on the plateau around the château, 24 percent. "It's a little like Burgundy, with the best parcels of Cabernet located on the mid-slope in front of the estuary," explains Delmas. Vinification is traditional, with the wine aged in 60 percent new oak barrels.

Given the generally high standard of the wines, is there room for further improvement? Delmas and his technical director Nicolas Glumineau certainly believe so. "In the past, the same parcels were systematically harvested in the same order. But we're now following each more closely to pick at optimum ripeness, and even separating the edge of certain parcels from the center, since there's a qualitative difference," explains Delmas.

FINEST WINES

Château Montrose

Going back a few years to 1990, one of the more memorable tastings for me was a vertical of old vintages of Montrose that had been bought at auction by a friend. The 1970 started the ball rolling, and although offering smoky, black-currant aromas, the palate seemed a little tired. The 1964 and 1959 were also out of condition, but the 1947 and 1945 were still on form, the latter with considerable depth and concentration. The sensations, though, were the 1928★, still with astonishing color, youthful fruit, and length on the finish; and the 1921★, a rich, velvety elixir that offered undeniable pleasure. Like Latour, Montrose has made its reputation with wines that are deeply colored, firm, powerful, and austere in youth but that age amazingly well. This ideal slipped at Montrose in the 1970s and early 1980s, due to a combination of difficult vintages, overcropping, and a problem with grape moth in 1983. Since 1986, however, the solid Montrose style has been back, with an added element of ripeness and opulence in the most notable years—among which must be included 1986, 1989★, 1990, 1996, 2000, and 2003. What the new management hopes to achieve is consistent ripeness at this level, as well as a purity and quality of texture and tannin that suits the modern age.

1998 Deep color. Solid and meaty on the nose, with a density of fruit on the palate and firm—if slightly austere—finish. This is classic Montrose, without the extra layers that have come with full maturity. It will undoubtedly age well, though.

2008 Although only tasted from barrel, this gives a clear indication of the direction in style. Little aromatic definition at this early stage, but deep color, ample fruit, and dense but rounded tannins. Altogether purer in expression. Still good length.

Right: Jean-Bernard Delmas, whose experience and expertise, acquired at Haut-Brion, now shows in the more refined Montrose

Château Montrose
Total area: 250 acres (100ha)
Area under vine: 173 acres (70ha)
Average production: grand vin 220,000 bottles; second wine 80,000 bottles
33180 St-Estèphe
Tel: +33 5 56 59 30 12
www.chateau-montrose.com

Calon-Ségur

Château Calon-Ségur may be one of the oldest properties in the Médoc, with a history that can be traced back to the Middle Ages, but the owners are definitely looking to the future these days. Vintages in the new millennium have been outstanding, the 2006 ushering in an exciting new era in which an extra twist of elegance and complexity has been added to the habitual density and structure of the wine.

The redoubtable Madame Denise Capbern-Gasqueton, assisted by her daughter, Madame de Baritault, took things in hand in 1995, on the death of her husband Philippe. A stricter control of the individual parcels in the vineyard was introduced, and the density of new plantings increased to 8,000 vines/ha. The majority of the vineyard had been planted at 6,500 vines/ha until then. In 1999, a new *cuvier* was inaugurated, equipped with stainless-steel tanks and installed within the walls of an 18th-century building.

Since 2006 there's been another leap in progress, which has coincided with the arrival of new technical director Vincent Millet. Previously the quality controller at Château Margaux for eight years, Millet's credentials speak for themselves. There have been two notable changes in the wines since his arrival: a gradual increase in the proportion of Cabernet Sauvignon (66 percent in 2006; 80 percent in 2008) and of new oak barrels (60 percent in 2006; 90 percent in 2008).

The changes all relate to the vineyard. As Millet says, "Calon-Ségur has a great terroir for Cabernet Sauvignon." The vineyard comprises three entities: a large walled-in block that surrounds the 17th-century château, with a rise in the land to the east and soils composed of gravel, sand, and a fair proportion of clay; two parcels outside the wall located either side of the cemetery, with a similar soil profile; and a block farther east toward the estuary known as La Chapelle, where the land is closer to the limestone bedrock and the soils have

a higher proportion of sand and clay. The first two provide finesse; the third, power.

A major program of replanting and restructuring (improved densities and rootstocks) is in progress and due to last another ten years. Only 114 acres (46ha) of the 136 acres (55ha) of vineyard are presently planted. This, to a certain extent, dictates selection for the grand vin. "My conviction is that the heart of Calon is within the walled section in front of the château, but much of it is being replanted at the moment," says Millet. The selection for Calon-Ségur, therefore, comes now from some of the younger Cabernet Sauvignon (10–15 years old) within the walled sector and the older Cabernet (25–35 years old) in La Chapelle. "We found that Cabernet planted in La Chapelle in 2001 was superior to Merlot planted there in 1940," adds Millet.

As well as the increase in Cabernet Sauvignon, the control of individual parcels has been further tightened to obtain optimum maturity (but not overripeness) before picking. The parcels are then vinified separately, the extraction of a gentle nature. There has also been considerable progress in the aging of the wines. A single cooper provided all the barrels in the past, but now there are four, the barrels from each adding further complexity. As we have seen, the proportion of new oak has also risen steadily. "The increase in Cabernet Sauvignon permits a higher proportion of new oak barrels and a longer *élevage*, because the oak is more readily absorbed," explains Millet. The wines are now egg-white fined but not filtered.

FINEST WINES

Château Calon-Ségur
The name Calon is thought to have been derived from the word *calones*, the sobriquet given to the small rowboats that at one time carried lumber across the estuary. Indeed, until the French Revolution, the village of St-Estèphe was known as St-Estèphe-de-Calon. In the 18th century, the

estate was owned by Nicolas-Alexandre, Marquis de Ségur. He also owned Lafite and Latour and is credited with the saying, "I make wine at Lafite and Latour, but my heart is at Calon"—hence the heart on the label of bottles of Calon-Ségur to this day. The reputation of Calon-Ségur was extremely high in the first half of the 20th century, then waned until the 1982 vintage. Thereafter, there were notable successes in 1986, 1988, 1990, and 1996, but not quite the consistency and panache of the wines now appearing in the new millennium (2000, 2003, 2005). The grand vin represents approximately 60% of the production; the second wine, Marquis de Calon, roughly 25%; and the third label, La Chapelle de Calon, roughly 10%, with the rest being sold off in bulk to négociants. These are wines to age, the structure impressive but increasingly refined, the texture and fragrance pure. "It bothers me that St-Estèphe has a reputation for biting tannins, so my aim is to have tannins that

are silky and fine," avows Vincent Millet.

2006★ Fragrant and precise, with firm but noble tannins. Real length, line, and backbone, but the texture is pure and fine. Marked minerality.

2008★ Tasted from barrel but worth a mention. Ripe, sweet, and *gourmand*, with a spicy, exotic fragrance and a wonderfully long, fresh, thirst-quenching finish.

Above: Château Calon-Ségur, with a long and proud tradition, is again producing wines to win the hearts of connoisseurs

Château Calon-Ségur
Total area: 185 acres (75ha)
Area under vine: 114 acres (46ha)
Production: grand vin 150,000–180,000 bottles; second wine 50,000–80,000 bottles
33180 St-Estèphe
Tel: +33 5 56 59 30 08

Lafite Rothschild

L afite Rothschild's time-honored reputation is impossible to ignore. This, after all, is the property that topped the list of first growths in 1855, and it maintains a cellar with vintages that pre-date even this event. The style has rarely changed, with elegance always being to the fore. Terroir is the dominant factor, aided and abetted by the continuity and tradition that persist at the estate.

Château Lafite Rothschild is at the northern limits of Pauillac, the Jalle de Breuil stream separating it from St-Estèphe beyond. The pagoda *chai* of Cos d'Estournel is clearly visible on a rise ahead. This is the largest of the first growths, the vineyard spanning the D2 road as one heads north, the major portion spreading west, down to the land of stablemate Château Duhart-Milon. Behind a screen of weeping willow trees, the homey-looking château and gardens are visible from the road.

There are three core areas to the vineyard. The most important in terms of size (over 125 acres [50ha]) is the plateau behind the château. The land here rises steadily to 88ft (27m), forming a *fite*, one of many Médocain words for a hillock and the origin of the name Lafite. Southwest of this lies the Carruades plateau, which is shared with Mouton Rothschild. Lafite's second wine takes its name from here, but the fruit is destined more often than not for the grand vin. Finally, across the border in St-Estèphe, there is an 11-acre (4.5ha) parcel known as La Caillava, which has historically always been permitted in Lafite.

The exposure of the land is varied (north, south, southeast), but a soil chart shows all three zones to have one thing in common: extremely gravelly soils. This means that they have over 50 percent gravel, with a limited amount of clay, to a depth that can exceed 13ft (4m), above a bed of marl and, farther down, limestone, or *calcaire de St-Estèphe* as it is locally known. Cabernet Sauvignon is the principal variety planted in these zones, with two excellent plots of Merlot in Carruades. The poverty of the soils, limestone bedrock, variability of exposure, and

Above: Château Lafite, *primus inter pares* in 1855, and again commanding the highest prices thanks to demand from Asia

distance from the estuary (compared to Latour) all help explain the style of wine produced at Lafite.

Continuity for the past 140 years has been provided by the Rothschild family, with Baron James de Rothschild purchasing the property in 1868. Prior to this, Lafite had been owned by the influential Ségur family from 1670 to 1784. Nicolas de Ségur and his son Nicolas-Alexandre developing the property in the

early 18th century. Expropriated then sold as a *bien national* at the time of the Revolution, Lafite changed hands several times before being acquired at auction by the French branch of the Rothschild family. There are now several family shareholders, but since 1974 Baron Eric de Rothschild has overseen the administration of the estate.

The technical director since 1994 has been Charles Chevallier. The experience of managing Château Rieussec in Sauternes (another Rothschild property that he still oversees) for nine years opened Chevallier's eyes to the importance of good viticultural practice—particularly the management of individual parcels and precision at harvest. This is not to imply lowly yields, however, because the average at the estate is a fairly generous 50hl/ha. "I take pleasure in viticulture and the vineyard being well maintained, but I also like the vine to give what it naturally wants to produce," Chevallier explains. That said, the selection for the grand vin has become increasingly more severe, the average these days being just 40 percent of the production.

The harvest is of course a critical period, and the estate is geared up to pick quickly when optimum ripeness has been achieved. More than 450 people are taken on at this time, which means Lafite and Duhart-Milon can be picked in a mere 11 days. The grapes are sorted on tables in the vineyard then vinified in wooden and stainless-steel tanks in the traditional manner. "We start from the principle that good grapes will make good wine and that the cellar master is there principally to maintain their potential," says Chevallier.

Most of the modern methods of vinification have been trialed and rejected, a stronger emphasis placed on, say, the quality and importance of the press wine (15–17 percent of the blend) than on instigating the malolactic fermentation in barrel. The same sort of philosophy applies when it comes to investment. Lafite was one of the first châteaux to acquire a concentrator (now rarely used), but otherwise the *cuvier* is relatively devoid of gadgetry. A new set of underground tanks is planned for 2010, however, and let's not forget the stunning circular cellar designed by Ricardo Bofill and completed in 1988.

FINEST WINES

Château Lafite Rothschild

Elegance and finesse and, of course, its ability to age are the hallmarks of Lafite. The château cellar, with vintages dating back to 1797 (the oldest bottle) provide the proof of this. In more recent times, there was a less distinguished period in the 1960s through to the mid-1970s, but thereafter Lafite has been on form. Since 1995, the wines have gained in weight and structure, as well as purity of fruit and texture. Lafite is naturally Cabernet-dominated (to the tune of 81–89% of the blend for the vintages tasted below). The balance is Merlot, occasionally with a pinch of Petit Verdot (0.5% in the 2005). Aging is in 100% new oak barrels, supplied by the estate's own cooperage, and lasts 20 months.
1998 A mix of elegance and vigor. Deep, ruby color. A fragrant, complex nose, with notes of cedar and

spice. The palate is medium-bodied, sweet, and ripe but virile, the tannins firm and long. An assertive finish. Still needs time.
2001 Quite a bit of charm and accessible now (at a pinch). Smoky, cedar notes, with a touch of vanilla oak on the nose. Lovely caressing fruit on the palate, and a long, fresh finish. Vibrant and harmonious and will doubtless age well.
2005★ Rich and powerful and unquestionably for the very long term. A subtle, elegant nose, the depth and intensity of the wine apparent even here. Layered fruit on the palate, with a note of integrated, chocolaty oak. The tannins are dense and tight but refined. Long, powerful finish.

Carruades de Lafite

Lafite's second wine has a greater proportion of Merlot in the blend (40–45% is not uncommon), and the Cabernet Franc and Petit Verdot at the estate (3% and 2% respectively) are also often used. Aging takes place in a mix of new oak barrels (10%), one-year-old barrels, and wooden vats. There's an element of the Lafite elegance, but this is a more supple wine for earlier consumption. It lacks the intensity and complexity of the grand vin, the difference clearly evident when the two are tasted side by side.
1998 Ruby color. The nose opens to red and dark fruits with a note of tobacco. Round, crisp, and fresh on the palate. Drinking now.
2001★ My choice for drinking from 2010. This has a purity of fruit on the nose, while the palate is ample and round, but vibrant, with black-currant-lozenge notes and excellent balance.
2005 Having said that Carruades is a wine for earlier consumption, this looks to have more staying power. Sweet and ripe, with a good consistency of fruit and vanilla oak. A firm tannic frame and a peppery note on the finish, but beginning to close.

Right: Charles Chevallier, Lafite's technical director since 1994, is producing wines worthy of its 1855 ranking

Château Lafite Rothschild
Total area (Lafite & Duhart-Milon): 457 acres (185ha)
Area under vine: 282 acres (114ha)
Average production: grand vin 240,000 bottles; second wine 300,000 bottles
Le Pouyalet, 33250 Pauillac
Tel: +33 5 56 73 18 18
www.lafite.com

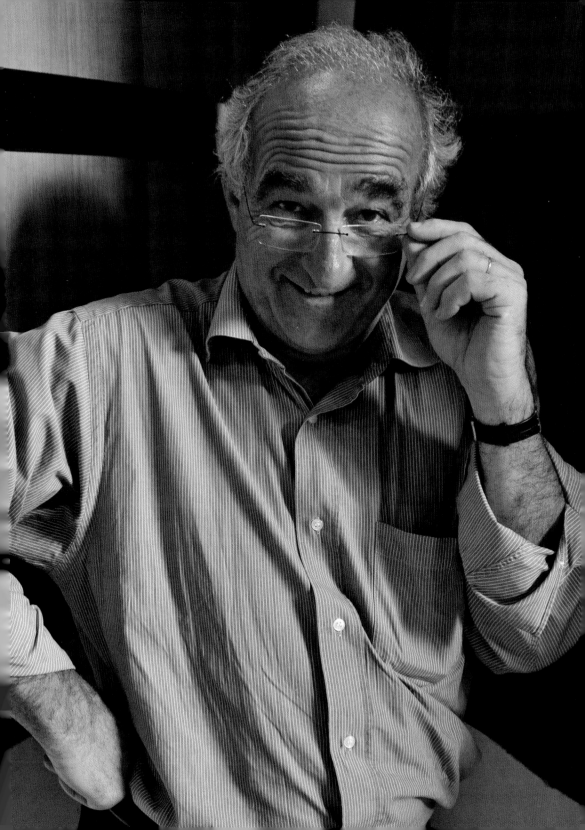

Latour

Heading north from St-Julien along the D2 road on a sunny summer day, there's the uplifting sight of the walled vineyard of Château Latour, with the estuary just behind. The winery sits low to the ground, and the modest château is partially obscured by trees, but the round 17th-century tower (actually a dovecote) is clear for all to see. The vineyard itself is bound to the north and south by streams and to the east by the *palus* of the estuary, the D2 forming the western limit. A map dating from 1769 at the winery shows that the profile has barely changed over the years.

This is the Enclos, or heart, of Latour—119 acres (48ha) used exclusively for the production of the grand vin. But the estate has other vineyards. Farther west near Château Batailley there are two other blocks totaling nearly 50 acres (20ha): Petit Batailley

Latour has shown remarkable consistency over the years. The present period is no exception, with the bar set, if anything, even higher in terms of quality

and Pinada, which contribute to the second wine, Les Forts de Latour (the name taken from a parcel in the Enclos). These were replanted in the 1960s but have been part of the property for over a century. Another block even farther west, Ste-Anne, partially dates from this time but has been expanded since 2000 with the acquisition of more land. Another 20 acres (8ha) have also been purchased to the north at Artigues. Again, the fruit is destined for the second wine, except for the very young vines, which since 1990 have supplied a third label, the generic Pauillac.

Returning to the origins of the Enclos, there were vines in the region as far back as the 14th century (as there was an original tower), but Latour, like Lafite, developed as a vineyard under the wealthy Ségur family in the 18th century. Demand for the wine

in England pushed the expansion of the vineyard; by 1759 it covered 94 acres (38ha), and by 1794 it had reached the 116 acres (47ha) it is today. Latour remained in the hands of the descendants of the Ségurs until it was acquired by a partnership between the British Pearson Group and Harveys of Bristol in 1963. The shareholding then went to Allied Lyons in 1989, before the company sold to the present owner, the wealthy French businessman François Pinault, in 1993.

The Enclos appears as a single undulating entity, but of course there are variations in the soils, as a very thorough study carried out in the early 2000s underlined. In the northern part of the vineyard, and to a certain extent in the south near the Juillac stream, the soils are heavier marly clay. Merlot is planted here but rarely makes the grand vin. The exception is the tiny parcel in the southwest corner that takes its name from the Juillac stream. The vines here are 80 years old and produce wine with the balance and concentration Latour demands.

The heart of the heart, if one can call it that, is the area surrounding the château and *chais*, where the soils are predominantly claylike gravel and the Cabernet Sauvignon is supreme. "The parcels on the left and right as you enter the property, Chêne Vert, Gravette, and Pièce de La Tour, give structure; Sarmentier, in front of the château, provides fruit and pleasure; while Pièce du Château and Socs on the eastern side offer aroma, since the soils here are more gravelly sand. All are vinified and tasted separately before a decision is made, the sum of all inevitably better than the individual parts," explains Frédéric Engerer, the general manager since 1995.

Engerer's quest for perfection, backed by a healthy budget from Monsieur Pinault, has led to even greater precision at the domaine. The parcels and occasionally their contours are harvested separately, as are the young vines that have been

Right: Latour's magnificent Enclos vineyard surrounding the secluded château and more emblematic dovecote

complanted within the vineyard. Only old vines are used for Château Latour. A brand-new gravity-fed *cuvier*, inaugurated in 2001, offers the luxury of 66 stainless-steel tanks of varying size to vinify the plots separately. The final selection is draconian, certain parcels even in the Enclos relegated to the second wine, Les Forts de Latour, which is itself considered as good as a second growth. Aging is in 100 percent new oak barrels; 50 percent for Les Forts de Latour.

FINEST WINES

Château Latour

The adjectives used to describe Latour invariably depict a masculine character. Words that come immediately to mind include powerful, vigorous, and muscular, with color, depth, and minerality helping complete the picture. There can be variations on this theme depending on the climatic conditions of the year, however, and this is what Frédéric Engerer wanted to demonstrate when he presented the three vintages below for tasting in October 2009. 2001 was the product of a year without extremes, with an Indian summer in early September. 2003 showed Latour's capacity to cope with the heat and drought of the year, while 2006 started well but was made difficult by alternate rain and heat in August and September. The proximity of the Enclos vineyard to the estuary has always been a mitigating factor. For one thing, the drainage is excellent. "You can take greater risks in the Enclos because the sanitary conditions are always better," says Engerer. The ripening cycle is also in advance, which helps during the harvest period. In 2005, Engerer explained, he started harvesting the Merlot in the Enclos on September 15, when the sugar level was 13.5°. About 1.25 miles (2km) farther west at Petit Batailley, the Merlot had reached only 12.5°, while 2.5 miles (4km) away at Ste-Anne the measure was 12°. Cabernet Sauvignon is, of course, the dominant variety, and if anything has progressed in the blend in recent years, the 94% in 2008 being the highest yet. "The Cabernet Sauvignon at Latour is so focused that the Merlot needs to be close in style to be included," declares Engerer. Having been lucky enough to taste several vats of Merlot just after the 2009 harvest, I can appreciate how acute the choice becomes.

Apart from a period in the mid-1980s, Latour has shown remarkable consistency over the years.

The present period is no exception, with the bar set, if anything, even higher in terms of quality.

2001 The elegant side of Latour. A fine, fragrant, perfumed nose, with a minerally, pencil-lead nuance. Silky texture on the attack, followed by impressive mid-palate fruit. Very smooth, with a long, fresh finish, minerality again to the fore. Precise, linear, and balanced.

2003 *Gourmand* in style. Dense, opaque color. The nose is full, rich, and ripe, positively oozing fruit, but with mocha and chocolate notes as well. The palate is ample, round, even sensual, again charged with ripe fruit. It still manages freshness on the finish and a tannin texture that is very fine. Flamboyant for Latour, it has garnered some high scores from influential critics, including Robert Parker, but this is less my preferred style.

2006★ The hallmark of Latour. Dark, powerful, and precise. The nose is closed but even now has a mineral presence. The palate is dense, firm, and long, with generous fruit on the mid-palate and an impressive tannic frame. Long, minerally, "pebble-sucking" finish. Considerable aging potential.

Right: The determined Frédéric Engerer, Latour's general manager since 1995, who is driving the quest for perfection

Château Latour

Total area: 320 acres (130ha)
Area under vine: 200 acres (80ha)
Average production: grand vin 132,000 bottles; second wine 144,000 bottles
33250 Pauillac
Tel: +33 5 56 73 19 80
www.chateau-latour.com

Mouton Rothschild

Above: The carefully maintained hedges and path leading to Mouton's Grand Chai are part of its carefully cultivated image

The story of Mouton is a well-documented tale, but it is no less fascinating for that. Its narrative focuses on the ambition and exploits of Baron Philippe de Rothschild, who almost single-handedly achieved for his estate something that no other estate has managed before or since: promotion to first-growth status.

The change took place in 1973. For the 118 years since the 1855 Classification, Mouton had been classed as a second growth. As might be expected, the promotion was commemorated in some style: Picasso was commissioned to produce the artwork for the wine's labels that year, and there was a new take on the house motto: *Premier je suis, second je fus, Mouton ne change* ("First I am, second I was, I Mouton do not change").

Philippe had taken over the property in the early 1920s at the age of just 20. It had come into his family's hands some 70 years before, when Baron Nathaniel de Rothschild acquired Brane-Mouton, as it was then known, from the English branch of the family in 1853. The name was swiftly changed, and in 1870 Baron Nathaniel's son, James, inherited the estate and built the château, which these days is partially hidden from view.

A résumé of Philippe's achievements shows just how far ahead of the times he was. In 1924, he introduced château bottling well before it became compulsory in Bordeaux. Investment in a new barrel cellar saw the completion of the striking Grand Chai, some 330ft (100m) long, in 1926. Shrewd marketing was also employed, and it was Philippe, in 1945, who began the series of artists' labels that has since included some of the world's greatest painters. Philippe was also a pioneer of wine tourism, which may be all the rage today but was barely talked about when he opened the Museum of Wine in Art and other parts of the Mouton property to visitors in 1962. Since his death in 1988, Mouton has been managed no less imaginatively by his daughter, Philippine.

Mouton's strength, today as then, lies in the relatively homogenous nature of the terroir. The core of the vineyard lies on what is known as the Grand Plateau, which dovetails with some of the vineyards of Lafite and lies just to the west of the winery. The soils are deep gravel and the exposure southerly. There's a slight dip before the land rises gently to the Carruades plateau, again joined with Lafite and also a source for the grand vin.

Baron Philippe de Rothschild achieved for his estate something that no other estate
has managed before or since: promotion to first-growth status. Since his death,
Mouton has been managed no less imaginatively by his daughter, Philippine

I was informed by Philippe Dhalluin, the technical director since 2003, that tastings consistently show the wines from the two plateaux to be superior to those from the dip. These latter parcels are therefore reserved for the second wine, Le Petit Mouton, introduced in 1993.

Cabernet Sauvignon is the principal variety, to the tune of 80 percent, with the proportion in the blend even higher. Merlot (12 percent) and Cabernet Franc (8 percent) are the other varieties, the latter omitted from the grand vin since 2006. Dhalluin explains that the average age of the vineyard is high at 50 years and that 37–50 acres (15–20ha) contain vines that are up to 70 years old. Within these parcels are complanted younger vines, and in 2004 the decision was made to harvest them separately.

Other elements of fine-tuning have been introduced since Dhalluin arrived from Branaire-Ducru. These are carried out not with the idea of changing the style but, rather, to introduce a little more depth and elegance and, in this most competitive of fields, to keep pace with the other

first growths—hence, the harvest is now carried out parcel by parcel with greater precision within each. A new *cuvier* with additional wooden vats (planned for 2011) should take this process a step further. Fermentation temperatures have been lowered to 82–84°F (28–29°C) to soften extraction and provide a purer grain of tannin. And since 2000, the toasting of the new oak barrels (100 percent) has been lighter—a measure introduced by Dhalluin's predecessor, Patrick Léon.

Above all, the selection for the grand vin, and even for the second wine, has become more draconian. In the 1980s and '90s, the proportion of production destined for Mouton consistently hovered around 80 percent, sometimes even more (91 percent in 1982 and 1989). In 2000 it was still 85 percent, but compare this with the figures for 2008: Mouton 54 percent, Le Petit Mouton 25 percent, the rest destined for the négociant arm of the company. Even in 2005, only 64 percent made the grand vin. This has been the trend since 2004, and it looks set to continue, the wines clearly gaining in stature.

Mouton also makes a tiny quantity of the lush but expensive white wine Aile d'Argent (10,000 bottles yearly). This is produced from three separate parcels on the estate that cover a total of 11 acres (4.5ha) and were planted in the 1980s. Semillon is the dominant variety in the vineyard (57 percent), followed by Sauvignon Blanc (42 percent), and rounded off with a little Muscadelle.

FINEST WINES

Château Mouton Rothschild

Mouton has always been the most exuberant of the first growths in Pauillac, its exotic, voluptuous nature contrasting with the refinement of Lafite and the steeliness of Latour. A Pauillac it clearly remains, though, the color, power, and minerality well defined, and its ability to age undisputed. In 2002, I tasted the 1961★ and was amazed by the

Left: Philippe Dhalluin, Mouton's capable technical director, with a reveler who has escaped from its outstanding museum

virility and youth of the wine, albeit an exceptional year, when frost reduced the yield to 16hl/ha. At the same tasting, the 1982★ was rich, generous, and assertive; the 1983, in comparison, supple and fresh but reserved. The 1989 appeared strict and tannic, while the 1990 was the opposite; opulent and perhaps overripe, it looked advanced for its age. The 1996★ was big and brooding, charged with cassis fruit, still with a long way to go.

Vintages in the new millennium have a little more purity and precision, the oak element being less overt but still contributing to the complexity and spicy fragrance of the wine. The bar has clearly been set higher. The following wines were tasted at the estate in September 2009. They had been double-decanted four hours before the tasting.

1986★ This wine has always had an incredible reputation, and now I can see why. Rich, dense, and sensuous, it's a monumental wine that has barely broken from its youthful shell despite being over 20 years of age. Deep, opaque color, with just a hint of brick at the rim. A magnificent bouquet—perfumed, complex, with a mix of spice, mineral, cassis, and tobacco. The palate is ripe and dense, with an incredibly opulent texture. Almost over the top but pulled back from the brink by a lingering, minerally freshness. Still has plenty of tannic bite. (Label by Bernard Séjourné)

1995 Flamboyant and exotic, but perhaps a touch of greenness lurking in the depths? Deep ruby-red color. A striking nose of cedar and spice, with some leafy notes following with time in the glass. The palate is full, bold, and masculine but appears slightly more evolved than the nose. Still a powerful, almost robust, tannic frame and a minty note on the finish. (Label by Antoni Tàpies)

2005★ Magnificent wine. Powerful, but at the same time, harmonious and finely textured. Wonderfully fragrant and typically Mouton, with that exotic, spicy touch. Rich, ripe fruit on the palate but produced at a perfect pitch. Fresh and minerally on the finish, with a grain of tannin that is long, powerful, and pure. (Label by Giuseppe Penone)

Château Mouton Rothschild

Total area: 210 acres (85ha)
Area under vine: 210 acres (85ha)
Average production: grand vin 170,000 bottles; second wine 100,000 bottles
33250 Pauillac
Tel: +33 5 56 73 21 29
www.bphr.com

Pichon-Longueville

Château Pichon-Longueville was once a part of the greater Pichon estate. But on the death of Joseph Pichon-Longueville in 1850, it was divided in two. One part became what is now commonly known as Pichon Lalande. The remaining two fifths (with 69 acres [28ha] of vines) was inherited by Pichon-Longueville's son Raoul and became the basis of what we now know as Château Pichon-Longueville or, occasionally, Pichon Baron. It was Raoul who built the existing château, one of the most distinctive in Bordeaux, with fairy-tale turrets, on the southern edge of Pauillac and now with a large pond in front. Below and out of sight is the latest investment—a barrel cellar that was built in 2007.

The modern history of the property really dates from 1987, the year Pichon-Longueville was acquired by AXA Millésimes, the viticultural investment arm of the French insurance company. The previous ownership had let the estate decline (due to lack of investment and absence of direct control), and it had been underachieving from the 1960s into the 1980s. The AXA team of general manager Jean-Michel Cazes and winemaker Daniel Llose instantly turned this around, with new investment and greater rigor and selection in the vineyards accounting for the splendid 1988, 1989, and 1990 vintages.

The 1990s proved to be a period of expansion and consolidation. More land was acquired and planted, but the image of the metamorphosis was the brand-new and somewhat controversial winery that was completed in 1991. A Franco-American team of architects—Jean de Gastines and Patrick Dillon—produced the design, which has a circular *cuvier* with a central dome and pillars, accompanied by an adjacent barrel cellar and bottling line. Technically efficient and mostly underground, it is the dramatic, highly contemporary exterior

Right: Pichon-Longueville's fairy-tale château has basked in the sun for years but has never reflected it more in its wines

The style of Pichon-Longueville is typically Pauillac; rich, powerful, sober, and long.
The color is dark, the density of fruit impressive, and there's a structure
that implies considerable aging potential

that has courted both indignation and admiration in equal measure.

In 2000, Cazes retired, and management of the AXA wine investments, including Pichon-Longueville, passed to the dapper Englishman Christian Seely. Since then there's been a retreat back to the historic core area of the vineyards for the production of the grand vin. This is the rolling section of land just opposite Château Latour on the other side of the D2 road, representing roughly 60 percent of the total surface area. The soils are deep gravel, and many of the vines are 50–60 years of age. Complantation is used to replace any that are missing or unproductive. "Our tastings consistently confirm that the best wines come from this terroir," declares the affable but astute Seely, adorned with his trademark bow tie.

The modern history of the property really dates from 1987, the year Pichon-Longueville was acquired by AXA Millésimes

Despite the glow of modern technology, the winemaking here is fairly traditional. There's increased emphasis on plot-by-plot management these days, all the way through to vinification. A greater number of smaller vats have been brought in since 2005 to accomplish the task. The winemaker, Jean-René Matignon, who has been at Pichon-Longueville since 1987, then adjusts the winemaking to suit each individual parcel. The *élevage* lasts for 18 months in 80 percent new oak casks. The new barrel cellar is fully air conditioned and allows the barrels to be arranged on a single level. Contrary to the design of the *cuvier*, there are no pillars in the structure and just one wide arch.

FINEST WINES

Château Pichon-Longueville

The style of Pichon-Longueville is typically Pauillac: rich, powerful, sober, and long. The color is dark; the density of fruit, impressive—and there's a structure that implies considerable aging potential. The vineyard is planted with 65% Cabernet Sauvignon, but there's usually more than 70% in the blend, the rest Merlot. The small amount of Cabernet Franc that existed has been grubbed up, and some Petit Verdot has recently been planted. The return to the historical vineyard as the exclusive source for the grand vin and stricter selection have meant a drop in the volume of wine. Christian Seely mentioned that production in the 1990s was over 300,000 bottles yearly—the unspoken comment being a schoolmasterly "room for improvement here." Now with yields at around 40hl/ha (36hl/ha in 2008), the wines of the new millennium have been of consistently high quality. The second wine, Les Tourelles de Longueville, has more than 50% Merlot in the blend. In the main, it is grown in the other sector of the vineyard known as Ste-Anne, which is located farther west near Batailley. It's a rounder and more tender wine that's accessible earlier on.

2004 Dark and firm, with a pronounced cassis aroma. There is a little less density and vigor on the palate than in the 2005 or 2006, but the wine is still solid and long-aging.

2005 Dense and pure on the nose. Powerful and seamless on the palate, with substantial depth and length.

2006★ Endowed with a certain noble classicism. Pure and firm on the palate, the acidity contributing freshness and length. This reminds me of the 1996 vintage. Long-aging and close to the 2005 in quality—so in that respect, good value.

Right: Christian Seely, whose commitment to quality has led to a focus on Pichon's historic vineyard for the grand vin

Château Pichon-Longueville

Total area: 217 acres (88ha)
Area under vine: 178 acres (72ha)
Average production: grand vin 200,000 bottles; second wine 150,000 bottles
33250 Pauillac
Tel: +33 5 56 73 17 17
www.pichonlongueville.com

Lynch-Bages

The family saga began in 1939, when Jean-Charles Cazes officially acquired Château Lynch-Bages. It continued with his son André, then grandson Jean-Michel, the succession eventually passing to his great-grandson and namesake Jean-Charles in 2006. The success of Château Lynch-Bages is bound to the efforts of the Cazes family over several generations. Once considered a lowly fifth growth, it has been raised to the level of a deuxième cru due to its quality and reputation.

The name Bages refers to a geographical entity, the plateau of Bages, but as the Lynch handle suggests, there was once an Irish interest in the property. A certain Thomas Lynch, whose father had arrived in Bordeaux in the late 17th century, married the heiress to the domaine, Elizabeth Drouillard, in 1740. The property passed into the hands of the Lynch family, where it remained until 1824. Several changes of ownership followed before Jean-Charles Cazes arrived on the scene, first as manager of Lynch-Bages in 1934, then as owner five years later.

Cazes, who already owned Les Ormes de Pez in St-Estèphe, replanted and improved the vineyard and enhanced the reputation of Lynch-Bages with a number of excellent postwar vintages, particularly in the 1950s. "He took risks and waited longer to pick than most," recounts his grandson, Jean-Michel Cazes. André Cazes took over the management from 1966 and further expanded the property, but his business as an insurance broker and his position as the mayor of Pauillac also occupied much of his time—hence his son, Jean-Michel, who had been living and working in Paris for 20 years, was persuaded to join him in 1972.

From 1974, Jean-Michel Cazes was effectively running the show, assisted at a later date by his sister Sylvie. Funds for investment were limited, but he began modernizing the winery and restructuring the vineyard. He also hired a brilliant young winemaker, Daniel Llose, who helped confirm the style of the wine and improve quality. A second wine, Haut-Bages Averous, was created to rectify the selection for the grand vin (the name changed to Echo de Lynch-Bages in 2008). The changes and improvements were crowned by a string of excellent vintages in the 1980s. Since then, Lynch-Bages has been regularly on form.

The two principal blocks of vineyard that constitute the historical heart of Lynch-Bages are located on the plateaux of Bages and Monferan. Both have classic Günzian gravel soils. The former surrounds the château and underwent a program of replanting at the end of the 1980s; the latter is situated a little farther west, on either side of the road that runs to Batailley. There are some venerable 80-year-old vines here, as well as parcels that are presently being grubbed up and replanted. Farther south at Trintaudon, on the limit of the Pauillac border, another block of vineyards also contributes fruit to the grand vin. The soils are composed of finer gravel and were planted in the 1960s.

Since Jean-Charles Cazes took over general management in 2006, the vineyard has been the main focus of attention. As well as an agenda for replanting, a soil study has been undertaken, and a program of massal selection for the Petit Verdot and Cabernet Sauvignon has been launched. Individual parcels are now harvested in a more selective way, and the style of the white wine, Blanc de Lynch-Bages (36,000 bottles yearly), has been altered by harvesting earlier in order to give added freshness to the wine. "Lynch-Bages is like a large seagoing tanker whose course needs occasional rectification," he says. On a grander scale, he's mulling over the possibility of a new *cuvier* in the years to come.

Right: Jean-Michel Cazes and son Jean-Charles, who continue the *de père en fils* tradition through to the fourth generation

FINEST WINES

Château Lynch-Bages

The length and power are also apparent, but Lynch-Bages has always been admired for its richness and opulence of fruit. There's more of the swagger of Mouton than the elegance of Lafite. Jean-Charles Cazes provided the outline in the 1950s by harvesting later and riper than most, and the style has been perpetuated by the continued search for optimum ripeness and by the relevant vinification techniques. *Délestage* was introduced by Daniel Llose in 1981 and can be used up to eight times in the nonalcoholic phase of fermentation in order to extract the fruit. Cabernet Sauvignon is the dominant variety, with 73% planted in the vineyard and yields respectable rather than restrained. Aging lasts for up to 16 months in 70–80% new oak barrels. In September 2009, I had the privilege of tasting a vertical of the wines at the estate. The one underlying factor was the consistency since 1982. As Stephen Browett of London fine-wine merchant Farr Vintners exclaimed: "Lynch-Bages is stronger than the vintage, because I know it will never let me down." Below is a

selection of the highlights from the tasting.

1959★ Fresh and elegant in style, the fruit and acidity still apparent. Lacy, complex, and long.

1966★ Powerful wine. Deep color, with a little brick at the rim. Still ripe, rich, and spicy. Currant, mineral, and roasted notes. Sweet middle palate.

1970★ Powerful but balanced. Rich and ripe with loads of exuberant fruit and a firm finish. Still plenty of reserve.

1982 Deep color. Dense, sweet, lush, and round. Certainly Pauillac in style, but with the Lynch-Bages fruit and flourish.

1988 Spice, dark fruit, and tobacco notes. Firm and pretty substantial.

1989★ Huge density of fruit, with power and complexity as well. Quite backward and reserved still on the palate.

1990★ Deep color. Rich, full, and perfumed. Lovely balance. Delicious, but will age.

1993 Leafy, tobacco notes but with surprising reserve. Lively, fresh, and balanced on the palate.

1994 Firm, long, and just a little austere, with tannic grip on the finish.

1996★ Fruit and charm on the nose, the palate sweet, round, and generous. Acidity adds balance on the finish.

1999★ Pure, ripe, and perfumed, with a touch of creamy, zesty oak. Mouth-filling fruit on the palate. Drinking well now.

2000★ Sweet, smoky, and exotic on the nose. Very pretty fruit. Long and racy, still well within itself.

2001 Similar to the 2000 but with more immediate charm.

2004 Lovely depth of fruit and a long, zesty finish. Handsome, medium-bodied wine.

2005★ Dense, long, and firm. Powerful but refined tannins. Huge *matière*. Evidently for the long term.

2006 A firm and powerful wine in the style of the vintage, the acidity adding length and line.

Left: One of the new shops around the square in the village of Bages, which the Cazes family is gradually reconstructing

Château Lynch-Bages
Total area: 260 acres (105ha)
Area under vine: 240 acres (97ha)
Average production: grand vin 420,000 bottles; second wine 200,000 bottles
33250 Pauillac
Tel: +33 5 56 73 24 00
www.lynchbages.com

Pichon Comtesse de Lalande

When the Rouzaud family acquired Pichon Longueville Comtesse de Lalande in 2007, most observers greeted favorably what looked like a sound decision for all concerned. After all, as owners of Roederer Champagne, the Rouzauds had already proved themselves committed to the highest standards, and this grand old estate had surely passed into good hands. All the same, the news was not without its note of pathos. The acquisition marked the end of a highly distinctive era for the estate—a period during which it was dominated by the resolute personality of the previous occupant, May-Eliane de Lencquesaing. And if Pichon Lalande, as it is more generally known, has been riding high since the late 1970s, much of that is due to her dedication and energy.

Merlot represents 35 percent of plantings. It's this that gives the wines their succulent charm and elegant, velvety texture. They are also accessible earlier

As I explain elsewhere in this book, the great estate of Pichon was divided in 1850, with one part going to the son, Raoul, and the remaining three fifths, including 104 acres (42ha) of vines, to three daughters. The two estates were initially managed as one property, but on the death of Raoul in 1860, his sister Virginie, Comtesse de Lalande, decided to run the sisters' portion separately, eventually acquiring all the shares. The château had been built earlier, in 1840.

Pichon Lalande remained in the same family until 1926, when it was sold to Edouard and Louis Miailhe, familiar figures in the Bordeaux trade. Edouard's daughter, May-Eliane, inherited the property in 1978, and after a nomadic existence as the wife of an army officer, she finally settled in Bordeaux to run the estate. It was de Lencquesaing who oversaw, among many other things, the construction of the two *cuviers* equipped with stainless-steel tanks, the extension of the existing barrel cellar, and the building of a second in 1986. She also brought in the present winemaker, Thomas Dô Chi Nam, and manager Gildas d'Ollone, as well as reprising the peripatetic existence she had led as an army bride by traveling the world as an untiring ambassador.

The château and *chais* are situated on the estuary side of the D2 road as one heads north into Pauillac, and from a landscaped terrace there's a splendid view of Château Latour and the estuary beyond. It is easy to assume that the surrounding vineyards belong to Pichon Lalande, but this is not the case: all but a parcel are owned by Latour. The vineyards, in fact, lie to the other side of the D2, the core area of about 160 acres (65ha) to the west and south of those of Pichon-Longueville. This includes 27 acres (11ha) that are geographically in St-Julien but historically have always been permitted in Pichon Lalande.

Another 30 acres (12ha) are located farther west at Ste-Anne, close to Batailley. This sector was planted in the 1980s but was already part of the property. The grapes rarely make the grand vin. Farther north, near St-Sauveur, are another 22 acres (9ha) in Pauillac, part of the purchase of the cru bourgeois Château Bernadotte in 1997. These have been incorporated into Pichon Lalande, and the fruit occasionally makes the top wine.

At present it is difficult to tell whether the Rouzauds have made any significant changes at the property. I was assured that attention has mainly been turned toward the vineyard. Soil studies have been carried out, drainage inspected, and the amount of staff and man-hours increased for green work and tilling the soils. As d'Ollone puts it, "The Rouzauds don't want to rock the boat but have said they will provide the means to improve."

FINEST WINES

Château Pichon Longueville Comtesse de Lalande
The style of Pichon Lalande has always been associated with a high proportion of Merlot in the blend. The Miailhe brothers adored the variety, planting it extensively in the 1920s and '30s. The oldest parcel in the vineyard today was planted in 1939, and all told Merlot represents 35% of plantings. It's this that gives the wines their succulent charm and elegant, velvety texture. They are also accessible earlier, notwithstanding the structure to age. A little Petit Verdot and Cabernet Franc (8% and 12% of the vineyard respectively) are usually in the blend, adding color, freshness, and further complexity. Cabernet Sauvignon represents 45% of vineyard plantings, but this is likely to increase. Vintages since 2000 have had a stronger Cabernet influence (63% in 2008), and winemaker Thomas Dô Chi Nam admits, "The tendency now is to reinforce the Cabernet Sauvignon, because it ripens better than in the past." The benchmark wine appears to be the 1996, which had 75% Cabernet Sauvignon in the blend, so expect future vintages to be denser, tighter, and more powerful—in short, more typically Pauillac. The winemaking is traditional, the grand vin aged for 18 months in 50% new oak barrels.

1985★ Beautiful now. Powerfully aromatic, with notes of cigar box, humus, and dark fruit. A lingering freshness on the palate, the finish a touch dry.

1996★ Very Pauillac in style. Notes of cassis, cedar, and cigar box. The palate is dense but fine and upright, with length and freshness on the finish.

2001★ Quite sensual and exotic, the palate round, sweet, ample, and spicy. Notes of licorice and mocha on the nose. Accessible but will age.

Château Pichon Longueville Comtesse de Lalande
Total area: 227 acres (92ha)
Area under vine: 215 acres (87ha)
Average production: grand vin 230,000 bottles; second wine 180,000 bottles
33250 Pauillac
Tel: +33 5 56 59 19 40
www.pichon-lalande.com

Above: The classically proportioned rear facade of Pichon Lalande reflects the elegance and harmony of the wine

Pontet-Canet

Two things have made Pontet-Canet a topic of conversation for Bordeaux lovers in recent years: the dramatic rise in the quality of the wine, and the decision to work the vineyard biodynamically. To my knowledge, Pontet-Canet is the only Médoc classed growth to have taken this bold initiative. Others have ongoing trials in parcels of vines, but none has around 200 acres (80ha) worked in this way. The question, however, remains: are these two talking points related? Alfred Tesseron, Pontet-Canet's owner, certainly hopes so. As he says, "The leitmotif is not the organics but making better wine."

It was Alfred's father, Cognac merchant Guy Tesseron, who bought the estate in 1975. Prior to that, Pontet-Canet had been owned by the négociant Cruse since 1865. The wine was well known in France (particularly on French railroads) thanks to the distribution network of the Cruse family. But until 1972 it was bottled at the merchant's cellars in Bordeaux, occasionally without a vintage date, and the property and wine were treated generally as just another brand.

Above: One of the horses now employed in Pontet-Canet's vineyards, where they compact the soil less than tractors

Alfred Tesseron admits that after the purchase, in the 1970s and '80s, there was little money for investment. The vineyard was in poor shape, and a program of grubbing up and replanting was initiated; this lasted into the 1990s. A second wine, Les Hauts de Pontet-Canet, was introduced in 1982 to improve selection, and green-harvesting was trialed in 1989, becoming systematic, until recently, from 1994. A new *cuvier* was also created.

Since 1999, investment in the winery has been on a much larger scale. Buildings for bottle storage and agricultural equipment have been constructed, the barrel cellar enlarged and renovated, and the *cuvier* redefined. This now contains 16 wooden vats and 32 conical 80hl concrete vats, as well as sorting tables for the harvest.

The vineyard is divided into two blocks. The core area, representing two-thirds of the plantings, surrounds the 19th-century château on a plateau opposite Mouton Rothschild. In fact, there are two undulating *croupes* here that rise to a high point of 100ft (30m). These elevated sections with deep Günzian gravel soils are considered the noblest terroir, the inclines having a greater proportion of sand and clay. The other sector is located just north of the town of Pauillac. The soils are more varied and principally Merlot is planted here.

The move to biodynamics was initiated and has been driven by Jean-Michel Comme, the technical director at Pontet-Canet for the past 20 years. "On reflection, it seemed the best solution to avoid chemicals and maintain quality," he says. The process, though, has been gradual. Pesticides were abandoned in 2001 and weedkiller in 2003, with an initial 35 acres (14ha) converted

Above: Pontet-Canet's owner Alfred Tesseron, who has boldly backed the move to convert his vineyards to biodynamics

to biodynamics in 2004. Since 2005, the whole vineyard has been biodynamic, with the process to full conversion delayed by a decision to spray for mildew in 2007. "We regretted it in the end, since other properties took a loss like us, but 15 days after spraying, we'd returned to biodynamics," Comme explains.

According to Comme, the vineyard has found a natural balance since 2008. They now do very little green-harvesting or trimming and are trialing horses to work the vines. He pointed to one parcel that produced a natural 45hl/ha in 2008 and said it would be the same in 2009. It is in this parcel that the link between practice and quality is most apparent—a link that Comme describes succinctly: "It's knowledge of the terroir by observation that counts, which means being morally and physically present all the time." Comme is a hard-bitten convert; Alfred Tesseron, I suspect, less so—but while the quality is there, he's happy to take the road.

FINEST WINES

Château Pontet-Canet
The vineyard is 60% CS, 33% M, 5% CF, and 2% PV. The grapes are gravity-fed and crushed over the tanks. In keeping with the natural approach, only indigenous yeasts are used, and the temperature of each tank is regulated manually. Aging is in 60% new oak barrels. The wines themselves are deep in color, dense, and powerful—the masculine side of Pauillac in full cry. Patience is needed before they can be broached. The nearest comparison would be a wine like Pichon-Longueville. Quality has been particularly high since 2000.

2001★ More immediate charm than some recent vintages but still has the tannins to age. Black currant notes and a minerally freshness on the finish.

2003 Deep color. Rather closed, with a robust tannic frame. Fresh for the vintage. Needs time.

Château Pontet-Canet
Total area: 300 acres (120ha)
Area under vine: 200 acres (81ha)
Average production: grand vin 250,000 bottles; second wine 100,000 bottles
33250 Pauillac
Tel: +33 5 56 59 04 04
www.pontet-canet.com

Grand-Puy-Lacoste

Grand-Puy-Lacoste is the connoisseur's wine and a quintessential Pauillac to boot. Rich and vigorous but balanced and poised, it has the black currant, cedar, and mineral notes that characterize the wines of the appellation. Owner François-Xavier Borie avoids the razzmatazz and speculation of neighboring superstars but produces a long-aging, richly satisfying wine.

There's been recent investment in the cellars and *cuvier*, but the essence of the wine is down to terroir and good vineyard husbandry. *Puy* in local parlance means hillock (like *cos* or *fîte*), and the Grand-Puy-Lacoste vineyard sits in one block on a gravel mound inland from the estuary. Visually, the land appears flat, but behind the 19th-century château to the west there's a fairly steep incline to a park indicating good natural drainage.

Grand-Puy-Lacoste is the connoisseur's wine and a quintessential Pauillac to boot. Rich and vigorous but balanced and poised, it has black currant, cedar, and mineral notes

The property was acquired by Jean-Eugène Borie of Ducru-Beaucaillou in 1978 and has since been run by his son, François-Xavier, the outright owner since 2003. There were initially only 75 acres (30ha) under production, so a further 60 acres (25ha) were added over the course of time. This is typical Cabernet Sauvignon country, and the grape variety represents 75 percent of the vineyard, with 5 percent Cabernet Franc and the rest Merlot. The average age in 2009 was 38 years. Much of the vineyard is planted on *riparia* rootstock, which, along with the early-ripening nature of the terroir, helps with the consistency of production.

Investment in the winery includes a renovated *cuvier* in 1997, with the addition of temperature-controlled stainless-steel tanks of varying size; a new barrel cellar in 2003; and an updated system for receiving the harvest (vibrating sorting tables and so on) from 2006. The vinification is as classic as it could be. After three weeks of cuvaison, the wine is run off and the press wine (which represents 10–12 percent of the final blend) carefully selected. The malolactic fermentation is in tank, the wine aged in 65 percent new oak barrels for 16 months. The second wine, Lacoste Borie, has existed since 1982.

FINEST WINES

Château Grand-Puy-Lacoste
This is classic Pauillac made in traditional fashion. The guardians of that temple, the Boissenots (father and son), are retained as consultant oenologists.
1982★ As with so many 1982s, an example of a great wine made from fairly high yields (62hl/ha). Arriving at full maturity but still with an abundance of delicious fruit and a solid tannic frame.
1990 Ripe and sensuous, the color dark, the nose redolent of sandalwood, spice, and dark fruit. The palate is sweet and dense, the tannins smooth.
1996★ Vinous and vigorous, the nose expressing the black currant and pencil-lead notes typical of Pauillac. Lovely freshness, minerality, and length.
2003 There's a curranty note on the nose, indicating the dry, hot conditions of the year, but minerality as well. Supple fruit on the palate, with a robust tannic frame. Solid rather than fine.
2004 More loosely structured but still with length. Black currant and blackberry notes. Supple fruit, the tannins still a little grippy.
2005★ Savory and complex, the cassis and cedar notes clear on the nose. The palate is dense and long, with balancing acidity. A very complete wine.
2006 Close to the 2005 in quality. A little less complex, but plenty of savory character. The palate is powerful, the tannins fine and long.

Château Grand-Puy-Lacoste
Total area: 235 acres (95ha)
Area under vine: 136 acres (55ha)
Average production: grand vin 185,000 bottles;
second wine 100,000 bottles
33250 Pauillac
Tel: +33 5 56 59 06 66
www.chateau-grand-puy-lacoste.fr

Léoville-Las-Cases

The heart and soul of Château Léoville-Las-Cases is the 131-acre (53ha) *grand enclos*, which lies between the village of St-Julien and the boundary of Château Latour to the north. A recently refreshed stone wall surrounds this vineyard area, the lion-topped gateway serving both as a distinctive landmark and as inspiration for the emblem used on the Las-Cases label.

This is the core of the old Léoville estate that was divided in the early 19th century (Pierre-Jean, Marquis de Las Cases, retained half the original holding) and provides the fruit for Léoville-Las-Cases today. A parcel on the southern outskirts of the village and one opposite the famous gateway on the other side of the D2 road occasionally contribute to the grand vin. The rest of the vineyard, though cultivated in the same manner, is considered another property, the Clos du Marquis little more than just a second label.

A walk in the *grand enclos* with the production manager Michael Georges, while I was researching this book, was an enlightening and uplifting experience, taking me right to the epicenter of the Las-Cases universe. The land forms two gently undulating mounds, with the slope down to the *palus* if not vertiginous then certainly marked. The estuary, at less than 0.6 miles (1km) away, appears remarkably close. Underfoot, the deep gravel soils comprise a complex matrix, the depth and proportion of sand and clay varying throughout the terrain.

A combination of the south-southeasterly exposure, the microclimate provided by the estuary, and the gravelly soils make this the ideal terrain for Cabernet Sauvignon, which accounts for 70 percent of vines within the *grand enclos*. Merlot is planted at the foot of the slope (oriented to the east and the north so as to ripen at the same time as the Cabernet) and in parcels in the middle.

Right: One of the most evocative landmarks in Bordeaux, the defiant lion gate that compensates for the lack of a château

There's no doubt that Léoville-Las-Cases is one of the finest wines of the Médoc.
Its track record since the mid-1970s has been nothing short of exemplary.
The wines are rich and concentrated

Above: Jean-Hubert Delon, as committed to quality as his predecessors but seeking more "balance, finesse, and mystery"

Some of the oldest vines, a plot of 80-year-old Cabernet Franc, are closer to the D2 road.

The vineyard is in a balanced state, Georges explained to me as we walked, the vigor very much under control. One or two parcels require grass cover, but the soils are mainly plowed in the traditional fashion. Green-harvesting and deleafing is more a question of removing the suckers in spring. Weedkiller is avoided, and pesticides were abandoned in the 1990s.

If the vineyard is in remarkable condition today, it is in part due to the continuity at Las-Cases for the past 100 years. In 1900, the estate was formed into a company, and Théophile Skawinski, then general manager, took a share. His great-great-grandson, Jean-Hubert Delon, is now the administrator and, with his sister Geneviève d'Alton, the outright owner of Las-Cases. In the years between, three other generations of the Delon family managed the estate, gradually accumulating a majority share.

The Clos du Marquis label was created as early as 1902 for wine produced from land outside the original Léoville land registry (parcels farther west). This is still the case today, with the addition of lots from the *grand enclos* (such as young vines) considered of insufficient quality for Léoville-Las-Cases. Michel Delon, who ran the property from 1976 until his death in 2000, was known for his uncompromising attitude to quality, and his son Jean-Hubert follows in a similar vein—hence the fluctuation in the volume of the grand vin.

Léoville-Las-Cases is vinified in traditional manner and aged in 65 percent new oak barrels. That said, the Delons have always availed themselves of the latest technology if it has proved its worth. A reverse-osmosis concentrator has been used for some years, and when I visited during the 2009 harvest, an optical grape-sorting system was in action, combined with a new-generation destemmer. The system had been trialed at the other Delon properties—Nenin and Potensac—the previous year.

FINEST WINES

Château Léoville-Las-Cases

There's no doubt that Léoville-Las-Cases is one of the finest wines of the Médoc. Its track record since the mid-1970s has been nothing short of exemplary. The wines are rich and concentrated, with a Pauillac-like power and structure (not surprising, given the geography of the vineyard) and are definitely built to age. Cabernet Sauvignon dominates the blend, the proportion increasing in the truly great years (87.6% in 2005). Cabernet Franc and Merlot are the other components used in roughly equal share (one of the differences with the Clos du Marquis is that it has up to 40% Merlot). Michel Delon used to add a tiny proportion of Petit Verdot to the grand vin, but this is now reserved for the Clos du Marquis. "My father favored power in the wine, but I'm looking for a little more balance, finesse, and mystery," explains Jean-Hubert Delon, his gravelly voice giving away a penchant for cigars. These are wines to be served and enjoyed at table; the Delons would have it no other way.

The following tasting took place at the estate in September 2009. The only addition is the 1989, a wine consumed with pleasure (in 2009) to celebrate my daughter's 20th birthday.

1962 Tawny color. Distinctive *sous-bois* notes but still with a hint of fruit on the nose and sweetness on the palate. Gentle and caressing.

1966 Brick hue but dense at the core. Herbal, leafy notes. The acidity provides some length, but the fruit is beginning to dry.

1975 Dark-brick hue. Curranty, empyreumatic notes on the nose register the hot, dry year. The palate is firm, dry, and subdued.

1979 The first bottle was corked; the second, a little out of condition. The fruit is still apparent, but I found a greenness running through the wine.

1985 Probably the most drinkable vintage at the moment. Ruby red with a hint of brick at the rim. Ripe, round, and generous on the nose, sweet and densely fruited on the palate.

1986★ An enormous wine. Definitely Pauillac in style. Powerful, complex, and restrained. Huge extract but wonderful balance as well. Michel Delon's greatest vintage?

1989★ Beautiful weight and texture. Plenty of mouth-filling fruit and a powerful tannic frame, but less massive than the 1986. Definite black currant notes with a hint of cedar and cigar box. Lovely balance. Well within itself. The last vintage with Emile Peynaud as consultant (now the Boissenots).

1994 The first vintage Jean-Hubert Delon made with his father. Restrained and backward in style. Plenty of dense extract. Powerful—even robust—tannic frame. Wait a while.

1996★ Dense and powerful, but fine and complex as well (comparisons with Lafite). A clear Cabernet signature—and minerally, too. Beautiful length and balance.

2000★ Dark, ripe, and dense. A powerful tannic frame but swathed in rich, generous fruit. A hint of classy oak. Definitely needs time.

2002 An impressive wine for the vintage. Pure and aromatic, with cassis and licorice notes. Medium to full-bodied, fleshy with a fine tannic grain. Vanilla oak apparent. Has a certain charm.

RÉCOLTE 2002

Grand Vin de Léoville

du Marquis de Las Cases

SAINT-JULIEN-MÉDOC

Château Léoville Las Cases
Total area: 250 acres (100ha)
Area under vine: 240 acres (97ha)
Production: grand vin 120,000–240,000 bottles; second wine 180,000–300,000 bottles
33250 St-Julien-Beychevelle
Tel: +33 5 56 73 25 26

Léoville Barton

I f the spirit of a wine can be embodied by its owner, then the charismatic Anthony Barton will have worked wonders for Château Léoville Barton. His debonair charm and wit have lightened the aura of the Médoc, while his careful nurturing of the property and sensitive handling of pricing have earned respect from consumers and his peers in the trade.

The vineyards of Léoville Barton were once part of the vast Léoville estate, which made its reputation under the ownership of Blaise Alexandre de Gasq in the 18th century. On de Gasq's death, in 1769, it was bequeathed to four heirs and, in the early 19th century, split, with a portion going to Hugh Barton of Irish descent in 1826. He had already purchased Château Langoa in 1821, and the elegant château of this property now serves both as Anthony Barton's residence and as the inspiration for the image depicted on the label of Léoville Barton. The winemaking facilities for both properties are also shared.

Anthony Barton took the reins at Léoville and Langoa Barton in 1983, his uncle Ronald having donated the properties to him. Born in Ireland, he'd worked for the family négociant, Barton and Guestier, on arrival in Bordeaux in 1951 before setting up his own négociant business in 1967. Les Vins Fins Anthony Barton is now run by his daughter Lilian, who also assists with the two estates.

There's been no revolution at Léoville Barton, merely a continuous process of fine-tuning to improve the wine. Particular attention has been given to the vineyard. A program of complantation was put in place from 1985 to replace missing vines (but maintain age), while the soils were tended with organic material. The vineyard is now in a balanced state, and yields are regulated by the use of judicious

Right: Anthony Barton and his daughter Lilian, whose estates have been in family ownership longer than any others

*If the spirit of a wine can be embodied by its owner, then the charismatic
Anthony Barton will have worked wonders for Château Léoville Barton.
His debonair charm and wit have lightened the aura of the Médoc*

pruning. Green-harvesting is avoided for all but the youngest vines, and even with those it is minimal. The unsung hero of all this work has been Michel Raoult, technical director from 1984 until his retirement in 2008.

A proportion of the vineyard is located on the estuary side of the D2 road running north from the agricultural buildings and offices of Léoville Barton toward a walled section of Léoville-Las-Cases. The soils are particularly stony here, the clay component conspicuous at various levels. Curiously, a large portion of the Merlot is planted in this sector, the oldest dating from 1962. There's also a little Cabernet Sauvignon, but the majority of this variety is in parcels running west toward Château Talbot. The gravelly soils here have slightly more sand.

The Léoville Barton team tends to pick a little earlier than is elsewhere considered the norm these days, but never before adequate maturity is reached. There's a traditional approach to winemaking, the grapes fermented with natural yeasts in temperature-controlled wooden vats that Anthony Barton has steadily replaced over the years. The malolactic fermentation is also executed in the same vats. Aging is in 60 percent new oak barrels and lasts for 18–20 months. A second barrel cellar was added in 1990.

FINEST WINES

Château Léoville Barton

The wine is classic in style, Cabernet Sauvignon dominant (just over 70% in the vineyard, with 23% Merlot and the rest Cabernet Franc), lively, harmonious, and well structured, with refreshingly attractive fruit. It is generally firmer than its stablemate Langoa Barton. The consistency is remarkable, particularly since the mid-1990s. I have tasting notes of vintages from the 1990s taken in February 2003 and for the 1986★ that Anthony Barton served at lunch. The latter seemed an eternal sort of wine, firm and vigorous, with great balance and length and a pebble-sucking freshness and minerality. The 1991 still had fruit and verve and a certain complexity of aroma. The 1992 and 1993 had not defied the difficulty of the years, my preference being the lightly fragrant 1992 over the greener 1993. The 1994 was a definite step up. It seemed to have avoided the abrasive tannins of the year but lacked the Léoville charm. This I found in abundance in the 1995★, a wine redolent of dark fruit with a long, firm finish. The 1996★, though, was one step better, being more concentrated and powerful (almost Pauillac-like) but still with the Léoville trademark balance and length. The 1997 was round and juicy and already starting to drink;

Above: The characteristically elegant facade of Château Langoa Barton, whose image also adorns Léoville Barton

the 1998 was at the opposite end of the spectrum, rich but firm and tannic and in need of time. The following wines were tasted at the estate in September 2009:

1999 Supple, medium-bodied wine with a certain charm. Dark-fruit and truffle notes. Drinking now.

2000★ Dark, ripe, and complex. Rich and concentrated, with defined black currant aromas. Big-boned but with balance and length. Long-aging. Very complete.

2001 Full-bodied and savory. Rich but less concentrated than the 2000. Firm tannic structure that will need time to open.

Château Léoville Barton
Total area: 370 acres (150ha)
Area under vine: 119 acres (48ha)
Average production: grand vin 250,000 bottles; second wine 90,000 bottles
33250 St-Julien
Tel: +33 5 56 59 06 05
www.leoville-barton.com

Ducru-Beaucaillou

The most striking thing about the vineyard of Ducru-Beaucaillou is the eclectic and multicolored range of quartz and flint stones found in its soils. Distinctive enough, at any rate, to have inspired part of the estate's memorable name: Beaucaillou. The Ducru part was added by Bertrand Ducru when he acquired the estate in 1795. Ducru was also responsible for the construction of what is now the middle section of the château, though the two square towers at either end of the château—strikingly apparent on the wine's label—were added in the latter part of the 19th century by the owner at the time, négociant Nathaniel Johnston. The property also includes an extensive area of pasture, marsh, and forest.

Since 1941, the estate has been in the Borie family. Jean-Eugène Borie took over from his father Francis in 1953 and, with the help of consultant oenologist Emile Peynaud, enhanced the estate's reputation with glorious vintages in the 1960s, 1970s, and early 1980s. His son, François-Xavier, joined him in 1978 to help run the expanding family portfolio, and he continued to manage the estate following Jean-Eugène's death in 1998. In 2003, there was a redistribution of the properties, which led to François-Xavier taking over at Grand-Puy-Lacoste and Haut-Batailley, while his brother, Bruno, took over the reins at Ducru-Beaucaillou.

The heart of the vineyard is the 136 acres (55ha) planted at 10,000 vines/ha that surround the château and descend to within 2,600ft (800m) of the estuary. "The terroir or ecosystem is dictated by the proximity to the estuary and deep Günzian gravel soils," explains Bruno Borie. His selection for the grand vin is taken principally from here, with a further 50 acres (20ha) situated inland near Talbot reserved for the second wine, Croix de Beaucaillou, introduced in 1995.

In recent times, the only rocky patch Ducru-Beaucaillou has had to endure was the late 1980s, when TCA contamination was found in the cellars.

This affected vintages in the late 1980s and early 1990s, resulting in the construction of new semi-underground cellars. Since 1995, however, the wines have been clean and without fault. What's more, since Bruno Borie took over, the estate has undoubtedly scaled new heights. The selection has become more draconian, with a maximum of 144,000 bottles produced annually, compared to 180,000 previously. Complanted vines are now harvested separately, new presses have been purchased to improve the press wine, and another St-Julien property, Château Lalande-Borie, is used to test new techniques before they are applied at Ducru-Beaucaillou. As Borie says, "It's the little details that help improve the wine."

The vinification, though, remains traditional, with gentle extraction and fermentation temperatures that do not exceed 86°F (30°C). As far as possible, there is parcel-by-parcel vinification, with the alcoholic and malolactic fermentation taking place in vat. The wine is then aged in barrel for 18 months, with up to 90 percent new oak used in vintages from 2005. Cabernet Sauvignon is the mainstay of the blend, Borie increasing the proportion to 85–90 percent (in 2007 and 2008) from the previous tally of 65–75 percent. Merlot is the complementary component.

FINEST WINES

Château Ducru-Beaucaillou

The style of Ducru-Beaucaillou is one of elegance combined with the balance and fruit character one expects from a St-Julien. The Léovilles can be more powerfully structured, and Gruaud-Larose occasionally richer, but Ducru-Beaucaillou leads with its finesse and length and freshness on the finish. These are wines that are generally slow to develop, needing a good ten years before all the components are in tune. In recent vintages, Bruno Borie seems to have pushed the ripeness further (but to an acceptable degree) to gain greater

Right: Twin towers have embellished the château since the 19th century, the magnificent whole appearing on the wine's label

Above: The artistically minded Bruno Borie, whose attention to detail has improved Ducru since he took over in 2003

purity and quality of texture. A "modern classic" is what I wrote of the 2008★ en primeur. I have rarely tasted older vintages, but a visit to the château in 2008 provided the opportunity to taste two of the celebrated years. The 1961★ was brilliant. Still dark, rich, and concentrated, with a volume of fruit on the palate, it belied its years. The secret, apparently, was a small, hot harvest and the fact that Ducru-Beaucaillou was one of the few estates to have an efficient cooling system (for fermentation) at the time. The 1970★ showed more evolution, with a brick hue and tobacco notes, but the texture was velvety smooth, the fruit still sweet and vibrant.

1996 A little less precision from a vintage I generally admire. Slight brick to the rim, with leafy, cassis notes on the nose. Medium-bodied, with the freshness and length of the cru and the vintage.

2003 Lots of fruit but less vibrancy and charm. Plum, currant, and roasted notes on both nose and palate, and a robust tannic frame.

2005★ Rich, ripe, and complex. A note of confit on the nose, but not jammy. Dense but harmonious on the palate, the acidity offering length and line. More power than finesse for now. Needs time.

Château Ducru-Beaucaillou
Total area: 545 acres (220ha)
Area under vine: 185 acres (75ha)
Production: grand vin 108,000–144,000 bottles; second wine 120,000–144,000 bottles
33250 St-Julien
Tel: +33 5 56 73 16 73
www.chateau-ducru-beaucaillou.com

Beychevelle

Legend has it that the name Beychevelle has nautical origins. When ships on the Gironde used to pass by the estate in the late 16th century, they would lower their sails (*baisse-voile*) in deference to the powerful owner of the property, the Duc d'Epernon, a French admiral. This story also explains the estate's label, which features an emblem of a sailing ship.

Today, the recently restored Beychevelle, with its landscaped gardens and park leading down to the estuary, is no less worthy of such respect. Originally built in the 17th century, it was reconstructed in the 18th and extended with various Baroque-style adornments in the 19th. It's a magnificent property that has been in the hands of Grands Millésimes de France, a company established by GMF insurance and the Japanese group Suntory, since 1986, when it was sold by the Achille-Fould family, the owners since 1890.

The style of Beychevelle is one of balance, elegance, and freshness, and the wines are more delicate than those of the other St-Julien classed growths

This is one of the Médoc's stronger brands, though its progress hasn't always been plain sailing. The wines, price, and image were strong in the 1950s and 1960s, but poor vintages in the 1970s and inconsistency in the 1980s (largely attributable to the heavy yields and a neglected vineyard) tarnished Beychevelle's image. Following the difficult years of the early 1990s, Philippe Blanc was brought in as general manager in 1995, and there has clearly been considerable improvement since. Indeed, as Blanc himself says, any "accusations of greenness these days are unfounded, because the fruit is harvested ripe and the quality is infinitely better than before."

The vineyard is quite dispersed, a distance of some 3.5 miles (6km) dividing the most northerly and southerly parcels. The core, however, remains the 50 acres (20ha) or so on the plateau behind the château. These are planted with equal portions of Merlot and Cabernet Sauvignon and, according to Blanc, "the land is as good as anything you'll find at Ducru-Beaucaillou or Léoville Barton." There are other parcels close to Gruaud-Larose and Léoville Barton, as well as 54.5 acres (22ha) in Cussac in the Haut-Médoc. Historically (pre-1855), this land has always been part of the estate, and a decree in 1946 officially tied it to St-Julien for as long as it should remain the property of Château Beychevelle.

Under Blanc's direction, yields have been reduced to an average 42hl/ha (the density of planting is 10,000 vines/ha), and the selection has become much more severe. Only 55 percent of the production now goes into the grand vin and 40 percent into the second wine (Amiral de Beychevelle), while 5 percent is sold off in bulk. To understand just how much of a change that is, compare those figures with 1982, when 96 percent of the production went into the grand vin and the yield was 70hl/ha.

The style of Beychevelle is one of balance, elegance, and freshness, and the wines are more delicate than those of the other St-Julien classed growths, though they do nevertheless have a surprising ability to age (as the notes below confirm). Those looking for power and volume will be disappointed, however. "Our philosophy at Beychevelle has been to correct deficiencies and to progress but to remain faithful to the character and style of the cru," says Blanc. For that reason, he adds, Jacques and Éric Boissenot were hired as consultant oenologists soon after his arrival in 1996. Along with Blanc, the Boissenots have ensured that Beychevelle has continued on its steady course.

of the older vintages were long past their best (1906, 1937) or disappointing (1929). The 1914 was also tired and gone, though the significance of the year made for an emotional experience. Moving forward in time, there was an amber-colored, fully mature, but still sweet 1961 and a solid but fresh 1970★. The 1975 and 1978 were unimpressive, the latter reconditioned and the addition of sulfur overdone. The 1982★ was rich and exuberant, the 1986 perfumed but still reserved and austere on the palate. The 1989★ was one of the highlights—complex, vinous, and long. Blanc admitted that he hadn't served the 1983, 1988, or 1990 because the vintages are underwhelming. His first vintage, however, the 1996★, was spicy and elegant on the nose, the palate rich and round with good acidity. The 1999 **[V]** surprised everyone with its elegance and harmony, though it's not for the long haul.

The blends at Beychevelle vary considerably—from almost 50/50 Merlot/Cabernet Sauvignon with a little Cabernet Franc (as in 2005 and 2008), to 59% Cabernet Sauvignon, 29% Merlot, 7% Cabernet Franc, and 5% Petit Verdot (as in 2006), the latter a formula that Blanc says he prefers.

2000 Sweet, round, and generous; just about ready to drink. Truffle notes on the nose but the tannins still firm on the finish.

2001 Similar to the 2000 but livelier and perhaps more elegant, the tannins finer.

2002 Lighter in style but gently perfumed, fresh, and balanced. Lacks a little length.

2003 Full, round, and easy, marked by the heat of the year. Plum and fig notes on both nose and palate, and a little warmth on the finish.

2004 Medium-bodied, fresh, and fruity, the oak still present and the tannins a touch austere.

2005★ Rich and complex, with a finesse of tannin and texture. Among the best from this estate.

2006 Rather strict and austere at present, but there's a purity of fruit and line and length that bodes well for the long term.

Above: Sails may no longer be lowered in respect, but Philippe Blanc has raised standards since his arrival in 1995

FINEST WINES

Château Beychevelle

A retrospective tasting of 24 vintages covering 100 years was held at the property in May 2009 and served to define the style of Beychevelle. Some

Château Beychevelle
Total area: 620 acres (250ha)
Area under vine: 222 acres (90ha)
Production: grand vin 250,000–280,000 bottles; second wine 130,000–150,000 bottles
33250 St-Julien-Beychevelle
Tel: +33 5 56 73 20 70
www.beychevelle.com

Branaire-Ducru

That Patrick Maroteaux, current owner of Branaire-Ducru, has the presence of a cautious corporate baron is perhaps to be expected of someone who was once an important figure in the sugar industry. One might also add modesty to the list of his qualities, since Maroteaux readily admits he knew little about Bordeaux in the early days of his tenure at the estate 21 years ago. All the same, he has ushered in a period of consistent quality at a property that had been through uneven times for much of the 20th century.

When Maroteaux and his family acquired Branaire-Ducru in 1988, he immediately entrusted the management and winemaking to Philippe Dhalluin, who must also take his fair share of the credit for the estate's subsequent performance. Dhalluin brought much greater precision to the vineyard and cellars but departed for Mouton Rothschild in 2002. His successor, Jean-Dominique Videau, has continued in the same vein. Today, the vineyards are either plowed or have grass cover, and the trellising has been raised, which helps with ripening, particularly in parcels to the west. Yields have been reduced to an average 45hl/ha, and from the outset, a second wine, Duluc, was introduced to improve selection.

In 1991, a gravity-fed *cuvier* was inaugurated. Innovative at the time, it still looks up to date in every respect, except for the large size of the vats. More recent developments have included the introduction of sorting tables before and after the destemmer, and better supervision of the press wine, which can be up to 14 percent of the blend.

Jean-Baptiste Braneyre acquired part of the old Beychevelle estate in 1680. His grandson Laurent du Luc (Duluc following the Revolution) extended the vineyards. It was his two sons, Louis and Justin, who built the château in 1824. By 1873, the property had passed to Gustave Ducru and his sister Zélie Ravez.

The estate's vineyards are widely scattered but remain practically unchanged since the 1855 Classification. There's a block adjacent to the château and another close to the buildings of Château du Glana, opposite Ducru-Beaucaillou, with other parcels farther west near Château Lagrange and in the commune of St-Laurent (the latter existing in 1855 and permitted in the wine).

FINEST WINES

Château Branaire-Ducru

The aim, as described by Patrick Maroteaux, is to produce wines that have "fruit, freshness, and finesse." In this, Branaire-Ducru generally succeeds. Another unspoken message is not to expect the weight or power of the other classed growths in St-Julien. Indeed, Branaire-Ducru is careful about extraction. The cuvaison lasts approximately three weeks, and the emphasis is placed on harmony, the press wine added to build length. These may not be big wines, but they have fruit and vivacity and are enjoyable to drink with a little bottle age. My only reservation is the slightly angular finish displayed in some vintages. Cabernet Sauvignon is the dominant grape variety (70% in the vineyard), with Merlot and a tiny amount of Petit Verdot and Cabernet Franc. The wine is aged in 55–65% new oak barrels.

2000★ A lovely wine, true to the Branaire style. Black currant and red-fruit notes, lively and long. Medium-bodied concentration. Ready, but will age.

2001★ Similar to the 2000 but less concentrated. Spicy, cedar notes, supple, balanced, and long.

2003 Slightly disjointed, the oak still dominating the easy, red fruit. A curranty note reveals the heat of the year. Palate soft and sweet, but a dry finish.

2004 A rustic note on the finish is highlighted by the acidity. Otherwise, fresh and perfumed, with notes of berry fruit.

2006 More stuffing than the 2004 but a little austere at present. Black currant and licorice aromas. Palate round and full, the finish firm. Definitely needs time.

Château Branaire-Ducru
Total area: 125 acres (50ha)
Area under vine: 119 acres (48ha)
Average production: grand vin 150,000 bottles;
second wine 90,000 bottles
33250 St-Julien
Tel: +33 5 56 59 25 86
www.branaire.com

Gruaud-Larose

Château Gruaud-Larose has always been one of the most accessible of the Médoc second growths, thanks to its size, price, and availability. From my days in Paris in the 1980s, I can remember vintages from the 1970s, then in high-necked, Haut-Brion-style bottles, available in restaurants throughout the French capital. The négociant Cordier, owner until 1983, was largely responsible for this, the company's system of distribution helping to make Gruaud-Larose a recognized brand around the world.

Cordier sold the estate to the Suez banking group, which in turn sold to Alcatel Alsthom ten years later in 1993. The industrial conglomerate invested heavily in the property, improving drainage, renewing agricultural equipment, modernizing the *cuvier* (new wooden vats were added), and renovating the 19th-century château. It proved a costly sideline, and in 1997 Alsthom sold to the present owners, the Taillan group, a négociant business owned by the Merlaut family.

From 1971 until his retirement in 2006, Georges Pauli remained the one constant factor at Gruaud-Larose, taking on the roles of general manager and winemaker. Under his direction, the wines maintained a rich, vigorous, full-bodied, fruit-driven style. Since 2007, the oenologist Eric Boissenot has been brought in as consultant, and the tendency today is to aim for a little more refinement, the extraction less pushed (Pauli liked the fermentations to "simmer"), the length and structure of the wine built instead with the careful selection and addition of press wine.

The style of the wine also owes much to the terroir. The vineyard has a southeasterly exposure and is located in a single block on deep gravel soils with a higher proportion of clay than elsewhere in St-Julien. Since 2000, there's been considerable restructuring, with the new plantings at a high density of 10,000 vines/ha, the older ones from 6,500 to 8,500 vines/ha. The presence of the young vines explains the impressive volume of the second wine, Sarget de Gruaud-Larose.

At present, the vineyard is planted to 61 percent Cabernet Sauvignon, 29 percent Merlot, and 5 percent each of Cabernet Franc and Petit Verdot. The plan is to increase the Cabernet Sauvignon and Petit Verdot and reduce the other two varieties. In recent vintages, the wine has been aged in 50 percent new oak barrels for 18–20 months.

FINEST WINES

Château Gruaud-Larose

Over the years, Gruaud-Larose has been somewhat distanced by the other second growths in St-Julien. The gap is relative, though, and there's still margin for improvement. On the positive side, the wines remain good value, are enjoyable, and age remarkably well. A tasting at the estate in 2004 highlighted the successes of the 1980s and 1990s. The 1982★ has always been immense, rich, full, and fleshy, the palate oozing fruit but maintaining length and definition. The 1986★ was powerful and impressive, the density and structure auguring well for long age. Of the duo 1989 and 1990, I preferred the long and intense 1989★ to the slightly sweeter, softer 1990. Another significant duo were the 1995 and 1996, the former offering fruit and charm, the latter complexity and length. The 2000 has the ripeness and density of fruit typical of Gruaud-Larose, the tannins firm and long.

1996★ A Cabernet Sauvignon year and a reference in terms of style for future vintages of Gruaud-Larose. The fruit is evident, but there's length and freshness and a great deal of complexity. Mineral, spice, and sandalwood aromas. Lovely balance.

2007 [V] Lighter in weight but honest and pure. The fruit is apparent but finer and less punchy in style, while the delicate tannic frame gives the wine some lift and length.

Château Gruaud-Larose
Total area: 320 acres (130ha)
Area under vine: 200 acres (80ha)
Average production: grand vin 180,000 bottles; second wine 240,000 bottles
33250 St-Julien-Beychevelle
Tel: +33 5 56 73 15 20

Lagrange

The resurrection of Château Lagrange owes much to present owners Suntory and general manager Marcel Ducasse, who ran the property until he retired in 2007. A thriving estate of 690 acres (280ha) in 1840, Lagrange was in pitiful condition when the Japanese beverage group took over in 1983. The property had dwindled to 388 acres (157ha), of which only 138 acres (56ha) were planted with vines (including a disproportionate amount of Merlot). The buildings and château were in ruins.

Marcel Ducasse was set the task of restoring the property, and it's very much his oeuvre (under the patronage of Suntory finance) we see today. The vineyard has doubled in size (the proportion of Cabernet Sauvignon increasing to 65 percent), the buildings and *cuvier* have been renovated, and additional barrel cellars have been built. The large proportion of young vines led to the introduction of a much more severe selection and the creation of a second wine, Les Fiefs de Lagrange, from the outset (first vintage 1985). In 1997, a white wine, Les Arums de Lagrange, was also launched.

The vineyard is located across two gravel *croupes* in the most westerly sector of St-Julien. A program of soil analysis is to be launched in 2010, but the best sites have already been identified. These include areas of small, stony gravel that produce rather fine Merlot and Petit Verdot, as well as parcels that include larger stones and traces of iron oxide and produce structured Cabernet Sauvignon. "There's also a more modest sandy-gravel terroir with older vines planted in the 1980s that's beginning to be of interest," explains Bruno Eynard, who succeeded Ducasse as general manager but has been at the estate since 1990.

Eynard is working on further improvements at Lagrange. Apart from soil analysis, there are experiments with organics and biodynamics, and since 2009 still more precision has been brought to the picking. The *cuvier* has been modified to include a greater number of smaller stainless-steel tanks, and during the 2009 harvest, an optical grape sorter and new-generation destemmer were trialed. In the long term, a budget of some $11 million has been earmarked for a new *cuvier*, bottling line, and reception area for visitors.

FINEST WINES

Château Lagrange

Due to the number of young plantings, vintages of Lagrange in the 1980s and early 1990s had a greater proportion of Merlot (45%), and much of the Cabernet Sauvignon went into the second wine. This has gradually changed since 1996, and Bruno Eynard sees the ideal blend for the grand vin as 60–70% Cabernet Sauvignon and 25–30% Merlot, with a complement of Petit Verdot. The wine is aged in 60 percent new oak barrels for 18–20 months.

A vertical tasting of recent vintages in 2008 showed just how consistent Lagrange has become. The wines are structured and balanced, with an attractive density of fruit. The only thing lacking is a little aromatic complexity. Older vintages on view included a lean but elegant 1996 and a sumptuous, fruit-driven 1990★ that was very much in St-Julien mode.

2000★ Dense, rich, and balanced, with cedar and spice notes. One of the best from this estate.
2001 Soft and balanced, with a lively mineral note, the finish a touch hard.
2002 [V] Medium-bodied, spicy, and fine. More harmonious than the 2001.
2003 Sweet but fresh and balanced. Avoids jamminess and tough tannins.
2004 Medium-bodied, with plenty of charm, if not the density of a top year.
2005★ An opulent and powerful wine, with lovely fruit concentration.
2006★ Classic in style, long and linear, with good acidity—but the fruit is ripe and pure.

> **Château Lagrange**
> Total area: 388 acres (157ha)
> Area under vine: 290 acres (117ha)
> Average production: grand vin 300,000 bottles;
> second wine 420,000 bottles
> 33250 St-Julien-Beychevelle
> Tel: +33 5 56 73 38 38
> www.chateau-lagrange.com

Léoville Poyferré

Château Léoville Poyferré has been owned by the Cuvelier family since 1920 and managed by Didier Cuvelier since 1979. It was once part of the vast Léoville estate, and this portion of the property was bestowed on the wife of the Baron du Poyferré in the early part of the 19th century.

In the 1980s and early 1990s, Poyferré was very much a work in progress, and the wine was very far behind the other two Léovilles, Barton and Las-Cases. Didier Cuvelier inherited 119 acres (48ha) of vines and soon decided to grub up and replant 50 acres (20ha) because of the deficiency of the rootstock. He also added a further 80 acres (32ha), taking the vineyard to the present total of just over 200 acres (80ha). "The vineyard has been ripening in regular fashion since 2000," he says.

Two thirds of the terroir is exceptional, the best parcels opposite the *enclos* of Léoville-Las-Cases and either side of the D2 road just south of the village of St-Julien. Another 54.5 acres (22ha) are located farther inland at Moulin Riche. The majority of grapes from this vineyard are used in the second wine (Château Moulin Riche), but the best Petit Verdot goes into the grand vin. A third label, Pavillon Poyferré, is reserved for wine downgraded from the other two labels.

The gradual increase in the age of the vineyard, the improvements in cultivation, and the steady investment in the cellars have helped give the wine greater depth and expression. Michel Rolland has been the consultant since 1994, so ripeness and precision in the blending are guaranteed. The wine is made from a field blend of 65 percent Cabernet Sauvignon, 25 percent Merlot, 8 percent Petit Verdot, and 2 percent Cabernet Franc; it is aged in 75 percent new oak barrels for up to 20 months.

FINEST WINES

Château Léoville Poyferré

I tasted vintages from the 1980s and 1990s at the estate in April 2001. Certainly there was less consistency than today. The weaker years (1981, 1984, 1992, and 1993) came across as rather green and weedy, while vintages like 1983, 1985, and 1988 lacked real conviction. The 1989 and 1990 were sweet and ripe and still firmly tannic, the 1990 having the edge in terms of elegance and finesse. My preferred wine from the 1980s, though, was the 1986★, a powerful, brooding wine of some substance that looked set for long age. The 1990s started poorly but improved with the 1996★, which seemed to have less robust tannins, as well as vibrancy and a good depth of fruit. The 1997 was soft and light; the 1998, fruit-driven and robust. Vintages in the new millennium appear rich and vigorous, but with a suave texture and tannins that are more refined. The style is definitely St-Julien but occasionally with a muscular, Pauillac edge.

1999 Fine, medium-bodied wine, with minty, black-currant notes. Smooth-textured and with a certain charm but with sandy tannins on the finish.

2000★ Rich, round, and opulent, with plenty of St-Julien fruit. Suave texture and tannins. Has the elegance that was missing previously.

2003★ Remarkable for the year. Dense, mouth-filling fruit, a touch *méridional*, but there's notable balancing acidity. Tannins are powerful but smooth.

Château Léoville Poyferré
Total area: 222 acres (90ha)
Area under vine: 200 acres (80ha)
Production: grand vin 216,000–240,000 bottles; second wine 84,000–156,000 bottles
33250 St-Julien
Tel: +33 5 56 59 08 30
www.leoville-poyferre.fr

St-Pierre

Château St-Pierre is a small estate with a long and complicated history. The property dates back to the 17th century but was purchased by the Baron de St-Pierre, who gave it his name in 1767. On his death in 1832, the estate, which totaled some 100 acres (40ha) of vineyard, was divided between his married daughters Mme Bontemps-Dubarry and Mme de Luetkens. The latter sold her half of the vineyard, and following a second sale, it fell into the hands of a Monsieur Sevaistre.

The two halves were classified in 1855, and wines continued to be produced under two labels: St-Pierre-Sevaistre and St-Pierre-Bontemps-Dubarry. The vineyard of the latter, though, was gradually sold off, and by 1920 all that remained was the château, cellars, brand name, and 2.5 acres (1ha) of land.

The same year, Château St-Pierre-Sevaistre purchased the Bontemps-Dubarry name, uniting the two halves, while the cellars were acquired by a cooper, Alfred Martin. In 1981, his son Henri Martin, the creator of Château Gloria, bought the château; the following year, he acquired the brand names and 42 acres (17ha) of Château-St-Pierre-Sevaistre.

The wine was renamed Château St-Pierre, and work started on improving quality and establishing the brand. "It has taken time because the wine was renamed, volumes are small and were previously not well distributed, and we had a lot of catching up to do with regards to the leading classed growths in St-Julien," explains manager Jean-Louis Triaud, Henri Martin's son-in-law and president of the Girondins de Bordeaux soccer club (French champions in 2008).

If one were to be frank, the wine lacked consistency and precision through the 1980s and '90s, and it's only since the new millennium that St-Pierre has been at the top of its game. The parcels of vineyard are widely spread—from close to the cemetery in St-Julien, to the château in St-Julien-Beychevelle—the soils sandy gravel and gravel with a proportion of clay. The average age is some 40 years,

complantation employed to replace missing vines. A stricter process of selection has been one of the keys to greater consistency. There's no second wine as such, but rejected parcels and wines are used in another label, Château Peymartin.

The wine is vinified in cellars shared with Château Gloria. These were modernized in 1991 and further improved in 2008 with the addition of smaller stainless-steel tanks and integrated temperature control. One of the problems in the past was the use of older wood for aging, but in 1998 the barrel park was renewed, and now the wine is aged in 60 percent new oak barrels.

FINEST WINES

Château St-Pierre
A tasting at the domaine in 2004 highlighted 1990 and 1995 as the two most memorable wines of the inconsistent and rather rustic 1980s and '90s. Recent vintages have been tremendous: full, round, and refined, with a good concentration of fruit. St-Pierre now comfortably warrants its fourth-growth status. The blend is made from 70–85% Cabernet Sauvignon, Merlot, and tiny amounts of Cabernet Franc and Petit Verdot.
2002 [V] A success in a difficult year. Ripe, fresh, and harmonious, the fruit generous and the tannins finely honed.
2004 Attractive fruit expression, the palate lively and long. Fine and linear in style.
2005★ Superb wine. Impressive density and texture. Powerful, structured, and long, the fruit wonderfully *gourmand*. Perhaps the greatest wine ever produced at this estate.
2006★ Overshadowed by the 2005 and a little more austere, but dense, ripe, and finely textured, the acidity adding freshness and length. Long-aging.

Château St-Pierre
Total area: 42 acres (17ha)
Area under vine: 42 acres (17ha)
Average production: grand vin 65,000 bottles
Domaines Henri Martin
33250 St-Julien-Beychevelle
Tel: +33 5 56 59 08 18
www.domaines-henri-martin.com

Margaux

A visit to Château Margaux on the eve of the 2009 harvest initially offered few surprises. The neoclassical château stood imposingly at the end of its plane-tree-lined alley, and the village of farm buildings alongside had its usual calm. Approaching the cellars, though, there was something new. The paved courtyard had been concreted over and a tent erected, under which a new reception system for the grapes was being assembled by engineers. This included sorting tables, the latest destemmer, and a system of mini-tanks and pulleys for gravity-feeding into vats.

The constancy that Château Margaux exudes is rarely disturbed by modern gadgetry (even temporarily; the system I saw on my visit was to be dismantled after the harvest and the concrete removed—this is, after all, an Historic Monument).

The wine combines an elegance of aroma with density and purity of fruit. This is a wine of poise and class that rouses the senses with its fragrance and harmony on the palate

The wine here is a product of its terroir, and technology is applied only when careful tests and trials indicate that it may be worthwhile. Detail, however, counts, and if general manager Paul Pontallier and the technical team were persuaded to forsake the old hopper and pumps, then it was evidently to gain another notch in quality.

The origins of the estate date back to the 12th century, when it was known as La Mothe de Margaux. It started to assume its present form toward the end of the 16th century under the Lestonnac family. By the end of the 17th century, Château Margaux covered the 647 acres (262ha) it still holds today, of which a third was under vine. "We have a document in our archives, dating from 1715, that shows that the parcels that make Château Margaux today existed in the 18th century," explains Pontallier. It was during this period that the reputation of the estate was established.

Château Margaux was seized during the Revolution and, in 1802, sold to the Marquis de la Colonilla, who was responsible for the construction of the present château. Alexandre Aguado, Marquis de las Marismas, a wealthy Parisian banker of Spanish descent, was the owner for a while, then the château changed hands a number of times before being acquired by a group of shareholders in the 1920s and the Ginestet family in 1950. The difficult economic period of the early 1970s eventually obliged the Ginestets to sell, and in 1977 Margaux was acquired by André Mentzelopoulos, a Greek-born businessman who had made his fortune by developing the Félix Potin supermarket chain. His daughter Corinne is the owner today, and since her father's death in 1980 she has had a hands-on role in running the estate.

The 1960s and '70s were difficult for Château Margaux, a number of vintages bettered by those of neighboring Château Palmer. The restructuring brought by André Mentzelopoulos seemed to cure the problem overnight. The 1978 was a great success, and quality has been maintained ever since. André Mentzelopoulos's projects were long term: better drainage and management in the vineyard, severe selection for the grand vin (with the assistance initially of consultant Emile Peynaud), and plans for a new cellar, which was constructed in 1982.

The vineyard remains the same. Part of it can be found within a walled enclosure that surrounds the château, another sizable chunk sits on an adjacent plateau to the north, and the rest is made up of parcels to the south near the church and opposite the *chais*. The soils are mainly gravel and sand with a not-insignificant proportion of clay, but there are also veins of limestone-clay and

Right: At the end of its long drive, Château Margaux boasts the most classical and most photographed facade in Bordeaux

sandy gravel. "There is some variation in the soils, but the essence of Château Margaux is the grand Cabernet Sauvignon grown on deep gravel soils with a proportion of sand and clay," says Pontallier.

The average age of the vineyard is 35 years, but vines range in age from one to 70 years, since every year 10,000–15,000 vines are complanted and a small parcel replanted. Green-harvesting and deleafing are adapted to the parcel. There has been a move toward organic practices, insecticides were abandoned 20 years ago, and "sexual confusion" was adopted in 1996. There are ongoing trials to find a more "green" treatment for mildew and oidium.

The winemaking is traditional. "When you have quality grapes, the vinification should simply provide their best expression," says Pontallier, who has headed the winemaking team since 1983. Old 150hl wooden vats are used for the fermentation, supplemented in 2009 by an additional 27 stainless-steel and new oak vats of varied but smaller size. These have been brought in for the more detailed management of parcels. Aging is usually in 100 percent new oak barrels and lasts 18–24 months. Pontallier gained his doctorate in oenology on the subject of oak aging, which is always handled with care at Château Margaux.

FINEST WINES

Château Margaux
The wine combines an elegance of aroma with density and purity of fruit. The tannins, if not powerful, are vigorous and fine. This is a wine of poise and class that rouses the senses with its fragrance and harmony on the palate. The fruit is ripe but never overripe and is always balanced by an agreeable freshness on the finish. Cabernet Sauvignon is by far the dominant variety (90% in 2006; 87% in 2007 and 2008). The complement is Merlot, with small amounts of Petit Verdot and Cabernet Franc. The selection has become far more draconian in recent years, the grand vin

Left: Margaux owner Corinne Mentzelopoulos, whose hands-on management since 1980 has raised standards ever higher

representing 36% of production in 2006 and 2008, 32% in 2007. The rest is destined for the second wine, Pavillon Rouge (mostly Cabernet but with up to 45% Merlot in the blend), or sold off in bulk.

2006★ Overshadowed inevitably by the 2005 but has the class and classicism of a great bottle of Margaux. Fragrant and refined on the nose, delicate but profound. Hint of teasing spice. Dense and rich on the palate but balanced by a fine tannic frame. Very pure and long, with freshness on the finish.

2004 Similar to the 2006 but a touch less density and refinement. A subdued nose, palate round and tender, with fine tannins and minerally freshness.

Pavillon Blanc de Château Margaux
Of the 225 acres (91ha) planted at Margaux, 27 acres (11ha) are given over to Sauvignon Blanc for this white wine (around 33,000 bottles yearly). The vineyard is on cooler soils to the west of the village of Margaux and was planted some 30 years ago. Frost can be a problem—hence the anti-frost system installed in the early 1980s. The wine is barrel-fermented then aged on lees for 6-7 months. It's a powerful wine (up to 15% ABV), with heady, pungent aromas (citrus and pear) and richness on the palate. Recent highlights are the frost-afflicted but complex 2006★ and the sumptuous 2007.

Château Margaux
Total area: 647 acres (262ha)
Area under vine: 225 acres (91ha)
Average production: grand vin 150,000 bottles; second wine 200,000 bottles
BP31, 33460 Margaux
Tel: +33 5 57 88 83 83
www.chateau-margaux.com

Palmer

The wines of Château Palmer are as celebrated as its black-and-gold label or its turreted château with its British, Dutch, and French flags. Second only to Château Margaux in the pecking order in Margaux (and a notch above in the 1950s, '60s, and '70s), Palmer performs well above its third-growth status, and this is reflected in the price. Thomas Duroux, managing director since 2004, has a theory as to why Palmer wasn't ranked any higher. "The heart of Palmer today is the plateau behind the château, but in 1855 it wasn't part of the estate," he explains.

The property gained its name and reputation from the English Major General Charles Palmer, the owner from 1814 to 1843. He bought the property, then named Château du Gasq, and expanded the vineyard to 200 acres (80ha), much of it on the Cantenac plateau and west of the village of Margaux in the *lieu-dit* Boston.

Placed on the market because of mounting debts, Château Palmer was eventually purchased by the banking Péreire family in 1853. The vineyard had been reduced to 67.5 acres (27ha), and it was probably during the Péreire's ownership that the land on the plateau was obtained. They also built the château before selling it on in 1938 to a consortium that included the négociants Sichel, Mähler-Besse, and Ginestet, as well as the Miailhe family. Today, the property is owned by Sichel (34 percent) and the descendants of Mähler-Besse.

The Palmer plateau, just south of Château Margaux, consists of gravel and sand, with clay 16–20in (40–50cm) below the surface. "It's particular to Palmer and partly explains the depth and finesse of the wines, especially the Merlot," says Duroux. The area constitutes 50–60 percent of the vineyard and provides the body of Château Palmer. There are other parcels closer to Château d'Issan, with deeper gravel soils (some of the best Cabernet Sauvignon comes from here), and on the sandy gravel soils of the Cantenac plateau.

Palmer is known for its Merlot content—47 percent of the vineyard, with an equivalent share of Cabernet Sauvignon, the remainder Petit Verdot. Since 2007, the parcels of each have been further dissected by an in-depth study of the soils. The resistivity, morphology, and vigor were studied, as well as the nitrogen and water content, in order to adapt management techniques to individual plots.

Continuity at Palmer has also had a human dimension. From 1945 to 1996, the Chardon family (Pierre and his sons Claude and Yves) maintained the vineyards and were responsible for the winemaking, while Bertrand Bouteiller held the role of general manager for 40 years, until his retirement in 2004. His successor Duroux (formerly the winemaker at Tenuta dell'Ornellaia in Italy) is proving a brilliant choice.

With its new *cuvier* built in 1995, Palmer has been technically up to speed for a while. Nonetheless, there's been more fine-tuning since Duroux's arrival. The 200hl stainless-steel tanks have been divided to allow the receipt of smaller volumes; vertical presses have been introduced to improve the quality of the press wine; and a new system been has put in place to receive the harvest, with sorting tables and an up-to-the-minute destemmer. Experiments in 2009 included the fitting of a mechanism within a number of the tanks to regulate the *remontage*.

Duroux has also been amusing himself with the production of two special cuvées, neither of which has the right to the appellation Margaux. There's a rare volume of Palmer blanc (essentially Muscadelle and Sauvignon Gris)—Viognier-like on the nose but livelier on the palate—and a wine labelled Historical XIX Century Blend, which includes 10 percent Syrah (bought from an undisclosed source in the northern Rhône) and equal portions of Merlot and Cabernet Sauvignon.

Right: The confident, international appearance of a property that has long outperformed its official ranking in 1855

FINEST WINES

Château Palmer

The hallmark of Palmer is its opulence and quality of texture, the result of wonderfully fine tannins. With time, its fragrance is also marked. The terroir (see above) is responsible in part, as is the proportion of Merlot, though recent vintages feature less than in the past. The average in the blend these days is more like 40% Merlot to 55% Cabernet Sauvignon, with an additional 5% Petit Verdot. The precise, voluptuous nature of the wine makes it instantly appealing, but Palmer is built to age and closes up over a period of time. Over the past couple of years (most recently in September 2009), I've had the chance to taste and drink the 1985★, which is splendid—suave, perfumed, fresh, and balanced, it still has abundant youthful zest.

2005★ Magnificent wine. Clearly one of the great vintages of Palmer. Round, opulent, seductive, complex, and long, and the tannins are amazingly fine and persistent. Superb balance.

2006★ Less *gourmand* than the 2005 but still suave and precise. Again, great length and balance.

Alter Ego

The second wine of Palmer is treated as a different entity with its own personality. There's still precision and finesse, but the accent is on fruit and earlier accessibility. In general, the Merlot is dominant.

2005 Ripe, round, even a little *méridional*, with a marked expression of red fruit. Ready for drinking.

2006 [V] Less weighty than 2005 but plenty of exuberant fruit, even if the oak needs a little more time to integrate, and an appreciable freshness and length on the finish. (It includes some Petit Verdot.)

Above: Thomas Duroux, Palmer's managing director, who has edged quality ever higher since arriving from Ornellaia in 2004

Château Palmer

Total area: 136 acres (55ha)
Area under vine: 136 acres (55ha)
Average production: grand vin 120,000 bottles; second wine 96,000 bottles
33460 Margaux
Tel: +33 5 57 88 72 72
www.chateau-palmer.com

Rauzan-Ségla

The stakes are high for the Wertheimer family. The two brothers Alain and Gérard and their half-brother Charles Heibronn were already owners of the Chanel fashion house (their grandfather having created Chanel No 5 for Coco Chanel in 1924) when, in 1993, they attempted to buy Château Latour. Their bid failed, so they turned their attention to Château Rauzan-Ségla the following year. This time they were successful.

Chanel Inc is therefore now the owner of Rauzan-Ségla, but this is less a corporate takeover than a private concern. The situation suits general manager John Kolasa, a British national with more than 30 years' experience in Bordeaux, including stints at Libourne-based négociant Janoueix and nearly ten years as manager of Château Latour. He has direct contact with the Wertheimers and none of the tedious rounds of reports and ingrained working systems of a large corporation.

In the 1855 Classification, Rauzan-Ségla was placed just after Mouton Rothschild in the pecking order of second growths. Quality was high until the 1930s but suffered thereafter. Investment by the administrators, Eschenauer, led to fine vintages in 1983, 1986, and 1988, but the property had lost a little soul under the ownership of English businessman George Walker. "It needed investment and a new philosophy," claims Kolasa.

Part of the vineyard was affected by eutypiose and had to be replanted. There was also a need to improve the drainage. "The system had been neglected for 50 or 60 years. There was also a wider implication for the commune of Margaux itself, because the water needs to drain through the village to the estuary beyond," says Kolasa. The Wertheimers commissioned a satellite survey of the commune that later benefited other producers, and 9 miles (15km) of drains were laid.

Below: Despite the rather forbidding lion from another era, the Wertheimers have made Rauzan-Sélga a hospitable home

Another key decision was to plant Petit Verdot. The estate's archives had revealed that up to 8 percent of the variety had been used in blends in the 19th century, and it has now been brought back to 4 percent. Yields for all varieties were cut, bringing production down from up to 204,000 bottles in the Eschenauer era to the present 120,000–144,000. In the winery, new equipment was brought in, the barrel cellars were rebuilt, and a storage facility was created. Finally, the château was renovated to be used as a family home.

The major part of the vineyard is located on the Plateau de Cantenac, with additional parcels just to the north of the village of Margaux. Since 2006, this core area has been augmented by acquisitions. These include 3.7 acres (1.5ha) of 50-year-old vines near Château Margaux, formerly owned by Château Marquis d'Alesme-Becker, and 22 acres (9ha) in Arsac, the grapes so far destined for the second wine, Ségla. "We need to continue the renovation of the vineyard, and the expansion helps balance things out," explains Kolasa.

FINEST WINES

Château Rauzan-Ségla

John Kolasa is a traditionalist when it comes to the style of wine he and the Wertheimers want to produce. Balance and drinkability are prerequisites, so there is rarely excess at Rauzan-Ségla. The extraction is relatively tame, the separation of parcels providing the choice for the grand vin. The structure is built by the addition of press wine, up to 13% according to the vintage. Cabernet Sauvignon accounts for 55–65% of the blend, Merlot 35–40%, then there's a little seasoning from Petit Verdot or Cabernet Franc or both. Aging is in 50% new oak barrels for 18–20 months. A tasting of vintages since the Wertheimer purchase, held in March 2004, gave an idea of the progress made. The 1994 wasn't really the new team's work. I found it Cabernet-dominated but a touch green, the tannins edgy on the finish. The 1995★ was

Left: John Kolasa, whose experience and expertise have helped the remarkable renaissance at Rauzan-Ségla

a great success—soft and perfumed, with fine tannins behind. The 1996 was fine and long, the structure a little muscular, though I had a question mark about the quality of the bottle. The 1997 was light and easy drinking and now probably passed its best. The 1998 was relatively closed, but there was plenty of flesh on the palate and a structure that indicated aging potential. The 1999 seemed a little dull, the tannins rustic and dry. The 2000★ was wonderful—poised and elegant, with a depth of fruit and fine-but-firm tannins behind. Fragrance, length, balance, and suppleness of texture are the hallmarks of Rauzan-Ségla. The vintage character is clear, but there's more consistency than before, and quality can only improve further.

2001 Plenty of charm. Tender and delicately perfumed, the accent on the fruit. The palate is lively and balanced. Readily accessible today.

2004 Deep color. Seems a little more austere than usual, the acidity evident. Medium-bodied and savory; the tannins a touch pinched on the finish.

2006★ A real classic—perfumed, long, and fresh, the tasty oak still a little pervasive. A smooth, refined texture, the tannins firm but civilized.

GRAND CRU CLASSÉ

Château

RAUZAN-SÉGLA

MARGAUX
APPELLATION MARGAUX CONTRÔLÉE

2000

CHÂTEAU RAUZAN · SÉGLA · PROPRIÉTAIRE A MARGAUX · FRANCE

13 % vol.　MIS EN BOUTEILLE AU CHATEAU　750 ml

PRODUCT OF FRANCE-BORDEAUX

Château Rauzan-Ségla

Total area: 185 acres (75ha)
Area under vine: 153 acres (62ha)
Production: grand vin 120,000–144,000 bottles; second wine 144,000 bottles
BP56, 33460 Margaux
Tel: +33 5 57 88 82 10
www.chateaurauzansegla.com

Brane-Cantenac

Henri Lurton's admirable résumé matches his discreet, bookish mien. It features a master's degree in biology and a DEA (*diplôme d'études approfondies*) in ampelology/oenology (researching vineyard soils with Professor Seguin), as well as a diploma in oenology. More surprising is his adventurous "work experience," which includes time in Australia, South Africa, and Chile in the early 1990s. In fact, Lurton may well have spent considerably more time on the road had it not been for his father Lucien's decision to hand over the family properties to his children. And so, in 1992, Henri suddenly found himself returning home to take the helm at Château Brane-Cantenac.

Elegance and breed are the words that come to mind here, particularly regarding aroma and structure. Henri Lurton has gradually added density and quality of texture

The heart of the estate he inherited is the 111-acre (45ha) block that surrounds the château—in particular, the 75 acres (30ha) to the front on the Plateau de Cantenac. The soils here are deep, free-draining Günzian gravel with a fair amount of clay, and they regularly produce the best lots of wine—a fact reconfirmed each year when it's time to make the blend. The 37 acres (15ha) behind the château have more of a sandy gravel composition and a higher water table than those on the plateau (10ft [3m] rather than 16–20ft [5–6m]). They were extensively replanted in 1998, but—at least for the moment—the wines rarely make the grand vin.

There are two further vineyards, though these principally supply the second wine, Baron de Brane: La Verdotte, next to the land behind the château; and Notton, close to Arsac and Château du Tertre, which has deep, coarse gravel and was drained and replanted in 1994.

Under Henri Lurton's careful supervision, the quality of Brane-Cantenac has clearly risen since 1995. There's greater selection, detailed plot-by-plot management, and a more "natural" approach. The density of planting is between 6,666 and 8,000 vines/ha, but the trellising has been raised to improve the canopy cover. Plowing was reintroduced in 1994, as was manual harvesting and the use of organic material, but Lurton says he'll "never be entirely organic, because I'm wary of the excessive use of copper-based solutions."

Ecology and the environment are nonetheless clearly a concern, and when the new winery was built in 1999, it was constructed on sustainable lines. It's both spacious and pragmatic, the wooden and stainless-steel vats corresponding to the size and number of parcels of vines. Lurton is happy to vary the method of vinification according to the situation, using techniques such as *pigeage*, cool pre-fermentation maceration, and malolactic fermentation in barrel as and when he feels they are required. "I sometimes go for more extraction to improve the quality of the tannins, in which case the press wine isn't used," he explains. The wine is aged for 18–20 months in 70 percent new oak barrels. Bookish he may be, but Henri Lurton is clearly an astute technician, too.

FINEST WINES

Château Brane-Cantenac
Elegance and breed are the words that come to mind here, particularly regarding aroma and structure. Henri Lurton has gradually added density and quality of texture, as well as providing a more reliable wine. On the whole, the vintages from the 1980s were disappointing, though the weaker years did hold up, showing the potential that was there. Ripeness, excessive yields, and quality of extraction were the most likely problems at the time. The two exceptions were the 1983★, which showed a little more depth and aromatic finesse, and the 1989★, which had real elegance, poise, and length. The 1986 had solid fruit, but I found it coarse and chunky. The

Above: Henri Lurton, whose meticulous, studious approach has helped raise standards at Brane-Cantenac since 1995

1982 was not shown. The early 1990s were again underwhelming, including a sweet but rather short 1990. Improvements started with the 1994, which had better fruit, even if it lacked some charm. Then came two splendid years, 1995★ and 1996★, the former ripe, round, and seductive; the latter long, fresh, and minerally, with the Cabernet Sauvignon character clearly marked. The 1997 was soft and simple but drinking well; the 1998 a more forceful style, with dense texture and robust tannins. The 1999 still had a note of chocolaty oak but appeared forward in style. The 2000★ showed class and finesse with a modern weight of fruit. The field blend for Brane-Cantenac is 55% Cabernet Sauvignon (this can rise to 70% in vintages like 2008), 40% Merlot, and 4.5% Cabernet Franc, with an experimental plot of Carmenère.

2004 [V] Fine, medium-bodied wine. Balanced and smooth and beginning to open now.

2005★ Perfumed and dense. Fine tannins and texture. Fresh and long. Complete and satisfying. On a par with, or better than, the 2000.

2006 Long and linear, but rather austere at present. Will benefit from food and age.

2007 Lighter style but ripe and balanced. Lots of red fruit, with a veneer of chocolaty oak. Early drinking.

PRODUCT OF FRANCE
GRAND CRU CLASSÉ EN 1855
CHÂTEAU
BRANE-CANTENAC
MARGAUX
2000
APPELLATION MARGAUX CONTRÔLÉE
13% vol. — HENRI LURTON, S.C.E.A. DU CHATEAU BRANE-CANTENAC — 750 ml
A CANTENAC · GIRONDE · FRANCE
MIS EN BOUTEILLE AU CHATEAU

Château Brane-Cantenac
Total area: 250 acres (100ha)
Area under vine: 183 acres (74ha)
Average production: grand vin 180,000 bottles; second wine 120,000–144,000 bottles
33460 Margaux
Tel: +33 5 57 88 83 33
www.brane-cantenac.com

Giscours

A major theme of this book is the benefit Bordeaux accrues from a constant stream of investors and how, thanks to their resources, ailing properties are turned around and the quality of their wines is transformed. A classic example is Château Giscours, which Dutch entrepreneur Eric Albada Jelgersma acquired in 1995.

Château Giscours is a magnificent estate, with an extravagant 19th-century château, a park, a forest, an arboretum, and, of course, vineyards. The maintenance must be colossal. Wine was produced here as far back as the 16th century, the château built later by the Comte de Pescatore, a Parisian banker. The Cruse family owned it for a while at the beginning of the 20th century, then in 1952 it was acquired by Nicolas Tari.

By then it was in a terribly run-down state, but Tari and his son Pierre did much to revive the prestige of former days, until financial difficulties in the early 1990s made them sell. Two companies were formed around the property, a *groupement foncier agricole*, which owns the land and buildings, and a *société anonyme d'exploitation*, which has the right to rent the land and produce the wine on a long-term basis. The Tari family retained the former, while Albada Jelgersma bought the latter.

As well as dealing with this somewhat complicated ownership structure, Albada Jelgersma has also had to contend with a scandal involving the exchange of appellation wines perpetrated by a former winemaker. But neither problem has distracted him from his main concern— the improvement of Giscours, in which he has invested heavily. Following the 1996 harvest, over 130,000 missing vines were complanted and the trellising was overhauled. Manual picking was reintroduced, and the young vines were initially harvested and treated separately. Buildings have been renovated, the *cuvier* modernized and extended, and the barrel park completely renewed.

Jacques Pélissié, a former cellar master at Cos d'Estournel, was brought in as technical director, and the Boissenots as consultants, the role of general manager going to Alexander Van Beek. Didier Foret, who has been at Giscours since 1998, is now the winemaker. Much the same team has also been involved in the revival of Château du Tertre, which Albada Jelgersma bought in 1997.

FINEST WINES

Château Giscours

The heart of Giscours is the 100-acre (40ha) gravel *croupe* that lies alongside the château. Another sector of importance is the Pujau vineyard in Arsac. The soils here are extremely stony and contribute to the firm, concentrated character of the wine. A third section is located on sandier soils close to Château Dauzac. The proportion of Cabernet Sauvignon in recent vintages (2007, 2008) has increased to 60%, the complement being Merlot. A little Cabernet Franc and Petit Verdot are also cultivated and occasionally used in the grand vin. My first encounter with Giscours was the 1979 served by the glass at Willi's Wine Bar in Paris in the mid-1980s. I can still remember the lingering fragrance, an element occasionally absent from the much-improved wines of the current era.

2000★ Deep color typical of Giscours. A pleasing fragrance and very gentle palate, supple, fresh, and clean. Ready for drinking now.

2003 Round, supple, and forward. Leafy, plummy notes. No great complexity and sandy tannins, but it has the freshness often missing in this vintage.

2005 Dense, rich, and powerful. The nose is reserved at present. It lacks a little elegance, and the tannins are firm, but it is clearly for the long haul.

Right: Alexander Van Beek, the general manager at Giscours, who has played an important role in its return to form

Château Giscours
Total area: 750 acres (300ha)
Area under vine: 210 acres (85ha)
Production: grand vin 225,000–275,000 bottles; second wine 75,000–115,000 bottles
Labarde, 33460 Margaux
Tel: +33 5 57 97 09 09
www.chateau-giscours.fr

Issan

The picturesque moated château here was built in the 17th century, but its roots go much deeper: early references to the property date from the 12th century, when the English ruled in Aquitaine. Its name comes from the contracted title of the founder of the building, the Chevalier d'Essenault, but since 1945 it has been in the hands of the Cruse family. The present generation is represented by general manager Emmanuel Cruse, who also answers to the rather grand title of *grand maître* of the Commanderie du Bontemps de Médoc et des Graves, Sauternes et Barsac.

From the beginnings of their tenure, the Cruse family have busied themselves with the seemingly endless task of recreating the vineyard, which had fallen into serious decline before and during World War II. The historical core of the vineyard lies close to the estuary within the *enclos* and now represents 65 percent of the area under vine. The soils are gravel but with limestone and clay at varying depths. A mix of these diverse parcels constitutes a good proportion of the blend.

Two other vineyards complete Issan's surface area in Margaux. A parcel on the fine, gravelly soils of the Plateau de Cantenac, between Prieuré-Lichine and the rail line, usually provides grapes for the grand vin. A third zone is located in Arsac and was considered to be in the Haut-Médoc until the 2007 re-delimitation of the boundaries of Margaux. At present, the grapes go into the second wine, Blason d'Issan, but some 20-year-old Merlot is destined eventually for the grand vin.

Until the mid-1990s Issan underperformed, which was due, at least in part, to the reluctance of the family to invest when the succession of the property was unsure. When this was resolved, the Cruse family launched a number of projects to help improve quality and recoup lost time. In the vineyard, a new system of drainage was put in place from 1993, and a program of replanting and restructuring was instituted under the guidance of technical director Eric Pellon. The

Above: Emmanuel Cruse, of the owning family, has overseen the improvements in vineyard and winery since the mid-1990s

second label was created in 1995 to accommodate the young vines.

Investment in the winery followed. The *cuvier* was extended in 2002, and the number of vats of varying size was increased from 26 to 37 to facilitate parcel-by-parcel vinification. Sorting tables and a system of gravity feeding were also introduced. A new barrel cellar was inaugurated in 2000 to complement the others built in 1978 and 1985, each with a capacity of 500 barrels. The wine is vinified in the traditional manner and aged in 55 percent new oak barrels for 18 months.

FINEST WINES

Château d'Issan

The rather weedy offerings of the 1980s and early 1990s (due to overcropping and problems with ripeness) have been left behind, and Issan is now performing like a true Margaux. The wines are fragrant and refined, with supple texture and a modern density of fruit. There have been improvements, but without a loss of style. "We strive for elegance and finesse but have also improved the structure and concentration of the wines," says Emmanuel Cruse. This results from severe selection and the decision to maintain a high proportion of Cabernet Sauvignon: 65% in the vineyard and up to 70% in the blend, the complement being Merlot. There's little speculation, so the wines remain good value.

2000 Ripe, firm, and concentrated, but with supple texture and fine tannins. Attractive dark fruit and mocha aromas. Should age well.

2003 Less complex aromatically—red fruit and vanilla—and less vivacious than the 2000 or 2006, but decent balance and relatively civilized tannins.

2006★ Dark hue. The nose is fine—dense but reserved. The fruit appears pure, the palate ripe, the texture delicate, and the tannins fine. Supporting acidity gives added length and freshness. Needs time to fill out but is potentially a fine bottle.

Château d'Issan

Total area: 292 acres (118ha)
Area under vine: 111 acres (45ha)
Production: grand vin 96,000–120,000 bottles; second wine 84,000–108,000 bottles
33460 Cantenac
Tel: +33 5 57 88 35 91
www.chateau-issan.com

Chasse-Spleen

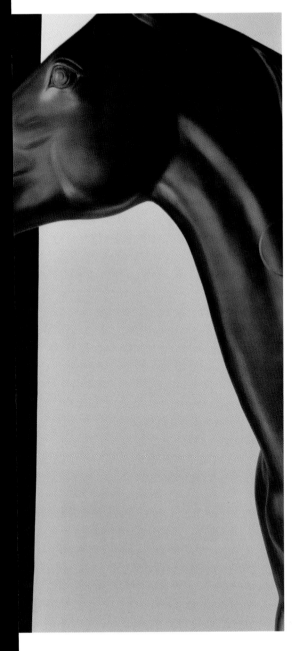

The romantic conjecture used to be that one of two poets—Baudelaire or Byron—was the inspiration for the name Chasse-Spleen, which roughly translates as "chase away the blues." Rather disappointingly, the more likely and prosaic explanation is that it was merely a brand name thought up for presentation to the British market at an exposition in 1862. Either way, Chasse-Spleen has long been the source of an impressive volume of fine Bordeaux, often of classed-growth standard, and always of appetizing value.

Chasse-Spleen has long been the source of an impressive volume of fine Bordeaux, often of classed-growth standard, and always of appetizing value

From 1922 to 1976, the property was owned and well maintained by the Lahary family, thanks in no small part to additional funds from their lumber company in the Lande. Négociant Jacques Merlaut then acquired the estate, which was run by his daughter, Bernadette Villars. Villars was responsible for expanding the property from 100 acres (40ha) to 210 acres (85ha), until an accident brought a tragically abrupt halt to her tenure in 1992. Her daughter Claire then took over, followed by Claire's sister Céline and her husband, Jean-Pierre Foubet, in 2000. Since 2007, Céline Villars-Foubet has become the sole owner.

The vineyard has now been extended to just over 250 acres (100ha), with a core area of some 173 acres (70ha) on Günzian gravel soils. This includes the original 100 acres purchased in 1976, as well as a 37-acre (15ha) zone known as Granins, added by Bernadette Villars, and a further 37 acres from Château Gressier Grand Poujeaux, purchased

Left: Céline Villars-Foubet, who has overseen improvements at Chasse-Spleen since 2000 and been sole owner since 2007

in 2003. The latter used to be part of the property until division in the early part of the 19th century, so for Villars-Foubet it's the logical repatriation of some very good land. (Château Gressier Grand Poujeaux continues, but at a reduced size.)

There's been considerable investment at the property since 2000, not only in newly acquired land but also in replanting the vineyard. Densities are high, at 8,000–10,000 vines/ha. Cabernet Sauvignon equates to 62 percent of the vineyard and normally 55–60 percent of the blend, but with the increased proportion of young vines, this dropped to 50 percent from 2000 onward. It will climb again as the recently planted vines grow older. The other varieties are Merlot (35 percent) and Petit Verdot (3 percent).

Other recent changes include an extended *cuvier* with the addition of cement tanks (2007) and a new barrel cellar (2003) that, with barrels stacked four high (manipulated by forklift truck), has the air of a Riojan bodega. The grapes are mostly hand-picked (though some parcels destined for the second wine—Heritage de Chasse-Spleen/Oratoire de Chasse-Spleen—are machine-harvested) and are vinified in a traditional manner. Aging is in 40 percent new oak barrels for 14–18 months.

FINEST WINES

Château Chasse-Spleen
The wines are classic Médoc with depth, structure, flavor, and the ability to age admirably well. Older vintages have a slightly stricter line. Improved maturity and the increase in Merlot in recent years have given the wine a rounder, warmer feel.

2000★ Ripe and full-bodied, the quality of the vintage showing. Dark-fruit and tobacco notes on the nose; full, round, and savory on the palate.

2001 A little leaner than the 2000, but fresh and lively and with a certain elegance.

2003 Medium-bodied, soft, and easy drinking. No great complexity.

2004 Firm and long, but with ample fruit. Quite classic in style, but still some spicy, vanilla oak present. Satisfying mid-weight wine from 2011.

2005★ Dark and dense, with generous fruit and a long, lingering finish. Full-bodied and vigorous, with evident aging potential.

2006 [V] Round and supple on the palate, with a firm, dry finish. Chocolate and dark-fruit notes on the nose. Plenty of charm but needs time.

Château Chasse-Spleen
Total area: 272 acres (110ha)
Area under vine: 257 acres (104ha)
Average production: grand vin 400,000 bottles; second wine 150,000–200,000 bottles
Grand Poujeaux
33480 Moulis-en-Médoc
Tel: +33 5 56 58 02 37
www.chasse-spleen.com

Clarke

When Baron Edmond de Rothschild acquired Château Clarke (the name bestowed by a 19th-century Irish owner) in 1973, he did so with a view to creating a classic Médoc wine of grand cru classé level. His ambition was backed by colossal investment. The vineyard was totally replanted, with an even split of Merlot and Cabernet Sauvignon (on the recommendation of the Chambre d'Agriculture), and the buildings and cellars were entirely renovated.

It was a good thing, however, that the baron had patience commensurate with his ambition and bank balance. To begin with (the first vintage was 1978), the wines proved inconsistent. And with the help of soil analysis, it soon became apparent that the soils were not gravel, as had been thought, but cool clay and limestone. This meant that much of the Cabernet Sauvignon was unsuited to the terrain and had difficulty ripening. So, yet more replanting ensued, with the Merlot increased to the present level of 70 percent by the mid-1990s. Working practices also changed, with grass cover replacing traditional plowing in a bid to reduce vigor.

The arrival of Michel Rolland as a consultant in 1998 further oriented cultivation and winemaking toward a Right Bank approach. Green-harvesting has become systematic in certain parcels, as has deleafing throughout, and yields have consequently been lowered by 10 percent to the present average of 45hl/ha (the vineyard planted at 6,600 vines/ha). Manual picking has replaced machine-harvesting for the majority of the vineyard.

In the winery, Rolland introduced a cold prefermentation maceration, intensified the practice of *saignée* for concentration, and brought in wooden vats. Yann Buchwalter, the technical director, had already started using microoxygenation *sous marc* during the maceration. Another Rolland-inspired change was to carry out malolactic fermentation and aging in 80 percent new oak barrels, with limited racking and a certain time on lees.

As well as the estate red wine, there's also the Sauvignon Blanc-dominated white Le Merle Blanc de Château Clarke and a second wine, Les Granges des Domaines Edmond de Rothschild, produced from wine from Château Clarke and two other estates (Haut-Médoc). But it's the estate red wine that commands most attention, and while the wine today is probably a far cry from the baron's original aspiration, it's still a clear leader in Listrac—rich and suave with a modern flamboyance.

FINEST WINES

Château Clarke

Emile Peynaud was the first consultant here, and he advised a trial bottling of 100% Merlot, which took place in 1982. Opened recently at the estate, it was reportedly still good. Clearly Peynaud was one step ahead of everyone! The modern-day Clarke is most evident from 2000 onward; prior vintages are less ripe, fleshy, and colored, the tannins more rustic.

1999 A transitional vintage. The nose is open but lacks complexity. The palate shows decent maturity of fruit for the vintage, but the tannins are a little sandy and coarse.

2002 Surprising ripeness, if a little flat and broad. Full and fleshy on the palate, Clarke's inherent tannic character showing on the finish.

2003 Rich, full, and opulent, the tannins well handled and in no way drying. Suave rather than fine.

2004 [V] Deep color. Discreet, dark-fruit nose. Pleasant balance, length, and freshness on the palate. A little more classical and linear in style, the tannins firm but fine.

2005★ [V] Probably the greatest vintage here so far. Full-bodied, rich, and modern, with ample fruit and integrated oak. The tannins are powerful but refined.

Château Clarke

Total area: 445 acres (180ha)
Area under vine: 133.5 acres (54ha)
Average production: grand vin 250,000 bottles; second wine 250,000 bottles
Compagnie Vinicole Baron Edmond de Rothschild
33480 Listrac-Médoc
Tel: +33 5 56 58 38 00
www.cver.fr

La Lagune

Traveling north from the city of Bordeaux along the D2, *la route des châteaux*, La Lagune is the first of the Médoc classed growths along the road. The 18th-century *chartreuse* and state of-the-art winery are partially hidden by trees, but a traffic roundabout and large sign give full warning of its presence, as does the sea of vines to the side of the road.

La Lagune has been undergoing a second renaissance since 2000, the year the property was acquired by Jean-Jacques Frey, a businessman who also owns Domaines Paul Jaboulet Aîné in the northern Rhône. There's been considerable investment in the vineyard, with an extensive program of restructuring, while the technical facilities have also been modernized with the inauguration of a new high-tech *cuvier* in 2004.

Frey's daughter Caroline, a trained oenologist, manages the estate, giving both a youthful and feminine luster to the property. She has the experience of Patrick Moulin, a figure at the estate since 1972, to lean on, as well as consultant oenologist Denis Dubourdieu, her former professor at Bordeaux's Faculté d'Oenologie.

La Lagune's first revival happened in the late 1950s. The estate had been going to seed during the early part of the century, and by the time Georges Brunet acquired the property in 1958 there was barely a vine in production. Brunet totally replanted the vineyard and built new cellars before selling the property in 1962 to René Chayoux, the owner of Champagne Ayala, who continued the restoration.

The majority of the vineyard (150 acres [60ha]) lies adjacent to the winery and takes the form of four *croupes*, or hillocks, the principal rising to 50ft (15m) above sea level (a considerable height in the Médoc), the others being 33–40ft (10–12m). The soils are free-draining sandy gravel, with a greater proportion of sand in the lower land. It's an early-ripening site (La Lagune is often one of the first to harvest in the Médoc) and bears a closer similarity to Pessac-Léognan than to Pauillac or St-Julien.

Farther east there are another 50 acres (20ha) in the proximity of Château d'Agassac. The parcels here were purchased in 1964, so they were not part of La Lagune at the time of the 1855 Classification. Nonetheless, the fruit, from 40-year-old vines grown on sandy gravel with a subsoil of clay, is often included in the grand vin.

The principal purpose of the restructuring in the vineyards has been to raise the trellising height to compensate for the lower density of plantings (6,666 vines/ha) and thus improve maturity. Altogether, 50 acres (20ha) have been replanted since the purchase in 2000, and the fruit is at present destined for the second wine, Moulin de La Lagune. Some of the Merlot on top of the primary hillock was grubbed up and replanted with Cabernet Sauvignon. This is destined to make its way into the grand vin, so there's still a margin for progression.

The new *cuvier* allows for parcel-by-parcel vinification in stainless-steel tanks that are gravity-fed. The winemaking, though, is traditional and without excess, the press wine rarely being used in the grand vin. Aging is in 50 percent new oak barrels and lasts for 12 months.

FINEST WINES

Château La Lagune

La Lagune began to hit its stride in the Frey era with the 2004 vintage. The philosophy is to produce wines of harmony and finesse, compatible with the terroir, rather than to push for power and substance. This seems to have been achieved, the maturity of fruit greatly improved at the same time. The new plantings augur well for the future. The field plantings of 60% Cabernet Sauvignon, 30% Merlot, and 10% Petit Verdot are more or less representative of the blend. "The Petit Verdot really has a place here, adding color, freshness, and aroma while giving lift to the Merlot, which can sometimes be a little flat," says Caroline Frey.

2000 The Freys' first vintage—but they only took over for the harvest. Soft and supple, but it lacks some punch. A more old-style claret, with a hint of green on the finish.

2004 Definitely more presence than the 2000. Attractive fruit, weight, and balance, with fine tannins and a point of acidity on the finish. Almost accessible after five years, but it will age.

2005★ A little more spice and complexity on the nose. The oak is still present but integrated. Medium-bodied, minerally, and long. Beautifully constructed. Takes on volume in the glass.

Above: Caroline Frey, ideally qualified through family interest and her Bordeaux training to continue La Lagune's renaissance

Château La Lagune
Total area: 300 acres (120ha)
Area under vine: 200 acres (80ha)
Production: grand vin 80,000–140,000 bottles; second wine 150,000–200,000 bottles
33290 Ludon-Médoc
Tel: +33 5 57 88 82 77
www.chateau-lalagune.com

Sociando-Mallet

The year 2009 marked the 40th anniversary of Jean Gautreau's ownership of Château Sociando-Mallet. He acquired the run-down 12-acre (5ha) property for the sum of 250,000 French francs in April 1969 and has since created one of the biggest commercial successes seen in the Médoc in recent times. Now with a flourishing 210-acre (85ha) vineyard and nominal fifth-growth standing, Gautreau vaunts independent status for his cru. *Ni classé, ni bourgeois... Sociando-Mallet, tout simplement*, runs the maxim.

The rags-to-riches success started on an impulse, the vineyard taking Gautreau's fancy while he was out looking for land for a Belgian client linked to his négociant business in Lesparre. In a dilapidated state, the property nonetheless

Jean Gautreau acquired the run-down property in April 1969 and has since created one of the biggest commercial successes seen in the Médoc in recent times

had a history. A document dating from 1633 refers to the *terres nobles* in the commune of St-Seurin-de-Cadourne owned by the Sossiondo [sic] family. In 1831, a naval captain named Achille Mallet married Marie-Elisabeth Alaret, the owner of Sociando, adding his name to the estate. The 1932 classification of the crus bourgeois lists Sociando-Mallet among the crus.

In 1969, though, the estate was practically abandoned, the commune of St-Seurin-de-Cadourne known simply as a source of inexpensive table wine. It was Gautreau's second vintage, the 1970, that he claims revealed the quality of the terroir and motivated him to expand the property. Sociando-Mallet stands on a mound of Günzian gravel, the *croupe* de Baleyron, over a limestone-clay subsoil. It also benefits from proximity to the tempering influence of the estuary. The profile is similar to that of the river-hugging crus of St-Estèphe and Pauillac and is the most northerly point in the Médoc where this occurs.

Gautreau purchased more land and planted—first with Cabernet Sauvignon, then gradually with more Merlot—to reach today's balance of 48 percent Cabernet Sauvignon, 47 percent Merlot, and 5 percent Cabernet Franc. The average density of the vineyard is 8,333 vines/ha, and with that, Gautreau maintains a grand vin can be produced with yields of up to 60hl/ha. There's no green-harvesting at Sociando-Mallet and only a little deleafing, the yields determined by pruning.

Sociando-Mallet is in all respects a traditionally run estate, the soils plowed and the grapes harvested manually. In the cellar, the wine is fermented in stainless-steel and cement tanks using natural yeasts, the cuvaison lasting 25–30 days. The malolactic fermentation takes place in tank, and the wine is then aged in 100 percent new oak barrels for 12 months, the maturation lasting 18 months in total. The wine is lightly filtered but not fined before bottling.

FINEST WINES

Château Sociando-Mallet

In June 2009, Jean Gautreau (then a sprightly 82-year-old) invited me to a tasting of his 40 vintages at Sociando-Mallet. The highlights are described below. Stylistically, the wine seems to have experienced three different passages in time. The early vintages until 1981 appear dominated by Cabernet Sauvignon, are upright and old-fashioned, and are perhaps a little green and pinched. From 1982, there's more Merlot in the blend and extra sweetness and volume in the wines. The 2000 marks the beginning of a new era of greater purity, concentration, and finesse. But there is always good vintage expression and the potential to age.
1969 Jean Gautreau's first vintage. Rust colored. Still a glow of fruit on the nose, the palate fresh and linear with minerally, leafy notes. Antique but still holding up.

1975★ A hailstorm decimated the crop, cutting the yield to 21hl/ha. A dark inner core with brick to the rim. A complex nose that still has a resonance of fruit. The palate is fresh, clean, and minerally, but with impressive concentration and power and a firm tannic grip on the finish. This is drinking well but will age longer.

1982★ The vintage that launched Sociando-Mallet. Still going strong. Deep ruby color. Impressive depth of fruit (with yields at 71hl/ha!). Smoky, mineral, black currant and blackberry aromas. The palate is ripe and round but also concentrated and intense. Powerful tannic frame. Accessible but still with great aging potential.

1986 Deep, bright, youthful color. A monolithic wine. Intense and brooding on the nose, with a smoky note. Immense power and depth. Huge tannic structure. Enormous reserve but lacks the finesse. Could age 50-odd years, but will it ever loosen up?

1989 Deep, dark hue. Less opulent than the 1990 but wonderful balance, depth, and length. Complex, stony, mineral, dark-fruit nose. Medium- to full-bodied. Powerful but fine tannic frame. Long, linear finish. Very complete.

1990 Color still dark, solid, and opaque. An opulent and almost exotic style of wine, with an exuberant nose and palate. Ripe black currant and dark-fruit aromas, with a hint of licorice. The palate is sweet, lush, and fleshy, with powerful tannins behind.

1996★ An immense wine. Still dark and opaque in color. An aromatic nose with black currant, mineral, chocolate, and vanilla notes. Rich, ripe, and full-bodied, with powerful but well-honed tannins. Long, fresh, smoky finish.

1998 Dark color, with little sign of evolution. Quite steely and austere in style. Attractive, dark-fruit nose, with pronounced mineral notes. Good concentration on the palate, with balancing freshness and length. A touch backward but still plenty in reserve.

2000★ Dark, firm color. A solid, powerful wine with definite Pauillac pretensions. The nose is ripe and dense but closed. Oozes concentration within a firm, tannic frame. Definitely for the long haul.

2001 Deep color. Very harmonious wine. Dark- and red-fruit aromas, with a hint of toast and vanilla. The palate is supple, but structured at the same time. Gentle, pure, and long.

2003 Deep, dense color. Rich and *gourmand* on the nose with an enormous concentration of fruit. Black currant notes. The palate is full and fleshy, with a powerful tannic frame. Big, robust style but with freshness to keep it in balance.

2004 Deep color. Elegant and poised in style. Long and linear, with lovely purity of fruit. Supple, medium-bodied wine with fine, fresh tannins. In the classic mold.

2005★ Deep, opaque color. Huge intensity and depth of fruit but very pure and nothing overbearing. Tight and closed at present. Palate dense, rich, and structured but harmonious. Tannins present but ripe and smooth. Shows power and finesse. Undoubtedly one of the greatest wines from this estate.

2006 Dark hue. Fine, classic, linear style. The fruit has purity and freshness, with well-integrated spicy, zesty oak. Medium-bodied in terms of weight. Firmness on the finish. A serious wine that will age.

2008 (Barrel sample) Deep purple/crimson hue. Appreciable ripeness on the nose: rich and spicy, with an almost exotic note. Pure and appetizing on the palate, and a dark-fruit exuberance. Surprisingly firm in structure, with good length.

Château Sociando-Mallet
Total area: 285 acres (115ha)
Area under vine: 210 acres (85ha)
Production: grand vin 400,000–500,000 bottles; second wine 75,000–100,000 bottles
33180 St-Seurin-de-Cadourne
Tel: +33 5 56 73 38 80
www.sociandomallet.com

Rollan de By

In the context of the northern Médoc, this wine has been a revelation since the first vintage in 1989. The vineyard was then only 6 acres (2.5ha) and has since been expanded to more than 125 acres (50ha). The fully planted extent of Domaines Rollan de By is 215 acres (87ha) if one includes the other properties in the same stable: châteaux La Clare, Tour Seran, and Haut Condissas.

Rollan de By is the brainchild of Parisian interior designer Jean Guyon, whose main occupation now is to market and sell the wine. The parcels of vines are located on claylike gravel soils close to the estuary, on terrain that is slightly more undulating than the typically flat northern Médoc. The high proportion of Merlot (70 percent) suits the soil, giving the wine a rounded, accessible charm, Petit Verdot (10 percent) and Cabernet Sauvignon adding color, vigor, and freshness.

The grapes are machine-harvested, but the techniques of cultivation permit optimum ripeness, an important factor in the quality and consistency of the wine. The density of planting is 8,500–11,000 vines/ha, with production around 45–50hl/ha. Trellising has been raised to allow 3ft (1m) of leaf canopy, and most of the parcels have been set to grass cover to curb vigor. Deleafing is practiced on the Merlot, while lateral shoots are removed from the Petit Verdot and Cabernet.

Jean Guyon has surrounded himself with plenty of technical expertise, including consultants Riccardo Cotarella and Alain Reynaud, as well as technical manager Emmanuel Bonneau, formerly at Château La Tour Carnet. Vinification techniques are modern and include a pre-fermentation cold soak (6–8 days at 8°C [46°F]), *pigeage*, *remontage*, and *délestage* during the alcoholic fermentation (the lees put into suspension at the end) and a maceration that lasts 15–21 days. The malolactic for the Merlot and Petit Verdot is completed in barrel (65–70 percent new oak) and the Cabernet in tank, the maturation lasting 12 months.

FINEST WINES

Château Rollan de By
Rollan de By has a rounded charm that makes it accessible relatively early on. There's a sweetness to the fruit that makes it enticing, but also the sort of freshness and vigor that correspond to the Médoc. The oak adds spiciness and seems relatively well absorbed. I prefer the balance of this wine to the more distinctly opulent Haut Condissas.
2004 Deep color. A generous, fruity nose, the palate supple and fresh, with a hint of chocolaty oak. The tannins are a touch angular on the finish.
2005★ [V] Same as the 2004 but riper and more profound, the tannins firm but fine. All in balance.

Château Haut Condissas
This is the show-stopper—a more voluptuous creation with an international dimension when it comes to oak and extraction. The 30-acre (12ha) vineyard has a higher clay content. Petit Verdot represents 20% of the blend (with 60% Merlot, the rest Cabernet Sauvignon and Cabernet Franc). The maturity and extraction are pushed a little further, and the wine is aged in 200% new oak barrels for 18–24 months (the Petit Verdot in American oak). Average production is 65,000 bottles.
2001 Deep, dark color. A quite complex nose, the oak still apparent. Full, round, opulent palate, the tannins muscular and firm. A little dry on the end.
2002 A simpler wine. Quite a bit of stuffing, but the extraction may be pushed a bit too far in this more delicate year, leading to an edgy finish.
2003 Big, rich wine, definitely more international in style. Dark, almost black in color. Creamy oak and layers of plump ripe fruit. Powerful tannins but polished and long. A hint of freshness gives surprising balance overall.

Right: Jean Guyon, whose carefully crafted wines have consistently delivered impressive results in blind tastings

Château Rollan de By
Total area: 125 acres (50ha)
Area under vine: 125 acres (50ha)
Average production: grand vin 250,000 bottles
3 Route de Haut Condissas
33340 Bégadan
Tel: +33 5 56 41 58 59
www.rollandeby.com

Pessac, Graves, and Entre-Deux-Mers

Although Pessac-Léognan and the rest of the Graves have far more in common than either does with Entre-Deux-Mers, its proximity makes it sensible to discuss them together.

Pessac-Léognan

In 1987, the northern Graves split from the rest of the region, creating a new appellation: Pessac-Léognan. These had always been the two most prominent communes, close to the city of Bordeaux, and contained all the crus classés of the Graves. Since then, a synergy of new ownership and investment has elevated quality in the region, making it one of Bordeaux's most progressive appellations. This is also Bordeaux's oldest viticultural zone, the vineyards existing from at least the Middle Ages. The best soils for Cabernet and Merlot are the gravelly *croupes* and bands of clay; for Semillon and Sauvignon Blanc, limestone and clay. The vineyard, much reduced by Bordeaux's urban development, has expanded recently to 3,420 acres (1,385ha) for reds and 620 acres (250ha) for whites. Red Pessac-Léognan places the emphasis on balance and finesse and maintains an earthy minerality that is the signature of the Graves. There is a distinct similarity with the wines of the Médoc but generally a higher proportion of Merlot. The limited production of barrel-fermented, dry white wine is the finest in Bordeaux, on a par with good white Burgundy at the very top end.

Graves

The Graves appellation extends along the Left Bank of the Garonne, from La Brède in the north to Barsac and Sauternes, with a pocket of vineyards farther south around the town of Langon. It's a fairly large appellation, with nearly 6,900 acres (2,800ha) for reds and a further 2,470 acres (1,000ha) for whites, the majority dry, but 25 percent sweet Graves Supérieur. As the name suggests, there's a dominance of gravelly soils, with silt and sand and occasionally clay. Limestone can also be found at Pujols-sur-Ciron, where the calcareous soils of Barsac extend into the commune. The region has its difficulties, the separation from Pessac-Léognan robbing it of its locomotives; the absence of a cooperative, of an instrument to help regulate quality and production; and the generally low prices, of the incentive to invest and improve. But there are interesting, good-value wines: the whites, crisp and dry, or more complex, barrel-fermented versions; the reds, fresh and appealing.

Entre-Deux-Mers

Entre-Deux-Mers is both an appellation and a geographical zone. The latter is the wedge of land bounded by the Dordogne and Garonne rivers. The AOC is for dry whites from Sauvignon Blanc, Semillon, and Muscadelle. Production has been fairly constant, an average 75,000hl yearly from 3,700 acres (1,500ha), indicating a stable market for this simple, fresh, fruity, and generally well-made wine. On the western rim, bordering the Garonne, the AOC Premières Côtes de Bordeaux stretches north–south for 37 miles (60km) and 3 miles (5km) across at the widest point. Just over 7,400 acres (3,000ha) produce the aromatic, lightly structured Cadillac reds that will be labeled under the new AOC Côtes de Bordeaux from the 2008 vintage. The rest of the region is the source of much of Bordeaux's generic wines. Historically, it is an area of mixed farming, hence the importance of cooperatives. The terrain is of gently rolling hills, with very varied soils: clay-limestone, sandy gravel, gravel, and the silty soils (*boulbènes*) better suited to whites. Producers sell reds under the AOC Bordeaux or Bordeaux Supérieur labels, the latter demanding an extra half a degree minimum alcohol, a slight reduction in yield, and longer maturation. Quality is mixed and depends on investment, expertise, and distribution, as well as access to good terroir.

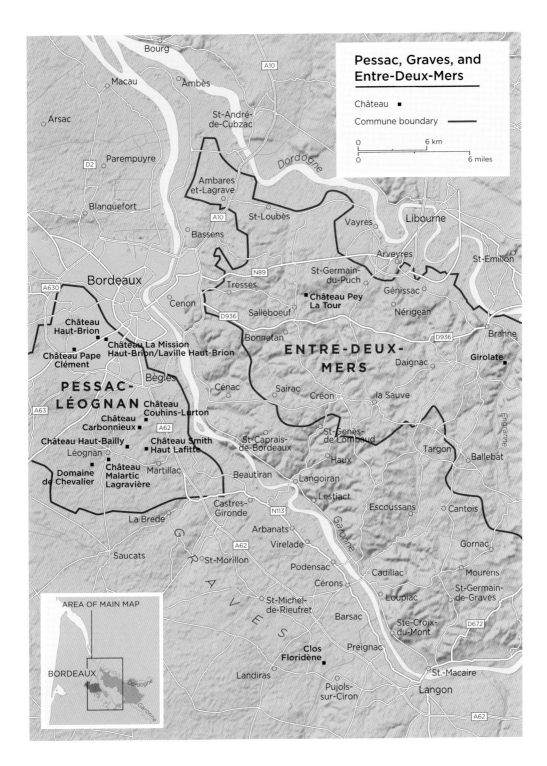

Pessac, Graves, and
Entre-Deux-Mers

■ Château
—— Commune boundary

0 ———— 6 km
0 ———— 6 miles

Bourg

Macau

Arsac

Ambès

St-André-
de-Cubzac

A10

Dordogne

Parempuyre

D2

Ambares-
et-Lagrave

A10

Blanquefort

St-Loubès

Vayres

Libourne

Bassens

St-Emilion

Bordeaux

A630

N89

Arveyres

Tresses

St-Germain-
du-Puch

Génissac

Cenon

**Château Pey
La Tour**

Nérigean

**Château
Haut-Brion**

D936

Salleboeuf

Branne

**Château La Mission
Haut-Brion/Laville Haut-Brion**

Bonnetan

D936

**Château Pape
Clément**

**ENTRE-DEUX-
MERS**

Daignac

Girolate

Bègles

**PESSAC-
LÉOGNAN**

Cénac

Sairac

Créon

la Sauve

Engranne

A63

**Château
Couhins-Lurton**

**Château
Carbonnieux**

A62

**Château Smith
Haut Lafitte**

St-Caprais-
de-Bordeaux

St-Genès-
de-Lombaud

Targon

Ballebat

Château Haut-Bailly

Léognan

Haux

**Domaine
de Chevalier**

**Château
Malartic
Lagravière**

Martillac

Beautiran

Langoiran

Escoussans

Cantois

Lestiact

La Brede

Castres-
Gironde

N113

Gornac

Saucats

Arbanats

Virelade

Garonne

Cadillac

Mourens

St-Morillon

A62

Podensac

St-Germain-
de-Graves

G

Cérons

Loupiac

St-Michel-
de-Rieufret

Barsac

Ste-Croix-
du-Mont

D672

A

V

E

S

Preignac

**Clos
Floridène**

Landiras

Pujols-
sur-Ciron

St.-Macaire

Langon

A62

AREA OF MAIN MAP

BORDEAUX

Dordogne

Garonne

Haut-Brion

Château Haut-Brion is possibly the oldest wine estate in Bordeaux. It was certainly the first property to be known by its place name and, in the 17th century, was responsible for fashioning the "New French Claret," the prototype of classic red Bordeaux. Over the years, the estate has continued to lead from the front, thanks to a combination of terroir, committed ownership, and the intelligent use of technology.

The property is now locked inside the suburban sprawl of Pessac to the southwest of the city of Bordeaux. The vineyard is formed on two southeast-facing sand and gravel knolls and has the essential elements of gently sloping hills; deep, poor, gravelly soils; and a well-drained subsoil composed of limestone and clay.

In certain areas, the gravel has been eroded by the passage of two streams, the Serpent and the Peugue, allowing the limestone and clay to outcrop. In others, sand has been moved by gravity and erosion and deposited at the bottom of the slopes. This adds to the complexity of the terrain. Climatically, the "inner-city" location provides slightly higher average annual temperatures, making Haut-Brion an earlier-ripening site.

Terroir is one thing, but it needs to be nurtured by man, and in this respect Haut-Brion has been well served. Successive proprietors and managers have provided continuity and direction, always with the aim of improvement.

Initial success and renown can be attributed to the de Pontac family, which owned Haut-Brion until the Revolution. Founded by Jean de Pontac in 1533, the domaine gained notoriety in the 17th century under the ownership of Arnaud III de Pontac, a wealthy and politically powerful figure. He oversaw improvements in the winemaking and, with his son François-Auguste, established a market for the wine in England. The 1660 cellar ledger of King Charles II

Right: The entrance to one of Bordeaux's oldest wine estates
Over: The defiant leonine guardian at Château Haut-Brion

Château Haut-Brion is possibly the oldest wine estate in Bordeaux. Over the years, it has continued to lead from the front, thanks to a combination of terroir, committed ownership, and the intelligent use of technology

Above: General manager Jean-Philippe Delmas and a map of the vineyards that have resisted the encroachment of the city

bears witness to this, as do the words penned by the diarist Samuel Pepys in 1663: "I drank a sort of French wine, called Ho Bryan [sic], that hath a good and most particular taste that I ever met with."

The post-Revolutionary years were less stable, but in 1836 the estate was acquired by Joseph Eugène Larrieu, who consolidated and expanded the property. It was under his stewardship that Haut-Brion, a leader in terms of prestige and market price, was classified premier cru in 1855.

The present owners, the American Dillon family, have provided further continuity since 1935, when the estate was bought by Clarence Dillon. His great-grandson, Prince Robert of Luxembourg, holds the role of president today. These latter years have also been marked by the commitment of the estate managers, the Delmas family—first Georges (1923), then his son Jean-Bernard (1961), and since 2004, his son Jean-Philippe.

The use of new technology and techniques in both viticulture and winemaking is another reason Haut-Brion has been able to keep ahead of the game. In the 17th century, the proximity to the city of Bordeaux and the power and wealth of the de Pontac family permitted the progression. *Ouillage* and *soutirage* were current practices, as was the use of sulfur for sterilizing barrels. A greater effort in the vineyard probably raised quality, too.

More recently, in 1961, Haut-Brion took the "revolutionary" step of introducing stainless-steel fermentation tanks, then in 1991 built an ultra-modern *cuvier*. In the vineyards, a groundbreaking program of clonal selection has been running since the 1970s. Progress today continues under Jean-Philippe Delmas and the experienced team of cellar master Jean-Philippe Masclef and vineyard manager Pascal Baratié, both at the property since 1988.

FINEST WINES

Château Haut-Brion
Elegance, more than anything, is the hallmark of Haut-Brion, and this is evident even in lesser years (the consistency is impressive). The quality and finesse of tannin are exceptional; the bouquet, complex but harmonious, with roasted, burned cocoa-bean and caramel notes and an almost overripe fruit character. The blend usually includes a healthy proportion of Merlot (up to 55%), which contributes to the smooth, round, unctuous texture that is typical of the cru. Cabernet Sauvignon (around 40%) and Cabernet Franc (up to 10%) are the complementary varieties. Seductive when young, it also has a considerable ability to age, the underlying depth and power of the wine often deceptive. The following notes were penned at Haut-Brion in October 2007.

1982 ★ Good color. Aromatically complex with notes of confit fruit, cedar, and tobacco. Velvety texture. Still plenty of youth, charm, and finesse.

1996 Long, fine, and classic in style. Fresh, minerally finish. Balanced. Perhaps a little lacking in intensity. Beginning to open.

1997 Brick rim. Evolved, but has fruit and poise. Mineral, tobacco, and red-fruit aromas. Soft and round.

1998 ★ Plenty of energy and vigor in this wine. Deep and dense. Lovely weight, length, and structure, with a fresh, balanced finish.

1999 Youthful color. Beginning to open. Earthy, roasted nuance on the nose. The palate is ample, generous, and finely textured, with a firm finish.

2000 ★ Quintessential Haut-Brion: sumptuous fruit and texture; great finesse. A splendid nose, with notes of cedar and red fruit. Fine, filigree tannins and huge length and persistence.

2001 ★ Generous, appealing wine, but still with plenty of reserve. Deep color. Soft, lush, opulent fruit, silky texture, and firm-but-fine tannins.

2002 The antithesis of 2003. Firm, rigorous, even a little austere. Long and linear. Similar to 2004 but with less purity and precision.

2003 A difficult year for this early-ripening terroir. Less density and complexity than usual, but fine tannins. Sweet-fruited, aromatic, accessible.

2004 ★ Elegant wine. Classic in style. Harmonious and long, with very fine tannins. Plenty of minerality and freshness. An unusual 61% Merlot in the blend.

2005 ★ Exceptional wine from an exceptional vintage. Subtle and restrained but with immeasurable power and complexity. Velvety texture, layered fruit, tannins powerful but refined.

Le Clarence de Haut-Brion
This is the new name for the second wine of Haut-Brion. Until the 2007 vintage it was known as Château Bahans Haut-Brion. The style mirrors that of Haut-Brion, with gentle aroma, supple fruit, and a fine tannic structure for mid-term aging.

Château Haut-Brion (white)
The tiny quantity of dry white wine is rich, full, and intense, clearly marked, at least in youth, by the dominance of Sauvignon Blanc (usually at least 50%). En primeur, I usually find it a little richer, weightier, and oakier than stablemate Laville Haut-Brion. As with the latter, there were a few vintages in the late 1990s that seemed to evolve prematurely, but recent offerings have been sublime. A discreet amount of a sort of second wine—Les Plantiers de Haut-Brion, renamed La Clarté de Haut-Brion in 2009—is made from rejected lots from both Haut-Brion and Laville Haut-Brion.

Château Haut-Brion
Total area: 126 acres (51ha)
Area under vine: 126 acres (51ha)—
7 acres (3ha) white; 119 acres (48ha) red
Production: (white) grand vin 9,000 bottles;
(red) grand vin 120,000–144,000 bottles,
second wine 96,000–120,000 bottles
135 Avenue Jean Jaurès, 33608 Pessac
Tel: +33 5 56 00 29 30
www.haut-brion.com

La Mission Haut-Brion

Château La Mission Haut-Brion has been in the possession of the American Dillon family since 1983. They also own the neighboring Château Haut-Brion across the road, and the winemaking team is shared. The fact that there is such a divergence in styles between the two interrelated properties often comes as a surprise, but historically this has always been the case.

The majority of the La Mission vineyard lies in the suburb of Talence, though there are a couple of parcels intermixed with those of Haut-Brion in nearby Pessac. The land is generally flatter, more plateau-like than at Haut-Brion. The soils are also slightly richer—still gravelly, but with a little more clay and a subsoil that is chalky sand. This has permitted a higher density of planting than at Haut-Brion: 10,000 vines/ha.

The vineyard has recently been replanted and expanded. Some 5 acres (2ha) were recuperated from Château Laville Haut-Brion in 1990 and the vineyard that was formerly Château La Tour Haut-Brion (12 acres [5ha]) incorporated from 2006. Laville Haut-Brion is now reduced to three small parcels planted in 1934, 1960, and 1961.

The name La Mission hails from the 17th and 18th centuries, when the property was owned and run by Lazerite priests, also known as the Congregation de la Mission. They built the recently renovated chapel and château. Confiscated at the Revolution, it was eventually acquired by Célestin Chiapella from New Orleans in 1821. He and his son Jérôme helped establish the name, improved the vineyard, and enclosed the property, constructing the iron gate that is still in use today. They also developed markets for the wine in the United States and Great Britain.

From 1884, La Mission changed hands several times before being acquired by Frédéric Woltner in 1919. His son Henri renovated the property and

Right: The tranquil setting of La Mission, where the architecture reflects its 18th-century monastic origins

*If Haut-Brion is all about elegance, finesse, and polished texture, then
La Mission represents power and concentration, with a lushness of fruit
and force of tannin that hand it a masculine tag*

helped further its reputation. La Mission actually produced four vintages of wine in 1927, 1928, 1929, and 1930 from white varieties planted after the purchase, but with the acquisition of the tiny Clos Laville vineyard in 1931, the two were amalgamated, resulting in the first vintage of Château Laville-Terroir du Haut-Brion, renamed Château Laville Haut-Brion in 1934.

The latter part of the Woltner era was less glorious. Investment became limited to the extent that new oak barrels were not even purchased. Since the arrival of the Dillon family, the property has been steadily put back on track. A new stainless-steel *cuvier* was built in 1987, and more recently, in 2007, the *chai* was completely redesigned to include new barrel cellars (80 percent new barrels each year) and bottling and storage areas. The vineyard, of course, remains the priority.

FINEST WINES

Château La Mission Haut-Brion

If Haut-Brion is all about elegance, finesse, and polished texture, then La Mission represents power and concentration, with a lushness of fruit and force of tannin that hand it a masculine tag. This is very much the case in exceptional years (1929, 1955, 1959, 1961, 1978, 1982, 1989, 1990, 2000, 2005), though La Mission maintains consistency in lesser vintages as well. There's usually a high proportion of Merlot in the blend, 55% the norm, complemented by Cabernet Sauvignon and up to 10% Cabernet Franc. Aging potential is at least 30–40 years. A tasting of recent vintages (1996–2005) held at the estate in October 2007 showed the remarkable consistency of the wine, with only one poor vintage, the 1997, on display. The 2000★ and 2005★ were, needless to say, outstanding, but I also enjoyed the fragrant, minerally 2004★ and the broader, muscular 1998★, which had a distinct cigar-box aroma.

1996 Fine, harmonious, medium-bodied wine. Not quite the depth and intensity of a top year. Approachable now.

Left: Vineyard manager Pascal Baratié (left) and cellar master Jean-Philipe Masclef, who both play crucial roles at La Mission

La Chapelle de la Mission Haut-Brion

The second wine of La Mission was created in 1991. Prior to that, Château La Tour Haut-Brion was considered the second wine of the estate. In 2006, the latter's vineyard was incorporated into La Mission, and much of the production now finds its way into La Chapelle. This has helped provide a more refined, fragrant Graves character and given far more interest to the wine.

Château Laville Haut-Brion

This tiny and monstrously expensive dry white wine, renamed La Mission Haut-Brion Blanc from the 2009 vintage, owes much of its character to the unusually high proportion of Semillon in the blend. The norm is 80% (though it was 86% in 2006), with a complement of Sauvignon Blanc. The wine is opulent and intense in youth, with balancing acidity, a marked note of citrus fruit, and a kiss of vanilla oak. Greater purity of fruit has been the defining factor in latter years. The wine's ability to age is also part of the legend: 30–40 years is the potential for some vintages, the Semillon maintaining freshness but providing a creamy texture on the palate and panoply of aroma that varies from biscuity to waxy, honeyed notes and even crystallized fruits. The nearest comparison is a fine white Burgundy. Vintages in the late 1990s (1997–2000) seem to have aged somewhat prematurely, but the problem has evidently been taken in hand, but vintages from 2004 showing Laville Haut-Brion at its summit. These days, fermentation is started in stainless-steel tanks and completed in oak barrels, 50% of which are new. There's no malolactic fermentation, but the wine is matured in barrel, with *bâtonnage*, for ten months prior to bottling.

2006★ Pale, lemon hue. Absolute precision—long, linear, and pure. Citrus spectrum of aroma, with just a hint of oak. Cool, clean, crystalline finish.

Château La Mission Haut-Brion

Total area: 72 acres (29ha)
Area under vine: 72 acres (29ha)—
6.5 acres (2.5ha) white; 65.5 acres (27ha) red
Production: (white) grand vin 9,000 bottles
(Laville Haut-Brion / La Mission Haut-Brion Blanc);
(red) grand vin 48,000–72,000 bottles,
second wine 48,000–60,000 bottles
67 Rue Peybouquey, 33400 Talence
Tel: +33 5 56 00 29 30
www.mission-haut-brion.com

Haut-Bailly

American banker Robert G. Wilmers, like many new owners, had achieved wealth and respectability in another field when he decided he would like to own a vineyard in Bordeaux. "You have to be foolhardy on the one hand and a dreamer on the other, but I had a little change in my pocket and decided to go out and search," he says whimsically.

The hunt led him to Château Haut-Bailly, where he met and was smitten by the then-proprietor Jean Sanders. Château Haut-Bailly was by no means in a neglected state and had continued to produce the elegant, medium-bodied red wines that had made the reputation of the château. But divisions within the family meant the inevitable sale of the 80-acre (32ha) property, and a deal was struck in 1998.

I can confirm the consistency, freshness, and harmony of the wine. Haut-Bailly has stuck with a style that suits, and everyone is happy that it stays that way

The sale now seems providential, since Haut-Bailly has not only gained a steadying hand but has progressed, while maintaining its hallmark style of wine. Wilmers lends a calm reassurance, financial security, and business acumen from his base in Buffalo, New York, while the daily management is left to Jean Sanders's capable granddaughter Véronique, who has undertaken the task with passion and dedication. She is ably supported by technical director Gabriel Vialard, previously the winemaker at Château Smith Haut Lafitte.

Fine-tuning has been the name of the game in the Wilmers era, allowing a little more precision and purity in the wines, particularly from 2004. An in-depth study of the land has allowed a better understanding of the vineyard and revealed a mosaic of different soils. The parcel of possibly pre-phylloxera vines, planted before 1907 (15 percent of the vineyard with a mix of Cabernet, Merlot, Petit Verdot, Malbec, and Carmenère), is still held in great esteem, but other quality parcels have been revealed, the best with only 30in (75cm) of gravel and then a compact, clay-based subsoil. The density of planting is exceptionally high (for the appellation), at 10,000 vines/ha.

Plot-by-plot management is strictly applied, and consequently the *cuvier* has been modified to allow a greater number of vats. Only 50 percent of the production is used for the grand vin, and the press wine, considered too rustic, is never included. The second wine, La Parde de Haut-Bailly, represents another 30 percent, the remainder going to a third label, a generic Pessac-Léognan.

FINEST WINES

Château Haut-Bailly
The property produces only red wine, principally from Cabernet Sauvignon (64%), with a complement of Merlot (30%) and Cabernet Franc (6%). The parcel of mixed varieties planted pre-1907 usually represents 20% of the blend. The wine is aged in oak barrels, 50–65% of which are renewed yearly. I've been lucky enough to participate in a number of vertical tastings at the property over the years and can confirm the consistency, freshness, and harmony of the wine. Haut-Bailly has stuck with a style that suits, and everyone from owner to consumer is happy that it stays that way. The notes below were made in October 2008.

1978 (Magnum) Amber-brick color. Clearly a grand old bottle. An attractive, earthy, leafy nose. The palate is still quite savory. Noted acidity. Fragile but still has presence.

1988 (Magnum) Developed, brick color. Long and linear with marked acidity. Light style. *Sous-bois* notes and a touch of green.

Right: Véronique Sanders, whose enlightened appointment as manager of Haut-Bailly continues her family's involvement

1996 ★ Long and powerful, with a marked Cabernet Sauvignon expression. Minty menthol notes on the nose, with a hint of warm brick. The palate is intense, structured, fresh, and long, with definite black currant flavor.

1998 This has 43% Merlot in the blend and is correspondingly broader in style. Deep, garnet hue. Quite fine, minerally nose. Full and round, with slightly grainier tannins. Acidity offers freshness and length on the finish.

1999 Garnet, with brick at the rim. A developed nose, definitely less refined. Easy and open on the palate, the tannins drying on the finish. The weak link at the tasting.

2000 ★ Merlot is to the fore here, making up 50% in the blend. Deep color. This is still quite closed on the nose, but it eventually reveals licorice and spice aromas. A dense, full, supple texture on the palate, with firm, tannic structure—muscular for Haut-Bailly.

2001 ★ A very appealing nose. Dark fruits, even black currant, with a smoky, mineral nuance. Less fulsome than the 2000, but there is a sweetness on the palate and tannins that are fine and long.

2002 A fine effort for a difficult year. Dark fruit with a slight empyreumatic character on the nose. The palate is light to medium-bodied but supple, fresh, and open.

2003 Evolved color. Less complexity and finesse than usual. A curranty nose. Broad, open palate. Lower acidity. Tannins a touch robust and drying.

2004 [V] Purple color. Smoky, earthy Graves nose with a hint of spicy oak. Soft, caressing fruit on the palate—pure, fresh, and long. More tender than 2006 and less structured than 2005, but very fine.

2005 ★ Impressively deep color. Restrained at present but with plenty of reserve. Ripe and dense, with a firm tannic frame. Acidity on the finish provides freshness and balance. Big for Haut-Bailly and obviously for the long haul.

2006 ★ Deep, purple hue. Nose complex but subdued. Crisp acidity, but the fruit is pure, dense, and fleshy. Less power than 2005 but very fine. Long, linear, and classical in style. Will age.

Above: The compact, discreet château at Haut-Bailly, with roses in the vineyard to give early warning of disease

Château Haut-Bailly

Total area: 81.5 acres (33ha)
Area under vine: 76.5 acres (31ha)
Average production: grand vin 80,000 bottles; second wine 50,000 bottles
33850 Léognan
Tel: +33 5 56 64 75 11
www.chateau-haut-bailly.com

Malartic Lagravière

This estate has undergone a rapid transformation since being purchased by Belgian businessman Alfred-Alexandre Bonnie in 1997. It's a clear example of what good terroir, application, and deep pockets can attain in a relatively short period of time. From underachieving also-ran, Malartic Lagravière is now one of the stars of the Pessac-Léognan appellation, the market price for the red equated with that of a Médoc fourth growth.

The previous owners, Champagne Laurent-Perrier, had maintained the well-exposed, gravelly, 47-acre (19ha) vineyard, but yields had been generous and selection limited. The production facilities needed renovating, and the management and winemaking teams also required a shake-up, the property run from a distance at the time.

An impressive budget of $20 million was earmarked for the revival of Malartic Lagravière. Almost overnight, a new state-of-the-art gravity-fed winery containing stainless-steel and wooden vats, as well as cellars with the capacity to stock 1,400 barrels, was constructed for the 1998 vintage. A new château also saw the light of day. Soils were analyzed to permit plot-by-plot management, yields were reduced, and a replanting program was introduced.

Of the original 47 acres situated behind the cellars, 5 acres (2ha) were grubbed up and extra parcels planted. This is still the heart of the vineyard, though, the gravel terrace as much as 26ft (8m) deep in places. Some 27 acres (11ha)

Below: M and Mme Alfred-Alexandre Bonnie with son Jean-Jacques and daughter-in-law Séverine, who now run the estate

of a neighboring vineyard known as Château Neuf were purchased and planted; likewise a 17-acre (7ha) parcel called Marquet that had once been part of the Lagravière estate. On the other side of the town of Léognan, a further acquisition of land that had not been cultivated since the 1950s was made, at a site known as Laguloup.

In terms of personnel, a young *maître de chais* with work experience at Haut-Brion, Philippe Garcia, was engaged, a vineyard manager was "trained up," and Michel Rolland was retained as consultant oenologist. In 2003, the overall management was placed in the hands of Monsieur Bonnie's son Jean-Jacques and daughter-in-law Séverine, who remain in charge today.

increased this to 15–20% of the blend. The wine is fermented in barrel (30–40% new oak) then aged for 10–12 months. The use of skin contact prior to fermentation was abandoned in 2000. There's no doubt that the addition of Semillon, together with riper fruit, has given the wine a more unctuous, fuller feel, as well as introducing an exotic note. My feeling is that this is probably a wine to be enjoyed relatively young.

2002 Perhaps not the best example of the new style, since there seems to be a lack of freshness and the color is rather advanced for its age (tasted July 2008). There is plenty of fruit extract, with the oak still apparent, but it seems to miss that zip of acidity. Perhaps I was unlucky with this particular bottle and it was not representative?

Château Malartic Lagravière (red)

The red used to be rather lean and severe but now has greater vigor, length, weight, and finesse and—at least since 1998—a remarkable consistency, too. It is made from a varying blend of 45% Cabernet Sauvignon, 45% Merlot, 8% Cabernet Franc, and 2% Petit Verdot and aged for 15–22 months in 50–70% new oak barrels. With the considerable number of new plantings, the selection was particularly severe in the early 2000s, the grand vin representing only 45% of the production. It is now nearer 60%. The rest is destined for the second wine, recently rebaptized La Réserve de Malartic (the old name, Le Sillage de Malartic—*sillage* meaning the wake of a boat—not going down too well with English speakers).

2001 Classic ruby red. A fine, fragrant bouquet. The palate has a certain opulence and sweetness of fruit but also a characteristic Graves freshness and digestibility. Fine, supple tannins.

Left: The stately château and grounds at Malartic Lagravière, where substantial investments are paying off handsomely

FINEST WINES

Château Malartic Lagravière (white)

In the 1970s and '80s, the Malartic Lagravière white was more highly esteemed than the red. In those days, it was made from pure Sauvignon Blanc, crisp and citric, and with the aid of a highish dose of sulfur dioxide (typical of the time), it had a certain potential to age. Laurent-Perrier grafted a little Semillon in 1992, and the Bonnies have since

Château Malartic Lagravière
Total area: 150 acres (60ha)
Area under vine: 131 acres (53ha)—
17 acres (7ha) white; 114 acres (46ha) red
Average production: (white) grand vin 12,000 bottles, second wine 6,000 bottles; (red) grand vin 100,000 bottles, second wine 80,000 bottles
43 Avenue de Mont de Marsan, 33850 Léognan
Tel: +33 5 56 64 75 08
www.malartic-lagraviere.com

Pape Clément

Pape Clément derives its name from celebrated medieval owner Bertrand de Goth, who in 1305 became Pope Clement V and took up his papal seat in Avignon. The owner today, Bernard Magrez, is also a noted figure but more for his entrepreneurial activities and string of wine estates around the world. Pape Clément is the jewel in the crown.

The property is located within the suburban sprawl of Pessac, not far from Bordeaux's busy bypass, the *rocade*. The nearest neighboring vineyard is that of Haut-Brion, closer to the city center, but the harvest at Pape Clément is usually a week or so later and more closely aligned with activities in the Médoc. The site is at the core of

Pape Clément is assertive and seductively modern in style, the texture smooth and opulent. Rich, ripe, and oaky when young, it gains in aromatic complexity

the old vineyards of the Graves (a large portion since devoured by the developers), the soils being essentially Pyrenean gravel with varying proportions of sand, clay, and pebbles.

Bertrand de Goth donated the property to the church, in whose hands it remained until the Revolution. It then changed ownership several times, expanding gradually toward its present size. The château was built in the 19th century but extensively remodeled later on, the medieval ramparts and gothic elements being subsequent additions. Property developers nearly claimed the site in 1938, but Pape Clément was saved when Paul Montagne acquired it a year later. The wines remained highly regarded throughout this period, as they were in the 1950s and 1960s. Due to a lack of investment and overcropping, a leaner spell ensued in the 1970s and early 1980s.

The modern revival of Château Pape Clément dates from 1985 and coincides with a change of management and the arrival of Bernard Magrez. New winemaking facilities were built, the barrel cellar was restored, and in 1986 a second wine, Le Clémentin, was introduced to improve selection. Michel Rolland was brought in as a consultant from 1993. Of more long-term importance, a program for replanting and restructuring the vineyard was put in place in 1990 and has since seen 60 percent of the surface area renewed.

There's been further change and innovation in the new millennium. During the harvest, an army of nearly 150 people sort and hand-destem the grapes. These are picked parcel by parcel, the separation continuing through to vinification in a bank of brand-new wooden vats, where manual *pigeage* is employed for extraction. The use of pumps is avoided, the grapes and later the wine being gravity-fed. Aging is in 100 percent new oak barrels and lasts 20–22 months for the red.

FINEST WINES

Château Pape Clément (red)

Pape Clément's reputation is built firmly on its red wine, which is generally produced from an equal share of Cabernet Sauvignon and Merlot (though the vineyard is 60% Cabernet Sauvignon and 40% Merlot). Dark in color, it is assertive and seductively modern in style, the texture smooth and opulent. Rich, ripe, and oaky when young, it gains in aromatic complexity, with smoky, spicy notes becoming more apparent with age. The palate is firm and forceful, the sweetness of fruit underpinned by a strong tannic frame and a marked minerality that provides balancing freshness and length.

1995 Garnet hue, with a touch of evolution at the rim. Smoky and spicy on the nose, with a touch of Burgundian fragrance, the fruit still youthful and fresh. The palate has solid definition, with a sweetness of fruit, firm, long tannins, and freshness

Right: Bernard Magrez, whose ambition for Château Pape Clément has been backed by generous investment since 1985

on the finish. Quite punchy and masculine in style—more La Mission than Haut-Brion.

Château Pape Clément (white)

I have little experience of the white other than at the annual en primeur tastings. Here it always appears rich, full, and exotic, the fruit clearly super-ripe but the oak a tad overpowering. Obviously, the wine needs a certain time in bottle, and even then, I suspect, the style won't please everyone. It is produced from a field blend of 45% each Sauvignon Blanc and Semillon, with an additional 5% each of Sauvignon Gris and Muscadelle to round it off.

Château Pape Clément

Total area: 89 acres (36ha)
Area under vine: 81.5 acres (33ha)—
7.5 acres (3ha) white; 74 acres (30ha) red
Average production: (white) grand vin 10,000 bottles, second wine 5,000 bottles; (red) grand vin 100,000 bottles, second wine 60,000 bottles
216 Avenue du Docteur Nancel Penard
33600 Pessac
Tel: +33 5 57 26 38 38
www.pape-clement.com

Smith Haut Lafitte

Daniel and Florence Cathiard acquired Château Smith Haut Lafitte in 1990 and have since transformed both the property and the quality of the wines beyond recognition. The visible evidence of change is everywhere—from the renovated 18th-century *chartreuse*, which is their permanent home, to the remodeled 16th-century tower and new cuverie and barrel cellar for white wine, not to mention the adjacent hotel-spa complex, Les Sources de Caudalie. The vineyard, too, has been restructured and restored.

The history of Smith Haut Lafitte can be traced back to the 14th century, and as the name suggests, there was once an "Anglo-Saxon" owner, the British négociant George Smith, proprietor in the 18th century. By the mid-19th century, it was owned by the Mayor of Bordeaux, Monsieur Duffour-Dubergier, who is credited with bringing the quality of the wines up to classed-growth standard. The négociant Louis Eschenauer owned the property prior to the sale in 1990. There had been considerable investment through the 1970s, including the construction of a vaulted underground cellar that can hold 2,000 barrels, but the estate was still underachieving.

This was the situation when the Cathiards took over the property. Their first decision was to end the Eschenauer method of cultivating in an industrial manner. Hand-picking was reintroduced for the first harvest in 1991, as was the practice of plowing

Below: Daniel and Florence Cathiard, former Olympic skiers who have brought much-needed investment and panache

the soil. Smith Haut Lafitte is not officially organic, but the practices and philosophy veer in that direction. Herbicides were banned from 1992, and artificial pheromones have been used in the fight against grape-berry moth since 1995. The estate has produced its own organic compost since 1997.

A program of replanting has seen 30 percent of the vineyard reconstituted since the 1990s. Two important decisions were made. Some 12 acres (5ha) on the present site of the hotel-spa were grubbed up, and Cabernet Sauvignon was replanted on more suitable gravelly soils close by. In the northern part of the estate, Cabernet

Sauvignon that had difficulty ripening on clay soils was replaced with Merlot. Needless to say, yields were drastically cut and now average just over 30hl/ha for both red and white.

There has been change in the winery, too. A cooperage supplying 60 percent of the château's needs was opened in 1995, and from 2000 only truncated wooden vats have been used for fermenting the reds. A barrel cellar for the white wine was created in 1995 and the red cellar improved. The reception of the harvest is more selective, with sorting tables from 1999 and a laser-optical sorting machine from 2009.

The Cathiards take great comfort from the land and live the adventure, but they've also harnessed their considerable management skills to make the project a success. The right personnel have been hired (winemaker Fabien Tietgen and consultants Michel Rolland and Stéphane Derenoncourt), marketing and communication applied adroitly, and a business plan executed. It's a professional approach to excellence that Daniel Cathiard summarizes with a competitive air. "The contest is all about what's in the glass, so there's no point talking a lot of hot air. You just have to make the best wine possible."

FINEST WINES

Château Smith Haut Lafitte (white)
The barrel-fermented white wine was the first to enhance the reputation of Smith Haut Lafitte under the Cathiard regime, the 1993 receiving particular praise. The wines were fuller and richer than in the past, the oak and maturity of the fruit adding a riper and more complex character. The addition of Sauvignon Gris (from 1993) to the Sauvignon Blanc (planted in the 1960s) also added floral aromas and more opulence and power. Since 2002, Smith Haut Lafitte white has achieved further aromatic complexity with the addition of 5–10% Semillon.
2006★ Aromatically complex, with notes of pear, citrus, and vanilla. The palate is round and succulent, with a Burgundian buttery note and acidity on the finish. Lush and generous in style but not flabby. Drinking well from three years of age.

Château Smith Haut Lafitte (red)
The red took a little longer to find form but, from 1995, has been reassuringly consistent. Produced from a varying blend of 55% CS, 34% M, 10% CF, and 1% PV, this is a generous wine, modern to a degree, with toasted oak in youth but a finish that's pure, minerally Graves. Vintages in the 1990s were perhaps more overtly ripe and opulent, the amount of Merlot generous, but since 2003 the Cabernet Sauvignon has been on the increase (64% in 2005 and 2006) and the Petit Verdot added to give the wines greater finesse, freshness, and length. Aging is in 60–80% new oak barrels.
2004★ Dark garnet hue. Ripe and fragrant on the nose, with notes of red and black fruit. The palate is supple but with a fine tannic structure and freshness on the finish. Well-integrated and classy toasted oak. Accessible, with the structure to age.

Left: The distinctive profile of Château Smith Haut Lafitte, the sculpture of the bounding hare symbolizing its progress

Château Smith Haut Lafitte
Total area: 300 acres (120ha)
Area under vine: 165.5 acres (67ha)—
27 acres (11ha) white; 138.5 acres (56ha) red
Average production: (white) grand vin 33,000 bottles, second wine 12,000 bottles; (red) grand vin 120,000 bottles, second wine 78,000 bottles
33650 Martillac
Tel: +33 5 57 83 11 22
www.smith-haut-lafitte.com

Domaine de Chevalier

Domaine de Chevalier sits in splendid isolation, the gently undulating vineyard surrounded on three sides by pine forest without a neighbor in sight. It's a particular terroir, on the limit for ripening Cabernet and prone to frost but, with human assistance, capable of producing distinctive wines.

The soil is mainly black sandy gravel over a subsoil of clay and gravel mixed with iron-rich sandstone. This provides an adequate base for viticulture, provided there's a guiding hand. A system of drainage was put in place by previous owner Claude Ricard in 1962, but since 1983 the property has been run by Olivier Bernard and new initiatives have been introduced.

Although not overtly powerful or aromatic, the wines have digestibility and finesse, coupled with a distinctive earthy, minerally character and the ability to age

Amounting to only 44 acres (18ha) when purchased by the Bernard family, the vineyard has since been expanded to the present 111 acres (45ha). Some 12 acres (5ha) are planted with Sauvignon Blanc (70 percent) and Semillon (30 percent). A steady program of restructuring and planting has seen the density of planting increase to 10,000 vines/ha, the Sauvignon Blanc consigned to cooler zones and the Cabernet Sauvignon located on deeper, warmer, gravelly soils. In the sectors prone to spring frost, wind machines have been installed, the trees in close proximity cut down, and smudge pots introduced.

Winemaking for the white wine has been taken to a rare level of precision. Only golden bunches are selected by successive *tries*. The grapes are then pressed (with CO_2 added at the press) and the juice cold settled. Fermentation takes place in oak barrels, 35 percent of which are renewed each year (down from the 50 percent used from the mid-1980s until 1999). The wine spends 18 months in barrel—longer than any other dry white in Bordeaux—where it takes on weight and texture and undergoes a natural clarification.

The red is produced in a circular cellar that was built in 1991. Cabernet Sauvignon (64 percent) is the principal variety, supplemented by Merlot (30 percent), Cabernet Franc, and Petit Verdot (each 3 percent). Work in the vineyard (plowing and sustainable practices) and restricted yields have enabled a longer hang-time and greater maturity in recent years. A second wine, L'Esprit de Chevalier, and even a third label provide the option of further selection, the grand vin representing less than half the production, as is the case for the white.

FINEST WINES

Domaine de Chevalier (white)

A blind tasting at the domaine in April 2005 allowed me to draw a number of conclusions about this mythical wine. First, it does have an incredible ability to age. The color stays bright and youthful, and there's a freshness and minerality that remain. The oldest wine in the series of five flights was the 1970, which was lively, fresh, and ready for drinking. My personal preference at this stage was for the 1979★, which was equally fresh but even more youthful, with complex citrus, wax, and almond flavors. The acidity was a constant factor throughout. From about 10 to 15 years the complexity of flavor becomes more pronounced. Altogether, 26 wines were served, and the consistency was high, even through the so-called *petits millésimes*. Of the latter I gave good notes to the 1984, 1987, 1991, and 1999★. From the classic vintages of the 1980s and 1990s, I found the 1986★ and 1996★ impressive. The last flight presented the wines of the new millennium from 2000 to 2004, and here the 2002★ and 2004★ were outstanding—limpid, poised, and harmonious, with a racy citric edge.

2001★ Pale lemon hue. A fine, citrus nose with just a hint of honey and brioche. The palate is suave

and sophisticated. Full and round on the attack, with acidity adding length and precision. Pure and crystalline, with a mineral note on the finish. Probably has another 20 years.

Domaine de Chevalier (red)

Another blind tasting, this time for the reds, was organized at Domaine de Chevalier in October 2005. As many as 29 vintages were shown, from 1959 to 2004. The general impression was that, although not overtly powerful or aromatic, the wines have digestibility and finesse, coupled with a distinctive earthy, minerally character and, like the whites, the ability to age. Vintages in the 1960s were particularly strong, my preference being for the powerful, creamy 1961★ and complex, minerally 1964★. The 1970s and early 1980s appeared a little weaker, though I liked the delicately fragrant 1983★, which is infinitely better than the 1982 (Chevalier was hit by the frost that year). The 1988 appeared light in style but harmonious, the 1989 a little more robust. The wines of the early 1990s were not shown, but the 1995 launched a period of greater consistency, the wines gradually gaining in ripeness, depth, and purity of fruit. I had particularly good notes for the elegant 1999★ and more powerful and intense 2001★.

2002 Subtle, elegant, with smoky, minerally notes. Lightish in weight but fine, fresh, and balanced.

Above: The modern winery at Domaine de Chevalier reflects the meticulous attention devoted to these remarkable wines

Domaine de Chevalier

Total area: 272 acres (110ha)
Area under vine: 112 acres (45ha)—
12 acres (5ha) white; 100 acres (40ha) red
Average production: (white) grand vin 15,000 bottles, second wine 8,000 bottles; (red) grand vin 90,000 bottles, second wine 70,000 bottles
33850 Léognan
Tel: +33 5 56 64 16 16
www.domainedechevalier.com

Carbonnieux

This is a sizable estate that produces a generous amount of wine, both red and white. Standards, though, are high (yields are not exaggerated), and the consistency and regularity are impressive. Add a competitive price, and Carbonnieux is an interesting option in Bordeaux's often heated market.

The property was purchased by Marc Perrin in 1956. At the time, there were only 75 acres (30ha) under vine, and following a severe frost that year, three unproductive years followed. The château (a fortified country manor of 13th-century origin) had been uninhabited since the 1920s, and investment was needed for the cellars and equipment. With a certain resilience, Marc Perrin and his son Antony restored Carbonnieux to its present state. Antony died in 2008, and his sons Eric and Philibert are now in charge.

The vineyard is situated on a gravel *croupe* with pockets of sand, gravel, and limestone as the slope falls away. The Perrins have endeavored to plant Sauvignon Blanc and Semillon on the clay-limestone soils, while the deeper gravel of the higher land has been reserved for Cabernet Sauvignon. Replanting was initiated immediately after the frost and intensified from 1962.

The Perrins were among the first in Bordeaux to embrace Denis Dubourdieu's premise on white-wine vinification, and they continue to retain him as consultant. Barrel fermentation, which is preceded by some skin contact and cold settling in tank, has been practiced since 1988. A quarter of the barrels are now renewed each year, the new oak reserved mainly for the Semillon, and the wine is aged for ten months.

As the vineyard has matured, so has the quality of the red wine, particularly after the inauguration of a new cuverie in 1990. As well as Cabernet Sauvignon (60 percent), the blend includes Merlot (30 percent), Cabernet Franc (7 percent), Petit Verdot and Malbec (3 percent). The *élevage* lasts 15–18 months.

FINEST WINES

Château Carbonnieux (white)

Lively, refreshing, direct, Carbonnieux white has a minerality that is always quite pronounced. A modern concentration of fruit has been added, but these are still not wines that can be described as opulent. Best to drink on the youthful fruit (at 2–5 years), but the wine can age.

2006 Fine, linear style. Fragrant nose of pear and mandarin. Crisp on the attack, then fills out on the palate. Minerally acidity. Clean, dry finish.

Château Carbonnieux (red)

The red is a typical Graves, with a fresh, well-structured palate, notes of dark fruit, and well-integrated oak. It ages well, despite a rumor to the contrary, and in recent years has gained in density and quality of tannin.

2005 [V] Firm, tight, but with ample fruit. Good aging potential. The nose is a little strict at present, but there's a notion of mineral and dark fruit. Well structured on the palate, with black currant notes, the rigor of the Cabernet Sauvignon showing. Long, fresh finish.

Château Carbonnieux
Total area: 346 acres (140ha)
Area under vine: 227 acres (92ha)—
104 acres (42ha) white; 123 acres (50ha) red
Average production: (white) grand vin 180,000 bottles, second wine 24,000 bottles; (red) grand vin 200,000 bottles, second wine 24,000 bottles
33850 Léognan
Tel: +33 5 57 96 56 20
www.carbonnieux.com

Couhins-Lurton

The creation of Château Couhins-Lurton resulted from the partition of the original Couhins estate in 1968. Owned by the Gasqueton family (of Calon-Ségur) at the time, the vineyard was under threat of being abandoned when André Lurton was contacted by an intermediary to see if anything could be done. Lurton agreed to lease the vineyard and—despite its lamentable state (missing wires and stakes and badly pruned vines), and with only a couple of hectares viable—produced his first white vintage here in 1967.

The following year, the Gasquetons decided to sell, the bulk of the land acquired by the Institut National de la Recherche Agronomique (INRA), along with the title Château Couhins, while the château and cellars were purchased by a local pharmacist. André Lurton continued with the rental agreement through to 1978, but in 1972 INRA sold him a 3.7-acre (1.5ha) parcel of vines, enabling him to launch the Couhins-Lurton label.

In 1992, Lurton was able to buy the 19th-century château, as well as the cellars. Renovation started in 1998, the château undergoing restoration, while the old cellars were dismantled and the stones used to build a new cellar and repair other buildings. The new cellar became operational in 2001, the wines until then produced at sister property Château La Louvière.

The vineyard for the white wine (100 percent Sauvignon Blanc) is located on gravel and sandy gravel soils on a limestone bedrock. There are two principal parcels—one located on top of a slope near the château, and the other lower down, beyond the cellars of neighboring Château Couhins. The grapes are hand-picked, pressed directly (no skin contact), then fermented and aged for ten months (with *bâtonnage*) in oak barrels. These are predominantly made from Vosges oak by a Burgundian cooper, some 25 percent renewed each year.

Since 2002, a red wine has also been produced at Couhins-Lurton, a reminder that Couhins was better known for its reds in the 19th century. (The reputation of the white was established in the early part of the 20th century.) The vineyard, which was planted in the late 1980s, is located a few miles away, near Château de Rochemorin, another Lurton estate. The wine has an unusually high proportion of Merlot (75 percent) and is supple, round, and fragrant.

FINEST WINES

Château Couhins-Lurton (white)
A pure Sauvignon Blanc, Couhins-Lurton blanc has a remarkable and somewhat surprising capacity to age. Lively and zesty in youth, with a dominantly citrus fragrance, it gradually fills out on the palate, gaining a minerally, nutty complexity, while at the same time preserving the fruit and freshness. Top vintages can age upward of 20 years, making this a somewhat exceptional white wine. An innovation (at least for Bordeaux at this level) launched in 2003 sees half the yearly production bottled with a screwcap closure, the rest with traditional cork.
2001 Pale gold hue. Crisp, fresh, and youthful on the nose. Broader on the palate but still with fine acidity. Just beginning to show some minerally complexity, but the fruit is still very present.
2005 Richer and denser in style. Pungent grapefruit and peach aromas. Firm acidity providing a long, linear finish.
2006★ Pure, fine, and long. Distinct citrus aromas tinged with a nuance of oak. Trademark acidity and freshness. Should age comfortably.

Château Couhins-Lurton
Total area: 62 acres (25ha)
Area under vines: 57 acres (23ha)—
15 acres (6ha) white; 42 acres (17ha) red
Average production: (white) grand vin 25,000 bottles; (red) grand vin 50,000 bottles
48 Chemin de Martillac
33140 Villenave d'Ornon
Tel: +33 5 57 25 58 58
www.andrelurton.com

Clos Floridène

Clos Floridène has been Professor Denis Dubourdieu's experimental playground for dry white wines ever since the inaugural 1982 vintage. While his research at Bordeaux University provided scientific corroboration, it has been the practical experience at his own domaine that has helped fine-tune his methods, making the wine a showcase example and one of Bordeaux's finest dry whites to boot. But this is not just a case of winemaking bravado, the terroir also having a say in the wine's personality and ability to age.

Pujols-sur-Ciron is a very particular corner of the Graves, as an extension of Barsac's limestone plateau. The soils, therefore, are a thin layer of red claylike sand atop a calcareous bedrock. The other influencing factor is the local climate, which is 5–7°F (3–4°C) cooler in the morning than the surrounding Garonne Valley—an aspect emphasized by the regular threat of frost (wind machines and smudge pots have been installed). "The great dry whites always come from calcareous soils, so this, plus the cool climate, convinced me I could make a dry white that would age," says Dubourdieu.

Only time would confirm the wine's longevity, but in the intervening years the winemaking process was refined in order to develop complexity and finesse. The 1982 was made uniquely from old-vine Semillon (the vineyard was only 6 acres [2.5ha] at the beginning), and initial vintages continued to have a bias toward the variety. "The Sauvignon Blanc was young at the outset—hence the dominance of Semillon—but by 1993 we were closer to the 50/50 blend we prefer today," explains Dubourdieu.

Techniques that have been perfected and adhered to include plowing the soils to drive the roots of the vines deeper, moderate use of skin contact prior to fermentation (variable according to the year), and the art of gentle pressing to avoid oxidation. Another practice Dubourdieu introduced was aging the wine on lees in barrel with *bâtonnage*, again to protect against oxidation and to stabilize the wine in a natural manner. From 1996, he also reduced the proportion of new oak for fermentation and aging, cutting back from 50 percent to the present rule of one-third for the Semillon and no new oak for the Sauvignon Blanc. "The great dry whites do not support a lot of new oak," he says. The *élevage* lasts eight to ten months.

Clos Floridène is one of the rare dry whites in Bordeaux not to have made its reputation on the back of the red. The latter is less distinguished but still has a distinct personality, the high proportion of Cabernet Sauvignon cultivated on limestone soils imparting a fresh, lithe character. Clos Floridène red has been vinified at the estate since 2005, while the white is still produced at Dubourdieu's property, Château Reynon, in the Premières Côtes de Bordeaux.

FINEST WINES

Clos Floridène (white)

In 2004, I had the chance to taste a vertical lineup of the wine from 2003 back to 1987. If the 1988 and 1987 were a little clumsy and fading, the 1989 and 1990 still had interest, the former lively with a petrol nuance, the latter more unctuous, with a touch of old Sauternes on the nose. The increase in Sauvignon Blanc in 1993 definitely gave more length and elegance. Thereafter, vintages that shone were 1996★, 1998, 2001, and 2002, all with length, freshness, balance, and, once the Sauvignon element had dissipated, an almost Burgundian complexity. "Floridène is the most Burgundian of Bordeaux whites because of the terroir," declares Denis Dubourdieu. The ability to age, I would say, was confirmed for a period of up to 15 years for the better vintages. There's been even greater purity and finesse in recent years.

1996★ Pale golden hue. The nose is quite rich, with butter, toast, and truffle notes—the Burgundian nuance. The palate is round and full but surprisingly fresh and young.

Above: Denis Dubourdieu and wife Florence produce some of Bordeaux's finest—and its most Burgundian—white wines

2001 Gold flecks. The nose is crisp and minerally, still with a Sauvignon Blanc grapefruit-zest nuance. The palate is long, fine, fresh, and still incredibly youthful.

2007★ [V] Pale, bright color with green flecks. Pure, refined, citrus aromas. The palate is round and smooth, again with a citrus/mandarin nuance, the acidity adding length and freshness. Lovely purity and balance.

Clos Floridène
Total area: 100 acres (40ha)
Area under vine: 100 acres (40ha)—
60 acres (24ha) white; 40 acres (16ha) red
Average production: (white) grand vin 90,000 bottles, second wine 8,000–10,000 bottles; (red) grand vin 60,000 bottles, second wine 15,000 bottles
33210 Pujols-sur-Ciron
Tel: +33 5 56 62 96 51
www.denisdubourdieu.com

Girolate

When it comes to energy and innovation, the Despagne family is a powerhouse in the Entre-Deux-Mers. Jean-Louis Despagne anticipated the brave new world of wine arriving in the 1980s, with its emphasis on quality and marketing, and has since transmitted his pioneering spirit and profound understanding of the need to move with the times to his son Thibault and daughter Basaline. They now head up a healthy concern of some 750 acres (300ha) and several different labels, including the revolutionary red wine Girolate.

The fact that the vineyards are located in the less reputable Entre-Deux-Mers makes it all the more commendable, Girolate being the ultimate challenge. "We basically want to show that there's no need to have a hang-up about the region and that, given the means, it's possible to make a *grand vin* in the Entre-Deux-Mers," explains Thibault.

The Girolate vineyard was chosen both for its south-facing clay-limestone site (there's a quarried limestone tunnel in the vicinity) and because wines from the old vines planted at 5,000 vines/ha were so good. The radical change came in 1999, when part of the vineyard was replanted with Merlot at 10,000 vines/ha (as in the Médoc), the vines trained low to the ground to absorb heat and the trellising lifted for adequate leaf exposure. Only four bunches per vine are kept, the target yield being 20hl/ha. "It may change when the vines are older, but at the moment we get the best results from this low volume," acknowledges Thibault.

The idea is that the grapes should ripen and concentrate in the vineyard and that in the winery there should be minimal handling—hence the next radical step, which sees the grapes vinified in 100 percent new oak barrels (225 liters), having been hand-picked, destemmed, and lightly crushed. Cultured yeast is added and the barrels turned on

Right: Brother and sister Thibault and Basaline Despagne, with a sculpture that symbolizes their modern approach

When it comes to energy and innovation, the Despagne family is a powerhouse in the Entre-Deux-Mers. Jean-Louis Despagne anticipated the brave new world of wine, with its emphasis on quality and marketing

Oxoline racks to aid gentle extraction, the period of maceration lasting three to four weeks. The press wine is then generally added to the free-run juice, and the malolactic fermentation is allowed to take place in spring. Aging in barrel can be anything from eight to 16 months, with minimal racking, the wines bottled since 2006 with a light fining and filtration.

At present, the wine is made from 100 percent Merlot, and quantities are limited. Production covered as little as 6 acres (2.5ha) in 2009. "We know we're not going to get to where we want to be overnight. This is a long-term project that still has a way to go," says Thibault. Already a nearby south-facing hillslope site has been purchased and cleared with a view to planting Cabernet and possibly other varieties. There's a certain folly to the whole scheme, but that's probably what makes it so intriguing.

FINEST WINES

Girolate
I find Girolate to be generally fine-textured, rich, and round but not overextracted. It's evidently modern in style, the quest for ripeness leading to a powerful constitution (14.5% ABV in most vintages) and an opulence of fruit. Aromatically, though, it would gain from a little more complexity. This could come with vine age and/or the addition of Cabernet, the latter also helping to rein in alcohol levels. Only time will tell if there is a real imprint of terroir. Girolate was not produced in 2004 or 2007.

2001 The first vintage of Girolate. Plum and red-fruit aromas. The palate is round and soft-textured. There's a warm glow of alcohol but also balancing freshness on the finish. The tannins are smooth and refined. Drinking now.

2002 This is the least convincing of the lineup to date. Plummy aroma with a nuance of caramel from the oak. Sweet on the attack but a little lean on the mid-palate, the tannins dry on the finish. There was even a touch of oxidation—possibly the bottle?

2003 Given the vintage conditions, this was surprisingly good. A *méridional* nuance to the nose, the oak apparent. The palate is round and full

but balanced, avoiding the cooked or dry flavors that are all too often found in this year. Still a virile tannic frame.

2005★ Clearly the best to date. Dense, but closed at present. Modern, round, and opulent, the tannins powerful but refined. Plenty of *matière* but still balanced.

2006★ A little more classical in style. The nose has a spicy lift, the aromas of ripe red fruit. The palate is again round and smooth but with a lingering acidity that provides length. The tannins are ripe but firm. Will benefit from some bottle age.

Château Mont Pérat
This is the Despagnes' 250-acre (100ha) property in the Premières Côtes de Bordeaux, acquired in 1998. A citation in the first volume of the Japanese manga comic book *The Drops of God* has provided a wealth of unsolicited publicity. The wine is again Merlot-dominated to the tune of 70%.

2005 Clean and modern in style. Red-fruit aroma and flavor, with a nuance of oak. Sweet and round on the attack, but balancing freshness on the finish. It's deliciously drinkable and digestible.

Girolate
Total area: 25 acres (10ha)
Area under vine: 25 acres (10ha)
Production: 5,000–12,000 bottles
Vignobles Despagne
33420 Naujan et Postiac
Tel: +33 5 57 84 55 08
www.despagne.fr

Pey La Tour

This is a splendid example of a good-value, quality-driven generic Bordeaux. Produced on a large scale, it is nonetheless a model in its practices and style. The volume evidently helps soften the price, but there are no shortcuts when it comes to the production of the wine. Two cuvées are offered: the early-drinking, fruit-driven regular bottling, which is aged in tank; and the superior Réserve du Château, which is aged in 40–50 percent new oak barrels.

The property was bought by Vignobles Dourthe, part of Groupe CVBG, in 1990 and has since expanded from the initial 62 acres (25ha) with additional acquisitions of land in the Entre-Deux-Mers. On such a large scale, the soils are inevitably varied, but this aids the selection process for the two different cuvées. The regular bottling is generally produced from grapes grown on sandy gravel and silty (known locally as *boulbènes*) soils, whereas the Réserve comes from clay-limestone soils (with a high proportion of clay) and the denser plots of gravel.

The vineyard is managed with the expertise and application usually reserved for a grand cru estate, and this is the principal reason for the quality and consistency of the wines. The density of planting runs to 5,200 vines/ha (whereas the minimum required for generic Bordeaux is only 3,300), and the trellising has been raised to provide a leaf canopy of 5ft 3in (1.6m) to help maximize sunlight. Soil management is adapted to the individual parcel, grass cover used in the more vigorous zones, and the techniques of deleafing and green-harvesting applied. Yields average 45–50hl/ha.

Machine harvesters are used for picking the majority of the vineyard, but these are equipped with an *égreneur* for the removal of stalks and other green matter, as well as split-level bins that allow juice and moisture to drain through to a separate container. The grapes are sorted at the winery and vinified by parcel, a total of 100 available for the final blends. Each parcel is treated separately, and modern winemaking techniques such as cold-soaking, microoxygenation, selected yeasts, or lees stirring are used only when deemed appropriate.

FINEST WINES

Château Pey La Tour Réserve du Château

The Réserve is usually produced from up to 90% Merlot with an addition of Cabernet Sauvignon and Petit Verdot. The wine spends between 12 and 14 months in barrel. This is a wine for drinking over a period of three to ten years, ideally at about five to six. It's distinctly Bordeaux but with a modern, fruity edge and impressive depth of color. There's admirable consistency, but vintage variation inevitably has a say.

2004 When tasted in September 2009, this was drinking well. Deep, bright hue. Pleasant fruitiness to the nose, with a hint of spicy oak. The palate is supple but defined, with a leafy, red-fruit note and freshness on the finish.

2005★ Deep, dark color. The quality of the vintage definitely comes through here. The nose is riper, denser, and more complex, with dark-fruit (black currant, blackberry), spice and mineral notes. The palate is rich and *gourmand*, with a bigger tannic frame. For those who like a little more maturity, this can certainly stand some bottle age.

2006 Deep color again. Very close to the 2004 in style. The nose is fresh and fruity, the oak evident but well integrated. The palate is smooth and supple on the attack, with freshness on the finish. Red-fruit and mint notes. The tannins were still a little edgy when tasted in September 2009 but will settle down with another year in bottle.

Château Pey La Tour
Total area: 500 acres (200ha)
Area under vine: 500 acres (200ha)
Average production: grand vin (Réserve du Château) 400,000 bottles; second wine 700,000 bottles
Vins et Vignobles Dourthe
33370 Salleboeuf
Tel: +33 5 56 35 53 00
www.dourthe.com

St-Emilion

Located on the Right Bank of the Dordogne River, some 25 miles (40km) northeast of the city of Bordeaux, this region is centered on the attractive medieval town of St-Emilion. There are 13,600 acres (5,500ha) under production, spread through nine different communes, but St-Emilion itself is responsible for the lion's share of two-fifths. In 1999, the whole area was declared a World Heritage site by UNESCO. Two appellations share the same geographical delimitations— AOC St-Emilion and the superior AOC St-Emilion grand cru (stricter production controls), which is responsible for two-thirds of the output.

This is a red-wine region with one principal grape variety: Merlot (over 60 percent of plantings). The tradition, though, as in the rest of Bordeaux, is of a blended wine, and here Cabernet Franc (known locally as Bouchet) is Merlot's partner, adding aromatic complexity and freshness to Merlot's generous fruit. Cabernet Sauvignon plays a minor role (around 10 percent of plantings).

A single style of wine might have been expected, but owing, above all, to the different soil types, as well as to the proportion of Cabernet Franc in the blend and variations in winemaking practices, there is considerable divergence.

St-Emilion has an intricate mosaic of terroirs, with six principal zones: the limestone plateau, Côtes, *pieds de côtes*, Quaternary gravel, ancient sands, and the alluvial Dordogne plain. They all produce different styles of St-Emilion, and confirm their status as great or mediocre terroir by one indubitable fact: the aging potential of the wines. An estate may have vines in more than one terroir.

The limestone plateau consists mainly of fossilized marine life, the *calcaire à astéries* (starfish limestone). It covers the center of the region, running west to east from the town of St-Emilion to the commune of St-Etienne-de-Lisse. The clay-loamy topsoil is generally thin, sometimes no more than 50cm (20in), though there are areas of deeper red and brown clay. The style of wine is one of finesse, with a more limited but quality-oriented tannin, lithe fruit, cool freshness, and subtle aromas that gain in complexity with age. It is perhaps no surprise to find that a good number of St-Emilion's top growths (including Belair-Monange, Canon, Clos Fourtet, and Trottevieille) have vineyards on this terroir.

The Côtes around the plateau are composed of a deeper clay-limestone mix over a fine-textured loamy clay known as *molasse du Fronsadais*. These soils are poor but have a high water-retention capacity, allowing a slightly greater water uptake than the plateau above. The slopes to the south and west are steeper; those to the east, more broken in relief. Those with a southerly or southeasterly exposure have the greater benefit of aspect. The wines have fresh-fruit aromas and are more tannic in style and, again, long aging. Those with a strong Côtes profile include Ausone (but with a high proportion of Cabernet Franc) and Pavie.

The *pieds de côtes* can be divided into three sectors. At the foot of the hill, below the town of St-Emilion, lies a band of deep, sandy (siliceous) soil. The water supply is less restricted and the terroir not as favorable as the plateau or Côtes, but with efficient vineyard management (grass cover in the vineyard to absorb nitrogen and control vigor), successful results can be achieved (as at Canon-la-Gaffelière). Northeast of St-Christophe-des-Bardes, the clay and loam soils and northerly exposure provide a cooler, later-ripening site. South around St Etienne-de-Lisse, the better aspect ensures the harvest is usually a week earlier than in the northeast. The soils are clay and sandy silt and the wines fresher and a little less rustic.

The Quaternary gravel is in the northwest of the appellation, on the border with Pomerol, and principally concerns two estates—Cheval Blanc

Right: The Jurade of St-Emilion, atop the impressive tower that dominates the landscape of this picturesque medieval town

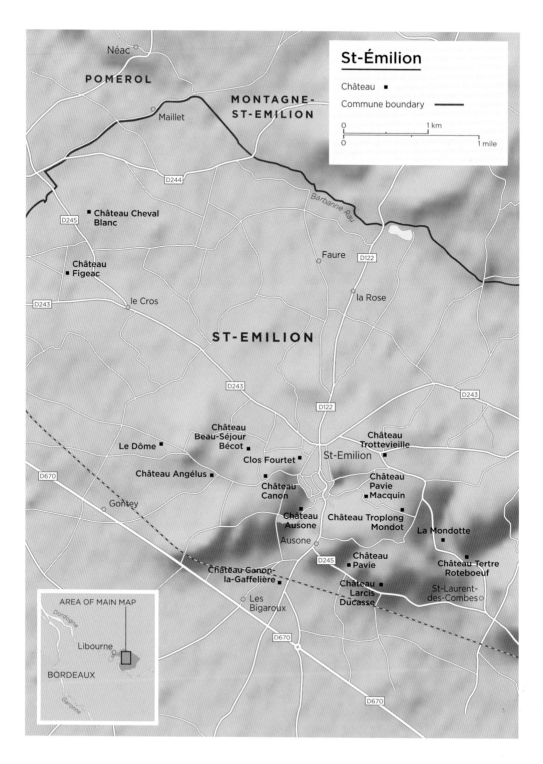

Néac

POMEROL

MONTAGNE-
ST-EMILION

Maillet

D244

D245

■ Château Cheval
Blanc

Barbanne Rau

Faure

D122

■ Château
Figeac

le Cros

la Rose

D243

ST-EMILION

D243

D243

D122

Château
Beau-Séjour
Bécot

Château
Trottevieille

Le Dôme ■

Clos Fourtet ■

St-Emilion

Château Angélus ■

Château
Pavie
Macquin

D670

Château
Canon

Château Troplong
Mondot

Gontey

Château
Ausone

La Mondotte

Ausone

Château Canon-
la-Gaffelière

D245

Château
Pavie

Château Tertre
Roteboeuf

Château
Larcis
Ducasse

St-Laurent-
des-Combes

Les
Bigaroux

AREA OF MAIN MAP

Dordogne

D670

Libourne

BORDEAUX

Garonne

D670

and Figeac. Gravelly soils from the Quaternary period, identical to those found in the Médoc, are located here in gently undulating ridges. These soils are the predilection of Cabernet, providing firm, tannic wines with a complex aromatic range. Figeac benefits most from these soils and, with a vineyard planted to one-third each of Cabernet Sauvignon, Cabernet Franc, and Merlot, produces wines that are more Médocain in style. Cheval Blanc, with 60 percent Cabernet Franc and 40 percent Merlot, is aromatically complex but has an opulence that makes it accessible earlier, the influence of clay in part of the vineyard also coming into play.

The ancient sands that cover a fair proportion of the northwest of the appellation are wind-blown sands devoid of any gravel. Water control is less efficient, and the wines are based more on a fine, fruity floral aroma and delicate structure. There are, however, areas within this zone where the clay content is greater, offering a little more density, structure, and longevity to the wines. This is generally the case for the majority of the wines with "Corbin" in the name.

The area between the *pieds de côtes* and the Dordogne River is generally poor viticultural land. The relief is flat, the land relatively fertile, the drainage poor, and the water table high. It needs a considerable amount of investment and astute vineyard management to achieve high standards, but it can be done, as Gérard Perse has proved at Château Monbousquet. For those with less exhaustive means but the will to curb vine vigor and excessive yields, a lighter-framed, fruit-driven wine can be produced on these soils. A vein of gravel follows the river from Vignonet to Libourne and, being better drained and warmer, offers the greatest potential in this zone.

As an indicator of quality (to a degree), St-Emilion has its own classification. The first edition appeared in 1955, exactly 100 years after that of the Médoc, but with the proviso that it should be revised every ten years by a reviewing committee. Twelve estates were nominated premier grand cru classé and 63 grand cru classé. An amendment in 1958 to the first growths lifted Ausone and Cheval Blanc to A status, the others designated B. Since then there have been official reviews in 1969, 1986, 1996, and 2006. Estates have been promoted and demoted, and in recent years the classification has certainly been a motivating force.

The problem is that financial considerations have become more acute—demotion leading to a drop in land prices and a crisis in confidence along the chain of distribution. There may also have been a change of ownership in the interim, the new owner paying the price for previous neglect—hence, the 2006 edition was challenged in court (on procedural grounds). After lengthy litigation, a compromise was finally achieved in 2009. The 1996 classification has been reinstated, so those demoted in 2006 still hold their place. Those promoted in 2006 have been allowed to keep their new ranking. This is the state of affairs until a new classification is announced in 2011, assuming a fresh set of rules can be agreed upon by then. There are presently, therefore, 15 premiers grands crus classés and 57 grands crus classés.

Winemaking trends have had a strong influence on wine style in St-Emilion. In the 1990s, Right Bank producers—including the so-called garagistes—were at the cutting edge of advances in viticulture and vinification in Bordeaux, all this leading to a darker, riper, richer style of wine. There were excesses, of course: a tendency to overripeness and extraction, and heavy use of oak. In the new millennium, this proclivity has somewhat settled down, but there's still divergence between the more "classical" styles and the bigger, bolder wines that represent "modern" St-Emilion. Overall, given the varying parameters, St-Emilion is riper and better made than in the past.

Ausone

In *Decanter*'s 2009 Bordeaux supplement, Château Ausone was voted one of the ten most improved châteaux of the previous decade. Given the lofty prices and pedigree of the property, this may have come as a surprise to some. But take a look at the changes instigated by owner/manager Alan Vauthier, as well as the present consistency of the wines, and the accolade is amply merited.

The tiny 17-acre (7ha) vineyard is located on the edge of the town of St-Emilion, partly on the shallow soils of the limestone plateau (25 percent) and partly on the clay-limestone *côtes*. This, coupled with an east-southeasterly exposure and protection from cool northerly winds, makes an exceptional terroir but one that needs nurturing and investment.

The name is taken from the Roman poet Ausonius, who is thought to have owned a villa on the site. Historically, the property was variously referred to as Château Ausone, Tour d'Ausone, Cru d'Ausone, and Cantenats (after the owner of the time) through the 16th to 18th centuries, before reverting to Château Ausone in the early 1800s. In 1892 the estate was inherited by Edouard Dubois, later Dubois-Challon when he married. He established Ausone's reputation as one of Bordeaux's finest and also acquired neighboring châteaux Belair (now owned by Etablissements Jean-Pierre Moueix and rebaptized Belair-Monange) and Moulin St-Georges.

Ausone passed to his children—Cécile Vauthier and Jean Dubois-Challon—and after the heyday of the 1920s, the château entered a less regular patch. This was offset by some notable vintages, namely the 1947, 1949, 1953, 1955, 1959, and 1964. During the period 1974 to 1996, Ausone was jointly owned by Jean Dubois-Challon's widow Heylette and the Vauthier family. Relations between the two sides were acrimonious, and little investment was made. Quality remained irregular, the high points being the 1982 and 1989 vintages.

This all changed in 1997, when the Vauthier family took full control of Ausone, and Alain Vauthier was given free rein to make the wines. A frank and thoughtful man, Vauthier had already been making wine at Ausone since the 1970s but under the restraints imposed by co-ownership. And, as he says, "To produce great wines, you need the liberty to make decisions without debate; otherwise, you'll always play safe."

The vineyard has been the focus of Vauthier's attention, and he has invested heavily to improve quality and consistency. A system of drainage has been installed and grass cover adopted to help with erosion and humidity. The retaining walls for terraces have been rebuilt, allowing Vauthier to recuperate tiny plots of land. Missing vines have been replaced, and nearly 2.5 acres (1ha) are planted at a density of 12,600 vines/ha (the rest of the vineyard is at 6,600 and 8,000 vines/ha). Ausone now has 55 percent Cabernet Franc, and Vauthier aims to take this to 65 percent over the next ten years using the estate's own selection.

The management is meticulous, with attention to every detail. Deleafing and green-harvesting are systematically carried out for aeration and to reduce yields down to an average of 30hl/ha. There's concern about the ecosystem—hence practices that run along organic and biodynamic lines. "We limit spraying, so we run a risk, but we now have the personnel and equipment to intervene rapidly when necessary," says Vauthier.

The procedure for harvesting has also changed considerably. Until 1995, itinerant workers were employed to harvest both Ausone and Belair, which made selective harvesting more difficult. Now Vauthier has a group of 70 pickers uniquely for the family properties he manages (Ausone, Moulin St-Georges, Simard, Fonbel). "It takes three

Right: Alain Vauthier has been a changed man, and Ausone a new wine, since he had the freedom to take risks from 1997 on

Above: An ancient name and exceptional terroir, the well-exposed, sheltered, clay-limestone *côtes* sloping down from the château

full days to harvest Ausone, but this is strung out over 15 days," explains Vauthier. The tailored approach is taken one step further with the use of tiny (6hl) refrigerated stainless-steel tanks to hold the fractionally picked grapes before transfer to larger fermentation vessels.

Investment has not been limited to the vineyard. The pillars of the 16th-century quarried limestone cellars have been strengthened and the ventilation improved. A 13th-century chapel has been restored, and renovation is under way on the 19th-century château that Vauthier hopes to inhabit one day.

In the cellars, a judicious blend of traditional and modern techniques is used for vinification. Oak vats, which have steadily been replaced and reduced in size to the present 54hl format, are the preferred recipients for the grapes. Following a cold pre-fermentation maceration, the alcoholic fermentation takes place using *remontage* and *délestage* for extraction. The total period of *cuvaison* is long—up to five weeks—so the press wine is never used in the grand vin. Since 1995 the malolactic fermentation has taken place in barrel, the wines aged in 100 percent new oak for up to 22 months.

Also in 1995 a second wine, Chapelle d'Ausone, was tentatively introduced, with the first vintage

Since the mid-1990s Ausone hasn't put a foot wrong, each vintage providing one of the wines of the year. The property has never looked better, and the succession appears assured with Alain Vauthier's daughter Pauline assuming a more important role

of any serious quantity being the 1997. It now represents about 25 percent of the production, a third selection equaling 5 percent (often the press wine) being sold in bulk to the *négoce*. Quantities of the grand vin have been considerably reduced since the 1980s—hence the confidential nature of the cru and lack of any attendant publicity.

Since the mid-1990s Ausone hasn't put a foot wrong, each vintage providing one of the wines of the year. Prices, too, have risen from below those of Cheval Blanc to well above during the same period. The property has never looked better, and the succession appears assured with Vauthier's daughter Pauline assuming a more important role.

oldest Ausone I have tasted is the 1964. In 2002 it was still vigorous and concentrated and holding up well. A vertical lineup at the same time showed the 1989★ to be powerful and intense—a real star. The 1988 was leaner and more austere, and the 1990 warm and *méridional* but less assertive than the 1989. The series 1992, 1993, and 1994 were disappointing and are probably best forgotten. The 1995 was sweet, supple, and generous. It appeared forward compared to the 1996, which had a minerally freshness and certain reserve. The 1997 was impressive for the vintage, when the new style began to show: deep color, attractive fruit, fine tannins, but not the intensity of a great year. The 1998★ was superb—rich, and powerful, with loads of extract and freshness and length on the finish. The 1999 was seductive, with ripe (almost overripe) fruit and a nuance of toasted oak that needed a bit more time to integrate.

1982 (30,000 bottles produced) Brick-red hue. Middling complexity on the nose, with leafy red-fruit and roasted notes. The palate is more impressive—still sweet, ripe, and round, but with fine tannins and freshness on the finish.

2000★ Still very young. Deep in color. An explosion of dark fruit on the nose, with spicy, sandalwood notes. Dense and firm on the palate, but with freshness and great length. Powerful and reserved.

2003 A big, powerful wine in a rich, extravagant style. Deep, black color. Full throttle on the nose, with dark fruit, spice, and chocolate notes. The palate is sweet, dense, and opulent, but with freshness on the finish. Tannins firm and assertive.

Chapelle d'Ausone

2001★ An elegant wine at the level of a classed growth. Plum, cherry, spice, and licorice aromas. Pure-fruited, with a minerally freshness and length. Lovely texture, the tannins firm but fine.

Left: Pauline Vauthier, who is gradually taking over from her father Alain as custodian of one of Bordeaux's greatest estates

FINEST WINES

Château Ausone

Reticent and reserved in youth, Ausone can initially be difficult to judge, but there's an ageless quality to the wine and a freshness and elegance that persist over time. Recent vintages have been charged and tense, with deeper color, complexity of aroma, dense ripe fruit, and dazzling texture. The

Château Ausone
Total area: 20 acres (8ha)
Area under vine: 17 acres (7ha)
Average production: grand vin 17,000 bottles; second wine 6,000 bottles
33330 St-Emilion
Tel: +33 5 57 24 24 57
www.chateau-ausone.fr

Cheval Blanc

This wine is something of an enigma, and perhaps that's its great appeal. Ripe, round, and fragrant in youth, Cheval Blanc has an accessibility and allure that's unexpected in a wine of this stature. And yet it has a considerable ability to age, gaining in complexity of aroma while retaining the hallmark traits of sweetness and opulence of texture balanced by a fine tannic frame. It really is a one-off—part St-Emilion, part Pomerol, perhaps a pinch of Margaux, the character defined by the terroir and the influence of Cabernet Franc.

Cheval Blanc really is a one-off—part St-Emilion, part Pomerol, perhaps a pinch of Margaux, the character defined by the terroir and the influence of Cabernet Franc

The property is located in the northwest corner of St-Emilion, a stone's throw from La Conseillante and L'Evangile in Pomerol. It was established in the 1830s by the owner of L'Evangile, a Monsieur Ducasse, with land purchased from Figeac and a few other parcels, including one from L'Evangile. By 1870 it had more or less acquired its present form, with an important system of drainage already in place. Ownership passed to the Fourcaud-Laussac family, proprietors until the purchase in 1998 by Bernard Arnault (who sold his share to LVMH in 2009) and Baron Albert Frère. Pierre Lurton remained as manager, having been engaged in 1991.

Under his volition, an analysis of the soils was undertaken in the early 1990s by Kees Van Leeuwen, technical director at the time and now viticultural consultant. The results revealed three distinct soil types: sandy clay over blue clay (the same as found at Pétrus), gravel, and sandy clay, representing 40, 40, and 20 percent of the surface area.

The surprise was the predominantly clay soils found in patches throughout the property.

Qualitatively they are the most regular, producing small, concentrated berries and wines with full, fleshy tannins similar to those in top Pomerol. The gravelly soils provide wines with a firm tannic edge and complex aromatic range, while wines from the sandy soils are usually deemed too light for the grand vin. The varietal characteristics are dominant for three or four years, but then the soil takes over.

The results of the soil studies led to a more thorough program of plot-by-plot management in relation to the grape varieties. Cabernet Franc, which represents 58 percent of plantings, has always been considered the grape variety at Cheval Blanc responsible for the wine's fragrance and finesse. It appears to have been planted here from as early as the late 19th century.

There are presently 20 acres (8ha) of Cabernet Franc that were planted pre-1956, the oldest dating from 1920. These old vines are the basis of a comprehensive program of replanting, the commercial clones being considered unsatisfactory. Since 2000, both Cabernet Franc and Merlot have been planted on the clay and gravel soils, and densities have increased to 7,700 vines/ha.

Overall, fine-tuning in the vineyard seems to have been taken up a notch in recent years, the competition exerted by Ausone (since 1995) and others exhorting greater efforts here. Denis Dubourdieu was brought in as a consultant in 2004 as a complement to Gilles Pauquet (consultant since 1985), and new vineyard manager Nicolas Corporandy, with ten years' experience at Château Laroque, was hired in 2006. There's been a fair amount of tweaking of viticultural techniques, such as pruning, deleafing, and the height of trellising, with a second green-harvest at the end of veraison also introduced. Evidently, this all paid off in 2008.

The vinification is as traditional as can be imagined—you won't see microoxygenation here.

Right: The discreet, partly secluded château at Cheval Blanc is fully in keeping with the enigmatic qualities of the wine

After sorting in the vineyard and cellars, the grapes are gravity-fed into cement vats. *Remontage* is used for extraction. In 2008 it was halted during the post-fermentation maceration for the first time. The malolactic fermentation takes place in tank and the wine is aged for 16–18 months in 100 percent new oak barrels, with racking every three months. The blend for the grand vin is ideally a 50/50 mix of Cabernet Franc and Merlot (as in 2006 and 2008) but is dictated by the year and can have a touch more Cabernet Franc (as in 2000 and 2004) or be predominantly Merlot (68 percent in 2001).

The second wine, Le Petit Cheval, was introduced in 1988 to allow a system of selection but now has its own standards to maintain. This means a third selection, roughly 10–25 percent of total production, which is sold to the négociants. Le Petit Cheval is also aged in new oak but for only 10–12 months.

There are plans for a new cuverie, which should be ready for the 2011 vintage. It will again be gravity-fed and equipped with concrete tanks, with a barrel cellar and storage space below ground. An environmentally conscious design will ensure that it blends in with the surrounding countryside.

FINEST WINES

Château Cheval Blanc

I have never tasted great old vintages of Cheval Blanc, but browsing the Sotheby's catalog for an auction of ex-château wines in 2009, it is fascinating to see the notes of Serena Sutcliffe MW, head of the international wine department. The overriding quality of the 1921 "is one of sweetness, almost liqueur-like." The 1929 was produced from a yield of 7.6hl/ha with 14.4% ABV and had "violet creams on the finish, with '29 silkiness." The 1947 is again 14.4% ABV and "something of a Bailey's cream of a wine!" The 1949 comes from a crop of 25hl/ha and has "unbelievable balance of fruit, acidity, and tannin." Yields were again tiny in 1961—only 11hl/ha—but the wine is "fabulously layered and firing on all cylinders."

Left: At once meticulous and mischievous, Pierre Lurton is responsible for both Cheval Blanc and Yquem

My only in-depth tasting took place at the château in 2001. The 1970s are not considered a great period for Cheval Blanc, and indeed I found the 1970 and 1971 tired and fading; 1978, a touch volatile but still with a nuance of soft fruit; 1979, fluid and evolved. The most interesting of the decade was the 1975, which had a complex nose of spice, jam, and tobacco, sweetness and volume on the palate, and a firm, cedary finish. Some 160,000 bottles of Cheval Blanc (more than twice the average today) were produced in 1982★ and it's still a sumptuous wine. The 1983, in contrast, was disappointing, with rather dry tannins. The 1985 was both complex and generous—a typical Cheval Blanc. The 1988 has high acidity, and it shows in the youthful color and freshness on the finish. Tasted again in 2009 (from magnum), there was still crispness on the finish and a good depth of fruit. The 1989 had the prune and raisin character of a hot year, with a touch of alcohol on the finish. The 1990★ was voluptuous and exotic—a real fruit bomb. The 1995 (Pierre Lurton's first "great" vintage) was again generous but polished and refined, with freshness on the finish.

1998 Rich, expressive nose of plum, chocolate, and spice. Round, opulent fruit on the palate. Firm on the finish, but attractive balance and freshness.

2001 Concentrated plum and cherry aromas with a hint of licorice. Generous fruit on the palate but tannins quite assertive. Lacks a little finesse.

2004 Leaner and linear in style. Violet and pepper notes on the nose. Medium-bodied, pronounced acidity providing a crisp finish.

2006 At an awkward stage. Deep purple color. Caramel, oak note on the nose. The attack is sweet, supple, and pure-fruited. Firm tannins bolstered by acidity. Greater depth and longevity than the 2004.

2008★ I've generally avoided using notes from en primeur tastings, but this struck me as a great Cheval Blanc. There's elegance, fragrance, opulence, and precision, as well as concealed power. Le Petit Cheval [V] is the finest I've tasted.

Château Cheval Blanc

Total area: 91 acres (37ha)
Area under vine: 84 acres (34ha)
Average production: grand vin 70,000 bottles; second wine 40,000 bottles
33330 St-Emilion
Tel: +33 5 57 55 55 55
www.chateau-chevalblanc.com

Tertre Roteboeuf

assionate, interrogative, and philosophical, François Mitjavile is the individualist who created Château Tertre Roteboeuf. A city boy originally, but with an ancestry linked to wine, he exchanged the role of businessman for vigneron in the hope of acquiring independence and a certain peace of mind. A two-year apprenticeship in the vineyard at Château Figeac gave him a basic grounding, and in 1978 he took over running 8.5-acre (3.5ha) Château du Tertre, as it was then known.

The property, which overlooks St-Laurent-des-Combes at the eastern end of St-Emilion's southern *côte*, was owned by his wife Miloute's family, who had used the 18th-century *chartreuse* as a vacation home. On the death of her father in 1961, the vineyard had been taken on by cousins at neighboring Château Bellefont-Belcier and the wine integrated into their label. Mitjavile had to restore the vineyard and relaunch the brand.

The potential of the terroir was never in any doubt. "Even a Parisian could see this was a grand terroir, but at the same time it's extremely fragile," says Mitjavile. The vineyard is in one block on the clay-limestone soils of the upper part of the *côte* and faces south-southeast. It's friable and therefore prone to erosion, and it is naturally free-draining to the point that it occasionally brushes with drought. "It's the most exotic terroir on the *côte sud*, so it can nudge fruit a long way down the road to confit while retaining freshness," Mitjavile adds.

He also realized that the property had to be run in a certain way. "Low production and high working costs meant an inexpensive wine was out of the question. I had to go for outstanding quality and sell expensively, or else go bankrupt," he explains. The quality factor would reside with the terroir and on viticultural perfection.

His work in the vineyard made him something of a groundbreaker at the time. Grass cover was—

Right: François Mitjavile in full flow at Tertre Roteboeuf, where he has succesfully realized his highly individual vision

Above: The favorably exposed but fragile sloping vineyard, the steepness of which exhausted the oxen, making them wheeze

and still is—used between the rows to curb vigor and halt erosion. With pruning, he dashed locally preconceived ideas by adopting the cordon rather than the traditional Guyot system. The vine is pruned low to the ground, approximately 9–12in (20–30cm) in height, to benefit from the heat of the soil, and the trellising is raised a further 4ft (1.3m) for an adequate leaf canopy and better photosynthesis.

The density of plantation is a fairly classical 5,555 vines/ha, "the best potential for this soil." Yields are low (20hl/ha in 2008; 34hl/ha in 2004), but Mitjavile doesn't green-harvest, performing only a little leaf removal, and is against the idea of overtly stressing the vine to achieve low yields. "I have low yields, but I'm not proud of it, since I have a very old vineyard with some virused vines (fan-leaf), which we're now in the process of rejuvenating," he says.

Late-harvesting was another characteristic for which he gained a reputation, but he likes to clarify his thinking on this crucial subject. "Some years, particularly the difficult ones, I harvest very late in order to have ripe tannins. But I never harvest as late as people think, because the Merlot [85 percent of the property] is all harvested in a single day, rather than over a spread of time."

There are two reasons for the late harvest: maturity of fruit and quality of tannin, the latter being one of his pet subjects. "I've always had a violent dislike of green, aggressive tannins. To me they are like a false musical note," he declares. What he wants is a loss of astringency and a *profondeur aromatique* in the tannins, which means harvesting at a knife-edge date when the grape skins are fragile but there's still opulence and freshness in the fruit.

Since the winemaking approach and the resulting wine style were so different under his ownership, Mitjavile believed that the estate needed a new name, hence the birth of Château Tertre Roteboeuf. Roteboeuf was one of the old *lieux-dits* at the property, so named for the belching, wheezing sound the oxen used to make when struggling up the slope with heavy loads. It was added as a suffix to distinguish the domaine from the other Tertres in St-Emilion and as a tiny snub to the status quo.

The changes in the vineyard occurred because Mitjavile already had an idea of the style of wine he wanted to make. He believes that the rather soft, easy-drinking wines of the 1970s were a style imposed by the négociants and oenologists of the time. What he wanted was a wine with more character, depth, and flavor. Viticultural practices changed, but so did the work in the cellars. "As early as 1979 I was arguing with the oenologist for an extension of the vatting time of up to three weeks to get more flavor," he says.

The 1982 was the first vintage to come close to his ideal, though today it seems a little rustic. It was aged in vat and 30 percent old barrels, because money was tight at the time. By 1985 (in Mitjavile's estimation, his first great wine), 50 percent new oak was being used; by 1986, 80 percent. Today, the figure is 100 percent.

Barrel maturation plays an important role in the style of the wine—and not just because of the 100 percent new oak content. Following a comparatively hot fermentation at 86–95°F (30–35°C) in cement tanks with classic *remontage*, the wine is aged for a lengthy period of up to 22 months in a fairly temperate cellar (no air conditioning) with regular aeration, initially by racking, then by microoxygenation. "The role of the winemaker is to place the wine in the bottle in a progressively evolving state in terms of flavor," he explains.

There's a risk factor working this way, because temperatures are high and acidities generally low (so, conducive to *Brettanomyces* and volatile acidity). The result, though, is a ruby-red color in youth (he is against the blue-black spectrum of modern St-Emilion and, by extension, pre-fermentation cold soaks) and a fairly exotic, sometimes Burgundian range of aromas and flavors. These characteristics, combined with an attractive opulence of fruit and a refined texture, make Tertre Roteboeuf extremely appealing in youth. Much to the surprise of some critics, however, the wines also age comfortably.

FINEST WINES

Château Tertre Roteboeuf

The following vertical held in 2008 gave ample demonstration of the luxurious nature of the great years, as well as the character of lighter vintages. Top vintages can age at least 20–25 years.

1981 (Aged in tank) Brick red. Typically Bordeaux in its expression. Leafy, tobacco notes but still some red fruit. Little complexity on the palate, but sweet, fresh, and quite refined. Drink up.

1982 (Aged in tank and old barrels) Mature, brick-edged hue. Still a red-fruit nuance but also more tertiary truffle notes. The palate is lively, fresh, and digestible, with a caress of fruit. The tannins are a touch robust, though, and the finish hard-edged.

1985 Deep red, bricking at the rim. An impressive wine for its age. A warm, ripe nose: very Merlot but still with a certain youthful zest. Soft and supple on the palate; mature but with an elegant frame.

1987 Brick-red hue. A savory, baked-earth aroma, still with a touch of fruit. The palate is round, fresh, and comforting but drying on the finish. Evidently past its best, but intriguing for the vintage.

1989★ Ruby color. Ripe, warm, and busy on the nose, with raisin, plum, and coffee-bean aromas. The palate is vigorous and meaty, with plum and currant notes. Amazing freshness for such a big wine. Strong, powerful tannins on the finish.

1990 Dark-red inner core, bricking at the rim. Rich, powerful, and heady on the nose. Notes of *sirop de cassis*, plum, licorice, and a hint of tobacco leaf. The palate is sweet, supple, and generous. Opulent weight and texture. Pure hedonism. But perhaps less staying power than the 1989?

1997 Ruby moving to brick at the rim. An attractive red-fruit and currant nose, with a gamey note. Still lively and fresh. Medium-bodied opulence on the silky-textured palate. A success for the vintage.

2001★ Ruby color. A lively, spicy nose. Burgundian in character. Sweet attack, round and caressing on the palate, with a lovely texture and filigree tannins. Opulence, power, and finesse.

Château Tertre Roteboeuf

Total area: 13.5 acres (5.5ha)
Area under vine: 13.5 acres (5.5ha)
Average production: 25,000 bottles
33330 St-Laurent-des-Combes
Fax: +33 5 57 74 42 11
www.tertre-roteboeuf.com

Angélus

Château Angélus is, in many ways, the symbol of modern St-Emilion. The wines are dark, rich, and concentrated. The brand is strong. Work practices in the vineyard and cellars have, since the 1980s, been cutting edge. And in 1996 progress was recompensed by promotion to premier grand cru classé—the first upgrading at this level since the inauguration of the classification in 1955.

The estate evolved throughout the 20th century. Maurice de Boüard inherited Château Mazerat in 1909. In 1921 he bought an adjacent plot of 7.5 acres (3ha) known locally as L'Angélus, because of the Angélus bell that tolled at three nearby churches. After World War II, the vineyards were amalgamated as Château L'Angélus (the "L" was dropped in 1990) by his sons Christian and Jacques. Other parcels were acquired, the largest being 7.5 acres on the *côte*, purchased in 1969 from what was then Beauséjour-Fagouet.

This was the estate Hubert de Boüard de Laforest took on when his father and uncle handed over management in 1985. De Boüard was born on the property, studied oenology at Bordeaux University in the 1970s, and returned to work at Angélus in 1980. He says his inspiration for what Angélus could achieve was the wines he'd tasted from the 1950s. "The 1960s and 1970s were not exceptional, but the 1953, 1955, and 1959 were great wines," he says.

The vineyard lies on St-Emilion's south-facing slopes, the vines tapering down from the upper reaches adjacent to Beau-Séjour Bécot and Beauséjour Héritiers Duffau-Lagarrosse. Here the clay-limestone soils are planted mainly to Merlot, the lower clay-sand-limestone to Cabernet Franc. "The warm, well-drained soils here are ideal for Cabernet Franc," says de Boüard. The variety is one of the characteristics of Angélus, with 47 percent in the vineyard and up to 56 percent in the blend. Some 25 acres (10ha) are more than 60 years old.

Right: Hubert de Boüard de Laforest, whose ambition and determination have taken Angélus into St-Emilion's top flight

Château Angélus is, in many ways, the symbol of modern St-Emilion. In 1996, progress was recompensed by promotion to premier grand cru classé—the first upgrading at this level since the inauguration of the classification in 1955

Angélus's metamorphosis started with changes in the vineyard. De Boüard was one of the first to use innovative practices and by the late 1980s had cut the use of chemical fertilizers, introduced grass cover in certain parcels, increased the leaf canopy, and was green-harvesting to control yields. "The work started to pay dividends from 1990 onward, but I think the vineyard reached a complete state of balance from 1995," he says. Late harvesting and ripeness have always been features. Cabernet Franc, de Boüard reckons, can never be picked too ripe, but Merlot becomes heavy and unrefined if a certain ripeness is exceeded. He now admits that the 1990 could have been even better if the Merlot had been picked a little earlier.

The empirical formula used in the vineyards is duplicated in the cellars. Everything has been tried and tested, and various winemaking options are left open—as can be seen from the selection of oak, stainless-steel, and concrete vats. The sorting process is meticulous, the grapes conveyor-fed to the tanks, where they are crushed before entry. A cold pre-fermentation maceration at 46°F (8°C), *pigeage*, *remontage*, and *délestage* are all possible extraction techniques. Microoxygenation can be used *sous marc* but not *cliquage*, which de Boüard considers a dangerous practice. Concentration by reverse osmosis was trialed during the 1993, 1994, and 1995 vintages but has not been used since.

The wine goes into barrel as early as possible— a technique de Boüard witnessed at Domaine des Comtes Lafon in Burgundy in the early 1980s, along with aging on fine lees. The latter, he feels, gives the wine its color, richness, and complexity of aroma. Only new oak barrels are used for Angélus, the wine spending eight months on lees before the first racking, the total maturation lasting 18–22 months.

Angélus is a very modern take on St-Emilion. There's a power and concentration that some will find excessive, but equally there's a precision and intensity that are undeniably impressive.

FINEST WINES

Château Angélus

I tasted two old vintages—1966 and 1976—at the property in 2001 and found them both well past their best. The 1985 showed well, still with expressive fruit on the palate. The 1990 was a very ripe, exotic wine with plum, currant, and confit-fruit notes to the fore. Tasted again in 2009 from a double magnum it was still dense, powerful, and decadent. The 1992 (an appalling year generally but a success for Angélus) showed the benefits of the work that had been done in the vineyard but is probably at its limit now. I was less impressed with the 1993 and 1994 but found the 1995 creamy and luxurious with a richness of fruit. The 1996 is made of sterner stuff, with a firm tannic frame, minerality, and Cabernet expression of dark fruit, spice, and mint.

A follow-up tasting in 2004 provided notes on later vintages. The 1998★ is Merlot-led, with plum and truffle notes, delicious fruit, and a zesty freshness. Angélus was hit by hail in 1999 and harvested 8–10 days earlier than planned. The result was a more brambly fruit aroma but decent concentration and slightly more angular tannins. The 2000 had the Angélus power and concentration but with harmony and balance. It is the epitome of the Angélus style. The 2001 had more plum and fig character, rich concentration, and supple texture.

2000★ Dark color. Rich, dark-fruit, spice, and cigar-box nose. Dense and concentrated on the palate but with freshness and persistence. Powerful tannic frame. Still in need of bottle age.

2001 Deep color. Rich and full but more accessible than the 2000. Plum and fig notes. Palate smooth and round. Firm, grainy tannins.

2004★ Purple-black color. A mix of power and charm. Fragrant, zesty nose of spice and dark fruit. Lovely texture, with a perfect pitch of fruit, balancing freshness, and firmness on the finish.

Château Angélus

Total area: 81.5 acres (33ha)
Area under vine: 80 acres (32ha), of which 58 acres (23.5ha) are premier grand cru classé
Average production: grand vin 90,000 bottles; second wine 20,000 bottles
33330 St-Emilion
Tel: +33 5 57 24 71 39
www.chateau-angelus.com

Beau-Séjour Bécot

Located on the *calcaire à astéries* of the St-Martin de Mazerat plateau, just to the west of the town, Château Beau-Séjour Bécot is the quintessential St-Emilion limestone-plateau estate. Merlot is the dominant grape variety on the 40-acre (16ha) vineyard, and the wines are imbued with the hallmark freshness, length, and structure that predispose them to long aging.

There's every probability that the vine was cultivated on the present site of Beau-Séjour Bécot as far back as Gallo-Roman times. In a corner of the property there are fissures in the limestone bedrock that suggest a certain type of cultivation as far back as the 3rd century AD. Certainly by the Middle Ages the monks of St-Martin de Mazerat and St-Emilion were tending parcels of vines in the vicinity.

Château Beau-Séjour Bécot is the quintessential St-Emilion limestone-plateau estate. The wines are imbued with a hallmark freshness, length, and structure

In the 18th century the property was owned by the Carles de Figeac family, the name Beauséjour acquired in 1787. Thereafter, it was whittled down in size. In 1849, 17 acres (7ha) were acquired by Pierre-Paulin Ducarpe, whose daughter was married to Dr. Duffau-Lagarrosse. This is the present Château Beauséjour Héritiers Duffau-Lagarrosse. The rest of the original Beauséjour estate was bought by another doctor, Jean Fagouet, in 1924. He extended the vineyard to the 26 acres (10.5ha) that was classified as Château Beauséjour-Fagouet in 1969.

The same year, the property was sold to Michel Bécot. The Bécots' history as vignerons in the region dates back to 1760. Since 1929 they had owned Château La Carte, an 11-acre (4.5ha) vineyard contiguous to Château Beauséjour-Fagouet, which in 1947 had been passed on to Michel.

The two estates were exploited separately, but in 1979 Michel Bécot, now assisted by his sons Gérard and Dominique, acquired another adjacent plateau property—4.5ha Les Trois Moulins—and a decision was made to amalgamate the three properties under one name: Château Beau-Séjour Bécot.

The merger was unauthorized, however, and the consequence was demotion to grand cru classé in 1986. Gérard and Dominique Bécot took over the running of the property and worked toward reclassification to premier grand cru classé, which they obtained in 1996.

The soils at Beau-Séjour Bécot are poor, a topsoil of 12–16in (30–40cm) all that covers the limestone bedrock. Below ground, quarried galleries run through 25 acres (10ha) of the total 46 acres (18.5ha) of the property. Elsewhere, it is solid limestone, the rock occasionally, as in one south-facing parcel, permitting the vine a slightly deeper rooting, down to 27in (70cm).

The vineyard is planted to 70 percent Merlot, 24 percent Cabernet Franc, and 6 percent Cabernet Sauvignon, the final blend usually a little heavier in Merlot, since the Cabernet does not always reach perfect ripeness. A second wine exists, Tournelle de Beau-Séjour Bécot, but as an indicator of the homogenous nature of the terroir, it represents a small proportion of the production and is not produced every year; the most recent vintages are 2001 and 2006.

Stylistically, Beau-Séjour Bécot manages a successful compromise between old and new. The young wines are dark-hued, rich, ripe, and oaky but never to the extreme of, say, Angélus or Troplong Mondot. Acidity and freshness are apparent whatever the vintage, and the tannic structure is firm. A minimum of eight years in bottle before drinking is advisable. Older vintages perhaps lack a little finesse, but the quality of texture and purity of fruit have gradually been improved and, from 2001 onward, seem on the mark.

Gérard Bécot puts much of this down to the gradual control of yields and perfection of the harvest. "In the 1970s, yields were not controlled and ripeness was wayward. In the 1980s and early 1990s, we were on a learning curve, bringing yields down to 40hl/ha. From 1998 we've been at 30–35hl/ha, and at this level it's easier to obtain a perfect pitch of ripeness. We also have a greater understanding of each parcel, and from 2001 we have been harvesting with more precision over a longer period of time. It's logistically difficult but worth it in the long term."

FINEST WINES

Château Beau-Séjour Bécot

The following tasting took place in October 2007.

1988 Mature, brick-edged hue. Medium to full-bodied, with the freshness and fruit characteristic of this cru. Evolved, leathery, red-fruit aroma, with a touch of undergrowth. The palate is round and supple, still with a good volume of fruit.

1989★ The standout wine of the series. Still youthful and well within itself. Exudes power, depth, and complexity, but there's elegance as well. Good, deep, garnet hue. Subtle, dark-fruit and spice aromas. The palate is dense, firm, and tight-knit. Wonderful length and freshness on the finish.

1990 Red, with a touch of brick at the rim. Ripe and generous in style. Open, aromatic, and drinking well. Plum, truffle, and gamey notes. Very expressive. Sweet, round, and warm on the palate. Quite hedonistic. Seemingly at its optimum.

1995 A ripe vintage that is beginning to open out. Combines attractive fruit with the fresh, minerally notes typical of this terroir. The palate is lively and complex, with a generous volume of fruit. Still with line and length and grip on the finish.

1996 Garnet color. Austere in form and fragrance. A little dark-fruit character on the nose but relatively inexpressive. Red fruit with a leafy, *sous-bois* note on the palate. Linear and quite strict in style, with grainy tannins. Maturity slightly compromised.

1998★ Superb generosity of fruit; Merlot at a perfect pitch. Fleshy but well structured, with ripe but robust tannins and a line of acidity on the

Left: Gérard Bécot, whose efforts helped secure restoration to premier grand cru classé status in 1996, with daughter Juliette

finish. The fruit makes it quite alluring, but this is for the long haul.

1999 Harvested on September 6 after a hailstorm. Starts promisingly, with a spicy, red-fruit fragrance and soft attack, but the finish is edgy, the tannins rather tough and foursquare.

2000 Deep, bright crimson hue. There's a rich concentration of fruit, but the spicy oak still dominates on both nose and palate. Round, smooth texture, a certain tannic grip, and acidity on the finish. All the components are there, but it's a little disjointed at present.

2001 Ample, generous wine with freshness and length. The fruit provides plenty of charm already, but there's a fine, firm tannic structure for aging.

2003 A wine of instant charm, complete with the balance so often lacking in this vintage. It oozes fruit on both nose and palate. Almost *liqueur de framboise*. Soft-textured, but there's grip and freshness on the finish to lift the palate.

2004 Clearly less volume than the 2005, but clean cut and precise. Has substance, though, in a "classic" way. Attractive fruit; fine, crisp tannins. Quite a graceful form and line.

2005★ Dark, dense color. Beautiful ripeness on the nose. Compote of red fruits, but complexity as well. Pure and *racé* on the palate. Fine-textured, with a powerful tannic frame. Superb balance and length. A wine that vibrates. A great Beau-Séjour.

SAINT-ÉMILION GRAND CRU

APPELLATION SAINT-ÉMILION GRAND CRU CONTRÔLÉE

Château Beau-Séjour Bécot
Total area: 46 acres (18.5ha)
Area under vine: 40 acres (16ha)
Average production: 65,000 bottles
33330 St-Emilion
Tel: +33 5 57 74 46 87
Fax: +33 5 57 24 66 88
www.beausejour-becot.com

Canon

Château Canon has been a work in progress since 1996. Such was the investment needed when the Wertheimers—owners of Chanel and Château Rauzan-Ségla in Margaux—bought the property in that year, that improvement was unlikely to happen overnight. The site on the limestone plateau just outside the town's walls, though, is exceptional, and much of the restructuring has now been completed. Since 2003, the wines have clearer definition, and quality and consistency have reached the level required.

The property takes its name from Jacques Kanon, an officer in the French navy who bought the estate in 1760. His successor, Raymond Fontémoing, was a Libourne négociant, and it was during this family's ownership that the name was changed from Domaine de St-Martin to Château Canon. The Fournier family owned the property from 1919 until the sale to the Wertheimers. During this period some memorable wines were made, latterly in the 1980s, but the issue of succession forced the sale.

The Wertheimers appeared to have bought a jewel, but there were several major problems that required urgent resolution, all with a considerable cost attached. John Kolasa, who was already managing Rauzan-Ségla, took over the estate's day-to-day running, and restoration began. Among the most pressing problems was the condition of the tunnels and quarries beneath the property, which were in danger of collapse. Two years were spent consolidating pillars and injecting concrete into the hollows to shore all this up.

The vineyard was also in a terrible condition. There had been no ongoing replanting schedule for a number of years. The old vines were ridden with viruses, and the soils infested with root rot (tree roots left in the ground from which bugs and bacteria migrate). A massive replanting program was launched, and at the time of writing, nearly

Right: The massive investment in Canon's vineyards since 1996 has been crucial in the gradual realization of its full potential

The philosophy of the owners—the Wertheimers—and manager John Kolasa, enhanced by the terroir, is to have elegance and finesse in the wine, and since at least 2003 they have managed to do just that

50 percent of the vineyard had been replanted. Kolasa says the program could have been even more radical, had the appellation laws allowed it. "We could have ripped out the whole vineyard in one go, but the St-Emilion classification stipulates no more than 30 percent young vines in the wines," he says.

The replanting has allowed densities to be increased from 5,600 to 7,000 vines/ha and the trellising to be improved. In 2000, Kolasa bought Château Curé Bon, a tiny grand cru classé next to Canon, and with the blessing of INAO integrated 8.5 acres (3.5ha) into the Canon estate. This has allowed a reasonable level of production with a proportion of older vines while the replanting has been going on. The average age of the vineyard was 25 years at the time of writing.

The winery was not exempt from difficulties, either. There was TCA (2,4,6-trichloroanisole) contamination in the cellars, which meant that, in November 1996, the winery had to begin the thankless task of removing every piece of wood from the winery before sand-blasting the walls and completely overhauling the ventilation system. The hard work was evidently worthwhile, because since 1997 all of the wines have been clean.

A system for gravity-feeding the grapes into the tanks was inaugurated with the 2002 vintage, as was an improved process of sorting and selection. Stainless-steel fermentation tanks were phased in from 2004, and Canon has been fully equipped with these since 2006. Winemaking is traditional, the grand vin aged in 50–80 percent new oak barrels for 14–17 months, with conventional racking.

The difficulties of the early 1990s and the work initiated since have meant a rocky period for Canon, during which the style of the wine was somewhat ill defined. But this is now very much in the past. The philosophy of the Wertheimers and John Kolasa, enhanced by the terroir, is to have elegance and finesse in the wine, and since at least 2003 they have managed to do just that.

FINEST WINES

Château Canon

Vineyard plantings are presently 80 percent Merlot and 20 percent Cabernet Franc, but John Kolasa hopes to boost the Cabernet Franc to 30 percent over time. Indeed, the 2008 already has 25 percent of this grape variety in the blend. A vertical tasting in October 2006 gave some idea of the progress that has been made during the Wertheimer era. I found the 1996 to be underripe and austere, and the 1997 brick-colored, soft, fluid, and at its limit. The 1998 seems to be the most successful wine of the 1990s, having complexity of aroma and depth of fruit. The 1999 is leaner and, again, austere, with tannins a touch foursquare. The 2000 is a more powerful, robust wine. There's clearly greater depth, but the textural elegance is not quite there. The 2001 has a leafy note but is soft and balanced. The 2002 is light and fresh but a touch vegetal. The 2003 is forward with a plummy note, but the texture is fine and there is freshness for the vintage. The 2004 is not a big wine but is elegant and harmonious. The 2005 is rich and ripe but refined. It's clearly the best to date—or was until the precise, streamlined 2008★. If the bottled version matches the en primeur sample, it will be a superb wine.

1998 Garnet hue. Quite complex mineral, red-fruit, and spice nose. The palate is supple, round, and generous. There is good depth of fruit and a fresh, harmonious finish. Powerful but refined.

2001 Red color. An elegant, red-fruit nose with a leafy hint. The palate is soft and round, but the finish fresh, with perhaps even a hint of green. Accessible now.

2004★ Ruby color. This is the epitome of Canon in a lighter year. Delicately fragrant, with spice and red-fruit notes on the nose. It is not big on the palate but is harmonious, ripe, and supple, with fine tannins.

Château Canon

Total area: 54.5 acres (22ha)
Area under vine: 48 acres (19.5ha)
Production: grand vin 36,000–45,000 bottles; second wine 30,000–40,000 bottles
BP22, 33330 St-Emilion
Tel: +33 5 57 55 23 45
www.chateau-canon.com

Pavie

If there's a wine and a personality that court controversy in Bordeaux, then they have to be Château Pavie and owner Gérard Perse. The full-on, concentrated style of Pavie attracts admiration from some and dismay from others, while Perse's perceived arrogance can ruffle feathers. Ten years on from Perse's acquisition of the estate in 1998, I'd say the wines are definitely powerful, occasionally excessive, but with a touch more charm in recent years. As to Perse's prickly character: it can in part be linked to his perpetual search for perfection. "Pavie is a great wine, but it's still not the Pavie I want to make," he told me while I was researching this book.

One thing is for certain and that is that Château Pavie has a magnificent terroir. Everyone in St-Emilion agrees. The property is large, at 100 acres (40ha), the vineyard spread over three zones. At the highest point, 37 acres (15ha) are planted on the clay-limestone plateau. The soils are thin, and because the topography twists and turns, the exposures are east and west. The vineyards below on the *côte* have a southerly exposure and a greater proportion of clay. Finally, at the foot of the slope there is an area of sandy clay.

A self-made man with a fortune gained from supermarkets, Perse already owned Château Monbousquet (1993) when he heard Pavie was for sale. "I didn't hesitate for a second. I saw the bankers and owners and made the decision in 24 hours," he recounts. A conflict of interest among the owning Valette family prompted the sale. Vintages in the 1960s and 1970s had been poor, and although there had been improvement in the 1980s, there was still plenty of scope for change.

In the vineyard, up to 25 percent of the vines were missing. This triggered an enormous program of replanting and trellising, which is still ongoing today. The proportion of Cabernet has been lifted to today's field planting of 30 percent Cabernet Franc, 10 percent Cabernet Sauvignon, and 60 percent

Above: The proud sign on what is universally recognized as a superb terroir, here the clay-rich south-facing slopes

Merlot. "I'm ultimately aiming for a 50/50 Cabernet/ Merlot split to add more finesse," says Perse.

In 2001, Château Pavie's surface area was modified with the blessing of INAO. Perse also owned neighboring châteaux La Clusière (6 acres [2.5ha]) and Pavie Decesse (22 acres [9ha]), respectively on the *côte* and plateau, and permission was granted to integrate the entire vineyard of the former and 16 acres (6.5ha) of the latter into Château Pavie. As compensation, 15 acres (6ha) of Pavie on sandier soils lower down in the *lieu-dit* Simard were declassified from the cru. The new configuration took form for the 2002 vintage.

Pavie is a late-ripening site, says Perse, and low yields are obligatory for the ripeness he wants to achieve. Deleafing and green-harvesting—

techniques he first used at Monbousquet—are systematic, and the yields are held to around 30hl/ha. The concentration is something Perse defends. "The great wines of Bordeaux are those that, above all, have the potential for long aging, and for that you need richness and substance in the bottle. I've tasted 1929 Pavie, which is unimaginably good, and my dream is that wines like the 2005 will also have the same splendor in 60 years' time."

The winemaking facilities were not to his taste, so changes were made from the outset. A new *cuvier* replaced the old one built in 1923, and 20 new temperature-controlled oak vats replaced the 300hl concrete tanks. The input of so much new oak at once has, I think, marked the inaugural 1998 vintage, which now appears extracted and dry. The old barrel cellar, quarried and built into the limestone slope, was considered too cold and humid, so was abandoned for a new cellar built next to the *cuvier*.

Winemaking techniques are on the modern side. After sorting and selection, the grapes are gravity-fed into oak vats, and if necessary, the juice is bled for further concentration. There's a pre-fermentation cold soak, while *pigeage* and *remontage* are used for extraction. The wine then goes straight into new oak barrels for the malolactic fermentation and aging on lees, with racking every three to five months. The total period of maturation ranges from 18 to 24 months.

Perse does little in moderation, and his next project, unveiled on my most recent visit, is for a new winery complex to be completed in 2012. The design includes a 21,200-sq-ft (600-sq-m) function room overlooking the vines, a tasting room, and additional cellars and storage space, all linked to the existing winery buildings. It is ambitious but inevitably contentious, so the responses are again likely to be mixed.

Left: Perfectionist Gérard Perse, who is sparing no expense to produce wines worthy of the greatest Pavies of the past

FINEST WINES

Château Pavie

Pavie's present blend is roughly 70% Merlot, 20% Cabernet Franc, and 10% Cabernet Sauvignon. I tasted all of the vintages from 1998 onward in Paris in March 2009 and felt the winemaking to be more discerning from the 2005 vintage. The 1998 appeared overextracted and marked by the oak. (As already mentioned, the use of 20 brand-new oak vats for fermentation probably accounts for this.) The 1999 was evolving and sweet but with some leafy notes—the reflection of a difficult year. The 2000 is a massive wine, sweet but firm and on the cusp of *surmaturité*. Apparent low acidity enhances the feeling of weight and mass. The 2001 was also very ripe and full, with plum and chocolate notes and a powerful tannic frame. The 2002 was lighter, with supple texture and red-fruit notes; the 2003, supple, round, and sweet, with less complexity, and tannins that were a little pinched on the finish. The 2004 was rich and textured but marked by the oak. The 2005★ is a great wine, complex, textured, and with endless depth. It also has wonderful balance. The 2006 was rich and structured but austere for the moment. The 2007★ is delicate for Pavie, more forward in style but fragrant and harmonious. A barrel sample of the 2008 showed power and depth of fruit, but balance and length as well.

1998 Ruby color. Muscular, with heavy extraction and marked by the oak. Drying on the finish.
2001 A big, broad-shouldered wine. Very ripe on the nose, with notes of damson and chocolate. Rich, full, and firm on the palate, with a powerful tannic frame.
2006 Dark crimson-purple color. A complex, spicy, dark-fruit nose. Rich, full extract, with fresh acidity behind. Powerfully structured and a touch austere. For long aging.

Château Pavie
Total area: 100 acres (40ha)
Area under vine: 91 acres (37ha)
Production: grand vin 80,000–96,000 bottles; second wine 35,000–50,000 bottles
33330 St-Emilion
Tel: +33 5 57 55 43 43
www.vignoblesperse.com

Troplong Mondot

Christine Valette achieved her goal in 2006, with the promotion of Château Troplong Mondot to St-Emilion premier grand cru classé. It had taken 26 years for the consecration, during which time she instigated a revolution in the quality and style of the wine.

The property stands at the highest point in St-Emilion, clearly visible from a distance, due to the rather ugly white water tower (owned by the local municipality) that looms over the attractive 18th-century château. The surface area of the vineyard—81.5 acres (33ha)—has remained the same since its creation in the 1850s by Raymond Troplong, owner of Mondot at the time. His nephew and successor Edouard added the name Troplong. In 1921, the property was acquired by Belgian merchant Georges Thienpont, who sold it on during the 1930s to Valette's great-grandfather, Alexandre.

Thrown in at the deep end in 1980 at a tender age, Valette took the advice of Michel Rolland, already consultant oenologist, who persuaded her that Troplong Mondot could aspire to greater heights. The vineyard lies on the clay-limestone plateau, with heavy clay in certain zones and thinner soils closer to neighboring Château Trottevieille. It's a late-ripening terroir, and one of the first decisions was to harvest later, riper, and with lower yields. This policy continues. The starting date for the Merlot in 2008 was October 9, and the average yield is 34hl/ha. The other significant change was the introduction of a second wine in 1985. "It was a rational upheaval, since it meant admitting there was variation in quality within the estate," says Valette.

Her husband, Xavier Pariente, joined in the running of the property from 1990, and the fine-tuning continued. The style of the new Troplong Mondot was now apparent: deep in color, rich, concentrated, powerful, structured, awkward in youth, and in need of bottle age.

Right: Christine Valette and husband Xavier Pariente, who won premier grand cru classé status for Troplong Mondot in 2006

Christine Valette achieved her goal in 2006, with the promotion of Troplong Mondot to St-Emilion premier grand cru classé. It had taken 26 years for the consecration, during which time she instigated a revolution in the quality and style of the wine

There are still some old parcels of vines dating from 1926, 1947, and 1948, but today the vineyard has an average age of 35 years following steady replanting in the 1990s and 2000s. This is an ongoing operation—hence the present area under vine totals only 54.5 acres (22ha). Merlot is by far the dominant variety, with 90 percent of the field plantings and often the same proportion in the final blend. There is a further 5 percent each of Cabernet Franc and Cabernet Sauvignon. "A parcel of Merlot near Trottevieille is to be grafted with Cabernet Franc in 2010, but we don't want the Cabernet element in the blend ever to surpass 15 percent," says Parente.

Investment in the cellars has also been ongoing, with the cuverie updated and modernized in 1990 and 2008 (new stainless-steel vats and a room for the malolactic fermentation) and a new barrel cellar in 2003. The winemaking (under the direction of cellar master Jean-Pierre Taleyson since the early 1980s) can resort to modern techniques like cold pre-fermentation maceration or microoxygenation *sous marc*, but nothing is systematic. Malolactic fermentation is in barrel and the wines aged 14–22 months in 75–100 percent new oak barrels with traditional racking when deemed necessary.

FINEST WINES

Château Troplong Mondot
The wines are certainly rich and powerful, but with a balancing freshness, thanks to the terroir, and greater purity of fruit from 2000. Top vintages are truly majestic. A vertical tasting in September 2006 gave some indication of the progress to date. I found the 1985 fresh and long but aromatically dull, perhaps a touch oxidized. The new style hadn't quite kicked in. The 1989 was rich and very ripe, the low acidity making it sweet and opulent but heavy. The 1998★ was superb, powerful, but poised; the 1999, less distinguished, with slightly angular tannins. The 2000 was big and brooding, with a mass of fruit and powerful tannic frame; the 2001 was also rich and firm but with a touch more charm. 2002 was admirable for the year, supple and spicy; the 2003, chunkier, broad, and round, with grainier tannins but freshness on the finish. The 2004 appeared to have a more gentle charm. A barrel sample of the 2008★ tasted in 2009 revealed a potentially stunning wine, dark, rich, and exotic, with beautiful balance.

1995 Dark inner core, with a touch of brick at the rim. An attractive nose with cedar, confit fruit, and mineral notes. The palate is rich but balanced, the tannins fine but firm, with freshness on the finish. Very complete.

2003 Ruby-red color. More *méridional* in style, with plum and currant notes. The palate is round and supple, simpler than the 1995 but in balance. Grainy tannins on the finish.

2005★ Rich, full, and powerful, with huge reserve. A firm tannic frame, so still in its shell at present. Dark fruit, and spicy oak notes on the finish.

2006 Dense, tight, and restrained. Again plenty of reserve, the opulent texture followed by firmness and length. Acidity heightens the minerally freshness on the finish.

Left: While there has been a revolution in the quality of the wine, much at the 18th-century château remains unchanged

Château Troplong Mondot
Total area: 81.5 acres (33ha)
Area under vine: 54.5 acres (22ha)
Production: grand vin 65,000–80,000 bottles; second wine 10,000–30,000 bottles
33330 St-Emilion
Tel: +33 5 57 55 32 05
www.chateau-troplong-mondot.com

Valandraud

I don't suppose there will ever be a monument to Jean-Luc Thunevin, but his place in the annals of St-Emilion is guaranteed. With a desire to make the best wine possible with limited resources and from vines in a less distinguished site, he unwittingly launched the garage movement in 1991. Little did he realize the ferment in Bordeaux that this would cause, that 20 years on he'd be the owner of 25 acres (10ha) in St-Emilion, or that Valandraud would be such a celebrated but controversial name.

A sometime *bistrotier*, disc jockey, and bank clerk, the Algerian-born Thunevin found his calling in St-Emilion in the mid-1980s. A négociant business that he still runs with great gusto became the cornerstone, enabling him and wife Murielle (very much part of the success story) to buy a parcel of

Thunevin's place in the annals of St-Emilion is guaranteed. With a desire to make the best wine possible with limited resources, he unwittingly launched the garage movement

1.5 acres (0.6ha) in a small valley close to the town of St-Emilion and another 3 acres (1.2ha) on the plain at St-Sulpice-de-Faleyrans. "We had a couple of plots of Merlot, limited finance, and virtually no equipment but wanted to make a stunning wine in a modern style, with wines like Le Pin, Tertre Roteboeuf, and Haut-Marbuzet as our reference," says Thunevin.

Only 1,280 bottles of Valandraud (the name is an amalgam of "val" for *vallon* and Murielle's maiden name Andraud) were produced the first year. Frost had ravaged the vineyard, and Thunevin green-harvested to select the best of what remained. The wine was made in a tiny garage, latterly a tradesman's workshop, abutting their house in St-Emilion. Destemming was carried out by hand, since they didn't have a destemmer, and *pigeage* was employed during fermentation because there was no pump

for pumping over. Money was spent, however, on a handful of new oak barrels for the malolactic fermentation (innovative at the time) and aging. The garage wine was born.

The volume increased to 4,500 bottles in 1992, with a further 12,000 bottles of a second wine, Virginie de Valandraud, named after his daughter. It was a terrible vintage with excessive rain, but the Thunevins spent long hours deleafing for aeration and crop-thinning to reduce the yield to 30hl/ha. The result was one of the few good wines made that year, and it was well received by critics. The focus on Valandraud intensified further when Thunevin released it on the Place de Bordeaux at the same price as Lafite, Margaux, and Mouton Rothschild.

The wine, the winemaking techniques, the price, the sheer bravado—all had ramifications throughout Bordeaux in the coming years. Other garage wines appeared on the scene. Speculation entered the equation as the price of Valandraud outstripped that of the Médoc first growths in the run-up to 2000. The Bordeaux establishment groaned. Others praised the Thunevins' methods and audacity and started to review viticultural and winemaking practices at their own domaines. "He woke us up and helped revolutionize Bordeaux," said Jean-Michel Cazes of Lynch-Bages in 2007.

The wine itself has always divided opinion: it's just too much for some, but for others it's a bravura display of modern ripeness and depth. Thunevin's personal penchant is for a rich, dense, opulent style, and there's an element of this in most vintages. But the wine has evolved away from one-dimensional concentration. The 1995 was produced mainly from a parcel he had purchased on gravelly soil and includes a proportion of Cabernet Franc. In 2007 it showed freshness, balance, and supple texture. With the 1998, Valandraud really stepped up a grade. As well as power and concentration, there's the racy edge of complexity that one expects from a grand vin. The wines are firmly structured and age well.

The Thunevin operation today is light-years away from the artisanal structure of 1991. There are now 60 acres (24ha) dotted around the appellation and three sites for vinification. The different plots provide different options according to the year, but with an eye to eventual classification, Valandraud is now generally made from selected parcels at the 20-acre (8ha) property bought in 1999 at St-Etienne-de-Lisse (formerly Château Bel-Air-Ouÿ) and the emblematic parcel in the *vallon* of Fongaban. Virginie de Valandraud (now an average 30,000 bottles) is also made from selected parcels and is no longer considered the second wine—indeed, in certain vintages (such as 2008), it's close to Valandraud in quality. A white wine, Blanc de Valandraud, was added in 2003.

The work in the vineyards is still as precise as ever, the grapes harvested late for perfect maturity, particularly on the later-ripening clay-limestone soils at St-Etienne-de-Lisse. The Merlot here was harvested October 15–20 in 2008, which is tardy by anyone's standards. Vinification techniques are a mix of traditional and modern. The juice is concentrated by *saignée* and sometimes by a concentrator, then given a cold pre-fermentation maceration. *Pigeage* and *remontage* are used during the alcoholic fermentation. Malolactic fermentation and maturation are in 100 percent new oak barrels for both Valandraud and Virginie de Valandraud, with classic racking when needed. The final blend is made just before bottling.

The garage movement may have waned, but Valandraud remains an established brand. Prices are less speculative than in the past and tend to yo-yo with the vintage (the *prix de sortie* for Valandraud 2005 was $220, but $100 for the 2004). Classification would certainly be the final consecration, but will the "bad boy" of St-Emilion really lay down his arms?

Left: Jean-Luc and Murielle Thunevin, both involved in the creation and evolution of Bordeaux's greatest new wine

FINEST WINES

Château Valandraud

The classic blend for Valandraud these days is 70% Merlot and 30% Cabernet Franc, occasionally with a tiny proportion of Cabernet Sauvignon.

2001★ Deep, bright color. There is depth and intensity on the nose: dark-fruit notes and a hint of cherry pit, perhaps a touch austere. The palate is round, flattering, and opulent on the attack, with refreshing acidity behind. Ripe, well-rounded tannins. This has both substance and charm. Superior to the 2000.

2003 Deep color. Ripe to overripe fruit on the nose, with a note of chocolaty oak. A round, supple palate but with a lift of freshness, the tannins a touch grainy on the finish. Accessible already but avoids the flabby, cooked nature of the vintage.

Virginie de Valandraud

2005 Dark purple-ruby color. Spicy, chocolaty oak apparent on the nose but zesty fruit behind. The palate is sweet and ripe but with balancing freshness and very fine tannins. Modern and structured, the oak still present, so, like most wines of the vintage, clearly in need of bottle age.

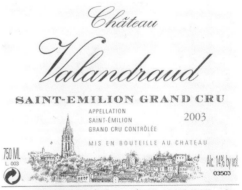

Château Valandraud
Total area: 25 acres (10ha)
Area under vine: 25 acres (10ha)
Average production: 15,000 bottles
BP88, 6 Rue Guadet, 33330 St-Emilion
Tel: +33 5 57 55 09 13
www.thunevin.com

Canon-la-Gaffelière

If there were a classification within a classification, then Canon-la-Gaffelière would be at the head of St-Emilion's grands crus classés. This has been the case since around 1989. Why the château has never made the final step to premier grand cru classé remains a mystery, since the wines are certainly of sufficient quality to be classed at that level. Displaying a modern density and expression of fruit, they also have an elegant, racy edge imparted by a substantial portion of old-vine Cabernet Franc.

The property is easy to find, located at the foot of St-Emilion's southern slope. The road up to the town winds past the winery and château and over the rail line that bisects the vineyard. The *pied de côte* soils are complex and varied, with a mix

The quality and health of the vineyard remain Stephan von Neipperg's principal concern. "My wish is to have a viticulture that lives," he declares

of clay-limestone and sandy clay, the clay more concentrated on the upper part of the slope (where the Cabernet Franc is found), the topsoil becoming sandier as the slope runs away. The vineyard needs careful management and a sensitive hand on the tiller, a task that Comte Stephan von Neipperg, a rather smart and urbane man in his early 50s, has accomplished with distinction in recent years.

The descendant of an aristocratic landowning family from Württemberg in Germany, von Neipperg officially took control of the family property in 1985, having studied economics and agronomy in Paris and Montpellier. Along with Clos de l'Oratoire, La Mondotte, and Château Peyreau, Canon-la-Gaffelière had been purchased by the von Neipperg family in 1971 and run by a manager until Stephan von Neipperg's arrival. His conclusion

following an audit of the estate was that it had been prudently managed but that there had been a clear drop in the quality of the wines since 1964.

The source of the problem, he felt, lay within the vineyard. The heart of the estate, as is the case today, resided on a core of old vines planted before 1953 (17 acres [7ha] of Cabernet Franc and 11 acres [4.5ha] of Merlot). But there was also a lack of balance created by a lot of young vines planted after the devastating frost of 1956, not always with the best rootstocks and clones. The other major issue was the heavy-handed use of chemical fertilizers throughout the 1960s and 1970s, which had led to excessive yields and an imbalance in the soils.

The quality and health of the vineyard remain von Neipperg's principal concern. "My wish is to have a viticulture that lives," he declares, and by employing a holistic approach he has steadily brought it back into balance. Herbicides, insecticides, and chemical fertilizers have all been abandoned, and any rectification of the soils is accomplished with the addition of natural compost. A system of drainage has been put in place, and grass cover is used to help curb vigor in the vines. The inspiration and execution are biodynamic, save for the occasional use of an anti-botrytis spray and a particular treatment for mildew.

The old plantings of Cabernet Franc (of which up to 45 percent can be used in the blend) remain the key to the quality and finesse of the wine. They also provide the source of a massal selection that is used for new plantings. When planted in blocks, these have a density of 10,000 vines/ha and are field-grafted on to low-vigor *riparia* rootstock. A proportion of old-vine Cabernet Sauvignon also achieves decent ripeness on the warmer, sandier soils. Overall, yields are restricted, principally by severe pruning, and kept to an average 30hl/ha for the grand vin.

The emphasis on viticultural harmony has not precluded a change in winemaking philosophy.

Stephan von Neipperg is forward-thinking and has been ready to embrace new ideas—but never with a fixed recipe in mind. The efforts in the vineyard can be seen to bear fruit from 1988 (though von Neipperg thinks they probably harvested too late in 1989), and changes in winemaking techniques can be felt in the wines from the mid-1990s. Buildings were renovated and a new cuverie established, with oak vats and a system for gravity-feeding the grapes.

Among the new practices are *pigeage* and microoxygenation. These were introduced in collaboration with Stéphane Derenoncourt, who is very much a soulmate when it comes to sensitivity in the vineyard; he was the winemaker at Canon-la-Gaffelière from 1996 until 1999, when he started his own winemaking consultancy. Von Neipperg had already introduced malolactic fermentation in barrel and started experimenting with aging on lees from 1990, but both practices progressed from the mid-1990s. The wine is now aged on lees in new oak barrels (80 to 100 percent), with little racking and limited use of *cliquage*.

FINEST WINES

Château Canon-la-Gaffelière

The blend for this wine turns around 55% Merlot, 40% Cabernet Franc, and 5% Cabernet Sauvignon. The dilution of the 1960s and 1970s has been replaced by ripe concentration and, since 1996, a vibrancy of fruit and greater finesse of texture.

1998 ★ Relatively deep color. A sublime wine that demonstrates the qualities of the cru. Engaging plum and spice nose. Delicious fruit on the palate, with racy, mineral notes. Full-bodied, with plenty of depth. Fine tannins give presence and length on the finish. Drinking well but has the reserve to age.

2000 Deep color. A lift of fruit on the nose again. Dark cherry and violet notes. Generous fruit on the palate, pure and round with a touch of cedar. Sweet but balanced. Only just beginning to hit its stride.

2004 Deep purple-crimson hue. A touch simpler on the nose—the aroma of red fruits. Medium-bodied, with a soft, silky texture. Pure-fruited and fresh, but with less depth and punch than in top vintages. Still needs a couple more years of bottle age.

Above: The crest of the von Neippergs, whose blue blood has been among the most welcome new blood in Bordeaux

Château Canon-la-Gaffelière

Total area: 48 acres (19.5ha)
Area under vine: 48 acres (19.5ha)
Production: grand vin 50,000–70,000 bottles; second wine 3,000–12,000 bottles
BP34, 33330 St-Emilion
Tel: +33 5 57 24 71 33
www.neipperg.com

Le Dôme

Jonathan Maltus is something of a mystery in St-Emilion. "I'm happy to be an outsider. It's a form of independence," he says. Locally he is known as *le businessman*—and in a sense, the villagers are not far wrong. His entrepreneurial skills have helped turn an average property on the Dordogne plain into a successful 300,000-bottle-a-year business that includes a line of single-vineyard wines, the most celebrated being Le Dôme.

An Englishman who has led a nomadic existence, Maltus sold his engineering consultancy and, in 1992, headed for France with his wife, Lyn. The wine bug bit while they were helping friends in Cahors, and after a search for a suitable property, they settled on the 13.5-acre (5.5ha) Château Teyssier in St-Emilion in 1994.

It soon became evident that Teyssier alone was going to be a struggle. The garage movement was under way, and motivated by the success of limited-edition wines such as Le Pin, Maltus raised a loan from the bank and purchased Le Dôme, now three parcels of vines on sandy soils next to Château Angélus. "I believe in terroir and never thought a garage wine could be made with grapes grown on the plain," Maltus says. The vines were planted in 1956 and 1970 and, unusually, are 75 percent Cabernet Franc, the rest Merlot (as in the blend).

The first vintage was 1996. Yields then and since have been kept low through careful pruning and green-harvesting, leaving only four bunches of grapes per vine. These are hand-picked into *cagettes* and then sorted again at the Teyssier winery via a multiple system of tables including a Mistral. The winemaking is contemporary but has evolved. "We're happy to use modern technology if it makes sense to us and produces better wine," he confirms.

The first two vintages were fermented in stainless-steel tanks, but these have since been replaced by wooden vats. Techniques include pre-fermentation maceration, *pigeage*, and *délestage*. Fermentation temperatures used to be as high as 88°F (31°C) but in recent vintages have come down to 82°F (28°C). The malolactic fermentation is in new oak barrels, and for vintages 1998 to 2001 inclusive, the wine was then racked into another set of new oak barrels for aging (200 percent new oak). The wine spends six months on lees with *bâtonnage* and is then aged with traditional racking and an egg-white fining to obtain the brilliant aspect Maltus prefers in his wines.

My experience of Le Dôme has been principally at en primeur tastings, where I've always found the wine dark, rich, pure-textured, and brooding but perhaps lacking a touch of vivacity. The 200 percent oak probably made for a chunkier style from 1998 to 2001, but perhaps the lower fermentation temperature has helped expression, since I've noticed more life and zest in vintages from 2004.

Le Dôme was sold exclusively by Justerini & Brooks of London for ten years but is now handled by Maltus's own distribution system. Its success helped finance the growth of Château Teyssier and to develop the single-vineyard range, which also includes Vieux Château Mazerat, Les Astéries, Le Carré, and the white Clos Nardian. Maltus now has similar ventures in the Barossa Valley (The Colonial Estate) and Napa Valley (World's End).

FINEST WINES

Le Dôme
2000 Deep color. Rich, full, almost meaty nose. Intense fruit on the palate, concentrated and brooding, with assertive structure and style.

2004★ Deep, dark, brilliant hue. Fragrant, elegant nose with distinct violet, zest, and spice notes. Beautifully textured, with smooth tannins. Violet hints again on the long, fresh finish.

Vieux Château Mazerat
This is the estate that supplied the parcels for Le Dôme. The wine is produced from 10 acres (4ha) of sandy and clay-limestone soils. The first vintage was produced in 2008★ from 65% Merlot and 35% Cabernet Franc. At the en primeur tastings, it

Above: Jonathan Maltus, whose entrepreneurial flare has established a diverse and impressive range of wines

showed fragrance, poise, and finesse. It could end up rivaling Le Dôme as the top of the line.

Les Astéries
Thin clay soils over limestone bedrock provide the hallmark minerality. Only 3,600 bottles are produced from the 2.7 acres (1.1ha) of 70% Merlot. **2004** Garnet hue, with a deep inner core. Red fruit with a touch of violets on the nose. Firm structure, marked minerality; long, fresh, and linear, with chocolate notes on the finish.

Le Carré
This is a Merlot-dominated parcel that belonged to Château Canon. Same production as Les Astéries. **2005** Dark, bright hue. Rich, ripe nose on the cusp of overripe. Notes of plum and dark cherry. The palate is firm, even slightly austere, and the tannins a little more angular.

Château Laforge
This is what Maltus labels an "estate wine"; it is produced from parcels dotted around St-Emilion. **2004** Rich, plummy nose. The palate is medium-bodied, supple, and smooth, but with a touch of leanness on the finish.

Château Teyssier [V]
This is Maltus's bread-and-butter wine—fruity but structured, for early to medium-term drinking. Production from the 50-acre (20ha) vineyard can be as high as 180,000 bottles in a good year.

> **Le Dôme**
> Total area: 7 acres (2.8ha)
> Area under vine: 7 acres (2.8ha)
> Production: 9,000–12,000 bottles
> Château Teyssier
> Vignonet, 33330 St-Emilion
> Tel: +33 5 57 84 64 22
> www.maltus.com

Figeac

Château Figeac is the atypical St-Emilion. The 18th-century château with adjacent wooded park and gardens could well be in the Médoc, as could the gravel soils of the vineyard. The same, up to a point, applies to the wine, which has a large proportion of Cabernet in the blend.

The property has a long and distinguished history dating to Gallo-Roman times. In the 18th century it was a large estate of more than 370 acres (150ha), but it was broken up in the 19th century, with parts sold to La Conseillante and Beauregard, and more than 75 acres (30ha) for the creation of Cheval Blanc. The present owner, the sprightly Thierry Manoncourt, inherited the estate in 1947, his ancestors acquiring it in 1892. Celebrating his 50th vintage in 1995, he is still an active ambassador, but the general management has been with his son-in-law, Comte Eric d'Aramon, since 1988.

The soils at Figeac are distinctive: three Günzian gravel ridges running north–south, which gently taper from a maximum height of 125ft (38m) to sandier soils to the west. To the east there's a corner of the property where the clay content is higher and the Cabernet Franc is at its best. The gravel mounds bear direct comparison with the better sites of the Médoc—a major reason for the high Cabernet content here. The present breakdown of grape varieties, reflected in the blend, is 35 percent each of Cabernet Franc and Cabernet Sauvignon, and 30 percent Merlot. "Any more Merlot, and the wine becomes flabby," says d'Aramon.

These are roughly the proportions Manoncourt found in 1947, with a little less Cabernet Franc and some Malbec since grubbed up. Logically, one would expect the Cabernet Sauvignon to be on the high points of the ridges, but this is not always the case. With a view to mechanization, Manoncourt planted east–west in the 1940s and 1950s; only since the 1980s, motivated by the idea of plot-by-plot management, have new parcels been planted north–south, Cabernet Sauvignon in the best zones.

Another result of mechanization was to plant rows wide, at 5ft (1.5m), but to plant vines 4ft (1.2m) apart for the requisite density of 5,500 vines/ha. The trellising was also raised, preempting today's modern trend. New plantings have a vine spacing of 3ft 7in (1.1m) and density of just over 6,000 vines/ha. The average age of the vineyard is 45 years. D'Aramon says he aims for yields of 45hl/ha, but the 2006, 2007, and 2008 vintages were well under, at 37, 32, and 26hl/ha.

In 2002, the family acquired two tiny properties from AXA Millésimes: Château Petit-Figeac (3.7 acres [1.5ha]) and La Fleur Pourret (11 acres [4.5ha]). Historically, the Petit-Figeac parcel was once part of Figeac, and on these grounds INAO granted the request to incorporate the land into Château Figeac in 2006. The brand, however, remains Château Petit-Figeac (an average 12,000 bottles a year), now produced from selected parcels at the estate with a mirror blend of grape varieties in order to produce a "junior" Figeac. The second wine, La Grange Neuve de Figeac, is produced from young vines, the blend varying from year to year.

The sand and gravel soils and high proportion of Cabernet contribute to Figeac's characteristic finesse, keeping it less broad-shouldered than the majority of its neighbors. This is not to say that Figeac hasn't evolved in recent times. As d'Aramon says, "In the 1990s we started to add a little more weight, *gras*, and color—but still with the will to preserve Figeac's traditional elegance."

As at many estates, the vineyard work became more precise and the organization of the harvest was reviewed. An itinerant group of workers used to supply the workforce, camping at the estate for the duration of the harvest. This has been abandoned, a local company now supplying pickers for the dates required, and the fruit picked a little riper. Sorting and selection have also been improved.

The vinification is fairly traditional, but again there have been adjustments to the process. A cold

Above: Comte Eric d'Aramon, who has been helping Figeac evolve while retaining the distinctive elegance of the wines

pre-fermentation maceration was introduced in 1995 and *pigeage* since 2000. This has allowed a reduction in the press wine (using a new vertical press) to 2–3 percent. At the end of the 1990s, the old wooden vats were replaced with new oak versions, the stainless-steel vats introduced in 1971 retained for storage, blending, and the second wine. Château Figeac is matured in 100 percent new oak barrels for 18–22 months, with traditional racking.

FINEST WINES

Château Figeac

The style of Figeac means that its young wines are often overshadowed in blind tastings by their Merlot-dominated peers. The estate also struggles a little in awkward years (the heat and drought of 2003 or rain of 1992 and 1993). This should not belie the fact that it can produce magnificent wines that have a remarkable capacity to age. The 1964

tasted during Vinexpo 2009 still had an amazingly youthful nose, surprising richness on the palate, and an exquisitely elegant texture.

1998★ A Merlot expression on the nose; ample, with blackberry and plum notes. Generous fruit on the palate, sweet and supple but with a point of acidity and firm Cabernet structure that bring it into line. Lovely balance. Just beginning to evolve.

2001★ Dark and fresh with a hint of mint. Blackberry and black currant notes with an edge of toasted oak. Fine, fresh palate. Dark-fruit notes. Good mid-palate weight and length. Plenty of charm.

2005 Dark, subdued, and intense. Generous fruit on the palate but everything in reserve. Firm but fine tannins. Closed at this stage but promising much

Château Figeac
Total area: 133.5 acres (54ha)
Area under vine: 100 acres (40ha)
Average production: grand vin 120,000 bottles; second wine 24,000–36,000 bottles
33330 St-Emilion
Tel: +33 5 57 24 72 26
www.chateau-figeac.com

La Mondotte

An overnight success story of a rags-to-riches nature, La Mondotte also became Stephan von Neipperg's parting shot at the French wine authority, INAO. Having been refused permission to incorporate the tiny 11-acre (4.5ha) vineyard of Château La Mondotte, as it was then known, into Château Canon-la-Gaffelière, he launched the rebaptized wine in 1996, determined to make a splash.

The property is situated in the southeastern sector of St-Emilion's plateau, close to Troplong Mondot. It was acquired by the von Neippergs in 1971, but the origins can be traced to the early 19th century. The vineyard has the classic profile of the plateau terrain, 16–32in (40–80cm) of clay-limestone soils reposing on the limestone bedrock. The vines were planted between the two world wars, an additional parcel purchased in 1988 giving the vineyard an average age of some 50 years.

Until the makeover in 1996, (Château) La Mondotte had remained a fairly mediocre wine, vinified and aged in a separate cellar at Canon-la-Gaffelière and treated as the also-ran of the von Neipperg stable. INAO's decision effectively implied the construction of an on-site cellar at La Mondotte, as did von Neipperg's decision to create something special. Yields were reduced to an average 20hl/ha (this can fall as low as 15hl/ha, as in 2008), the vineyard was given more attention, and the harvest date was pushed back for greater ripeness (usually early October for the Merlot).

The tiny scale of La Mondotte permits a certain amount of experimentation, and several of the winemaking techniques now used at the other von Neipperg properties were first trialed here. These include gravity reception of the grapes, the elimination of crushing, conical wooden vats, and *pigeage*. A cuvaison of 28–35 days is followed by malolactic fermentation in barrel and a maturation of 18 months in 100 percent new oak barrels on fine lees. The wine is neither fined nor filtered.

Timing, as they say, is everything, and the first vintage of La Mondotte hit the market when the garage movement was in full swing. La Mondotte got swept up in the resulting flurry of publicity and speculation, as von Neipperg remembers: "The 1996 La Mondotte sold surprisingly quickly, with the release price multiplying by ten on the open market, so the following year I went higher."

The fact that post-garagiste La Mondotte is one of the few solid brands to have survived says much about the intrinsic quality of the wine. Produced from a majority of Merlot (80 percent) with a complement of Cabernet Franc, this is a dense, powerful wine with a rich, ripe vein of fruit. The balance and notion of terroir is held by good acidity and low pH (3.5), which undoubtedly assists with the aging potential. Even the difficult years have been remarkably successful.

FINEST WINES

La Mondotte
1997 Ruby color with little sign of evolution. A peppery, spicy nose—almost a hint of the northern Rhône. Fruit and freshness on the palate, the tannins a little foursquare, but the wine remarkable for the vintage. Should drink well till 2015 or so.
2001★ Deep color. Rich and dense but with lovely balance and a distinguished, racy edge. Just opening on the nose. The palate is round and caressing, but with plenty of freshness, length, and reserve.
2003 Purple-crimson hue. A big, powerful wine on the verge of overripeness, at the plum and dark-cherry end of the spectrum. The palate is full, sweet, and supple, with a firm tannic frame. A low pH of 3.48 pulls it all into line and promises aging potential.

Right: Comte Stephan von Neipperg, the dashing visionary who recognized Mondotte's outstanding potential

Vignobles Comtes von Neipperg (La Mondotte)
Total area: 11 acres (4.5ha)
Area under vine: 11 acres (4.5ha)
Production: 5,000–13,000 bottles
BP34, 33330 St-Emilion
Tel: +33 5 57 24 71 33
www.neipperg.com

Pavie Macquin

The surprise of the 2006 St-Emilion classification was the elevation of Pavie Macquin to premier grand cru classé. The odds were long because, prior to the mid-1990s, the estate's reputation had been far from remarkable. But under the guidance of Nicolas Thienpont and Stéphane Derenoncourt, quality and consistency have prevailed and the classification looks merited, particularly in light of the excellent terroir.

Madame Maryse Barre managed the property from 1986 to 1994, introducing biodynamic cultivation and employing young *ouvrier viticole* Derenoncourt, who is now the consultant. The 1989 vintage was successful, but in 1993 two-thirds of the crop was lost to mildew. The upshot was the appointment of Nicolas Thienpont as manager and a return to more traditional methods.

Pavie Macquin takes its name from Albert Macquin, a pioneer of grafting vines on to American rootstock at the end of the 19th century, following the outbreak of phylloxera. It is now owned by his descendants, the Corre-Macquin family. Legend has it that villains used to be hanged on the estate where an oak tree now stands—hence the image of two oak trees and a noose on the label.

The vineyard is all on the limestone plateau, with Troplong Mondot to the west and Pavie to the south. The topsoil is rich in clay and varies in depth from 8in to 5ft (20cm to 1.5m) above the bedrock. As a result, the wines at Pavie Macquin are naturally powerful and structured (the acidity is quite marked), so the obligation is always to add a touch of finesse. This is achieved by the quality of fruit and gentle handling.

The vineyard is immaculately run, and biodynamics remains the inspiration, but with a pragmatic approach when it comes to disease protection. Yields are reduced by green-harvesting and kept around 30hl/ha. The harvest date is pushed to the limit to obtain optimum ripeness (October 18–23 for the Merlot in 2008).

The grapes are thoroughly sorted at the cellars, with an optical grape-sorting system added for the vintage in 2009, before going uncrushed to the vats. The vats are concrete or oak, modified for *pigeage*. Somewhat poetically, they have been given girls' names, such as Aglaée, Berthe, or Eliane.

Malolactic fermentation is in barrel, and the wines are then aged on lees, with minimal racking, for up to 18 months in 70 percent new oak barrels. The blend is made just before bottling. A second wine, Les Chênes de Macquin, allows a system of selection. In 2008 a rosé was produced instead.

FINEST WINES

Château Pavie Macquin
The wine is 84% M, 14% CF (massal selected), 2% CS. Ongoing experiments include ungrafted Cabernet Franc at 25,000 vines/ha. The wine needs 8–10 years in bottle. The 1996, tasted in 2007, was still well within itself, with a youthful color, depth of fruit, brooding power, and minerally freshness.

2000 Dark ruby hue. Notes of dark cherry and cherry stone on the nose. A firm tannic frame swathed in layers of dark, ripe fruit. Smooth and generous, with plenty of power and reserve.

2001 Dark-fruit aromas, but I also detected a leafy note and was informed that CS represents 5% of the blend this year. Supple fruit on the attack, the tannins a touch grainy on the finish.

2004 Deep color. Cherry-stone and spice aromas. The attack is frank and direct. Medium-bodied, fresh, and pure. The minerality shows.

2006 ★ Deep purple hue. In the same vein as 2004 but richer. Powerful structure heightened by natural acidity. Minerality and longevity.

Left: The level-headed Nicolas Thienpont has helped to raise quality at Larcis Ducasse as well as at Pavie Macquin

Château Pavie Macquin
Total area: 37 acres (15ha)
Area under vine: 37 acres (15ha)
Average production: grand vin 50,000 bottles; second wine 5,000–10,000 bottles
33330 St-Emilion
Tel: +33 5 57 24 74 23
www.pavie-macquin.com

Trottevieille

Just one look at this bijou property standing alone on the limestone plateau to the east of the town of St-Emilion, and you know there's the potential to make great wine. The well-exposed 25-acre (10ha) vineyard forms a single unit enclosed by a dry-stone wall. The clay-limestone topsoil is thin, with only 12–16in (30–40cm) over the limestone bedrock. The vineyard, now immaculately run, is old, with an average age of 60 years and a high proportion of Cabernet Franc. The combination of limestone and Cabernet Franc offers a recipe for wines of freshness and finesse and an appreciable ability to age.

The story of the name Trottevieille is somewhat folkloric, apparently originating from a time in the distant past when an old lady in the vicinity used to "trot out" to meet the passing stagecoach to enquire of the latest news. In 1949, Marcel Borie fell in love with the estate and purchased it complete with the attractive *chartreuse*. It now belongs to his descendants, the Castéja family, owners of the négociant house Borie-Manoux, and is managed by his grandson Philippe Castéja. "My grandfather was bowled over by the views of St-Emilion and the taste of the 1943 vintage," explains Castéja.

It has to be said that Trottevieille has not always performed consistently at its level of St-Emilion premier grand cru classé. Vintages of the 1950s and early 1960s were fine, but then there were indifferent years, the estate picking up only from the mid-1980s. Even then, the gains were somewhat overshadowed by the advances made at other châteaux, and there was still the feeling that the requisite spark of finesse had eluded Trottevieille.

Since 2000 this has no longer been the case. The wines have a linear freshness but with added elegance and purity of fruit. Denis Dubourdieu and Gilles Pauquet have been retained as consultants, and a certain amount of fine-tuning has been applied. There's now greater precision in the vineyard, as well as in the date and handling of the harvest.

Above: Philippe Castéja, under whose enlightened management favorably sited Trottevieille is again fully worthy of its status

Yields are low—only 25hl/ha for the grand vin in 2008—and the introduction of a second wine, La Vieille Dame de Trottevieille, in 2000 has offered the possibility of an even more severe selection.

A curiosity bottling of old ungrafted Cabernet Franc was also introduced in 2004. The 3,200 vines were planted toward the end of the 19th century and are now identified for selective harvesting within a mixed plot that also includes younger vines. A total of 135 bottles are produced each year.

Just one look at this bijou property standing alone on the limestone plateau to the east of the town of St-Emilion, and you know there's the potential to make great wine. The vineyard, now immaculately run, is old, with an average age of 60 years

FINEST WINES

Château Trottevieille
The blend is made from a field planting of 50% M, 45% CF, and 5% CS. The wine is aged in 100% new oak casks for 18–24 months.

1955 ★ Relatively deep color at the core, brick at the rim. Still incredibly youthful, with lively fruit on the nose. Rich and generous on the palate, with a long, fresh, minerally finish. An eye-opener.

2000 Rich, ripe, and powerful, with ample fruit on the palate and a firm, tannic frame. Balanced by a cool freshness on the finish. Definitely for long aging.

2003 Sweet, round, and accessible, with supple fruit on the palate. The tannins are a little grainy on the finish, but there's a freshness that gives balance in this difficult year.

2004 ★ Deep color. An elegant but discreet nose of dark fruits, with a delicate toasted note. The palate is ripe, fine, and fresh, with well-integrated oak. Harmonious. An apt demonstration of the estate's progression to a finer style. Mid- to long-term aging.

Château Trottevieille
Total area: 25 acres (10ha)
Area under vine: 25 acres (10ha)
Average production: grand vin 36,000 bottles; second wine 3,000 bottles
33330 St-Emilion
Tel: +33 5 56 00 00 70

Clos Fourtet

Visitors to St-Emilion inevitably get a glimpse of Clos Fourtet. The property, with its "homely" looking 18th-century château, stands on the edge of the town next to the Romanesque Eglise Collégiale and the vestiges of the town's fortified walls. The majority of the vineyard is in full view on the limestone plateau. Less visible below ground are the 30 acres (12ha) of quarried galleries that run along three levels—a section reserved for aging barrels.

Clos Fourtet was acquired by French businessman Philippe Cuvelier in January 2001. His son Matthieu runs the estate and has a solid team—including Tony Ballu, the winemaker since 1991. Consultants Stéphane Derenoncourt and Jean-Claude Berrouet, the winemaker for Pétrus and other J-P Moueix properties for more than 40 years, came on board during the year of purchase.

The wine has the characteristics typical of the limestone plateau: freshness, minerality, and the structure to age. What the new regime has added is a greater density of fruit and more finesse, as well as greater consistency. As Ballu says, "Philippe Cuvelier has provided the means for us to advance."

Lucien and André Lurton were the previous owners of Clos Fourtet. When they took over from their father, François, in 1973, the property was in a run-down state. A program of replanting was launched, and continues today: some 90 percent of the vineyard has been renewed. A block of 37 acres (15ha) surrounding the château provides the heart of the grand vin. An additional 12 acres (5ha) are located farther north between Fonroque and Cadet Piola, the grapes normally destined for the second wine (Closerie de Fourtet, since 2006).

During the Lurton ownership, other changes were instigated: grass cover in the vineyard (1991); malolactic fermentation in barrel (1995); and ventilation of the cellars (1997). Improvements since have been even more clinical. Sorting tables, including a Mistral, have made the grape selection more precise. And on the advice of Derenoncourt, the process of extraction has been softened, partly by the use of manual *pigeage*. The wine is now aged on lees for 12 months in 75 percent new oak barrels, with minimal use of *cliquage*.

The approach has been "softly, softly," the idea being not to change the style but rather to fine-tune the existing wine. Pricing, too, has been handled sensitively, and there have been no excessive hikes. This is a wine for the cellar and for drinking, rather than for speculation. And to add a touch of sociability, the château, uninhabited for nearly a century, has been renovated and is occupied when Cuvelier is down from Paris.

FINEST WINES

Clos Fourtet
The wine is 85% Merlot. The Lurtons deemed the Cabernet Franc clones inadequate, so a fair amount was grubbed up, reducing the grape to 5% of plantings. There are plans to introduce better clones in the coming years. The Cabernet Sauvignon (10%) is at the top of the plateau to help it ripen.

1989 Light ruby, with a little brick at the rim. This is a mature wine with a note of forest floor and a slightly rustic edge. Ballu points out that vinification at the time included sterner extraction, as well as plenty of racking and aeration and filtration prior to bottling. The palate, though, is fresh and satisfying.

2001★ Bright ruby. Fresh, fruit-driven nose. An engaging palate: round and supple on the attack, with good depth of fruit, finely honed tannins, and minerally freshness. A good expression of the cru.

2002 [V] A success for the vintage. Lighter in weight but very fine, with expressive fruit, delicate tannins, length, and balance. Elegant and harmonious. Drinking now but will age another six or seven years.

Clos Fourtet
Total area: 50 acres (20ha)
Area under vine: 44 acres (18ha)
Average production: grand vin 48,000 bottles; second wine 28,000 bottles
1 Chatelet Sud, 33330 St-Emilion
Tel: +33 5 57 24 70 90
www.closfourtet.com

Larcis Ducasse

It was an audacious move when Nicolas Thienpont set the en primeur price of 2005 Larcis Ducasse at $80, the same as Château Figeac. The négociants grumbled, but the wine sold. There's since been a drop to just over $27 ($33 in 2008), but that's still quite a leap from $17–18 in the late 1990s. Quality has been on the up and up, and the market has followed the upward curve.

The potential has always been there, and indeed, until the mid-1960s Larcis Ducasse had a sound reputation. It was one of the wines Jean-Pierre Moueix liked to drink. The 1970s were not a good era, as for a number of estates. There were improvements in the 1980s and '90s, but the wine remained old-fashioned, light and breezy with a mineral note, but lacking depth and distinction.

In 2002, owner Jacques Olivier Gratiot (his family has owned the property for more than a century), a former executive with l'Oréal, took on Nicolas Thienpont as general manager, with Stéphane Derenoncourt as consultant, and things began to change. "If the terroir is good, then the wine will speak if the winemaking and viticultural side are tightened," says Thienpont.

One look at the vineyard, and it is clear that Larcis Ducasse has something to offer. Contiguous with Château Pavie, it lies on a south-facing slope that runs from the limestone plateau through to the sandy-clay *pied de côte*. There are a couple of parcels on the plateau in the vicinity of Pavie Decesse and Troplong Mondot. The bulk of the vineyard, though, lies on the clay-limestone *côte*, much of it terraced.

The "tightening" in the vineyard was multifaceted, for much needed to be done. The system of drainage was overhauled, grass cover introduced where necessary, and trellising lifted for better leaf cover. A large number of vines were missing on the *côte*, and these have been replaced, bringing the density up from 5,500 to 7,500 vines/ha in certain parcels. The lack of vines and production here had meant overcompensation lower down the slope, which has since been rationalized. The work of deleafing, shoot removal, and green-harvesting has been intensified to help improve maturity.

The harvest is generally later now, with yields kept around 30–35hl/ha and *saignée* used for concentration. There's no second wine, but the "bled" juice and lighter cuvées are used to make rosé (7,500–10,000 bottles). Vinification follows the processes favored by Thienpont and Derenoncourt: the use of whole-grape clusters; *pigeage*; microoxygenation *sous marc* if required; malolactic fermentation in barrel; aging on lees in 60 percent new oak barrels for 16–20 months, the wine racked twice; and minimum use of *cliquage*.

FINEST WINES

Château Larcis Ducasse
The present blend of Larcis Ducasse is 85% M and 15% CF, but Nicolas Thienpont hopes eventually to increase the latter to 25%. The objective has been to maintain the natural elegance and charm of the cru but add a little more weight, fruit, and maturity.
1998 Old-style Larcis Ducasse from a good year. Red color. Notes of strawberry and other red fruit on the nose. The palate is light, fresh, and *aérien*. Satisfying, but a lack of depth and length.
2004 Deepish color. Ripe, plummy nose. Tender fruit on the palate, with a minerally freshness. Not weighty but fine, and almost accessible now.
2005★ Dark purple hue. A very tasty wine—you can see what the noise was all about. Cherry, plum, and cherry-pit aromas. The palate is ripe, but fine and harmonious. Minerally persistence. Big, ripe tannins, but it still has that racy edge.
2007 Deep color. The oak is still a little evident on the nose, but this should make a really pleasing bottle. Plenty of fruit extract, with a silky texture and tannins. Early-drinking charm.

Château Larcis Ducasse
Total area: 27 acres (11ha)
Area under vine: 22 acres (9ha)
Average production: 35,000 bottles
33330 St-Emilion
Tel: +33 5 57 24 70 84
www.larcis-ducasse.com

Pomerol

A prestigious name, Pomerol is tiny in comparison to the reputation it holds. Around 1,980 acres (800ha) is the sum total of the vineyard, planted on a fairly flat, anonymous terrain. Properties are small and unassuming, the average holding no more than 12 acres (5ha) and unadorned by the architectural splendor seen in the Médoc or, occasionally, St-Emilion. Even the most celebrated properties—L'Eglise-Clinet, Lafleur, Pétrus, Le Pin—are humble in appearance. The only landmark is the spire of the village church.

Merlot is the affirmed grape variety of the region. Before the great freeze of 1956, there was a greater proportion of Cabernet Franc, Cabernet Sauvignon, and even Malbec, but planting since has pushed Merlot to nearly 80 percent. This clearly affects the style of the wine, but also means that the pendulum can swing widely, according to climatic conditions, between favorable (1998) and less favorable (1996) Merlot years.

An earlier-ripening variety, Merlot has been harnessed to an early-ripening terroir, which explains the rich, lush nature of the wine. The area has a maximum altitude of 130ft (40m) and more of a gentle incline than a hill, so slope and exposure have little influence on maturity but may help with natural drainage in some locations. It's the soils that are the important factor here, explaining the character of the wines from the top estates.

Unlike in St-Emilion, there's no limestone in Pomerol; it's gravel, sand, and clay. The alluvium was deposited in stages thousands of years ago, during the Quaternary period, by the River Isle, a tributary of the Dordogne, and forms a series of terraces that rise gently away from the river. The soil structure is complex, but in simple terms there's an ascending order of quality, the high terrace or Pomerol plateau being the oldest sector, with more gravel and clay.

At the highest point of the Pomerol plateau, the dense blue clay rises to the surface over 7.5–10 acres (3–4ha), forming what is known as the Pétrus "buttonhole." These water-retaining clays help provide the deep color, power, and volume that are typified by Pétrus. Fanning out eastward, the high clay content also runs through sections of Vieux Château Certan, L'Evangile, and La Conseillante, and on into part of Cheval Blanc across the Pomerol border in St-Emilion.

Elsewhere on the Pomerol plateau, one finds a mix of soil profiles, including clay and fine gravel, gravel, and clay in equal portions; gravelly clay; and sandy gravel. The wines produced from these soils tend to have a firm tannic structure and benefit from bottle age. Examples include L'Evangile and La Conseillante, as well as the relatively recently created Hosanna. Lafleur and Vieux Château Certan should be included in the same family but make their individuality felt with a higher proportion of Cabernet. In the northwest corner, Trotanoy, Le Pin, and La Violette have deep gravel soils over clay, Trotanoy having another sector that is deep clay, the combination providing a wine that is dense but fresh and long aging.

The lower terraces to the west of the central plateau are also early-ripening, but the soils are sandier, with gravel of a finer texture. The wines can have an attractive ripeness of fruit and a certain structure but less power, volume, and complexity of bouquet than those on the central plateau. Farther west and south, the soils become sandier still, with a sandy-clay subsoil. The water table is higher, and there are more regular traces of what is known locally as *crasse de fer*, a ferruginous sand touted as a quality factor, though this has yet to be proved scientifically. The wines are lighter-framed and fresh in style and perhaps less typically Pomerol.

The fact that Pomerol has an international reputation owes much to one man: Jean-Pierre Moueix. Before World War II, the wines were virtually unknown beyond the traditional markets

Right: The landmark spire of the local church soars above the village, whose sleepy appearance belies its recent prestige

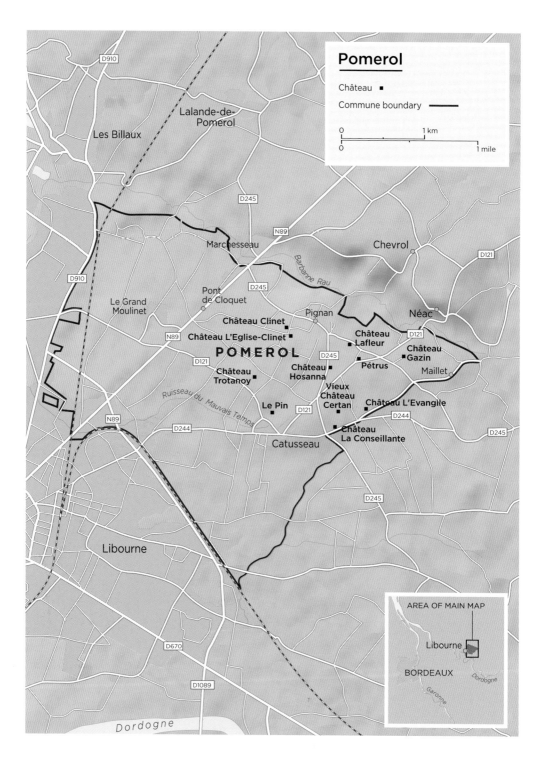

of northern France and the Benelux countries. Moueix, however, having established his négociant house Etablissements Jean-Pierre Moueix in Libourne in 1937, started investing in properties in the region in the 1950s and marketing the now-prestigious names overseas. The house remains a prime mover in Pomerol, thanks to its portfolio of properties (Pétrus, Trotanoy, La Fleur-Pétrus, and Hosanna, among others) and its high standards.

There's been a limited amount of investment in Pomerol recently, most of it private rather than corporate (Catherine Péré-Vergé at Le Gay and La Violette; Sylviane Garcin-Cathiard at Clos L'Eglise; the Delon family of Léoville-Las-Cases at Nénin), though AXA Millésimes owns Petit-Village, and

Above: Pomerol is close to St-Emilion but very much smaller, making up in reputation what it lacks in size and tradition

the Lafite Rothschild group owns L'Evangile. Land in the prime sites is expensive ($5 million/ ha was rumored for one transaction in the new millennium), and there's not much to go around.

Otherwise, many properties are owned by local vignerons, where the quality is variable. Some have other properties in neighboring appellations and vinify their Pomerol there. This practice will stop in 2019, a recent rule decreeing that from that date the wine will have to be produced within the delimited Pomerol zone. In that case, several small wineries are likely to mushroom in the interim.

Lafleur

It should go without saying that Lafleur is one of Bordeaux's greatest wines, but would I be out of turn in declaring it Pomerol's finest? Old vintages are legendary, those produced since 1982 exquisite, the vineyard tended like a garden by owners who can honestly flaunt the name vigneron. Pétrus appears to be the only rival, certainly on the secondary market. The trouble is Lafleur's rarity and the fact that so few have the chance to taste it.

Lafleur belies the notion that prestigious Bordeaux châteaux are the sole preserve of well-heeled and sometimes distant owners. Jacques and Sylvie Guinaudeau, their son Baptiste and his companion Julie Gresiak, work in the vineyard throughout the year and have a deep knowledge of the terroir. "We're farmers in our approach, and our objective is to guide rather than to dictate to the vine," explains Baptiste. Their great asset is a plot of land located on Pomerol's upper plateau, surrounded by Pétrus, La Fleur-Pétrus, Le Gay, Hosanna, and Vieux Château Certan.

It goes without saying that Lafleur is one of Bordeaux's greatest wines, but would I be out of turn in declaring it Pomerol's finest?

The 11-acre (4.5ha) vineyard is rectangular, with clay and fine gravel in the southeastern corner and equal portions of gravel and clay in the southwest. It's in this southern sector that most of the Cabernet Franc (50 percent of plantings) is located. The northwest corner has gravelly clay similar to that at Trotanoy and Le Pin, while the northeast has sand and gravel. It's this mix of soils that helps provide the complexity and structure in Lafleur. Through the center runs a crescent-shaped band of deeper silt and sand, used for the second wine, Pensées de Lafleur.

Baptiste's great-great-great-grandfather, Henri Greloud, acquired the land in 1872. Already the owner of neighboring Le Gay, he decided to create a separate property, naming the new estate after the *lieu-dit*, Lafleur. The house and cellars were built (visitors were received at Le Gay), together with an identical building across the road that is now La Fleur-Pétrus.

The property passed to Greloud's son Charles in 1888 and was then purchased by a cousin, André Robin, in 1915. His daughters Marie and Thérèse inherited the estate in 1946, along with Château Le Gay. Lafleur already had a certain reputation, but the wines produced during the sisters' 38-year tenure (1947, 1950, 1955, 1966, 1975, 1979) brought it international renown.

The sisters never married, and in 1984 Thérèse died, whereupon Marie leased the vineyard to her second cousin Jacques Guinaudeau. He already ran the family property, Château Grand Village (Bordeaux Supérieur), so he had a viticultural base. Jean-Claude Berrouet of J-P Moueix oversaw the 1982, 1983, and 1984 vintages, but Jacques and Sylvie Guinaudeau have made the wines since 1985. On Marie's death in 2001, the Guinaudeaus raised the capital to acquire the property outright and were joined by Baptiste and Julie.

Baptiste divides the Guinaudeau years into three periods. "When my parents took over, nothing much had been done in the vineyard for nearly 40 years. So between 1985 and 1990 they replanted something like 8,000 missing vines, corrected soil pH, improved trellising, and put in drainage." Only 10 percent of the vineyard pre-dates the 1956 frost, the rest planted shortly afterward, the Guinaudeaus replanting two tiny plots but relying mostly on complantation. New plantings of Cabernet Franc are from their own massal selection. Vintages during this period were exceptional.

Right: Jacques Guinaudeau at Lafleur, where meticulous attention to detail has helped take the wines to the top

The second stage of the Guinaudeau tenure was spent understanding the soils, managing the young vines, and settling yields. "We've always been more interested in the yield per plant, but the yearly average is around 38hl/ha, though the vintages 2005 to 2008 have been lower, at 32hl/ha," says Baptiste. The small size of the property and the permanent labor force, which moves between Lafleur and Grand Village, enable individual vines to benefit from unusual care and attention. The third cycle started at the end of the 1990s, when the vineyard was finally in balance and experience and knowledge attained.

This is clearly a wine that's made in the vineyard, the vinification achieved with a light hand. The harvest date for each parcel is given careful consideration, and blending decisions are made primarily in the vineyard, since there are only seven vinification tanks. Selection is also done at the vine, and sorting tables are notable by their absence. Once at the *cuvier*, the grapes are destemmed, lightly crushed, and placed in temperature-controlled concrete tanks. "We may add yeast, but we avoid long maceration, the idea being to let the vintage dictate extraction," explains Baptiste.

Malolactic fermentation in barrel was introduced in 1991. Only 40 percent new oak barrels are used for aging, and these are "prepared" at Grand Village with a wash of white wine. The blending is carried out early, with the final blend for the grand vin and second wine finished by the end of February. The wine is then aged for a further 15 months, with racking every three to four months and an egg-white fining before bottling.

Below: Jacques and Sylvie Guinaudeau, with son Baptiste and Julie Gresiak, in the vineyard that is the focus of all their efforts

FINEST WINES

Château Lafleur

One of the features of Lafleur is the high proportion
of Cabernet Franc in the blend—on average 40%,
the rest being Merlot. It's this that provides the
complexity and the hallmark mineral character
derived from the soils. A tasting of Lafleur held at
Grand Village in October 2005 gave me the chance
to appreciate the consistency and intensity of
vintages since 1986. The aging potential of most
was prodigious, the need for time in bottle absolute.
The 1986 had a mature nose of truffle and tobacco,
the palate still full and firm reposing on a powerful
tannic frame. The 1988 was fine if slightly austere,
with plenty of minerally freshness and length. The
1989★ was big, brooding, and powerful, the nose
warm and ripe with plum and fig notes, the palate
full-bodied with enormous depth and intensity,
capable of aging another 20 years. There was no
1990 for comparison, but the complex, aristocratic
1995★ had great intensity of flavor and, again,
powerful structure and length. The 1996 seemed a
little leaner and austere, the minerality coming to
the fore. The 1998 was reasonably accessible with
notes of chocolate and cassis, the palate smooth
and minerally, with tannic backbone but perhaps
a little less intensity than I expected. The 1999 had
unusual power and concentration for a difficult
year, the tannins steely firm. The 2000★ had the
power, density, and complexity of a great year, the
nose ripe and exotic, the palate rich with beautifully
layered fruit and amazing length and freshness.
The 2001★ was in the same vein, virile and
powerful, with a core of ripe fruit but still resolutely
closed. The 2002 was leaner and a touch austere
but "classic," harmonious, and focused. The 2003
was the opposite—open and exuberant, round and
ripe, but with a wisp of freshness to give it lift.
2000★ Dark hue. Intense, poised, the nose ripe
and minerally but fairly closed. The palate is fine-
textured, dense, and racy, while the tannins are
firm. Fresh and balanced, with great persistence
but in need of bottle age.

Pensées de Lafleur

The second wine is blended along the same lines
as Lafleur, except in unusual years like 2003, when
it was 100% Merlot. In top years (2005, 2000,
1995) it can be an impressive wine with a hint of
the intensity of the grand vin and the potential for
aging 20-plus years. Relative to Lafleur it is good
value, especially in vintages like 2004 and 2006,
but even then it is scarce.

Château Lafleur

Total area: 11 acres (4.5ha)
Area under vine: 10 acres (4ha)
Average production: grand vin 12,000 bottles;
second wine 6,000 bottles
33500 Pomerol
Tel: +33 5 57 84 44 03

Pétrus

Visitors expecting a temple to venerate the legend will be disappointed; the buildings at Pétrus are simple and low-key. Recent renovation has added a bit of luster, and the name Pétrus is clearly visible on the wall, but we are still talking basics here, a reception room and cellars comprising the principal construction. What really matters, though, is the surrounding vineyard, the clay soils responsible for Pétrus's celebrated power and ability to age.

All the same, it needs a sharp eye to detect the advantages, even standing amid the vines. The rows are immaculately tended, but the slope running gently away from a high point of 130ft (40m) is barely perceptible. The vines are planted in the sense of the slope, the natural drainage assisted since the early 1970s by a man-made system.

The soil is blue clay, the famous "buttonhole" of Pétrus, a sort of double layer of clay with traces of *crasse de fer* where, millions of years ago, the clay-like subsoil burst through the clay-gravel surface forming this unique terroir. "The clay has the advantage of limiting water uptake when it rains by expanding and creating a run-off, but it allows the rooting system to develop via fissures, providing moisture in dry periods, so avoiding hydric stress," explains Edouard Moueix, son of the celebrated Christian, and the face of the next generation at Etablissements Jean-Pierre Moueix.

The dense clay soil is not unique to Pétrus—the neighboring vineyards of Gazin, Vieux Château Certan, L'Evangile, and La Conseillante all have a proportion—but at Pétrus it covers virtually the whole property. Its preponderance explains the decision to plant so much Merlot, and the remaining 5 percent of Cabernet Franc rarely makes it into the grand vin (1998, 2001, and 2003 being the recent exceptions).

The vineyard was replanted after the 1956 frost, so the oldest vines are around 50 years old. Parcels have been steadily replanted since and a little complantation has been employed, but Christian Moueix prefers a rotation system whereby whole blocks are replanted. He was responsible, as far back as 1973, for trialing green-harvesting to aerate bunches and reduce yields, the practice becoming systematic from the late 1980s. There's now a green-harvest along with deleafing in July, followed by a second passage for what the Moueix call the *toilettage* (best translated as "tidy-up"), after the veraison.

The Moueix family has been involved with Pétrus since the 1940s, when the then-owner Madame Loubat granted Jean-Pierre Moueix the concession as sole agent for the wine. He acquired a major shareholding in the 1960s, along with 11 acres (4.5ha) from Château Gazin to supplement the existing vineyard, which was then little more than 17 acres (7ha). Jean-Pierre's son, Christian, and oenologist Jean-Claude Berrouet were responsible for the management and winemaking from this period through to recent times. A new structure has applied since 2009. Christian's elder brother, Jean-François, is now the official owner, and the management and winemaking are in the hands of Jean-Claude Berrouet's son Olivier, previously at Cheval Blanc. Distribution continues to be handled by Ets J-P Moueix.

Deciding the harvest date is probably the single most important decision of the year. As a company, Moueix has never advocated late-harvesting, in a bid to avoid the prune-and-jam end of the flavor spectrum. Because the soils are essentially cooler clay, however, albeit in an early-ripening zone, time is needed for full phenolic ripeness. In Jean-Claude Berrouet's last vintage (his 44th) in 2007, he and Christian Moueix disagreed on the date for the first time in 38 years, Berrouet advocating a longer wait. In 2008, one of the latest harvests, Pétrus was picked in the first few days of October.

Right: The eponymous St. Peter at Pétrus, with his rather oversized key to the heavenly gates, and undersized boat

The advantage, when the decision is made, is that Pétrus can be picked rapidly in two afternoons using the Moueix complement of 150 pickers.

The winemaking that follows is relatively straightforward and traditional. Fermentation takes place in concrete tanks (there are 15 in all, with an additional four in stainless steel) using *remontage* for extraction and a hotter temperature initially. The malolactic fermentation also takes place in tank, though a proportion was done in barrel in 2008 for the purposes of the en primeur tastings. Aging—for up to 18 months, with racking every three—is initially in 100 percent new oak barrels, the proportion of new oak either maintained or reduced according to the quality of the year.

FINEST WINES

Pétrus

The overriding sensation with Pétrus is power and strength, the inner core being tightly wound and reluctant to uncoil—hence its brooding nature when the wine is young, the reserves of tannin restrained. There's concentration but it's never heavy or monumental or over the top. Complexity in the great vintages comes from having the Merlot spot on, the ripeness and vivacity adding a further dimension to the wine. Despite the density and concentration, Pétrus stays clear of a modern stamp. The color is dark but never blue-black, the aromatic notes carefully pitched to avoid overripeness, and the palate at no time thick or dull. It's clearly a great wine, though these days its price means that it is largely the preserve of millionaires. Exceptional vintages have recently included 1998, 2000, 2001, 2005, and 2008, though I have a personal preference for the 1998.

2001★ Power, but charm and finesse as well, the nose full, fragrant, and generous. Notes of black currant, other dark fruit, and coffee. The palate has caressing fruit but a firm inner core, the tannins ripe and honed. Dense and rich, but balanced, with length and poise. It gives a little flourish now but is really for the long haul.

2005★ Aristocratic but slumbering. Concentrated but in no way dull. A complex spice, confit, and dark-fruit nose, with a hint of the exotic. The palate is full and generous, with a wonderfully smooth texture over a massive but ripe tannic frame. Freshness and length on the finish. There's power but balance as well. Will age for 50 or more years.

Left: Olivier Berrouet has succeeded his father Jean-Claude as winemaker. **Above:** Christian and Dionysian symbols coexist.

Pétrus
Total area: 28.5 acres (11.5ha)
Area under vine: 28.5 acres (11.5ha)
Average production: 30,000 bottles
33500 Pomerol
Tel: +33 5 57 51 17 96

La Conseillante

British importers and consumers have always had a soft spot for Château La Conseillante. It has the minerally dark-fruit notes and structure that remind them of their favorite wines from the Médoc. This is curious, since the wine is made with the traditional Pomerol blend of 85 percent Merlot and 15 percent Cabernet Franc.

As is often the case, it all comes down to the vineyard, the boundaries of which have not changed since 1871 in this instance. This is the date the ancestors of the present owners, the Nicolas family, acquired the estate, the name taken from previous owner Catherine Conseillan. Situated in one block, the vineyard lies to the south of Vieux Château Certan, a part touching Pétrus and L'Evangile, with an 11-acre (4.5ha) sector still farther south across the tiny RD244 road in what is effectively the commune of St-Emilion but part of Pomerol. The neighbors here are Cheval Blanc and Beauregard.

La Conseillante has the minerally dark-fruit notes and structure reminiscent of wines from the Médoc. As is often the case, it all comes down to the vineyard

There are two soil types that run north–south through this land mass: gray clay to the east, sandy gravel to the west, with *crasse de fer* almost everywhere 6.5ft (2m) below the surface. "The Cabernet Franc grown on stony gravel gives the minerality, and Merlot on gravel soils the finesse, the power coming from Merlot cultivated on clay," explains the winemaker and manager Jean-Michel Laporte.

An average age of 32 years has been maintained in the vineyard, with the oldest parcel dating back 57 years, though it is due for grubbing up and replanting in the next couple of years. New plantings have a density of 7,500 vines/ha, with the rest of the vineyard a respectable 6,000 vines/ha. Part of the inconsistency La Conseillante experienced in the 1990s was due to high yields, so since 2001 the aim has been 38–40hl/ha, the vines pruned to the *taille Bordelaise* and the leaf canopy improved.

This is a classic estate in every sense, the Nicolas family unwilling to change or rock the boat. After the ups and downs of the 1990s, however, when one of the family members oversaw the winemaking, it was clear that a more professional approach was needed. A manager arrived in 2001, to be replaced in 2004 by the level-headed and efficient Jean-Michel Laporte. His fine-tuning has improved quality, but he embraces the traditional Moueix school of winemaking (where he once had work experience), so the style of La Conseillante hasn't altered.

The harvest used to be carried out by pickers who were lodged at the estate (one of the last to do so). But since 2009 a specialist company has been retained, making it is easier to organize the selective picking and the stop-start approach that has now become de rigueur. The grapes are then sorted at the cellars and destemmed via a gentle destemmer known as an *égreneur*, which was purchased in 2003.

The vinification is fairly classic and takes place in stainless-steel tanks that were introduced in 1971. "My philosophy is to work the must early on in the absence of alcohol, so we do a cold soak, then add yeast and do a fair amount of *remontage* until the point of mid-density is reached," explains Laporte. There is no artificial concentration, *pigeage*, or microoxygenation, and the malolactic fermentation takes place in tank. In 2008, Laporte inoculated the must with lactic bacteria in order to speed up the malolactic fermentation. About 6–7 percent press wine is incorporated in the final blend.

Right: La Conseillante's able winemaker Jean-Michel Laporte, with wine-stained matting from a traditional vertical press

Aging takes place in 80–100 percent new oak barrels over 18 months, with classic racking and egg-white fining and filtering if needed. Laporte has changed the toasting of the barrels to "medium-long at a lower temperature"—what the coopers call a *chauffe Bourguignon*. Another change has been the introduction of a second wine, Duo de Conseillante, from the 2007 vintage. This is produced from young vines and a parcel on sandier soils close to Cheval Blanc. Rejected wine was previously sold to the négociants.

Plans for a new *cuvier* were well in hand when the world financial crisis hit in 2009. The work had to be postponed until 2010, but a glimpse at the architect's plan showed that smaller concrete tanks would replace the stainless-steel vats and that they will be aligned in an oval form.

FINEST WINES

Château La Conseillante

I have limited experience of older vintages at La Conseillante, and so does Jean-Michel Laporte, because there's precious little at the domaine. He assures me, though, that the 1928, 1949, and 1959 were superb and that the 1970 and practically all the vintages through the 1980s were excellent. On my most recent visit, he wanted me to taste the 2001 and 2006 in particular, since they epitomize for him La Conseillante's style—the 2005, for instance, being richer and more powerful. The estate has been on top form throughout the new millennium.

2001★ Dark hue. An almost Médocain nose of minerals, dark fruit, mint, and violets. A clean, fresh attack followed by generous mid-palate fruit, with balancing acidity. Long, firm finish. Very fine.

2006 Dark color. A slightly reserved nose, but fresh, with a note of creamy oak and cassis. Minerally palate, the freshness and acidity apparent. Smooth and intense. The tannins are firm but sleek and integrated, and there is good length on the finish. Long aging potential.

Above: The discreet gatepost reflecting the restraint of the wine, and the distinctive wrapping paper around a classic vintage

Château La Conseillante
Total area: 30 acres (12ha)
Area under vine: 30 acres (12ha)
Average production: grand vin 50,000 bottles; second wine 4,000 bottles
33500 Pomerol
Tel: +33 5 57 51 15 32
www.la-conseillante.com

L'Eglise-Clinet

This is one of those properties that you wouldn't give a second glance if you didn't know the quality and price of the wines. A simple farmhouse and cellar abut a local cemetery, the L'Eglise-Clinet signpost looking as if it has seen better days. It's the home of Denis Durantou, the quick-witted and perspicacious owner/winemaker, and his artist wife Marie Reilhac.

Durantou took over the family property in 1983, since when he has steadily improved quality and the estate's prestige has risen. With finances limited in the early years, efforts were (and still are) centered on the vineyard. This comprises a handful of parcels on clay and clay-gravel soils on the plateau by the house, as well as opposite the winery of neighboring Château Clinet. The heart of the wine comes from old vines that endured the 1956 frost, the Cabernet Franc being planted in 1935.

The other half of the vineyard was replanted after the 1956 frost, but Durantou has been steadily replanting again. "I should have started earlier, since the quality of the rootstock and vines used at the time was not good. But there were financial constraints, and I was also restrained by reverence for the work of my ancestors," he explains. All told, 6 acres (2.5ha) have since been replanted, some at a density of 8,000 vines/ha, with the fruit from the young vines now in the grand vin.

The use of fertilizer was stopped in 1989 to correct the balance of the soil. Organic compost is now occasionally used to make adjustments. Deleafing and green-harvesting are systematic, the harvest date selected to avoid *surmaturité*. "If temperatures are high, Merlot can change in 24 to 48 hours with resultant loss of aroma, so you need to move quickly, since there's no going back," Durantou says. Most of the selection is in the vineyard, though there are now two sorting tables at the cellar.

Contrary to appearance and temperament, Durantou is not a new-wave man when it comes to vinification, and he eschews practices such as cold-soaking, microoxygenation, and even malolactic fermentation in barrel. He prefers a long, slow fermentation at the relatively low

Below: The modest farmhouse at L'Eglise-Clinet reflects the authenticity but not the grandeur or reputation of the wine

temperature of 79–84°F (26–29°C). "The alcoholic fermentation must last seven days," he claims. The only items of modern technology visible are the small stainless-steel tanks he purchased in 2000 to vinify the parcels separately.

The other major change has been the use of new oak barrels. In the late 1980s Durantou was using only 30 percent new oak, and in 1989 he didn't use any. This increased to 50–65 percent from 1995 and is now at or close to 80 percent for vintages such as 2000, 2005, and 2008. The wine is aged for up to 18 months with traditional racking and egg-white fining.

Clearly the oak has added an extra edge of refinement and complexity to a wine that already had depth, intensity, and its own vital personality. There's the Pomerol richness of fruit, but also structure and acidity to give it balance. Remarkably, the price of L'Eglise-Clinet was only $11 a bottle en primeur in the early 1990s, but it spiraled from 1995 onward.

Durantou also produces a wine called La Petite Eglise, which is occasionally referred to as L'Eglise-Clinet's second wine. This is not the case: the grapes come from a separate 3.2-acre (1.3ha) parcel of Merlot grown on sandier soils. Given the price differential, though, it's relatively good value.

FINEST WINES

Château L'Eglise-Clinet
I'm indebted to Denis Durantou for organizing this tasting of double magnums during Bordeaux's biennial wine fair, Vinexpo, in 2009. Those invited were treated to some exceptional wines. The blend for almost all of them is roughly 85% M and 15% CF, though the 2005 has up to 90% M. The Cabernet Franc is uniquely from old vines.

1985★ Superb—at its apogee at the tasting. Red, with brick to rim. The first nose was hesitant, then it became exuberant, opening to dark- and red-fruit and truffle notes. Sweet, firm, and positive on the palate, with good density and length. Quite unctuous. Cassis notes. Still some reserve.

1988 This had the highest acidity in the lineup, with a pH of 3.5, and I guess it shows. Youthful red color. The nose has minerally, leafy, undergrowth notes, and there is a similar spectrum on the palate. Some sweetness on the attack, but lighter-bodied and fresh, the acidity evident. Finishes a little dry.

1989★ Powerful, complex, and ultimately fine. Red, with brick at the rim. A fragrant, aromatic nose, just like a fine Burgundy—violet, spice, and coffee notes. A wonderful palate—opulent, decadent even. Big structure but fine, ripe tannins.

1990 Rich and generous but not the complexity or stature of 1989. A dark inner core, with brick at the rim. Truffle and red-fruit notes on the nose. Round, sweet, and unctuous, but the tannins are a little more vigorous than in the preceding vintage.

1995 Lighter and less imposing. Bright, youthful red but limpid at the rim. Medium-bodied with leafy, *sous-bois* notes. Some sweetness, but the tannins are angular and a touch drying on the finish.

1998★ More classical in style. Deep, bright color. Dense, rich, but fresh and poised. Lovely fruit and texture. The tannins are firm but fine. Great length and balance.

1999 A great effort for the vintage. Deep red color. The nose is simpler than for the 1998, with dark- and red-fruit notes. The palate is surprisingly rich, with a vanilla-oak nuance. Assertive tannins. Beginning to drink but still with plenty of reserve.

2000 A powerful wine, with the highest level of tannins in the lineup. A rich but elegant nose with a note of *crème de cassis*, the oak adding an exotic touch. The palate is ripe, sweet, and complex. Big tannic frame. Long aging potential.

2005★ Modern, exotic, but so refined. Deep, dark color. Decadent, spicy, creamy nose with a note of *liqueur de fruits*. The oak is still present on the palate, giving chocolate and vanilla notes, but it is packed with fruit behind. Smooth, velvety texture. Powerful tannins but more finesse than in 2000.

Left: The dynamic, independent-minded Denis Durantou, in front of a mural painted by his artist wife Marie Reilhac

Château L'Eglise-Clinet
Total area: 12 acres (5ha)
Area under vine: 11 acres (4.5ha)
Production: 15,000–18,000 bottles
33500 Pomerol
Tel: +33 5 57 25 96 59
www.eglise-clinet.com

Le Pin

Jacques Thienpont still looks somewhat bemused by the whole thing. What started out as a hobby for the unassuming Belgium-based négociant has spiraled into the production of a mythical wine, the price equally fabled. He's now gotten his head around the pricing factor but insists that it is the market and scarcity that create the dizzy figures. As for tales of launching the garage movement, he just shakes his head and smiles.

The true story goes something like this. In the 1970s, the tiny 2.47-acre (1ha) property of Le Pin, complete with unprepossessing house and pine trees (two), came up for sale. Jacques's uncle Léon, then manager of Vieux Château Certan, recognizing the quality of the land and its proximity to his own estate, recommended buying it to bolster Vieux Château Certan. The Thienpont family decided it was too expensive, but urged on by his uncles Léon and Gérard, Jacques bought Le Pin on his own account in 1979.

Jacques had indulged in a little winemaking with Léon, but this was the chance to try it out on his own. Facilities and equipment for the first vintage, the 1979, were rudimentary: an earthen floor in the basement of the house, a single stainless-steel tank, a hand pump, a press, and a set of used barrels from Vieux Château Certan for the malolactic fermentation (in the absence of anything else) and maturation.

In 1978, 40 percent of the plot had been replanted, so it was not until 1981 that the entire vineyard was harvested for Le Pin. In 1984 and 1986, further acquisitions were made: the first a vegetable plot contiguous to Le Pin that Jacques then planted to vines; the second about half a hectare of vines owned by the local blacksmith.

The entire area is located on a high point of the Pomerol plateau, the soils gravelly with more sand as the land gently tapers away. There are

Right: The distinguished Belgian merchant Jacques Thienpont, whose wine started as a hobby but soon fetched record prices

What started out as a hobby for the unassuming Belgium-based négociant has spiraled into the production of a mythical wine. As for tales of launching the garage movement, he just shakes his head and smiles

a few pre-1956 vines, but replanting has given the vineyard an average age of 28 years and made Merlot the unique variety. Yields are kept to around 30hl/ha. A little less than an acre (about a third of a hectare) was grubbed up in 2008 and replanted in 2010.

Le Pin's notoriety spread from the mid-1980s. Robert Parker gave a high score to the 1982, while Swiss buyer René Gabriel and French journalist Jacques Luxey began to sing the wine's praises, the latter referring to it as the "DRC of Pomerol." Wine collectors began to show interest, and demand steadily increased for the new cult wine. The rest owes much to Le Pin's scarcity and to activity on the secondary market. In 2008, a magnum of the 2000 sold for $6,300, while the 1982 sells at around $30,000 a case.

The cellar and equipment may have improved, but the traditional style of winemaking has remained constant over the years. "It's a question of letting nature take its course and preventing accidents from happening," says Jacques. The grapes are hand-harvested in roughly a day and a half, the sorting done in the vines. Vinification is still in stainless-steel tanks, and natural yeast is used for the fermentation. The tanks may be lightly bled if concentration is required. New oak barrels from Seguin Moreau have been used for the malolactic fermentation and aging since 1981. There is a selection for the grand vin, the rejected wine sold to négociants in Belgium.

In 2009, plans were drawn up for a brand-new winery that may see the light of day in 2011. A tiny but sleek construction will replace the peculiar old house, but the pine trees will remain.

FINEST WINES

Château Le Pin
My experience of Le Pin is limited mainly to the en primeur tastings, where I've often found the Burgundian character to which Jacques Luxey refers. It's expressed in the wine's refined perfume and fragrance, its silky texture, and its vibrancy in certain years. There's always a concentration of fruit, but it's never blockbuster in style. An exotic note stems from the aging in new oak barrels. I suspect (but have no proof) that the wine is now more refined and less brash than in the past. Because it is produced uniquely from Merlot grown on gravel, weather conditions need to be just right, and in very dry years Le Pin does not perform to its best. Jacques Thienpont did not make a vintage in 2003 and prefers the refined and crystalline 2006★ to the rich, concentrated, but more one-dimensional 2005. I must say I agree. The 2008★ also has the makings of another fine vintage. One of the objections leveled at Le Pin is its questionable ability to age, but following a retrospective tasting (1979–2006) held in Los Angeles in 2008, Jacques Thienpont assures me that the older vintages are keeping well.

2001★ This is Le Pin in fine, digestible guise (2006 and 2008 are similar). Garnet hue. Concentrated fruit on the nose but with lift and zing. Red-fruit aromas. The palate is soft, smooth, and fleshy but with an acidity and structure that give it freshness and length. Beginning to open at around eight years of age but has plenty in reserve.

Above: The dramatically ordinary house and winery at Le Pin will soon be replaced, but the eponymous pine(s) will stay

Château Le Pin
Total area: 5.4 acres (2.2ha)
Area under vine: 4.7 acres (1.9ha)
Average production: 6,000 bottles
33500 Pomerol
Tel: +32 5 57 51 33 99

Vieux Château Certan

Vieux Château Certan is indisputably one of the leading Pomerols and has been since at least the mid-19th century. Its situation indicates the potential for excellence, the vineyard located at the heart of the Pomerol plateau alongside those of Pétrus, La Conseillante, and L'Evangile. Nor do the wines disappoint, being of a profound nature, firm but fine and upright, with impressive persistence. In style, there's a nuance of the Médoc rather than the fleshier and more exuberant side of Pomerol.

The property was acquired by the Belgian négociant Georges Thienpont in 1924 and has been immaculately run since, first by Georges, then by his son Léon, and now by his grandson Alexandre. The continuity has evidently played a part in maintaining VCC at the highest level; few vineyards of this size are in such perfect condition and have been managed from the beginning with a view to the very long term.

The vineyard, after all, is where the character of the wine lies. There are three soil types—heavy clay, clay-gravel, and gravel—each of which determines the grape variety planted. Merlot, which represents 60 percent of plantings, is located on the clay; Cabernet Franc, whose proportion has increased to 35 percent, on clay-gravel; and Cabernet Sauvignon, now 5 percent, on gravel. Fertilizer was last used 20 years ago, and spraying is kept to a minimum.

Two thirds of the vineyard was replanted after the 1956 frost, but there are still some old parcels dating from 1932 and 1948. A steady system of rotation has seen other parcels replanted in 1967, 1982, 1988, 1990 (using the estate's massal-selected Cabernet Franc), and 1998, the Thienponts aiming to maintain an average age of 40–50 years. Another 3.2 acres (1.3ha) will be replanted in 2010 and 2011. "The difficulty is choosing the parcels to replace, because they all produce good wines, but I have to think ahead to the future," explains Alexandre Thienpont. The new plantings have to bide their time for use in

the grand vin, so the 1982 parcel was included only from 2001, and the 1998 parcel is used systematically in the second wine for the moment.

Thienpont comes across as discreet and edgy on first encounter, but he has the family affinity for the land and the eye and intellect to set high standards. Following experience as the *régisseur* of Château La Gaffelière in St-Emilion, he took over the management at VCC in 1985 and has moved the property forward with the times. He introduced the second wine, La Gravette de Certan, reduced yields, and brought more precision to the cultivation. He has also insisted on systematic destemming and 100 percent new oak barrels for the grand vin.

He's adamant, though, about maintaining the character of the cru. "The greatest wines are those that are completely authentic, that respect the place they come from, and that avoid pretence and manipulation," he says. His views on winemaking indicate a traditional approach, though he's pragmatic enough to ensure that VCC is up to speed technically. Air conditioning was installed in the cellars in 2003, along with temperature control for the wooden vats. "The essential work is done in the vineyard," he says. "After that the wine is simply fermented grape juice that is matured in oak, fined with egg white, and not filtered."

FINEST WINES

Vieux Château Certan

The gravel soils and high proportion of Cabernet clearly have an influence on the style of the wine, but the expression can vary with the vintage, as can the blend. The 1998, a very Merlot year, had 85% M, 10% CS, and only 5% CF, which was not considered successful. In contrast, the difficult 2003 vintage was produced from 80% CF (but only 9,600 bottles were produced). Thienpont also highlights the fact that the blend can be virtually the same in vintages like 1995 and 1996 (a more classic 60% M, 30% CF, 10% CS) but the expression different—in this instance, Cabernet dominating in the refined 1996, Merlot in the 1995. The important feature is the authenticity of the wine and the vintage. As at many Bordeaux estates, the 1970s were a weak period at VCC, but quality returned in the 1980s with the magnificent 1982, 1986, and 1988. Recent vintages have been outstanding, particularly 2005 and 2006.

1998 Ruby color. Subtle red-fruit and laurel notes. Ripe but within reason. Open-fruited, but one can sense the reserve. The palate is round and fleshy but with a firm, linear structure to hold it together. Lovely balance, with plenty of freshness and verve.

2000★ Magnificent wine. Ruby red. A dense, minerally nose with violet, dark cherry, and coffee notes. Beautiful purity of fruit on the palate, the texture fine, the finish long and persistent. Really fresh, racy, and elegant. Long aging potential.

The important feature is the authenticity of the wine and the vintage. Recent vintages have been outstanding, particularly 2005 and 2006

Left: The intellectual and sensitive Alexandre Thienpont at VCC, his high aspirations reflected by the glider on his laptop

Vieux Château Certan
Total area: 40 acres (16ha)
Area under vine: 35 acres (14ha)
Average production: grand vin 48,000 bottles; second wine 14,400–18,000 bottles
33500 Pomerol
Tel: +33 5 57 51 17 33
www.vieuxchateaucertan.com

Clinet

Despite favorable references in the Cocks & Féret "Bordeaux bible" in the late 19th and early 20th centuries, Clinet did not make much of a splash until the mid-1980s. This was when Jean-Michel Arcaute took over the management from his father-in-law, the négociant Georges Audy, and in tandem with Michel Rolland started to produce wines in a luxurious, super-ripe, modern style. The property was sold to the GAN insurance company in 1991, but Arcaute stayed on, resigning only in 1999, after the sale of Clinet to the present owner, Jean Louis Laborde, in 1998. (Arcaute died in a boating accident in 2001.)

The Clinet style under Arcaute divides critics and consumers, the concentration palpable and a pleasure for some, but a little too excessive and with dubious longevity for others. The question is, which way hence? There seems to have been some indecision during the early years of the new management, but according to Ronan Laborde, son of Jean Louis and manager of Clinet since 2003, "the idea is to have more finesse in the wines."

The evidence is not completely conclusive yet, though I found the 2008 en primeur appealing in a modern but not overtaxed vein. Michel Rolland is still the consultant, but there's perhaps less *surmaturité* through slightly earlier picking, and since 2004 the new oak barrels have been reduced from 100 to 60 percent. Ronan Laborde and the new, young cellar master Romain Ducolomb (since 2006) are clearly on a learning curve, and it's my feeling that the wines can only get better.

The means for making good wine are clearly there. The vineyard is made up of a number of parcels, the majority on good terroir. There's a parcel on clay and gravel soils near the church and another in the same sector known as La Grande Vigne, with some old vines dating from 1937. A tiny plot near Vieux Château Certan is planted with Cabernet Franc, but it's not consistent, the feeling being that the clones used were not of good quality. The rest of the vineyard is located on the clay-gravel slope behind the winery and on the lower slope at La Soulatte, where there's more sand. Nearly 20 percent of the vineyard—3.7 acres (1.5ha)—was replanted in 2001 and 2006.

A brand-new cellar was inaugurated in 2004, equipped with nine 60hl oak vats and a modern vertical press. The grapes are gravity-fed into the vats, and after a cold soak, the fermentation takes place using manual *pigeage* and *remontage*. Malolactic fermentation is in barrel, and the wines are then aged for 16–18 months. A second wine, Fleur de Clinet, was introduced in 1997, but having missed a vintage in 2005, it has since become a négociant brand made from bought-in grapes.

FINEST WINES

Château Clinet

Clinet has an atypically high proportion of Cabernet Sauvignon for Pomerol: 10%, with a further 5% of Cabernet Franc, and the rest Merlot. Vintage conditions dictated 30% Cabernet in 2003 and 100% Merlot in 2001, but from 2004 to 2008 inclusive, the blend has reflected vineyard plantings.

2005★ The grapes were picked, chilled, then destemmed by hand this vintage. The maturity is clearly there, with notes of *liqueur de fruits* on the nose. A rich, opulent palate with freshness behind, the fruit attractive, but a little firmness on the finish.
2006 Dark color. Spice and compote of red fruits on the nose. The oak is present on the nose and palate, but the acidity provides a Burgundian freshness and nuance. Fresh but rather dry on the finish.
2007 Supple, soft, and round. Pleasant fruit, but the oak requires a little integration. For early drinking.

Right: The sign at Clinet may still date from another era, but the style of the wine has been evolving rapidly since the 1980s

Château Clinet
Total area: 22 acres (9ha)
Area under vine: 21 acres (8.5ha)
Average production: 35,000 bottles
33500 Pomerol
Tel: +33 5 57 25 50 00
www.chateauclinet.com

Gazin

The concept is relative, of course, but if any estate in Pomerol represents good value, then Gazin is surely it. The size of the property and a healthy production level certainly help, as does the sensible pricing policy of the owners. All the same, one shouldn't make the mistake of equating value with a drop in standards or an absence of terroir. Approximately 42 acres (17ha) of the 60 acres (24ha) planted are on the clay and gravel soils of the plateau alongside Pétrus and L'Evangile. And since 1988, considerable effort has gone into improving quality.

Gazin's establishment as a winery dates from the second half of the 18th century, the homely château built a little later in the early 19th. The négociant Louis Soualle, great-grandfather of the present owners, bought the property in 1917. On his death in 1946, his son-in-law, Edouard de Bailliencourt *dit* Courcol, took over the management. (The nickname Courcol, meaning "short neck," was bestowed by King Philip Augustus in 1214 for a feat of arms.)

The problems of succession hit the next generation. In 1969, Edouard's son Etienne was obliged to sell 11 acres (4.5ha) on the Pomerol plateau to Jean-Pierre Moueix of Pétrus, to maintain control of Gazin. He also had to relinquish his share in La Dominique, which was then part of the estate. The 1970s and 1980s were a difficult period for Gazin. The less interesting alluvial land below the château was planted, yields were pushed, and machine harvesting was the norm. "It was a period of convenience, with quality pushed to one side," says Nicolas de Bailliencourt, manager since 1988.

Gazin has steadily improved since then. Hand-harvesting was reintroduced, yields curbed (29hl/ha in 2006), and the process of selection tightened. Further progress occurred from 1996 with the inauguration of the new *cuvier*, which has permitted greater precision in the cultivation and vinification of individual parcels. Gilles Pauquet (also employed at Cheval Blanc and Canon) was subsequently retained as consultant oenologist from 1999, and since 2006 Mickaël Obert, formerly of Clos L'Eglise and Barde-Haut, has been responsible for the winemaking.

FINEST WINES

Château Gazin

The winemaking at Gazin is fairly traditional apart from a little manual *pigeage* for extraction and a proportion of the malolactic fermentation completed in barrel. Cold-soaking was to be trialed in 2009. Maturation is in 50% new oak barrels and lasts for up to 18 months. The blend is 85–95% Merlot, the rest Cabernet Sauvignon and Cabernet Franc. Nicolas de Bailliencourt says the Cabernet Sauvignon is not planted in the best sites but in good years is included in the grand vin. In the future he hopes to increase the proportion of Cabernet Franc. I've generally found the wines of Gazin full and satisfying, with enough structure for medium-term aging. The trio of 1988, 1989, and 1990 were successful, then there was a dip before a return to form in 1995. The 2000 appears to suffer from bottle variation. Vintages from 2004 onward have been particularly good and mostly underrated; 2003 was creditable but is for drinking now.

1995 Medium-bodied, round, and fleshy. Attractive fruit expression with a hint of leafiness creeping in. Adequate ripeness but not overly concentrated. A slight leanness on the finish. Fresh. Drink now.
2001 Deep color. Generous expression of dark fruits with a hint of leather and truffle. Sweet and full on the palate. The tannins are firm, if a little robust. Balancing acidity. Lacks some polish but plenty of fun.
2000★ [V] Definitely more refined. Deep purple color. Lovely purity of fruit. Blueberry, cherry notes. Chocolaty oak is apparent but integrated. Firm but fine tannins. Good acidity. Aging potential.

Left: The attractive 19th-century château at Gazin, whose much-improved wines represent some of the best value in Pomerol

Château Gazin
Total area: 65 acres (26.5ha)
Area under vine: 60 acres (24ha)
Production: grand vin 45,000–95,000 bottles; second wine 20,000–35,000 bottles
33500 Pomerol
Tel: +33 5 57 51 07 05
www.chateau-gazin.com

Trotanoy

In a region devoid of significant landmarks, the row of cypress trees leading down to the modest house and cellars of Trotanoy is a prominent feature. On the western edge of the Pomerol plateau, Trotanoy has the natural attributes to make fine wine: good drainage, a mix of soils, and sunny exposure—in short, an excellent terroir.

If Pétrus is the king of the Moueix stable, then Trotanoy is the prince pretender, the property acquired by Jean-Pierre Moueix in 1953. The wines can be every bit as dense and profound, with creaminess on the palate and a firmness, freshness, and minerality that belie the fact that the wine is made almost exclusively from Merlot.

Recent vintages show Trotanoy at the top of its game, the 2007 perhaps surpassing its august stablemate Pétrus. Trotanoy is clearly one of the greats of Pomerol

The vineyard comprises a single block but with two distinctive soil types. On the elevated sector in front of the château the soils are deep gravel over clay, the land as stony as certain areas of the Médoc. This is one of the earliest-ripening parts of the appellation, the gravel contributing to the complexity and minerality of the wine. The second section, on a slope behind the château, has deep clay soils that assist with the density and structure.

These heat-retaining soils helped Trotanoy withstand the devastating frost of 1956, and for a number of years the vineyard remained extremely old, with an average age of over 40 years. But an extensive program of replanting took place between 1985 and 1995, and the age of the vineyard had dropped to 21 years at the time of writing in 2009. "That's fine for us, since we feel that a vineyard in Pomerol is at its best between 17 and 27 years," explains Edouard Moueix, son of Christian.

The vineyard is cultivated meticulously in typical Moueix fashion, the soils plowed and a tiny zone of flatter land set to grass cover in alternate rows. The grapes are hand-harvested parcel by parcel in selective fashion and then sorted, destemmed, and vinified in a traditional manner. The maturation lasts for 16 to 20 months in 50 percent new oak barrels. "Trotanoy is so structured that too much new oak tends to dry it out," says Edouard Moueix.

FINEST WINES

Château Trotanoy
The reputation of Trotanoy was enormous in the 1960s and 1970s, with some spectacular vintages like 1961, 1967, 1971, and 1975. Following the magnificent 1982, there was a slightly hesitant period that a number of critics attributed to changes caused by a significant amount of replanting. This was brought to a close with a fine 1989. My notes from en primeur tastings of recent vintages show Trotanoy at the top of its game, the 2004 firm and imposing, the 2005 long, intense, and pure, the 2006 with classic elegance, and the 2007 perhaps surpassing its august stablemate Pétrus. Trotanoy is clearly one of the greats of Pomerol.
2001 Dark ruby-garnet hue. Slightly retrained on the nose, but fresh and minerally in tone. The palate is deep and intense, with a soft texture but firm tannic backbone. Notes of dark fruits, but also plenty of lift and freshness. Great overall balance.
2005★ Deep, dark color. Gentle, perfumed nose with a hint of pepper and spice. Fresh, elegant, and racy. The palate is deep and intense, with just a kiss of integrated oak and a firm but ripe tannic frame. Long, fine, and persistent.

Right: Brilliant, passionate, and professional, Christian Moueix and son Edouard are also the most powerful players in Pomerol

Château Trotanoy
Total area: 17 acres (7ha)
Area under vine: 17 acres (7ha)
Average production: 25,000 bottles
Etablissements Jean-Pierre Moueix
54 Quai du Priourat, 33500 Libourne
Tel: +33 5 57 51 78 96
www.moueix.com

L'Evangile

It's taken a while to get L'Evangile up to a consistent level, but the Rothschild (Lafite) family is finally getting there. Domaines Barons de Rothschild acquired 70 percent of the property from the Ducasse family in 1990, but the remaining shares were held by the formidable Madame Simone Ducasse, who in effect continued to run the show, ignoring the overtures of Baron Eric and technical director Charles Chevallier. Ducasse's only concession was the introduction of a second wine, Blason de l'Evangile. Otherwise there was little change, and the vintages of the 1990s were ultimately disappointing because the absence of investment hindered quality.

Then in 1999, the Rothschilds acquired the remaining shares, and work accelerated on renovation and improvement. A manager was brought in from Lafite, replaced in 2001 by the incumbent Jean-Pascal Vazart. The existing cellars were condemned, and a new *cuvier* and circular barrel cellar (somewhat Médocain in appearance) were inaugurated in 2004. In the vineyard a program of replanting was launched, and so far this has seen 11 acres (4.5ha) grubbed up and nearly 7.5 acres (3ha) replanted.

The vineyard is located at the southeast corner of the Pomerol plateau. There are a number of different parcels with varying soil types. Some are on clay soils in close proximity to Pétrus; others are on deep sand and gravel soils neighboring Jean Fauré and Cheval Blanc. The remainder are close to Gazin on gravel soils, including some with a higher silt and sand content—hence the need for selection and a second wine, which on average represents 30 percent of the production.

Parcel-by-parcel management in the vineyard is now more precise, the advent of the new *cuvier* allowing this process to be followed all the way down to the finished wine. Yields are held to an average 38hl/ha, those from the younger vines lower at 30hl/ha, with grass cover used to help curb vigor.

Some of the fruit from the young vines planted in 2003 has already been used in the grand vin.

Vinification is fairly traditional except for a cold pre-fermentation maceration for certain designated cuvées. The malolactic fermentation takes place in barrel, the different parcels of wine initially kept separate but progressively blended, ready for the en primeur tastings in early April. Between 75 and 100 percent new oak is used for the maturation, which takes 14–18 months. Sixty percent of the new oak barrels are supplied by the Rothschild's own cooperage in Pauillac.

FINEST WINES

Château L'Evangile

Clearly there were some very fine vintages in the pre-Rothschild era—1947, 1966, 1982, 1989, and 1990 to name only a few. The terroir is mostly admirable, and it shows in top years, the Rothschilds aiming for more consistency while rejuvenating a vineyard that was in decline. When on top form, the style is distinctly Pomerol: rich, round, and opulent with a density and structure for aging a number of years. The blend is usually 85–90% Merlot, the rest old-vine Cabernet Franc.

1998 There's a touch of elegance, but the wine lacks the panache of this exceptional Right Bank year. Fairly forward, berry-fruit nose with a leafy, herbaceous note. The palate is fresh and lively but not grand, and the tannins are angular.

2002 Garnet hue. Medium-bodied, with an attractive density of ripe fruit. Round and well balanced, but the oak is just a little excessive. A good effort.

2005★ Purple hue. This has all the density and power of a top year. Rich, ripe, and generous. Confit fruit, spice, and vanilla notes. The palate is full and concentrated, with firm, fresh tannins.

Château L'Evangile
Total area: 40 acres (16ha)
Area under vine: 32 acres (13ha)
Average production: grand vin 40,000 bottles; second wine 20,000 bottles
33500 Pomerol
Tel: +33 5 57 55 45 55
www.lafite.com

Hosanna

Its name may be somewhat pretentious, but Hosanna has impressed ever since its inaugural vintage in 1999. A glimpse at the location of the vineyard explains part of the reason why. Situated in a single block on the Pomerol plateau, it has as neighbors Lafleur, Vieux Château Certan, Pétrus, and Providence. The soils are deep clay in a third of the property, the rest gravel over clay and *crasse de fer*.

This is essentially the heart of what used to be Château Certan-Giraud, purchased by Etablissements Jean-Pierre Moueix in 1999 and rebaptized Hosanna (two other parcels were acquired by Château Nénin). Consistency at Certan-Giraud had been checkered in the past, and Moueix felt this was partly due to poor drainage. A drainage system has therefore been put in place, including two small wells with pumps to extract excess water.

It is passion all around at this jewel of a property. One feels it in their love of the place and of the wine, which despite its air of exclusivity has been a great market success

Methods of cultivation have also been revised, the soils plowed and now looking immaculate, and the leaf canopy improved. The Merlot, which represents 70 percent of plantings, was planted mainly after the 1956 frost, the Cabernet Franc—30 percent of the vineyard but 20 percent of the blend—in the 1970s. Roughly half a hectare was replanted in 2002 and 2003, with fruit from the young vines entering the grand vin in the 2007 and 2008 vintages.

Until the 2008 vintage, Hosanna was produced in the cellars of La Fleur-Pétrus, but it now shares the brand-new *cuvier* and cellars at nearby Providence. As for all the Moueix properties, the winemaking is traditional, with the only change—again from 2008—being that the malolactic fermentation was performed in barrel, a technique urged by Moueix's new technical director Eric Murisasco, with a view to making the wines more *aimable* at the en primeur tastings. Hosanna starts the period of maturation in 50 percent new oak barrels, the proportion of new oak either increasing or diminishing as the technical team sees fit.

FINEST WINES

Château Hosanna

The wine has all the power and opulence of a top Pomerol, as well as elegance and length. The guiding hand of the Moueix technical team means ripeness and concentration are never over the top, but the density and purity of fruit coupled with a note of oak do provide a slightly more modern allure. In general, Hosanna appears to take a little longer for the oak to integrate when in bottle. The quality was not deemed satisfactory in 2002, so Hosanna was not produced. Most of my notes are from the en primeur tastings, where I found the 2004 and 2006 similar in style, with good intensity but greater freshness and minerality. The 2005 had power and concentration; the 2007, a lighter weight and structure. The 2008 had elegance, density, and balance, and it promises much.

2001 Just beginning to open. Ruby color. Concentrated nose of damsons and spice, with a lick of vanilla oak on swirling. The palate is ripe, supple, and round with fine tannins and a reassuring glow.

2005★ Ruby-garnet hue. Restrained on the nose but an elegant red-fruit nuance. Vanilla oak apparent. Opulent fruit on the palate, with a firm inner core. Very Pomerol. The oak needs time to integrate, but this has the potential for long aging.

Château Hosanna

Total area: 11 acres (4.5ha)
Area under vine: 10 acres (4ha)
Average production: 18,000 bottles
Etablissements Jean-Pierre Moueix
54 Quai du Priourat, 33500 Libourne
Tel: +33 5 57 51 78 96
www.moueix.com

Rest of the Right Bank

The other Right Bank appellations have one thing in common with St-Emilion and Pomerol: the dominance of Merlot in the wine, with Cabernet Franc generally the foil. The terroir varies but, in some instances, can be similar, or even superior, to parts of St-Emilion. The one constraining factor is economic. Given the selling price of the wines, producers have to balance cost against return, meaning generally less investment in labor and material.

Fronsac and Canon Fronsac

In the 18th and 19th centuries, Fronsac sold at a higher premium than St-Emilion. Today, it is one of Bordeaux's most underrated zones and has difficulty marketing its name. Standards are not uniformly high, but the best wines are excellent, offering the power and generosity of a Pomerol, with the structure, minerality, and freshness of a good St-Emilion. The region is located to the west of the town of Libourne and forms a triangle bounded to the east by the River Isle and to the south by the River Dordogne. There are two appellations—Fronsac, with just over 1,980 acres (800ha) and, to the south, the tiny 750-acre (300ha) enclave of Canon Fronsac—but to all intents and purposes, this is a single zone. Only the higher, undulating ground is delimited, the flat alluvial river terraces reserved for generic Bordeaux. The soil structure is varied but is essentially clay and limestone on a base of fine-textured loamy clay known as *molasse du Fronsadais*. It's a late-ripening zone, and care is therefore needed with the maturity of the grapes to avoid the "rustic" label—dry, aggressive tannins exacerbated by a naturally high acidity and low pH. The best producers restrict yields and practice deleafing and green-harvesting to accelerate ripening and to aerate grape bunches. Sorting tables, softer extraction, and better-quality barrels have also helped lend more refinement to the wines.

Lalande de Pomerol

The 2,700 acres (1,100ha) of Lalande de Pomerol are located directly north of Pomerol, across the tiny Barbanne stream. There are two communal poles to the appellation—Lalande de Pomerol and Néac—each situated the opposite side of the busy N89 road. The soils vary considerably, with certain areas offering better-than-average potential for Merlot. These include the Chevrol plateau in Néac, an extension of the Pomerol plateau at the same altitude (115–130ft [35–40m]), the soils a mix of clay and fine gravel. On the edge of the Barbanne nearby, a small *coteau* has gravel and deeper clay, while a band of land on either side of the N89 offers a mix of stony gravel and clay with traces of *crasse de fer*. The farther west one goes, the sandier the soils become. Overall, Lalande de Pomerol has more gravel, but Néac has a greater proportion of clay. The appellation has traded on the Pomerol suffix for some time without setting the world alight, but new investment and better vineyard practice have helped progress in recent years. Forty percent of the producers own land in neighboring appellations and vinify and bottle outside Lalande's bounds.

St-Emilion satellites

The satellites are essentially the northern extension of St-Emilion's hillslope terrain. Four communes—Lussac, Montagne, Puisseguin, and St-Georges—totaling some 9,900 acres (4,000ha), have the right to append "St-Emilion" to their communal names. The family resemblance is close, the wines being Merlot-dominated, the grapes grown on a mix of limestone, clay, and sandy soils. The potential for quality and finesse is at its greatest where a cap rock of *calcaire à astéries* occurs. With only 500 acres (200ha) of south-facing, clay-limestone slopes, St-Georges

Right: The hilly hinterland of Fronsac, which, along with other less well-known Right Bank appellations, has been on the rise

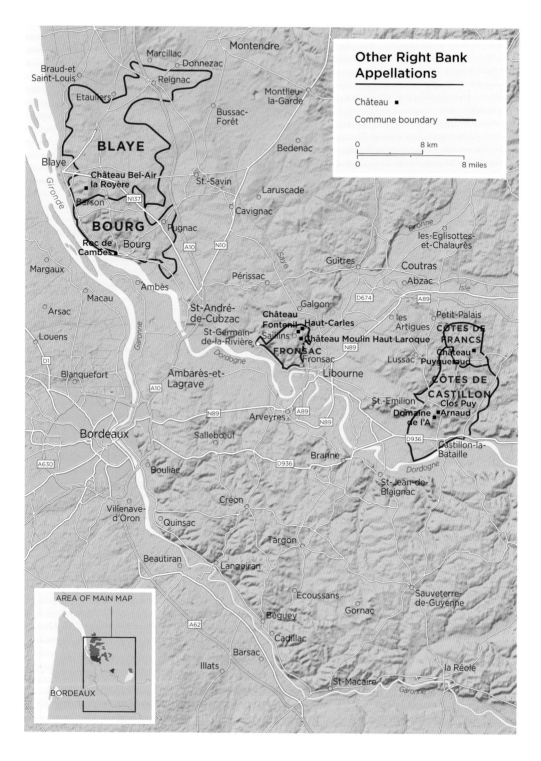

has the most homogenous terrain. Montagne, with 3,950 acres (1,600ha), has a good proportion of calcareous soil and, with it, the capacity for finesse, but there are also zones of heavier clay and sand. Puisseguin's 1,850 acres (750ha) have a dominance of clay-limestone, while Lussac's 3,630 acres (1,470ha) harbor the least propitious terrain, limestone outcropping around the village but elsewhere a preponderance of heavier clay and fertile sand. Fifty percent of the satellites' production is sold in bulk (the Lussac cooperative is a powerhouse in the region), and a large proportion of the rest by direct sale to local clients (export represents a mere 20 percent).

Côtes de Castillon and Côtes de Francs

Côtes de Castillon takes its name from the sleepy riverside town of Castillon-la-Bataille, the scene of the 1453 battle that marked the end of the Hundred Years War and English rule in Aquitaine. The 7,400-acre (3,000ha) region is basically the eastern prolongation of the St-Emilion hillslopes and, in many ways, has a similar profile to its neighbor. About 30 percent of the vineyards are located on the Dordogne plain, the rest on the limestone-clay slopes and plateau behind. Exposure is an important factor, with the harvest generally a good week behind St-Emilion. The simplest wines tend toward a briary fruitiness, while the better examples are rich and full, with a firm, fresh finish. In the late 1990s, the region benefited from an influx of investment, mainly from established producers in St-Emilion. Northeast of Côtes de Castillon, Côtes de Francs, with only 1,235 acres (500ha), is tiny in comparison. The close proximity and similar limestone-clay soils often make Francs a Castillon lookalike. With Cabernet Sauvignon and Cabernet Franc accounting for almost half the vineyards, however, there's a strong Cabernet influence that provides a touch of complexity and

a firm, linear presence on the palate. A little white is also made. From the 2008 vintage, Castillon and Francs (along with Côtes de Blaye and Premières Côtes de Bordeaux) have been part of the new appellation Côtes de Bordeaux, which is eventually set to replace the existing appellations. Cross-blending from these regions is permitted, but for those wanting to maintain the identity of a single terroir, stiffer controls permit AOC Côtes de Bordeaux with the suffix of the commune attached.

Côtes de Bourg and Côtes de Blaye

The 16,000 acres (6,500ha) of Côtes de Blaye—principally AOC Premières Côtes de Blaye—are spread over a vast geographical area but located essentially in three sectors: around the port of Blaye to the west; near St-Ciers in the north; and south at St-Savin. This used to be primarily a white-wine region (there's still a small production of mainly Sauvignon-based white), but it's now overwhelmingly red. Clay-limestone soils can be found around the hilly hinterland of the port of Blaye, but elsewhere there's a mix of sand, gravel, and clay on flatter land. The wines tend to be round, crisp, and lighter-framed. There's been considerable improvement in quality since the mid-1990s, thanks to new investment and a motivated younger generation. South of Blaye, the Côtes de Bourg (9,600 acres [3,900ha]) is made of sterner stuff. The wines tend to be chunkier and more substantial, with an earthy fruitiness and firm tannic structure. As in Blaye, Merlot is the major grape variety (70 percent), but the terroir is different. There's a greater abundance of clay-limestone soils, a hillier topography, a closer proximity to the warming waters of the estuary, and lower rainfall. Côtes de Bourg has decided to go it alone and, unlike Blaye, is not part of the new AOC Côtes de Bordeaux, which was launched with the 2008 vintage (see Côtes de Castillon and Côtes de Francs, *left*).

Domaine de l'A

Stéphane Derenoncourt won't forget the year 1999 in a hurry. He launched his winemaking consultancy Vignerons Consultants, married his wife Christine (also a winemaker), and produced the first vintage of Domaine de l'A. In those days he hadn't quite reached the level of renown and prosperity he enjoys today, so he came up with the novel idea of raising capital for his project by subscription. Two hundred members signed up for the venture, each paying $1,000, and they were reimbursed with 84 bottles of wine over the first four vintages. The subscribers invested well.

Derenoncourt's initial inclination was to look for land in favored Fronsac, the good terroir in St-Emilion being too expensive. But when nothing of interest came his way, he turned his attention to the Côtes de Castillon and found 6 acres (2.5ha) in Ste-Colombe. "The site is south-facing, and the limestone-clay soil is a little like the *tuffeau* of the Loire," Derenoncourt says. "Also, the previous owners had worked it organically, so the vines had not been saturated with chemicals."

The latter point was particularly significant, since Domaine de l'A has been run biodynamically from the outset. There's no official certification, and Derenoncourt reserves the right to use chemical treatment if necessary (an anti-botrytis spray was used in 2006), but otherwise the principles are respected, including the use of compost and *tisanes* and following the cycle of the moon.

The domaine has since grown to 20 acres (8ha), with further purchases of land in 2000, 2003, 2004, and 2006. The parcels are virtually all in one zone and located on south-facing slopes. "I set this as a priority, since Castillon is later-ripening due to its position east of St-Emilion and the greater proportion of clay," Derenoncourt says. Through the interplanting of rows and complantation, the density has been increased to 7,000 vines/ha.

Right: Stéphane Derenoncourt, whose excellent wines from Domaine de l'A have helped raise the stature of Castillon

In many ways Domaine de l'A is a model in work practices and ethics, cultivated at the level of a classed growth, with the luxury of a workforce of four permanent staff

Much else has been done to revive the land. Plowing is systematic, and one sector is plowed by horse. The old vines, some 50 to 70 years of age, have been maintained but retrained, the trellising and leaf canopy rectified. Yields are tiny in certain parcels, but overall, 35hl/ha is the average, with green-harvesting kept to a minimum. Cabernet Franc was planted in 2003 using massal selections from Pavie Macquin, L'Eglise-Clinet, and Vieux Château Certan. In many ways it's a model in work practices and ethics, cultivated at the level of a classed growth, with the luxury of a workforce of four permanent staff.

The first six vintages of Domaine de l'A were produced in a tiny makeshift cellar, but a new *cuvier* was inaugurated in 2005. The Burgundian-styled, vaulted barrel cellar was constructed along ecological lines using brick, stone, wood, and lime. "I indulged myself," says Derenoncourt with a smile. Winemaking and domestic effluent is now filtered and purified through pools with aquatic plants.

The harvest is lengthy, lasting up to three weeks, due to the repetitive *tries*. As one might expect, the winemaking practices follow the methods Derenoncourt advocates at many of his consultancies. These include the absence of cold-soaking and the fermentation of uncrushed berries in open-topped wooden tanks using *pigeage* for extraction. The malolactic fermentation is allowed to go naturally all the way through to spring, with the exception of en primeur samples. Aging is normally in 50 percent new oak barrels, with only limited racking.

FINEST WINES

Domaine de l'A

The interplanting of varieties (marked for selective hand-harvesting) makes it tricky to calculate the precise proportions, but the blend for Domaine de l'A is around 70% Merlot, 30% Cabernet Franc. Derenoncourt hopes to push the Cabernet Franc to 40% over the coming years. In the first few vintages there was a second wine—B de l'A—but that ceased from 2002. In terms of style, the wines have a similarity with those from St-Emilion's limestone plateau, the acidity and minerality apparent. The texture and tannins are fine, the rusticity associated with the Côtes de Castillon absent. The extraction is never excessive, and the oak is well integrated.

2005★ Deep, bright garnet hue. Superb nose of ripe, unctuous fruit. Quite complex, with notes of black currant and cedar. The palate is round and supple on the attack but refreshingly lively as well. A firm tannic frame and tight, chalky finish. Accessible, but will age.

2006 Castillon caught the full dose of harvest rain, so this was a difficult year. Despite plenty of *saignée*, the wine reflects the conditions, being lighter-hued, less finely aromatic, and more austere. The attack is full and supple, but the middle is a little leaner and the finish firmer. Will need time to round out.

2007★ [V] A great effort for the vintage; elegant and smooth. Lovely purity of fruit on the nose, with well-integrated oak. A silky texture and middling intensity, the acidity and minerality giving it lift and grip. Earlier drinking in the style of the vintage, but there is the structure for a little age.

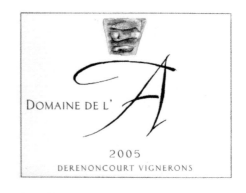

Domaine de l'A
Total area: 20 acres (8ha)
Area under vine: 20 acres (8ha)
Average production: 25,000 bottles
Lieu-dit Fillol
33500 Ste-Colombe
Tel: +33 5 57 24 60 29
www.vigneronsconsultants.com

Clos Puy Arnaud

"Organics used to be considered foolish. Now the concept is deemed good but not for the Bordelais," recounts Puy Arnaud owner Thierry Valette. There's been a change of mind-set in Bordeaux in recent years, but organic cultivation is still a minor cause. Valette purchased Château Pervenche-Puy Arnaud in 2000, converting to organic viticulture in 2001 and to biodynamics from 2005. He also changed the name of the grand vin to Clos Puy Arnaud.

Valette was a family shareholder in Château Pavie, its sale in 1998 enabling him to finance his own domaine. Originally set for a career in music and dance, he returned to Bordeaux in the 1980s, gaining viticultural and winemaking experience at Pavie, Tertre Roteboeuf, and Pavie Macquin. At the latter he was introduced to biodynamics by Maryse Barre and the young Stéphane Derenoncourt. "I was able to see at first hand the advances being made in the vineyard compared to Pavie, which was more conventionally run," he says.

The idea evidently gelled, because organic and, later, biodynamic principles were rapidly introduced at Clos Puy Arnaud, with Derenoncourt initially the consultant. The conversion has not been without incident, and a third of the crop was lost to mildew in 2007. "You need experience, technical ability, and good personnel to cope with the difficulties presented by Bordeaux's climate, so it takes time to master," says Valette.

Of course, a good terroir and a qualitative approach also help. The majority of the vineyard is located on a limestone plateau at Belvès de Castillon. The topsoil is thin, with only 8–28in (20–70cm) before the bedrock of *calcaire à astéries* appears. Wines from these soils tend toward finesse, but Valette believes that power has been added with the conversion to biodynamics. A further acquisition of 7.5 acres (3ha) on limestone (*tuffeau*)-clay slopes at St-Genès de Castillon has also added structure. Yields are maintained at a level of 30–35hl/ha.

Winemaking, as one might expect, has been strongly influenced by Derenoncourt, the one exception being the application of a cold pre-fermentation maceration. The grapes are uncrushed, native yeasts used, and the wine vinified in concrete and wooden tanks, with *pigeage* used in the latter. Aging is in 30 percent new oak barrels and lasts 12–14 months with limited racking. The second wine, Cuvée Pervenche-Puy Arnaud, changed to an unoaked, fruit-driven style from 2008.

FINEST WINES

Clos Puy Arnaud
As well as being expressive of their respective vintages, the three wines below represent stages in the evolution of the domaine. 2001 was Thierry Valette's second vintage, Stéphane Derenoncourt was the consultant winemaker, and the vineyard was only recently converted to organic cultivation. 2004 was the last year with Derenoncourt as consultant; biodynamic specialist Anne Calderoni took over in 2005. The official certificate of "biodynamic conversion" was granted in 2007. Stylistically, there's a generosity and purity of fruit that seems to prevail, balanced by the minerality of the terroir. The blend in most vintages is 70% Merlot, 25% Cabernet Franc, 5% Cabernet Sauvignon.
2001 Pure, linear, and long. Red-fruit aromas with a faint leafy note. Good mid-palate fruit. Fresh, minerally, and balanced. Drinking now.
2004★ [V] Excellent for the vintage. Dense, expressive fruit, with classic, minerally freshness. Black currant, licorice, and roasted notes on the nose. The palate is balanced, round, and supple, with a Cabernet-cassis nuance. Firm finish.
2007 Medium-bodied. Lacks the intensity of a top year, but balanced, fragrant, and pure. Cherry and other red-fruit notes. Supple and fresh, for earlier drinking than the 2004.

Clos Puy Arnaud
Total area: 35 acres (14ha)
Area under vine: 27 acres (11ha)
Average production: grand vin 25,000 bottles; second wine 7,000 bottles
7 Puy Arnaud, 33500 Belvès de Castillon
Tel: +33 5 57 47 90 33

Puygueraud

The Thienpont family have almost made the Côtes de Francs their fiefdom, and they now own some 10 percent of the vineyards in the 1,235-acre (500ha) appellation. Château Puygueraud, the largest and most prestigious of their properties, was bought by George Thienpont in 1946 and has been run by his son Nicolas (see Pavie Macquin and Larcis Ducasse) since 1983. The latter was the first vintage here for some time, the old vines having been grubbed up and the land turned over to mixed farming (cereal and cattle) in the 1950s and 1960s. Replanting resumed only in the 1970s.

George Thienpont was an admirer of the great Pomerol property Vieux Château Certan (in which he had a family interest), as well as of the wines of the Médoc, so he initially planted a high proportion of Cabernet Sauvignon. This worked in the warmer years but in retrospect was a mistake, the terroir being late-ripening (limestone-clay over a limestone bedrock on the plateau, with the addition of marl on the slopes). The altitude of 384ft (117m) is the highest in the Gironde. Nicolas Thienpont has steadily modified the plantings over the years and in 2004 grubbed up the last of the Cabernet Sauvignon, leaving the vineyard with a present-day total of 70 percent Merlot, 25 percent Cabernet Franc, and 5 percent Malbec. Some of the Cabernet Franc comes from the massal selection at Pavie Macquin.

In 2000, Nicolas Thienpont initiated the first vintage of the Cuvée George in honor of his father, who died in 1997. The wine, produced in selected years, has a high proportion of Malbec in the blend. Puygueraud's second wine, Château Lauriol, is made from the young vines and less successful parcels.

There is soon to be a white Puygueraud as well, some 10 acres (4ha) of Sauvignon Blanc and Sauvignon Gris having been planted in 2008 and 2009.

FINEST WINES

Château Puygueraud

In the years when Cabernet Sauvignon was still part of the blend, its influence is evident. Structured and firm, with a dark fruit character in warm vintages, the wines veer toward a slight rusticity and herbaceousness in cooler years. The Malbec offers a distinctive peppery note. The increase in Merlot has lent a touch more opulence and should improve consistency. These are wines constructed for aging and ideally would have at least six or seven years in bottle. The new oak component is about 25 percent.

2000★ Dark garnet hue. Shows intensity and depth of fruit. Firm and long on the finish, the palate displaying interesting complexity, with spice, mint, and pepper notes. The Cabernet element is ripe and present.

2004 A difficult vintage and the last with Cabernet Sauvignon in the blend. The attack is clean, the wine linear in style with a cassis note, but there's green pepper on the nose and sandy tannins.

2006 Purple-garnet hue. Spice, red fruit, and pepper notes on the nose. Supple fruit on the mid-palate, the tannins firm but fine. Marked acidity gives freshness and length. Harmonious, but it needs time to become fully resolved.

Château Puygueraud Cuvée George

This is a small production of 5,000 to 10,000 bottles produced in given years from selected batches of wine. The vintages 2000, 2001, 2003, and 2004 were produced with 35% Malbec, 35% CF, 20% Merlot, and 10% CS; vintages 2006 and 2007, from 50% Malbec, 30% CF, and 20% Merlot.

2004 Clearly a step up from the regular cuvée. Supple fruit on the palate, the tannins long and refined. Pepper and violet notes.

2006★ Intense but subdued, with a hint of violet on the palate. Tight, firm structure. A touch austere at present but should mellow with bottle age.

Château Puygueraud

Total area: 150 acres (60ha)
Area under vine: 85 acres (35ha)
Average production: grand vin 120,000 bottles; second wine 30,000 bottles
33570 St-Cibard
Tel: +33 5 57 56 07 47
www.puygueraud.com

Fontenil

As the world's most famous wine consultants, Dany and Michel Rolland require little introduction. But their property in Fronsac warrants further investigation. Château Fontenil doubles as family home and working domaine, as well as a site for experimentation, and all the elements of the Rolland philosophy of winemaking can be found here.

As fate would have it, the Rollands were in fact looking for a home rather than a vineyard when they came across the property in Saillans. "We wanted the house, but initially the owner would only sell the accompanying 8ha [20 acres] of vines," says Dany. And so it was that the vineyard was purchased first, in 1986 (Michel's consulting in the 1970s had given him a working knowledge of Fronsac), with the house following in 1990. It wasn't until 1997, however, that the Rollands were able to move in.

As the world's most famous wine consultants, Dany and Michel Rolland require little introduction. But their property in Fronsac warrants further investigation

In the interim, the cellars were steadily renovated, and Fontenil (the wine) was launched, the name taken from one of the parcels of land. The vineyard is located on a high point of the commune with a view over Libourne and Pomerol beyond. The soil is the classic limestone-clay of the region over a bedrock of *molasse du Fronsadais*, a limestone/clay/sandstone mix. But while the terroir is quite consistent, the exposures vary considerably: 12 acres (5ha) are south-facing, the rest are inclined to the east, northeast, and north.

The average age of the vineyard is high, at some 40 years. As one would imagine, it is managed in accordance with the now-famous Rolland tenets of low yields and optimum maturity. The trellising has been raised, and green-harvesting and deleafing (on both sides) are carried out systematically. In 2008, production fell as low as 20hl/ha—the lowest ever. Merlot is the principal grape variety, but there's also a little Cabernet Sauvignon. "It's been here since the beginning but is badly sited and rarely in the blend," explains Dany.

The renovated stone-built cellars are well stocked with an array of equipment: stainless-steel and wooden (for *pigeage*) tanks; barrels (60 percent new oak for Fontenil); Oxoline racks; sorting tables; and a brand-new vertical press. "The *cuvier* is really oversized for the domaine," Dany says with a hint of resignation. This becomes even more evident when I learn that, from 2008, a proportion of Fontenil and the entire production of Le Défi de Fontenil has been fermented in barrel (with dry ice used to permit a pre-fermentation cold soak).

There's a curious story behind the birth of Le Défi de Fontenil. In 1999, the Rollands decided, on an experimental basis, to use plastic sheeting under a parcel of vines to protect them from rain prior to the harvest. The French authorities acquiesced the first year but in 2000 refused appellation status to the grapes from the parcel. The Rollands, as a snub, bottled the wine as a simple vin de table, and the first vintage of Le Défi de Fontenil was launched. The sheeting was used again in 2001 and 2004, but since 2005 the wine has been produced more as a super-cuvée and as a vehicle for experimentation.

FINEST WINES

Château Fontenil

This is one of the leading wines in the appellation, the style ripe and opulent but not jammy, the generosity of the Merlot balanced by an inherent freshness. The tannins are polished and smooth. The wine is bottled without fining or filtration following 15 months in barrel, initially on fine lees.
2000 Ripeness is pushed to the limit, but it backs away from being overripe. Red-fruit and plum notes

on the nose; the palate is rich and concentrated but with balancing freshness. A suave texture but with the structure to age.

2001★ [V] This wine hits the button for me, offering just the right degree of ripeness, charm, and complexity. Spice, mineral, and red-fruit notes on the nose. A clean attack, good mid-palate fruit, and great balance.

2003 The roasted, curranty notes give a hint of the hot, dry vintage, but the wine holds up well. The palate is full, round, and supple, the tannins firm but not dry, giving decent length.

2005 [V] Rich and opulent but restrained at present. Attractive fruit with integrated spice. Structure firm and long. Powerful, long-term wine.

Le Défi de Fontenil

This is clearly not going to be everybody's cup of tea. Dark, rich, concentrated, flamboyant, the oak apparent—it's the antithesis of classic Bordeaux. However, there's an intensity and structure that suggest that, in the long term, the wine may settle into a subtler mode. The grapes used are from parcels of very old vines (more than 50 years old), and all manner of modern techniques have been used in the winemaking. Between 3,000 and 5,000 bottles are produced yearly.

2000 Whether it's a function of bottle age, or whether the techniques and the maturity of the grapes were less extreme, I found this a little more harmonious than the other vintages tasted. It's concentrated and structured but well knit.

2001 Dark, rich, and oozing fruit on the palate. The oak is still perceptible, providing chocolate and mocha notes. The tannins are round and smooth, while a touch of acidity adds a note of freshness.

2005 Perhaps one step too far? Black color. Sweet, ripe-to-overripe, confit fruit with an overlay of creamy oak. Massively rich and concentrated. Firm but polished structure. Time will tell.

Right: At home at Fontenil, Michel and Dany Rolland remain down to earth and fun-loving despite their consulting success

Château Fontenil
Total area: 30 acres (12ha)
Area under vine: 22 acres (9ha)
Average production: grand vin 35,000–40,000 bottles; second wine 15,000 bottles
33141 Saillans
Tel: +33 5 57 51 52 43
www.rollandcollection.com

Dark, rich, concentrated, and flamboyant, Le Défi de Fontenil is the antithesis of classic Bordeaux. However, there's an intensity and structure that suggest that, in the long term, the wine may settle into a subtler mode

Haut-Carles

Historically, architecturally, and now viticulturally, Haut-Carles is quite a remarkable property. The château, built in the 15th century, boasts fortified towers and cypress trees that conjure up a vaguely Tuscan air, while within the building, mosaics of tiles and scenes from North Africa offer further cultural surprise. More importantly for this book, the grand vin, Haut-Carles, has become a leading light in Fronsac and is fast approaching the level of the top crus in St-Emilion.

The owners, Constance and Stéphane Droulers, may live in Paris, where Stéphane is a merchant banker, but they are directly involved in the running of the estate. Constance's great-grandfather, Guillaume Chastenet de Castaing, a senator, acquired the property in 1900, and a sense of continuity is strongly felt. The commitment and investment are decidedly ambitious. "We want to make one of the greatest wines in Bordeaux, not just the Right Bank," says Stéphane.

In the 1980s Château de Carles was a sound but unexceptional wine marketed by Ets J-P Moueix. The Droulers' friend Robert Vifian of restaurant Tan Dinh proposed the idea of a special cuvée, and in 1994, 5 acres (2ha) of Merlot were set aside for special attention to produce the first vintage of Haut-Carles. The project has grown from there, with the entire vineyard now cultivated at the level of a grand cru (the whole gamut of "green" work, yields of 30hl/ha, new plantings at 10,000 vines/ha) but still with selected parcels for Haut-Carles.

A brand-new gravity-fed *cuvier* was inaugurated in 2003. Hygiene is at an optimum, and pumping is banned. A tiny proportion of Haut-Carles is now fermented in barrel, but the majority is in stainless-steel tanks. Following malolactic fermentation (in barrel), the wine is aged 18 months on fine lees in two thirds new oak barrels with minimal racking. The second wine, Château de Carles, is produced in a fruitier and less concentrated style. Since 2006, the technical expertise has been provided by Jean-Philippe Fort and Dr. Alain Reynaud.

FINEST WINES

Haut-Carles

The wine is produced essentially from Merlot (from selected parcels with the correct exposure and rootstocks), with an additional seasoning of a little very old Malbec. Cabernet Franc is grown but rarely makes the grand vin. It's perhaps the one component missing, since it would add greater aromatic complexity. A more-than-agreeable wine at the turn of the century, Haut-Carles took a significant step forward in 2003, with greater purity of fruit, then leapt again with the 2006 vintage. The wine has a wonderful depth of fruit and incredible texture, and it appears to mark the change toward a superior quality and style. These are wines that will definitely age.

2001 Lively, well-balanced wine with a good concentration of fruit. Plum and red-fruit aromas. Firm, tannic finish.

2002 In the same vein as the 2001 but with a lighter weight of fruit. Tannins a touch drier on the finish.

2003 Round, smooth, and supple. Has the plummy ripeness and warmth of the year, with a touch of well-integrated, chocolaty oak and a refreshing line of acidity. The tannins are firm but polished.

2005 Ripe but not overripe, opulent, and spicy. Greater aromatic complexity than previously. The palate is smooth, powerful, and intense, and the finish is firm and long.

2006★ A considerable step up, even from 2005. Deep color. Wonderful concentration of fruit. Distinguished mocha and dark-fruit notes. Gains in finesse of texture and opulence of fruit. Tannins powerful but smooth, the acidity adding length.

2007 A little fuzzy due to recent bottling but wonderful texture and tannins. Less powerful and more elegant than the 2006. Should be delicious.

Château de Carles
Total area: 50 acres (20ha)
Area under vine: 50 acres (20ha)
Average production: grand vin 25,000–30,000 bottles; second wine 50,000 bottles
33141 Saillans
Tel: +33 5 57 84 32 03
www.haut-carles.com

Moulin Haut Laroque

Jean-Noël Hervé has been at the forefront of the battle for greater recognition of Fronsac wines since he took over the family's property in 1977. Indeed, Moulin Haut Laroque could not be a better advertisement for the cause: impeccable maturity, admirable consistency, and the ability to age are all hallmarks of the wines.

It wasn't always the case. "The early days were difficult, because the wines weren't good and we lacked the means to invest," says the ever-garrulous, passionate Hervé. "But Michel Rolland gave us a bit of courage by saying that, if we improved our work methods, the future would be brighter." Thus inspired, Hervé set about the task of progressively overhauling the vineyard during the 1980s, with the trellising raised and the density increased to some 6,700 vines/ha. The next big step, at the end of the 1990s, was the use of grass cover to control vigor.

Impeccable maturity, admirable consistency, and the ability to age are all hallmarks of the Moulin Haut Laroque wines. But this wasn't always the case.

The vineyard is divided into two blocks. The Haut Laroque section is located at a high point in the appellation close to the vineyard of Haut-Carles. It's been in the family's hands since the late 19th century, and the soil has traces of magnesium within the clay. It also harbors the estate's oldest Cabernet Franc vines, planted before World War II. It forms the heart of Moulin Haut Laroque.

The Moulin portion lies on the plateau and the slope of the hill in front of the house and cellars. "The soils are limestone-clay, but there's more of a mosaic, the clay varying in depth within the zone," explains Hervé. Both sections have a stately age. The Malbec is 80 years old, some Merlot and Cabernet over 40, and the Cabernet Franc over 70.

A new *cuvier* was added in 1999, enabling the vinification to be handled more efficiently. The grapes are placed in stainless-steel vats by gravity, and pumping is kept to a minimum. Techniques are traditional, though there's a little manual *pigeage*, and Hervé often vinifies the old Malbec with the young Merlot—he feels it provides a better balance. Selection for the grand vin and second wine (Hervé-Laroque) is done purely by tasting, and if Hervé's not satisfied with a batch, then it's sold off in bulk.

FINEST WINES

Château Moulin Haut Laroque

Hervé admits that he places greater importance on the structure of the wine than on the aromatic expression. "I've had the privilege of tasting old vintages of Moulin Haut Laroque dating back to the 19th century, and that's given me the desire to produce wines that can age." Generally, all four grape varieties are used in the blend but not always from the same parcels. The wine is aged in 30–40 percent new oak barrels for up to 18 months.

1999 Medium-bodied, supple, and fresh, if a little austere. No great complexity but well constructed.
2001★ [V] Offers a lovely pitch of ripe, fresh fruit. Lively and harmonious, the palate dense, the tannins fine and long. A very engaging wine.
2003 Somewhat awkward but the same family structurally. Plummy expression with an overlay of creamy oak. Rich and full on the palate. Quite powerful and heady, but there's a nip of freshness to give balance and length.
2005★ Closed at present, but this has the intensity and structure of a grand vin. Rich and concentrated on the palate, with plenty of mouth-filling fruit. Big tannic frame. Great persistence and length.
2006★ [V] Less concentrated but livelier than 2005. The wine really dances. Long and linear, with real presence, good fruit, and length on the palate.

Château Moulin Haut Laroque

Total area: 44 acres (18ha)
Area under vine: 40 acres (16ha)
Average production: grand vin 50,000 bottles; second wine 10,000–20,000 bottles
33141 Saillans
Tel: +33 5 57 84 32 07
www.moulinhautlaroque.com

Roc de Cambes

In 1988, François Mitjavile acquired Roc de Cambes in the Côtes de Bourg. Worried by the financial fragility of owning a tiny, albeit successful, domaine in St-Emilion—Tertre Roteboeuf—he'd been looking for a solution when a friend told him about an estate for sale in Bourg. "I went with my wife, Miloute, on a filthy day in November. But as soon as we saw the property, we said, 'This is for us, because it's exactly the same type of terroir we've been working for the past ten years,'" Mitjavile recalls.

The 31-acre (12.5ha) vineyard forms an amphitheater overlooking the Gironde estuary, just on the edge of the citadel of Bourg. The soils are limestone-clay, the exposure south/southwest, the vines sheltered from the wind. Like Tertre Roteboeuf it has a dominance of Merlot (75 percent), but instead of Cabernet Franc the complement is old-vine Cabernet Sauvignon (20 percent) and Malbec. Mitjavile admits to being less convinced by the latter but has yet to have it grubbed up.

Roc de Cambes is cultivated and vinified in exactly the same way as its stablemate, without regard to cost. There is no second wine. The harvest, of course, is late but takes a little longer (three days, on average) due to the estate's larger size. Depending on the vintage, picking can be before or after Tertre Roteboeuf.

With a bank loan financing the project, Mitjavile's ambition from the outset was to transcend the commercial limitations of the Côtes de Bourg. He hoped that the combination of man, terroir, and a superb wine would be enough to seduce consumers, who would disregard the established hierarchy of appellations. The gamble actually took nearly 20 years to pay off, and one of Mitjavile's disappointments has been the time that it took for consumers "to open their minds" to the quality of the wine. Happily, they are doing so now.

FINEST WINES

Roc de Cambes

The following wines were tasted at Tertre Roteboeuf in 2008. This was convincing evidence that Roc de Cambes can stand with the best from St-Emilion and that, with time, application, and investment, the Côtes de Bourg has true potential. The wine has depth and intensity; an opulence of fruit, even in more "classic" years like 2004; an exotic touch; fine, silky texture; elegance, freshness, and length.

1988 (first vintage, aged in old barrels) Ruby hue. Mature Bordeaux in a classic style. Leafy, black-currant-leaf notes on both nose and palate. Fresh and persistent but a touch hard and austere.

1990★ Still well within itself. Ruby with a little brick at the rim. The warmth and ripeness of the year are appreciable in the aroma. Dark-fruit notes with a curranty, truffley nuance. The palate is full, fresh, and long, with an elegant texture.

1991 Brick-edged. Minerally notes on both nose and palate. A touch austere, firm, even hard, but proof that the terroir permitted a vintage this frosty year.

1995 Dark ruby hue. A powerful presence. Dense and full. Red-fruit, spice, and roasted aromas. Minerality shows, firm, fresh, and long on the palate. Coffee notes. The tannins are a touch robust on the finish.

2004 Firm ruby-garnet hue. Exotic nose of dark fruit, spice, coffee, toast, and orange zest. The oak is apparent but well integrated. The palate is supple with good fruit concentration and a confit nuance, but there is freshness, harmony, and finesse.

2005★ An impressive wine. Modern in style but rich, long, and elegant. Deep color. The nose has that exotic touch of spice, toasted oak, and dark fruit. Ripe and opulent on the palate, the wonderfully smooth texture backed by powerful but refined tannins. Freshness and length on the finish. A *grand vin*.

2006★ Deep color. An overriding impression of depth and intensity. An opulent palate, refined texture, and firm, linear structure. There is a vanilla hint, but the oak is well integrated. Creamy, ripe fruit but balancing freshness. Great potential.

Roc de Cambes

Total area: 33.5 acres (13.5ha)
Area under vine: 31 acres (12.5ha)
Average production: 60,000 bottles
33710 Bourg-sur-Gironde
Fax: +33 5 57 74 42 11
www.roc-de-cambes.com

Bel-Air La Royère

While most producers in Bordeaux were grubbing up their old Malbec, the Loriauds created their top wine, Bel-Air La Royère, around the variety. "Malbec is the soul of the property," says Corinne Loriaud. It has certainly helped to create one of the most distinctive wines in the Côtes de Blaye and to relaunch the variety in that region.

Corinne and Xavier Loriaud acquired the 22-acre (9ha) property at Cars in 1992 and, through leasing and further purchases, have expanded it to the present 58 acres (23.5ha). The original 13.5 acres (5.5ha) isolated for Bel-Air La Royère, however, remain the same. "The soil is a little like the *molasse du Fronsadais* with limestone, sandstone, and a high proportion of clay," says Xavier. "It's well drained, the water uptake is controlled, and consequently the vigor of the vine is restricted."

It's also where the old-vine Malbec is located. Plantings date from 1947, 1949, 1953, and 1965, with some complantation in 2009 to replace missing vines. The density is high, at 6,000 vines/ha. In the early years, the Loriauds commuted from their native Charente and sold the wine in bulk, but by 1995 they'd settled in the region and had decided to launch Bel-Air La Royère, giving Malbec the key role.

The 13.5 acres (5.5ha) receive special treatment, with a surplus of man-hours spent in the vines. Yields for the Malbec are around 25hl/ha; for the Merlot, 35–40hl/ha. Harvesting is late to achieve full phenolic maturity. The first vintage of Bel-Air La Royère to gain notoriety, the 1997 (a respectable wine in a difficult year) was harvested ten days later than most in the region. "The neighbors thought we weren't going to pick because we had no money to make the wine," says Xavier with a laugh.

The winemaking is fairly traditional up to the point of maturation. The malolactic fermentation takes place in barrel, and the wine is then aged on lees until the first racking in the spring. All told, the wine can spend up to 20 months in barrel, the new oak representing 80 percent of the final blend.

FINEST WINES

Château Bel-Air La Royère
The incidence of old-vine Malbec in the blend (up to 30%) gives this wine its distinctive character. The color is inevitably deep and dense, even black in youth, the aromatics redolent of dark fruit, spice, and pepper. The distinguishing feature on the palate is the acidity, which can be piercing, sometimes bitter—hence the need to push ripeness in order to create the opulence that fleshes it out and gives balance.
1996 Deep, dense color. Defies an estimate of age. Subdued aroma, with notes of pepper, spice, and cherry stone. An ample palate, fresh but with rounded tannins. The marked acidity provides a slightly hard and austere finish.
2002 [V] Dark hue. Rich and concentrated on the nose. Roasted, empyreumatic notes, with creamy, dark fruit. The palate is supple and fleshy, with well-rounded tannins, the Malbec providing freshness. A touch hard on the finish, but an excellent result for such a difficult year.
2005★ Powerful, brooding, and in need of time. Black color. The nose is intense but reserved, with subtle vanilla and chocolate notes. There is weight and depth on the palate, with acidity behind. Rounded tannins but a firm, tight finish.
2007 Purple-black hue. Round, supple, and forward. Attractive blueberry and vanilla-oak notes. Soft and lightly structured, the acidity adding a little zest. For early drinking.

Château Les Ricards [V]
I have no written tasting notes for the second wine, Les Ricards, but have come across it in restaurants and always found it appetizing and good value. It's approachable earlier than Bel-Air La Royère but still has line, length, and freshness.

Château Bel-Air La Royère
Total area: 58 acres (23.5ha)
Area under vine: 47 acres (19ha)
Average production: grand vin 20,000 bottles; second wine 45,000 bottles
Les Ricards, 33390 Cars
Tel : +33 5 57 42 91 34

Sauternes and Barsac

Bordeaux's sweet-wine zone is located 25 miles (40km) south of the city of Bordeaux. Production here takes place on both sides of the Garonne river—Cadillac, Loupiac, and Ste-Croix-du-Mont being the subordinate appellations responsible for output on the Right Bank (effectively in the Entre-Deux-Mers), with Sauternes, Barsac, and the more confidential Cérons on the Left. The French refer to these wines as *liquoreux*, including the notion that not only are they sweet and concentrated, but they have a character defined by noble-rotted grapes.

Sauternes and Barsac account for some 5,400 acres (2,200ha), encircled to a greater degree by the vineyards of the Graves. Separating Barsac from Sauternes, the cool waters of the tiny Ciron River flow into the warmer Garonne. This convergence assists with the development of early-morning mists—the perfect scenario for the onset of *Botrytis cinerea* or noble rot (*pourriture noble*). Humid conditions in Sauternes, where clay soils can be found, as well as a number of water springs, also assist with the development of fungal spores. In an ideal world, sun and wind in the afternoon then dry the grapes, assisting with concentration and preventing any malevolent rot.

As many as five communes are included in the delimitation of Sauternes: Barsac, Bommes, Fargues, Preignac, and, of course, Sauternes itself. Producers in Barsac have the right to bottle their wines with either the Barsac or the Sauternes label (and sometimes use both). Around Sauternes, Bommes, and Fargues, the terrain is hilly—about 260ft (80m) at the highest points. Soils are varied, a mix of sand, gravel, and clay, the clay found at a depth of 20ft (6m) but also outcropping in areas. Good drainage is essential, and most top growths have their vineyards artificially drained.

Vineyards in Preignac are situated on lower-lying land, the soils being sand and gravel with less clay. The Barsac plateau is also lower-lying but consists of a thin layer of red, claylike sand over a limestone bedrock. It's this that provides acidity, offering delicacy, freshness, and minerality in the wines. Power and opulence, to varying degrees, are the signature of Sauternes, while concentration is assisted by exposure to sun and wind, as well as the gravel and clay soils.

The three grape varieties cultivated in Sauternes are Semillon, Sauvignon Blanc, and Muscadelle. Semillon is by far the most important, its thin skin receptive to the attack of noble rot, whose spores feed on the liquid in the grape, concentrating the sugar, acid, and glycerine content by dehydration. Producers prepare the vineyards for this eventuality, the Semillon pruned *à cots* (a sort of spur-pruning with three to four canes, each with two buds) and green-harvesting and leaf plucking applied. Xavier Planty, part-owner and manager of Château Guiraud, informed me that noble rot developed less successfully with other systems of pruning, but he could not offer a scientific explanation for this observation.

Yields are limited to a maximum 25hl/ha and are generally lower at most top estates. The idea is to achieve "golden ripeness," with an alcohol potential of 12–14% before the onset of *Botrytis cinerea* in the autumn. Planty believes that the botrytis installs itself at flowering but remains dormant until the grapes are physiologically ripe.

The harvest is the key moment in the production of the wine. Noble rot develops in a haphazard fashion, and producers have refined the art of picking by selective *tries*. Ideally, they are looking for noble-rotted grapes with a potential of 21% ABV, which will then be turned into a wine with 13.5–14% ABV and residual sugar of around 120g/l. The art of efficient selective harvesting involves patience, a stop-start approach, and enough experienced pickers. The first *trie* is often to clean out grapes

Right: A plaque at Yquem commemorating the noble rot essential for all Sauternes, at once its greatest asset and risk

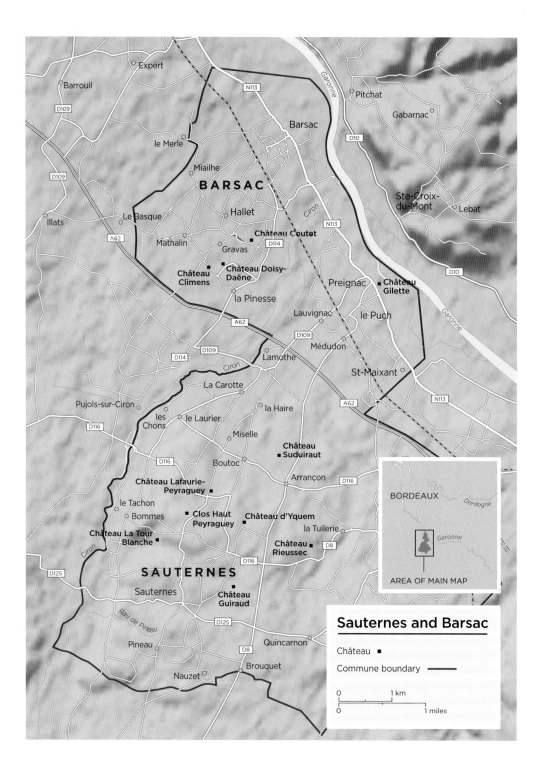

Expert

Barrouil

D109

D109

le Merle

N113

Miailhe

BARSAC

Le Basque

Illats

Hallet

A62

Mathalin

Gravas

Château Coutet

D114

Château Doisy-
Daëne

**Château
Climens**

la Pinesse

A62

D114

D109

Ciron

Lamothe

La Carotte

Pujols-sur-Ciron

les
Chons

le Laurier

D116

Miselle

D116

Boutoc

**Château Lafaurie-
Peyraguey**

le Tachon

Bommes

**Clos Haut
Peyraguey**

Château d'Yquem

**Château La Tour
Blanche**

Ciron

D125

SAUTERNES

Sauternes

**Château
Guiraud**

Rau de Pineau

D125

Pineau

D8

Quincarnon

Nauzet

Brouquet

Garonne

Barsac

Pitchat

D10

Gabarnac

Ste-Croix-
du-Mont

Lebat

N113

Preignac

**Château
Gilette**

Lauvignac

le Puch

Garonne

D109

Médudon

St-Maixant

A62

N113

D10

la Haire

**Château
Suduiraut**

Arrançon

D116

la Tuilerie

**Château
Rieussec**

D8

D116

BORDEAUX

Dordogne

Garonne

AREA OF MAIN MAP

Sauternes and Barsac

Château ■

Commune boundary ───

0   1 km

0   1 miles

Above: The vines that welcome visitors to the rather sleepy village of Sauternes, the capital of the sweet wine world

affected by gray rot (*pourriture aigre*) or even grapes where the noble rot is too mature and less refined. The harvest can then take anything from two weeks to three months. Rain, of course, can affect the harvest and quality, as it did in 2000.

In the winery, individual batches (date, site, and pressing) are kept separate until a final selection is made. Oak barrels are used for fermenting wines at the better estates. This practice was abandoned due to lack of investment in the 1960s and 1970s but has been back in use since the late 1980s. Sauternes is obviously an expensive wine to produce, the retail price in no way exaggerated, considering the labor and investment required, not to mention the risks of a product completely dependent on nature. The new millennium has been exceptionally kind, with great wines in 2001, 2003, 2005, 2007, and 2009.

The wines of Sauternes and Barsac were classified in 1855. Yquem was singled out for honor with the title Premier Cru Supérieur, the remaining 20 crus (now 25, as some have since been divided) classified as either first or second growths.

Yquem

I f the question lingers as to which Médoc first growth ultimately takes the supreme title, this has never been the case in Sauternes. Château d'Yquem stands head and shoulders above the rest and has done since the late 18th century. A eulogy from Thomas Jefferson at the time, and later the solitary ranking of premier cru supérieur in 1855, underline its reputation, as do any number of time-honored bottles the world has had the privilege to taste. Standards have rarely dropped, and even today, when rivals have seriously raised their game, Yquem remains the true benchmark.

Continuity has been one of the contributing factors—an asset provided by unchanged family ownership over an extended period of time. The Sauvage family originally acquired the tenure of Yquem in 1593, gradually consolidating the vineyard and obtaining full ownership in the early 18th century. In 1785, Françoise Joséphine de Sauvage d'Yquem married Comte Louis Amédée de Lur-Saluces, bringing Yquem as her dowry; from then on, Lur-Saluces descendants owned and ran the property. This was the case until 1999, when Moët Hennessy Louis Vuitton acquired a majority shareholding, placing Pierre Lurton—who was already running Château Cheval Blanc for the group—in charge from 2004.

Yquem takes pride of place at the center of Sauternes's first growths on a promontory that can be seen for miles around. There are, in fact, three *croupes* contained within Yquem's extensive vineyard that rise and fall over a height of 100–250ft (30–75m), the steepest slope facing north toward the Garonne. The soils are essentially sandy gravel over calcareous clay, with blue clay at a depth of 20ft (6m), but in varying proportions throughout the estate. It's this complexity that is one of the keys to Yquem, the different soils providing a varying nuance

Right: Château d'Yquem, its venerable walls recently renovated, stands literally, as well as metaphorically, above its neighbors

If the question lingers as to which Médoc first growth ultimately takes the supreme title, this has never been the case in Sauternes. Château d'Yquem stands head and shoulders above the rest and has done since the late 18th century

to the wines, the diversity allowing options for the grand vin most years.

The clay subsoil and presence of numerous springs mean drainage is essential, and since the 19th century, nearly 60 miles (100km) of drains have been laid. Needless to say, the vineyard is cultivated with care and exactitude, the soils plowed, the vines pruned in the Sauternes manner *à cots* (with three to four canes, each with two buds), and leaf-plucking and green-harvesting applied. "The idea is to bring a small volume to ripeness just before the noble rot sets in," says Pierre Lurton. The Yquem adage is "a glass of wine per vine." Each year, 5–7 acres (2–3ha) are replanted—with the property's own massal selection since 1992—giving the vineyard an average age of some 30 years.

Climatically, there can be local variation. The lower slope to the north can be cold and susceptible to frost in winter but the warmest zone in the summer months. Yquem's exposed position also allows the vineyard to be well ventilated, the easterly winds enabling concentration and evaporation in the ripening period and when noble rot sets in.

Selective harvesting at Yquem is practiced with precision and has been for many years. The 160 pickers are divided into four teams to provide flexibility when it comes to harvesting the 150-odd parcels. As usual, this is a stop-start process with several *tries*. "We now have the personnel and equipment to handle up to 80 barrels a day if necessary," explains Lurton. The equipment includes four pneumatic presses and three modern vertical basket versions.

Each day's harvest is kept separate for eventual blending or rejection. There is no second wine, the lots that are discarded sold in bulk. Since Pierre Lurton has been in charge, he and winemaker Sandrine Garbay, with advice from consultant Denis Dubourdieu, have made subtle changes to

Above: Sandrine Garbay, Yquem's winemaker, carefully controls sulfur dioxide levels, among myriad other details

the winemaking process. Adjustments to the nitrogen content in the must, with the addition of thiamine (vitamin B1), assist the yeasts, allowing fermentation at higher temperatures without the inconvenience of volatile acidity. Greater care is taken over the control of oxygen during maturation through hygiene, sulfur adjustment, and racking under nitrogen, while the conditions

for bottling have been improved. Fermentation still takes place in 100 percent new oak barrels, but aging has been reduced from 40 to 30 months.

These small rectifications have been aimed at gaining even greater purity in the wine. If the power and opulence of Yquem are generally taken for granted, then the direction these days has been toward greater freshness, purity, and precision in the aroma. The choice of lots for blending has also been oriented this way.

FINEST WINES

Château d'Yquem

The estate's exacting standards mean that in certain years no Yquem is released. This was the case in 1910, 1915, 1930, 1951, 1952, 1964, 1972, 1974, and 1992. Semillon dominates the blend to around 80%, with Sauvignon Blanc the complementary variety. Ideally, the balance shows an alcohol content of 13.5%, with residual sugar at around 125g/l. The aging potential of Yquem is legendary, and though my experience of older vintages is in no way extensive, I've occasionally had the chance

to taste some of the legendary wines. A tasting at the estate in 2003 presented an extremely distinguished line-up. The 1921★ was still long and persistent, with plenty of dried-fruit character. The 1929★ was darker, richer, and more concentrated but balanced by remarkable acidity. The 1937 had an orangey amber hue and still appeared harmonious and complete. The 1949★ was rich and complex with a wonderful depth of fruit. The 1955 was again rich but with dried-fruit character and a touch of alcohol on the finish. The 1962 was round and suave but missed a little balance on the finish. More recent vintages that appealed were the beautifully elegant 1990★ and the harmonious 1983★. In 2007 I was impressed by the powerful, creamy, but balanced 1989★ and complex, fresh, and zesty 1996★.

1988 Tasting remarkably well now. Aromatic, harmonious, and long. *Pain d'épices*, barley sugar, and caramel on the nose. The palate is suave and full, with refreshing acidity on the finish.

1997★ Honeyed gold hue. Rich and complex with clear botrytis character. *Rôti* nose. The palate is rich and concentrated, with fruit confit and caramel notes, then a zesty, bitter-marmalade finish.

2006★ Quite tight and closed on the nose at present. A touch of vanilla and pineapple with aeration. The palate is suave, pure, and precise, dense but very fine, with a beautiful balance.

Y

The name of Yquem's dry white wine is pronounced "ygrec." In the past, it was made on an irregular basis (first vintage 1959) from dry and partially botrytized grapes, which gave it a unique character: full-bodied and powerful, with a Sauternes nose but a dry finish. The new regime has ushered in more consistency,

and since 2004, Y is made regularly every year (production 5,000–10,000 bottles). The winemaking process has also been refined to add freshness and make Y less oxidative and oaky. The blend is now 50–60% Sauvignon Blanc, the rest Semillon, the Sauvignon picked at the beginning of the harvest, the Semillon (from clay soils) at an overripe stage. Fermentation takes place in barrel, the proportion of new oak radically reduced from 100 percent to a third. The maturation has also been shortened from 18 to 10 months, the wine remaining on lees with *bâtonnage*. After an initial trial with an almost bone-dry finish (less than 4g/l of residual sugar) in 2004, subsequent vintages have been given a fuller finish to maintain the individual style, the residual sugar at around 10g/l.

1966 Golden-amber hue. A nose of old Sauternes with crème brûlée and caramel notes. Then the surprise: an unexpectedly dry finish.

2006 Definitely livelier and purer on the nose than in the past. Pear and mandarin notes on the nose, with a spark of minerally vivacity. The palate is crisp on the attack, then smooth and full with a slight off-dry roundness to the finish. The question now is, how will it age?

Château d'Yquem
Total area: 470 acres (190ha)
Area under vine: 250 acres (100ha)
Average production: grand vin 120,000 bottles
33210 Sauternes
Tel: +33 5 57 98 07 07
www.chateau-yquem.fr

Climens

I n 1992, Lucien Lurton ceded his portfolio of properties to his ten children, the youngest, Bérénice, taking over at Château Climens. Only 22 at the time and fresh out of university, she was presented with a somewhat daunting task—particularly because weather conditions denied vintages in 1992 and 1993, the 1994 turned out to be poor, and economic prospects for sweet wines were anything but sure. "It's a humbling experience, because you must never lose sight of the fact that everything is dependent on the climate," states Bérénice Lurton.

Climens has amply reconfirmed its status as the leading property in Barsac, second only in the Sauternais to magisterial Yquem

Less than 20 years later, Climens had amply reconfirmed its status as the leading property in Barsac, second only in the Sauternais to magisterial Yquem. This is not to say that Climens should be compared in terms of power and opulence (the same applies to the likes of Rieussec and La Tour Blanche), but the balance, youth, and complexity make it an exceptional and exquisite wine with an inordinate ability to age.

The vineyard stands in one block around the simple 17th-century *chartreuse* (two pointed towers were added in the 18th century) on the highest point (60ft [18m]) of the Barsac plateau. The sandy clay soils are thin and relatively poor, the compact limestone bedrock responsible for the balancing acidity in the wines. All told, there are 20 different parcels, some subdivided and given grass cover to assist the natural drainage that is found in a greater part of the estate. Only one

Right: Even with the addition of its 18th-century towers, the modest château belies the golden splendor of its wines

grape variety, Semillon, is cultivated, a proportion replanted in recent years, replacing the poorer clones planted in the 1970s and 1980s.

Bérénice Lurton insists there's been no great revolution since she's been in charge. "It's been a question of observation, familiarization, and adaptability," she says. In concrete terms, this has meant permanent vigilance with regard to the quality and purity of the botrytis and greater precision at the harvest. The baskets of the pickers are numbered so that they can be followed, a sorting table has been introduced in the vineyard, and a financial incentive is offered for the quality of the work. All this falls under the watchful eye of technical director Frédéric Nivelle, who has been at the property since 1998.

The parcels are selectively picked and each day's (or half-day's) harvest kept apart and vinified as a separate lot. Only indigenous yeasts are used, the wines fermented in oak barrels, one-third of which are new, then aged for 20–22 months. The blending of the various lots has become a gradual process that now takes up to a year to complete—hence professionals and the press can taste only cask samples during the en primeur tastings in April. Once the decision for the grand vin has been made, the blend for the second wine, Cyprès de Climens, is decided, the remaining lots sold in bulk.

FINEST WINES

Château Climens
"In the past, concentration was a problem, but the tendency in recent years has been to try to curb it, because it is now obtained with relative ease," explains Bérénice Lurton. Certainly Climens has a concentration and *richesse* that set it aside from other Barsacs, particularly the traditional rival Coutet, but this is always offset by a vibrant acidity that provides balancing freshness and finesse. There's a consistency about Climens as well, the reputation solid since the early 20th century, the aging potential of the wines guaranteed. In fact, Bérénice Lurton feels that Climens needs time to show well.

1978 Deep golden hue but with a bright, lively aspect. The nose is soft and mellow and still relatively fresh, with chocolate and hazelnut notes. The palate is again fresh, with a slightly bitter finish. Lacks the concentration and complexity of a great year, but it is holding up well.

2002★ [V] A beautifully constructed wine—pure, long, and refined. Pale golden color. A very fine, spice and confit-fruit nose. Superb balance on the palate, the acidity offering freshness and drinkability, though the wine should also age well.

Cyprès de Climens
The second wine was originally created in 1984, a year that Climens was not produced. The precision of harvesting and winemaking are the same, so it's a question of the blend, Cyprès de Climens being less powerful than Climens and more aromatically expressive in youth.

2006 [V] True to the Climens style: pure and long, with a distinctive note of freshness on the finish. Floral rather than fruity. Medium-bodied, rich, but not heavy. Quite serious for a second wine.

Left: Bérénice Lurton, who has steadily raised the profile and quality of Climens since taking over at the tender age of 22

Château Climens
Total area: 75 acres (30ha)
Area under vine: 75 acres (30ha)
Average production: grand vin 25,000 bottles;
second wine 10,000 bottles
33720 Barsac
Tel: +33 5 56 27 15 33
www.chateau-climens.fr

Guiraud

Château Guiraud forms a sort of island state surrounded by forest and roads, with just the vines of Château Filhot touching in the southwest corner and the village of Sauternes to the west. The history of the property is less well documented than that of neighboring Yquem to the north—but nevertheless, it is long. The magnificent plane-tree-lined alley that forms the entrance to Guiraud used to be part of an old Roman road.

In 1766, the Maison Noble de Bayle, as Guiraud was once known, was bought by Pierre Guiraud. According to Xavier Planty—manager for the past 27 years and co-owner since 2006—this initiated a feud with the Lur-Saluces family, who also wanted the property, sandwiched between its estates of Filhot and Yquem. The rivalry lasted three generations, and when the Lur-Saluces side seemed finally to have acquired Guiraud in 1846, they were eventually outbid at auction by a syndicate of investors. Château Bayle was still the name recorded in the 1855 Classification.

In the 20th century, Guiraud was owned by Paul Rival from 1932 until 1981, when it was bought by Frank Narby, a Canadian businessman. More recently, in 2006, the Narbys sold to a group of investors including industrialist Robert Peugeot, Olivier Bernard of Domaine de Chevalier, Stephan von Neipperg of Château Canon-la-Gaffelière, and Xavier Planty, who remains as manager but in an expanded role.

The work undertaken since 1983 has been mainly to undo the legacy left by Rival. "The restructuring of the property after World War II was catastrophic," explains Planty. "Vines were planted at low density east to west instead of north to south, and red varieties were introduced because there was a lack of confidence in Sauternes."

Some 70 percent of the vineyard, which lies on sandy gravel soils with occasionally a little clay, has been drained and replanted at 6,660–7,200 vines/ha. Planty's biggest pride and joy, though,

Above: Xavier Planty, co-owner of Guiraud, and his daughter Laure Planty, happy to have the 2009 vintage in barrel

is the nursery, where they cultivate massal-selection vines sourced from the estate and other wineries. These have been used for replanting and complantation since 2002.

Planty has also steadily taken Guiraud in an organic direction. Herbicides were abandoned in 1996 and insecticides in 2000. In 2009, Guiraud was two years into its pursuit of official organic

certification. Several miles of hedges have also been planted to encourage a balanced ecological environment. The hedges are home to many insects, some of which are predators of vineyard pests such as red spider mites. "We're trying to overturn the inconveniences of a monoculture," Planty says.

Viticulturally, one of Planty's theories is that botrytis installs itself at flowering but remains dormant until the grapes are physiologically ripe—hence all treatments are avoided during the flowering period. As a result, he says, he harvests earlier than many estates but still picks Sauvignon Blanc with a greater degree of noble rot.

Some 210 acres (85ha) are devoted to the production of Château Guiraud and the second wine, Le Dauphin de Guiraud. A further 37 acres (15ha) are used for the production of G de Château Guiraud, a dry white Bordeaux produced from a dominance (70 percent) of Sauvignon Blanc.

FINEST WINES

Château Guiraud

The estate has an unusually high proportion of
Sauvignon Blanc, 35% in the vineyard, with 65%
Semillon. This can sometimes increase in the
blend, as in the 2001, where the Sauvignon Blanc
accounts for 45%. Nevertheless, the wines are still
rich, concentrated, and *rôti*, aromatically complex
but fresh and zesty on the finish. Since 2000,
Guiraud has been fermented entirely in new oak
barrels, which may have added a little more purity
to the wines. Chaptalization and cryo-extraction
are systematically avoided.

2000 A non-vintage for most Sauternes estates,
but the Sauvignon Blanc at Guiraud was picked
before the rain and represents an exceptional 70%
of the blend. Lighter and linear on the palate, with
definite marmalade and citrus tones. A surprising
120g/l residual sugar, though in tasting terms there
doesn't seem to be that concentration. Probably
not for the long haul but remarkable for the year.

2001 Deep in color, dense, rich, and powerful. Wax,
fruit-confit, and *rôti* notes on the nose. Enormous
weight and concentration on the palate, but
perhaps a little forward?

2002★ [V] Bright; gold hue. Exceptional for its
complexity, finesse, and balance. Full, suave texture,
with notes of apricot and chocolate and a lingering
minerally menthol note. Long, refreshing finish.

2007★ Pale yellow hue. Amazingly pure on the
nose, with definite citrus/mandarin notes. Rich and
concentrated but balanced and elegant as well. At
125g/l, the residual sugar is the same as the 2001.
Mandarin freshness on the finish. Simply delicious.

Above: Château Guiraud, in glorious isolation, the nearest
neighbors being Filhot to the south and Yquem to the north

Château Guiraud
Total area: 316 acres (128ha)
Area under vine: 210 acres (85ha)
Average production: grand vin 120,000 bottles;
second wine up to 36,000 bottles
33210 Sauternes
Tel: +33 5 56 76 61 01
www.chateauguiraud.com

Lafaurie-Peyraguey

I admit to having quite a soft spot for Château Lafaurie-Peyraguey. The 1983 had me enthralled from the beginning with its fruit, fragrance, and exquisite balance, and I bought a case en primeur (there are still a few bottles left). I've tasted some other notable vintages since, and Lafaurie-Peyraguey has remained remarkably consistent, but the 1983 made me a long-term fan.

The 18th-century château, with its 13th-century portal and fortified wall, is located in the commune of Bommes, but the vineyards are spread throughout the communes of Bommes, Sauternes, Preignac, and Fargues. Attached to the château and cellars is the 27-acre (11ha) walled *enclos* with claylike gravel soils. Higher up on the middle terrace opposite Clos Haut-Peyraguey lie another 12 acres (5ha) on clay soils, while continuing toward the village of Sauternes, a further 5ha are found on clay and gravel with limestone. There are also a number of parcels situated between Yquem

and Suduiraut and another 1.2 acres (0.5ha) near Rieussec, all with mainly sandy gravel soils.

"The variety of soils and, indeed, exposures is one of the strengths of Lafaurie-Peyraguey, allowing for balance and complexity in the wines," says manager Eric Larramona. The dispersed nature of the vineyard also helps with consistency. In 2006, the quality within the *enclos* was compromised, so the principal components of the blend came from the other vineyards.

Lafaurie-Peyraguey has been owned by the Suez Group since 1984; prior to that, it was in the hands of the négociant Cordier for nearly 70 years. The vineyards have always been well maintained, with complantation used to keep them fully planted (5,000 vines are replanted each year), the average age 40 years. Between 1998 and 2004, the cellars and château were completely renovated.

Below: Amber gold—bottles and magnums of venerable vintages maturing quietly in the château cellars

Responsibility for the winemaking from the 1980s onward was in the hands of Michel Laporte, who was then succeeded by his son Yannick. Eric Larramona was brought in as general manager in 2006, having previously run Château Pape Clément for Bernard Magrez. "I come from a world where rigor is applied to make great wine, but the risk and constraints are even greater here," he declares.

The botrytized grapes are selectively harvested (in anything between three and seven *tries*) then pressed, the first two pressings in pneumatic presses, the third and last in old vertical basket presses. "The advantage is that the

FINEST WINES

Château Lafaurie-Peyraguey

The style of the wine is typical of the great Sauternes: rich and concentrated, but with a harmony and balance that impart elegance. Residual sugar levels are usually around 125g/l and alcohol 13.5%, so there's less exaggerated power. Aromatically, the wines are very pure. Semillon is the principal variety (90%), the rest Sauvignon Blanc and just a pinch of Muscadelle. Yields average 18.5hl/ha, with second wine La Chapelle de Lafaurie-Peyraguey allowing further selection.

1983★ Pulled from my cellar. Still the same zesty expression and balance after 26 years. Honey-gold hue. Lively, expressive nose, with notes of confit fruit, apricot, and orange. Still extremely youthful. The palate is harmonious, sweet, and smooth but balanced by refreshing acidity.

1997 Deep golden hue. Creamy, caramel, and crème brûlée nose. Attractive crystallized fruit notes on the palate, again with a caramel/chocolate nuance. Harmonious, as usual, with freshness on the finish.

2005 Definitely richer and more concentrated than the 2006 or 2007, though the residual sugar (123g/l) is virtually the same in the 2006. Powerful and for the long term. A touch of confit fruit on the nose but aromatically reserved at present. A little heavy for my taste.

2006 Lively and expressive on the nose, with apricot and pineapple hints. Palate appears mid-weight but very pure. Lovely fruit but misses a bit of zippy acidity to give it extra length.

2007★ Picked over seven *tries* from September 13 to November 9. Golden hue. Nose still in retreat, with just a hint of citrus and pineapple. Palate smooth and creamy with a certain opulence but middling intensity and weight. Vivacity on the attack and finish. Very pure and precise.

Left: Château Lafaurie-Peyraguey surrounded by its enclosed vineyard, though parcels scattered elsewhere add complexity

pressure level is higher, and this is where we extract the richest juice," explains Larramona. Fermentation is in a mix of new (30 percent), one-year-old, and two-year-old barrels, with each lot adapted to the barrel. Aging then lasts 18–20 months, the racking less systematic since 2006 and applied only after tasting.

Château Lafaurie-Peyraguey

Total area: 117 acres (47.5ha)
Area under vine: 89 acres (36ha)
Average production: grand vin 65,000 bottles; second wine 25,000 bottles
33210 Bommes
Tel: +33 5 56 76 60 54
www.lafaurie-peyraguey.com

Clos Haut-Peyraguey

Martine Langlais-Pauly dropped the "château" tag in 2007, so the title is now closer to the reality. This is a small property with an unpretentious winery and walled *clos*. Until 1879 it was part of the greater estate of Château Peyraguey, which was classified as premier cru in 1855. Latterly, the domaine has proved that it is capable of producing some of the most refined wines in Sauternes.

Clos Haut-Peyraguey forms the upper part of the original estate, the rest now Château Lafaurie-Peyraguey. In 1914, the 20-acre (8ha) *clos* was purchased by Martine Langlais-Pauly's great-great-grandfather, Eugène Garbay, already the owner of Château Haut Bommes. Some 10 acres (4ha) on the opposite side of the road to the winery and bordering Château d'Yquem were added in the 1930s. Haut Bommes is not the second wine but a separate 12-acre (5ha) estate.

The terroir is probably one of the finest in Sauternes, the vines of the *clos* forming a single entity on a *croupe* at an altitude of just under 260ft (80m). The additional 4ha are at a slightly lower elevation. The exposure is northeasterly, the soils sandy gravel on a subsoil of clay, the gravel extremely stony in parts. The combination of soil and exposure helps provide a natural freshness that is always inherent in the wines.

Martine's father, Jacques Pauly, took over management in 1969 and was responsible for putting the property qualitatively on the map. Care in the vineyard and use of techniques gleaned from courses with Emile Peynaud eventually paid off, and by the 1980s the wines were winning critical acclaim. Improvements in harvesting and the increased use of new oak barrels in the 1990s pushed the quality along.

In 2002, the energetic and committed Martine took over from her father, convinced that the terroir was magnificent but that it "still hadn't been used to its full potential." As is so often the case, it's the attention to detail that's made the difference since. Certain parcels that were a little too vigorous have been given grass cover, weedkiller has been abandoned, and even more precision has been given to the timing of the harvest and the number of *tries*. The wine is fermented and matured in barrel, the proportion of new oak (50–80 percent) depending on the concentration of the pressed juice.

FINEST WINES

Clos Haut-Peyraguey

"The terroir provides a natural freshness and elegance in the wines, so there's less need for Sauvignon Blanc in the blend," explains Martine Langlais-Pauly. "We're working more on the richness and structure now," she adds. Semillon represented 92% of plantings in 2009 and was due to rise in 2010. These are some of the most harmonious wines to be found in Sauternes, the power inevitably balanced by freshness, the concentration and purity of fruit much improved since the mid-1990s and, in particular, since 2001.

1989 Less concentrated and full-bodied (92g/l of residual sugar) than recent vintages. Lacks a little punch. Fresh, soft-textured, and nervy on the finish. Currant, caramel, and confit notes.

2003 A wonderful example of the harmony of the cru. A bigger, richer, more powerful wine (13.5% ABV and 152g/l of residual sugar) but still the acidity on the finish to give balance. Confit-fruit aromas on the nose, the palate concentrated but fine.

2007★ Pale gold. Still recovering from bottling, so shy on the nose. Lovely purity of fruit, though. Opens gradually to a hint of pineapple. The palate is concentrated but beautifully balanced, the acidity providing freshness and length. Very fine and pure.

Right: The welcoming Martine Langlais-Pauly, whose attention to detail is fulfilling the promise of her privileged terroir

Clos Haut-Peyraguey
Total area: 30 acres (12ha)
Area under vine: 30 acres (12ha)
Production: grand vin 8,000–28,000 bottles
33210 Bommes
Tel: +33 5 56 76 61 53
www.closhautpeyraguey.com

Rieussec

The Rothschilds of Lafite took a majority interest in Château Rieussec in partnership with Baron Albert Frère (co-owner of Château Cheval Blanc) back in 1985. The baron has since sold his shares, so the property is now solely owned by Domaines Barons de Rothschild. Charles Chevallier ran the estate from 1985 until 1994, when he took over the management of Lafite and the other Rothschild acquisitions in Bordeaux. He still keeps a close eye on Rieussec, but the day-to-day running is now with Frédéric Magniez.

Rieussec lies just to the east of Yquem on another prominent hillock that rises to 256ft (78m), making it a relatively early-ripening site. A large proportion of the vineyard surrounds the château and winery, but there's another sector farther east near Château de Fargues. The soils are a variable

An impressively rich and opulent wine, Château Rieussec approaches Yquem in terms of power and concentration

mix of sand and gravel, with a subsoil of clay, the lower areas with less gravel, the clay occasionally outcropping in parts. The capacity for water retention is important (there are four springs on the property), and certain parcels have been drained.

The property has now attained a considerable size, additional purchases of land and rental agreements helping the vineyard expand from the initial acquisition of 153 acres (62ha) to today's total of 227 acres (92ha). Since 1993, 85 acres (35ha) have been grubbed up and replanted, leaving the vineyard with an average age of 25 years.

The foundations in place, Rieussec has shown steady progress, with a more spectacular leap in recent years. Chevallier puts this down to several factors. "We're better organized at the harvest,

we wait longer, stop and start if necessary, have a greater number of pickers—up to 120—and use *cagettes* [shallow plastic trays] to be more selective and protect the fruit."

There's also been change at the cellars, where since 2000, everything has been fermented in barrel. (From 1996, it was part barrel and part stainless-steel tank.) Selection for the grand vin and second wine (Carmes de Rieussec—a reference to the Carmelite monks who owned the property until the Revolution) is then made by tasting the 40-odd lots. Finally, Rieussec is aged for up to 30 months in a mix of new (60 percent) and one-year-old oak barrels, which all come from the Lafite cooperage with a longer but less intense "Rieussec" toast.

A dry white wine, R de Rieussec (5,000–50,000 bottles) is also produced from grapes picked before botrytis sets in.

FINEST WINES

Château Rieussec
An impressively rich and opulent wine, Château Rieussec approaches Yquem in terms of power and concentration. Considerable progress has been made since the initial Rothschild years, as was demonstrated at the tasting below, held at the estate in January 2009. There's now greater purity of fruit, more refinement, and an astonishing intensity and persistence, though the concentration of Semillon (96.5% in 2001) still makes it a vigorous wine. Vintages such as 2001 and 2005 are among the greatest ever produced at Rieussec.
1967 (Magnum) Orange-amber hue. Aromatically fading, the palate more impressive than the nose. A nuance of herbal tea (*tilleul*), fresh (more Sauvignon Blanc was used at this time), and delicately sweet— but past its prime.
1975 Dark amber hue—deeper than the 1967. Rancio and raisin notes on the nose evolving to orange and dried fruits. Palate more "Mediterranean" in style, with prune and dried-fruit notes. Still quite rich and lively—18% Sauvignon Blanc in the blend.
1988 ★ A reference vintage for Rieussec, the harvest finishing tardily on November 18. A beautifully elegant wine; fresh and balanced, with a linear purity of fruit. The palate has a delicate harmony,

the fruit and botrytis still apparent, the acidity adding vitality and length.

1989 Clearly superior to the 1990. Deep golden hue. Impressive depth of fruit and concentration. An initial touch of sulfur on the nose, but this dissipates, leaving fig, apricot, and honeyed notes. Good weight, balance, and texture; full and long.

1990 An evolved color. Mature nose with wax, caramel, dried fruit, and roasted notes. The palate is sweet but fading, the fruit and balance gone.

1997 Rich, concentrated, and drinking well. Full-bodied and powerful rather than overtly complex. Creamy caramel, crème brûlée, and toasted notes on the nose. Massive weight on the palate, but it finds balance on the finish.

2001★ Grand vin. Deep, bright, golden hue. Racy, complex nose, with orange zest and honeyed notes and overriding freshness. Palate suave and refined, with beautifully textured fruit and a long, lingering finish. Pure and harmonious, the acidity disguising 145g/l of residual sugar.

2002★ [V] The surprise of the tasting, given the moderate reputation of the vintage. Appears lighter in weight and substance but is fine, fresh, and balanced. Medium-bodied with confit fruit and honeyed notes on the nose.

2003 Rich, golden hue. Sweet, lush, and opulent in style. Aromatically complex, the notes of candied fruit, wax, and fruit drops defining the heat of the year. Full, fat, and unctuous on the palate. One of the richest wines ever, with 151g/l residual sugar.

2005 A powerful wine with plenty of reserve; the aging potential is enormous. Reticent on the nose but clean, pure, and dense. Some honeyed notes with aeration. Round and full on the palate—a true *liquoreux* with weight, power, and balance. Needs time and patience.

2007 A barrel sample, but it appears pure, rich, and long. Quality oak still present.

Right: The precious but fragile fruit shortly before harvest; more careful handling has helped edge quality higher

Château Rieussec
Total area: 338 acres (137ha)
Area under vine: 227 acres (92ha)
Average production: grand vin 110,000 bottles; second wine 67,000 bottles
33210 Fargues de Langon
Tel: +33 5 57 98 14 14
www.lafite.com

Suduiraut

Manager Pierre Montégut says that Suduiraut is "the most Barsac of Sauternes wines." I can see his point, since there's good acidity and an underlying minerality in most vintages. That said, Suduiraut still has the power and concentration of a top-flight Sauternes, the opulence particularly marked in hot years.

The property itself is lower-lying (165ft [50m]) than the majority of Sauternes first growths, all of which claim space on one or other of the region's hills. This gives it a later ripening cycle than, say, Rieussec or Yquem. The soils are mainly sandy gravel, with a limestone subsoil in parts but very little clay, except for a 25-acre (10ha) parcel located a little higher, near Yquem. Having lain fallow for several years, this was replanted in 1998 and 2004.

The bulk of the vineyard, though, lies around the splendid 17th-century château, with its gardens designed by Le Nôtre. The initial impression is of a flat plateau flanked by woods, but there's a gentle undulation that provides a subtle rise at several points. The grand vin usually comes from the various *tries* made on the higher ground, while the lower, sandier sections provide fruit for the second wine, Castelnau de Suduiraut.

Such precision has only been introduced since the property was acquired by AXA Millésimes in 1992. The company probably had second thoughts following the blighted years of 1992 (creation of the second wine), 1993 (when no Suduiraut was made), and 1994 (when it equaled 10–15 percent of production). More recently, there has been steady progress to attain the consistently high quality achieved since 1997. "The selection has been vastly improved, and we're picking riper, so there's no need to chaptalize," explains Montégut. The average yield is now 15hl/ha, down from 18–22hl/ha before 1992.

There's also been investment in the cellars, with an increase in the number of presses and an ingenious system of heat exchange, which allows individual barrels to be temperature-controlled during the fermentation. This is initially launched in stainless-steel tanks, the juice then racked to barrel (30 percent new oak) after one or two days. Aging lasts 18–24 months. There's a cold store for cryo-extraction, but it is used sparingly and the resulting lots incorporated into the second wine.

In 2004, the dry white wine S de Suduiraut (8,000–10,000 bottles) was launched. It is part barrel-fermented and usually has a dominance of Sauvignon Blanc, giving it a fresh, aromatic style.

FINEST WINES

Château Suduiraut
Semillon represents 90% of plantings at Suduiraut but 95–99% of the grand vin. Since 2001 the selection has become even more severe: 50% of production, while previously it was 60–70%. Most recent vintages show an impressive concentration of rich, botrytized fruit with an orange-zest or mineral finish providing excellent length.

1999 Deep, golden hue. Caramel notes on the nose but aromatically slightly withdrawn. The palate is rich but well balanced and still youthful, the acidity quite distinct. I suspect an interesting marriage with food. (Suduiraut proposes an Asian dish of steamed salmon with preserved ginger.)

2001 This is a rich, concentrated wine, with 150g/l of residual sugar. There's no mistaking the powerful Sauternes character here. Complex nose of apricot, mineral, and confit fruit. Palate lush and full. A twist of acidity on the finish. Long aging potential.

2007★ Less powerful than 2001, but I prefer the balance and elegance of this wine. Lovely purity of fruit and a long, fresh finish. Extremely refined. More of a mandarin/pineapple expression at present.

Right: The splendid 17th-century château at Suduiraut, sitting amid its landscaped gardens and surrounding vineyards

Château Suduiraut
Total area: 500 acres (200ha)
Area under vine: 227 acres (92ha)
Production: grand vin 30,000–120,000 bottles; second wine 30,000–90,000 bottles
33210 Preignac
Tel: +33 5 56 63 61 90
www.suduiraut.com

Coutet

The history of Coutet as a wine estate can be traced back to the 17th century. From 1807 until 1922—when it was sold to Louis Guy Mital, a wine-press manufacturer from Lyon—it was owned by the Lur-Saluces family of Yquem fame. Louis Guy Mital's daughter, Madame Rolland, took over on his death and ran the property until it was sold in 1977 to the present owners, the Baly family, originally from Alsace. Today, the family representatives are Philippe Baly and his niece Aline, who was brought up in the United States.

The property boasts the largest vineyard in Barsac, all in one unit surrounding the château and cellars, split only by a single country road. The soils are thin (8–20in [20–50cm]) and consist mainly of silt and sand with red clay in parts over a fissured limestone bedrock. It is the classic Barsac terroir that provides the delicacy, freshness, and minerality in the wines.

Vintages of Château Coutet in the 1970s and 1980s were generally light and unexciting. The Balys spent the first years of their tenure replanting and restructuring the vineyard and improving management techniques; their efforts began to pay from 1988 onward. In 1994, a contract was signed with Baron Philippe de Rothschild SA for distribution of the wines. The partnership also includes technical advice, so first Patrick Léon, then his successor as technical director at Mouton Rothschild, Philippe Dhalluin, have acted as consultants, particularly for the blending. The track record since 1996 has been consistently strong.

The vineyard is planted with 75 percent Semillon, 23 percent Sauvignon Blanc, and 2 percent Muscadelle, but I was told that the ratio of the blend is generally more like 84:14:2, except in 2005, when the Semillon rose to 90 percent. The estate still uses old vertical presses (as well as a more modern pneumatic), and the wine is fermented and aged in 100 percent new oak barrels for 18 months. The second wine is called La Chartreuse de Coutet.

FINEST WINES

Château Coutet

Coutet is often compared to Climens, its so-called rival in Barsac. Until the late 1980s, this would have done it a disservice, but qualitatively Coutet has raised the bar since. Both have the citrus freshness associated with the limestone terroir, but there's perhaps a little more intensity in Climens and more of a tangy zestiness to Coutet. The addition of up to 15% Sauvignon Blanc in Coutet possibly makes the difference. In 2005★, when the Sauvignon Blanc was only 8% and the Semillon 90%, Coutet was in a distinctly more powerful and *liquoreux* style.

1989★ Honeyed gold color. Caramel, crème brûlée, and gingerbread notes on both nose and palate. Shows some evolution, but lovely weight and texture, and trademark freshness on the finish.

1998 I tasted this in 2006, and it seemed dull and closed. Now there's a definite note of marmalade and confit fruit. Medium-bodied and balanced.

2003 Pale gold hue. Rich, round, and unctuous (150g/l of residual sugar) but reined in by a zesty, citrus freshness on the finish. Good balance for such a powerful year.

2004 Complete and harmonious. The nose is a little reserved at present, but good concentration and a fresh, minerally finish. Orange and exotic-fruit notes on the palate.

Cuvée Madame

This special cuvée was first produced in 1922 in honor of Madame Rolland. It has since been made in 1943, 1949, 1950, 1959, 1971, 1975, 1981, 1986, 1988, 1989, 1990, and 1995, the latest release. It seems to be at the discretion of the winemaker whether the wine is made, but when it is produced, it comes from two parcels of Semillon that are over 40 years old. Quantities are evidently limited. I've only ever tasted the 1995, which appeared incredibly rich and concentrated, with caramel and mocha notes and a little less zest than is normally found in Coutet.

Château Coutet

Total area: 104 acres (42ha)
Area under vine: 95 acres (38.5ha)
Average production: grand vin 42,000 bottles; second wine 5,000 bottles
33720 Barsac
Tel: +33 5 56 27 15 46
www.chateaucoutet.com

Doisy-Daëne

"My father has always had the instinct of a vigneron to guide him in his research at the Faculté d'Oenologie and in his role as consultant and winemaker," says Jean-Jacques Dubourdieu. Indeed, Professor Denis Dubourdieu is the third generation of the family to have owned and run Château Doisy-Daëne, where he has now been joined by his sons Fabrice and Jean-Jacques.

Denis's grandfather, Georges, purchased the property in 1924, when it was just over 10 acres (4ha). His father, Pierre, expanded it to its present size by buying and exchanging adjacent parcels, all from classed growths. He also replanted much of the property in the 1950s and '60s—hence today's excellent condition and density of 7,000 vines/ha. Denis then took over on Pierre's retirement in 2000.

The vineyard sits slightly higher than neighboring Doisy-Dubroca and Védrines on the thin, claylike sands of Barsac with a calcareous subsoil. The land is plowed and herbicides avoided. "Over the years we've observed that it usually rains in Bordeaux around September 15–20, so the vineyard is prepared to bring the grapes to 'golden ripeness' just prior to this date, so the botrytis can set in after, and we can harvest early, which is what we prefer," explains Jean-Jacques Dubourdieu.

FINEST WINES

Château Doisy-Daëne
Doisy-Daëne is always pure and elegant rather than opulent and heavy. This does not mean it lacks concentration. "We aim for around 140g/l of residual sugar, with relatively high acidity and low pH," declares Jean-Jacques Dubourdieu. "The maturation is not excessively long, to avoid oxidation, since this will hinder the potential of the wine to age." Doisy-Daëne is made principally from Semillon plus 10–15% Sauvignon Blanc. Fermented in barrel (a third new oak), it is aged for 12 months in barrel, followed by a further six months in vat.
1997 Rich and unctuous but a little less Doisy-Daëne in style. Deep, golden hue. Complex nose, with apricot, *rôti*, and dark-chocolate notes. Full and sweet on the palate, with acidity on the finish.

2006★ [V] A classic Doisy-Daëne. Light golden color. Aromatically pure, with a distinct citrus/marmalade expression and lemon-sherbet vivacity. Palate rich and succulent (140g/l residual sugar) but with driving acidity and fresh, tangy finish.

L'Extravagant de Doisy-Daëne
In 1990, Pierre and Denis Dubourdieu decided to renew the practice of making sweet wine with a high proportion of Sauvignon Blanc, as was the case in 1855. They were looking for concentration and aroma so left only two bunches on the vine after the initial *tries* to select grapes for the dry white wine. These were left to develop an incredible level of sugar—nearly 35% potential alcohol—then fermented to obtain a natural alcohol level for Sauternes (the winemaking still a secret), leaving a mass of residual sugar. The first vintage of L'Extravagant de Doisy-Daëne was born and has been followed by vintages in 1996, 1997, 2001, 2002, 2003, 2004, 2005, 2006, 2007, and 2009. The blend usually consists of an equal share of Sauvignon Blanc and Semillon fermented in 100% new oak barrels. The residual-sugar level is a minimum 230g/l. At around $250 per half-bottle, it is now the most expensive Sauternes after Yquem and, with a production of about 2,000 bottles, extremely rare.
2005★ (Half-bottle) The amazing thing is the lift and liveliness of the wine, despite the enormous concentration. Pale gold color. Fresh and almost zesty on the nose, with definite mandarin/citrus notes. Palate rich, smooth, and concentrated but no heaviness, a rapier-like acidity providing balance.

Château Doisy-Daëne Sec
The property is also known for its dry white wine. Introduced by Pierre Dubourdieu, it is made from Sauvignon Blanc grapes picked at "golden-color" stage at the beginning of the harvest. These are then fermented and aged for eight months in oak barrels (27% new). The style is crisp and fine, with a minerally acidity and subtle grapefruit/citrus aromas and flavor. There's definite aging potential.

Château Doisy-Daëne
Total area: 42 acres (17ha)
Area under vine: 42 acres (17ha)
Average production: grand vin 40,000 bottles
33720 Barsac
Tel: +33 5 56 62 96 51
www.denisdubourdieu.com

Gilette

F ate had a say in the creation of this extraordinary wine. On the outbreak of World War II, René Médeville joined the army, leaving a number of vintages from the 1930s unbottled and stored in concrete tanks. After the war he found them fresh and youthful in aspect and aroma, the wines preserved from oxidation by the form of maturation. He bottled the 1934, which became the first vintage of the new-style Château Gilette.

The property has been in the Médeville family hands since 1710, as has Sauternes stablemate Château Les Justices. More recently it was run by René's son Christian for over 40 years, before he in turn handed over to his daughter, Julie Gonet-Médeville, and her husband Xavier.

The vineyard forms a walled-in *clos* in the center of the village of Preignac. The wall helps harbor moisture, which can be beneficial for botrytis in dry years—1978, 1982, or 1985, for example—but conversely can be a handicap in wet years. The soils are free-draining sand and gravel over a subsoil of friable limestone, and the vines are old, with the average near 50 years in 2009. Complantation is the method used to replace vines.

Like all top Sauternes, this is a *vin de vendange*, the system of selective picking as important as anywhere else. René Médeville initially made a number of different styles of Château Gilette: Demi-Sec, Demi-Doux, Doux, and the top-of-the-line Crème de Tête. The latter has been the unique offering since 1963, but is not made every year.

The grapes are pressed in pneumatic presses, then fermented with natural yeasts at low temperature ($63°F$ [$17°C$]) in stainless-steel tanks. After a long alcoholic fermentation (10–12 months), the wines are sulfured, settled, then filtered, before being racked into concrete tank. Aging now takes 16–20 years, an empirical choice after years of trial and observation.

FINEST WINES

Château Gilette

The wine is produced principally from Semillon, but there is a smattering of Sauvignon Blanc and Muscadelle in the vineyard. "We don't look for enormous concentration, so residual sugar levels are usually around 100–110g/l," explains Julie Gonet-Médeville. Curiously, with this form of maturation some bottle age is still advisable, the absence of oxygen maintaining a youthful aspect but retarding the development of aroma. By 2010, the latest vintage to be bottled was the 1989. The following wines were tasted in November 2009.

1937★ The amber tint of an old Sauternes but a pungent, lifted nose and sweet but zesty palate. Crystallized citrus fruits the dominant aroma and flavor, with a menthol nuance. Attractive harmony and balance. Delicious at over 70 years old.

1953 Bottled after 27 years in vat. Delicately fragrant nose. Orange-zest aromas. Palate rather monumental. A concentrated block that doesn't seem to have aged. Definitively more powerful in style. Acidity less apparent. Needs more bottle age?!

1975★ Amber hue. Powerful, profound, and racy on the nose. Confit-fruit and almond aromas. Palate suave and round, with confit-fruit flavors and a dash of caramel. Balancing acidity gives a long, lingering finish. Poised and harmonious.

1979 Golden amber. A busy nose, with caramel, chocolate, crème brûlée, and apple notes. The palate is rich and creamy, again with that chocolate/crème brûlée nuance. Shorter, sweeter finish.

1983★ Bottled in 2000. Deep golden color. Rich and concentrated, but balanced by fine acidity. The palate is harmonious, suave, and *gras*, with a long, fresh finish. Crystallized-fruit and chocolate notes.

1985 Aromatically a little more floral. The palate is rich and ample but a touch less complex. The slightly bitter finish is typical of some aged Sauternes.

1988★ Pure, direct, and long, but it needs some bottle age. Fresh and youthful but closed. Appears similar in style to the 1983.

Château Gilette

Total area: 11 acres (4.5ha)
Area under vine: 11 acres (4.5ha)
Average production: grand vin 5,000 bottles
33210 Preignac
Tel: +33 5 56 76 28 44
www.gonet-medeville.com

La Tour Blanche

The vineyard of La Tour Blanche straddles the plateau of a hill that sits above the village of Bommes to the north. The Ciron is tucked in behind the village, its existence on a gray November day highlighted by wisps of mist that follow its trail. The vines on the sandy soils at the foot of the hill had been stripped of their leaves by frost but, in any case, are not used for La Tour Blanche. As the elevation increased and the soils became gravel and clay, so the leaf cover returned. Over on the other side of the hill, I could see the vineyard sloping away in the general direction of the village of Sauternes.

Nestling close to the vineyard, the winery and offices form part of a rambling complex that includes a viticultural college. On his death in 1907, owner Daniel Iffla bequeathed La Tour Blanche to the French state on condition that the college was built. Since then, the property has been owned and run by the French Ministry of Agriculture.

In the 1855 Classification, La Tour Blanche was placed top of the premiers crus, just behind Yquem. The quality of the wines for much of the 20th century, though, was fairly indifferent, La Tour Blanche gaining a second lease on life from 1988 onward. Much of this was due to a new director, Jean-Pierre Jausserand, who was appointed in 1983 and ran the property until retirement in 2001. He brought in new barrels for fermentation and instituted greater rigor in the vineyards and for selection. The second wine, Les Charmilles de Tour Blanche, was introduced at this time. His successor, Corinne Reulet, has carried on the good work.

FINEST WINES

Château La Tour Blanche

The style of La Tour Blanche is generally powerful, rich, and concentrated, with an aromatic nuance of spice and exotic fruits. This is due to the significance of Muscadelle and Sauvignon Blanc in the blend. The two represent, respectively, 5% and 12% of the plantings in the vineyard, are vinified and aged together in stainless-steel tank, and combined represent 17–21% of the eventual blend. In 2009, they were fermented separately to ascertain the true character of each and, eventually, to bring more precision to the blend. The Semillon is fermented and aged in 100 percent new oak barrels for 16–18 months. Since 2001, cultured yeasts have been systematically used. The average yield for the past ten years is 13hl/ha.

1990 Rich and powerful but with a smoky, mineral finish that gives the wine balance. Honeyed gold color. There's no missing the concentration on the nose. Aromatically, there's a toasted note (presumably from the oak aging), as well as fig and a smoky nuance. Full, fat, and creamy on the palate, with more of a caramel and crème brûlée flavor and a minerally bite to the finish.

2002 As much as 157g/l of residual sugar, which is pretty amazing for the vintage. Fragrant, aromatic nose, with notes of exotic fruit and apricot. Palate sweet and round with a similar aromatic spectrum. The finish is a little peppery. Personally, I would like a little more *nervosité*, but it's drinking well now.

2005 Decanted two days before tasting! All the same, the nose is still fairly reserved but pure. Just a hint of oak, indicating well-integrated wood. Impressive palate: rich and unctuous, with enormous concentration. Powerful but finely textured. Long, spicy finish. Definitely a bottle for aging.

Château La Tour Blanche
Total area: 173 acres (70ha)
Area under vine: 91 acres (37ha)
Average production: grand vin 45,000 bottles; second wine 20,000 bottles
33210 Bommes
Tel: +33 5 57 98 02 73
www.tour-blanche.com

Médoc and Graves 1855

	Appellation
First Growths	
(*Premiers Crus*)	
Château Lafite Rothschild	Pauillac
Château Margaux	Margaux
Château Latour	Pauillac
Château Haut-Brion	Pessac-Léognan
Château Mouton Rothschild	Pauillac
Second Growths	
(*Deuxièmes Crus*)	
Château Rauzan-Ségla	Margaux
Château Rauzan-Gassies	Margaux
Château Léoville-Las-Cases	St-Julien
Château Léoville Poyferré	St-Julien
Château Léoville Barton	St-Julien
Château Durfort-Vivens	Margaux
Château Gruaud-Larose	St-Julien
Château Lascombes	Margaux
Château Brane-Cantenac	Margaux
Château Pichon-Longueville	Pauillac
Château Pichon Longueville Comtesse de Lalande	Pauillac
Château Ducru-Beaucaillou	St-Julien
Château Cos d'Estournel	St-Estèphe
Château Montrose	St-Estèphe
Third Growths	
(*Troisièmes Crus*)	
Château Kirwan	Margaux
Château d'Issan	Margaux
Château Lagrange	St-Julien
Château Langoa Barton	St-Julien
Château Giscours	Margaux
Château Malescot St-Exupéry	Margaux
Château Boyd-Cantenac	Margaux
Château Cantenac Brown	Margaux
Château Palmer	Margaux
Château La Lagune	Haut-Médoc

	Appellation
Château Desmirail	Margaux
Château Calon-Ségur	St-Estèphe
Château Ferrière	Margaux
Château Marquis d'Alesme Becker	Margaux
Fourth Growths	
(*Quatrièmes Crus*)	
Château St-Pierre	St-Julien
Château Talbot	St-Julien
Château Branaire-Ducru	St-Julien
Château Duhart-Milon Rothschild	Pauillac
Château Pouget	Margaux
Château La Tour Carnet	Haut-Médoc
Château Lafon-Rochet	St-Estèphe
Château Beychevelle	St-Julien
Château Prieuré-Lichine	Margaux
Château Marquis de Terme	Margaux
Fifth Growths	
(*Cinquièmes Crus*)	
Château Pontet-Canet	Pauillac
Château Batailley	Pauillac
Château Haut-Batailley	Pauillac
Château Grand-Puy-Lacoste	Pauillac
Château Grand-Puy Ducasse	Pauillac
Château Lynch-Bages	Pauillac
Château Lynch-Moussas	Pauillac
Château Dauzac	Margaux
Château d'Armailhac	Pauillac
Château du Tertre	Margaux
Château Haut-Bages Libéral	Pauillac
Château Pédesclaux	Pauillac
Château Belgrave	Haut-Médoc
Château de Camensac	Haut-Médoc
Château Cos Labory	St-Estèphe
Château Clerc Milon	Pauillac
Château Croizet-Bages	Pauillac
Château Cantemerle	Haut-Médoc

Sauternes and Barsac 1855

	Commune		Commune
First Great Growth		**Second Growths**	
(*Premier Cru Supérieur*)		(*Deuxièmes Crus*)	
Château d'Yquem	Sauternes		
		Château de Myrat	Barsac
First Growths		Château Doisy-Daëne	Barsac
(*Premiers Crus*)		Château Doisy-Dubroca	Barsac
Château La Tour Blanche	Bommes	Château Doisy-Vedrines	Barsac
Château Lafaurie-Peyraguey	Bommes	Château d'Arche	Sauternes
Château Clos Haut-Peyraguey	Bommes	Château Filhot	Sauternes
Château de Rayne Vigneau	Bommes	Château Broustet	Barsac
Château Suduiraut	Preignac	Château Nairac	Barsac
Château Coutet	Barsac	Château Caillou	Barsac
Château Climens	Barsac	Château Suau	Barsac
Château Guiraud	Sauternes	Château de Malle	Preignac
Château Rieussec	Fargues	Château Romer du Hayot	Fargues
Château Rabaud-Promis	Bommes	Château Lamothe-Despujols	Sauternes
Château Sigalas Rabaud	Bommes	Château Lamothe Guignard	Sauternes

St-Emilion 1955 (reclassified 2006)

Premiers Grands Crus Classés (A)
Château Ausone
Château Cheval Blanc

Premiers Grands Crus Classés (B)
Château Angélus
Château Beau-Séjour Bécot
Château Beauséjour (Héritiers Duffau-Lagarrosse)
Château Belair-Monange
Château Canon
Château Figeac
Château La Gaffelière
Château Magdelaine
Château Pavie
Château Pavie Macquin
Château Troplong Mondot
Château Trottevieille
Clos Fourtet

Grands Crus Classés
Château Balestard la Tonnelle
Château Bellefont-Belcier
Château Bellevue
Château Bergat
Château Berliquet
Château Cadet Bon
Château Cadet-Piola
Château Canon-la-Gaffelière
Château Cap de Mourlin
Château Chauvin
Château Corbin
Château Corbin Michotte
Château Dassault
Château Destieux
Château Faurie de Souchard
Château Fleur Cardinale
Château Fonplégade
Château Fonroque
Château Franc-Mayne

Château Grand Corbin
Château Grand Corbin-Despagne
Château Grand Mayne
Château Grand-Pontet
Château Guadet
Château Haut-Corbin
Château Haut-Sarpe
Château l'Arrosée
Château La Clotte
Château La Couspaude
Château La Dominique
Château La Marzelle
Château La Serre
Château La Tour du Pin Figeac
Château La Tour du Pin Figeac (Giraud-Bélivier)
Château La Tour Figeac
Château Laniote
Château Larcis Ducasse
Château Larmande
Château Laroque
Château Laroze
Château Le Prieuré
Château les Grandes Murailles
Château Matras
Château Monbousquet
Château Moulin du Cadet
Château Pavie Decesse
Château Petit-Faurie-de-Soutard
Château Ripeau
Château St-Georges Côte Pavie
Château Soutard
Château Tertre Daugay
Château Villemaurine
Château Yon Figeac
Clos de l'Oratoire
Clos des Jacobins
Clos St-Martin
Couvent des Jacobins

Graves 1959

Classified Red Wines	*Commune*
Château Bouscaut	Cadaujac
Château Haut-Bailly	Léognan
Château Carbonnieux	Léognan
Domaine de Chevalier	Léognan
Château de Fieuzal	Léognan
Château d'Olivier	Léognan
Château Malartic Lagravière	Léognan
Château La Tour Martillac	Martillac
Château Smith Haut Lafitte	Martillac
Château Haut-Brion	Pessac
Château La Mission Haut-Brion	Talence
Château Pape Clément	Pessac
Château La Tour Haut-Brion	Talence

Classified White Wines	*Commune*
Château Bouscaut	Cadaujac
Château Carbonnieux	Léognan
Domaine de Chevalier	Léognan
Château d'Olivier	Léognan
Château Malartic Lagravière	Léognan
Château La Tour Martillac	Martillac
Château Laville Haut-Brion	Talence
Château Couhins-Lurton	Léognan
Château Couhins	Villenave d'Ornon

Liv-ex Bordeaux (2009)

Wine	Average (£)	2009 Classification	1855 Classification	2009 Ranking	1855 Ranking	Move
Latour	4,620	1st	1st	1	2	+1
Lafite Rothschild	4,197	1st	1st	2	1	-1
Margaux	3,773	1st	1st	3	3	0
Mouton Rothschild	2,941	1st	1st	4	5	+1
Haut-Brion	2,705	1st	1st	5	4	-1
La Mission Haut-Brion	2,225	1st	new	6	new	new
Palmer	1,085	2nd	3rd	7	29	+22
Léoville-Las-Cases	1,029	2nd	2nd	8	8	0
Cos d'Estournel	804	2nd	2nd	9	18	+9
Pape Clément	686	2nd	new	10	new	new
Montrose	672	2nd	2nd	11	19	+8
Ducru-Beaucaillou	664	2nd	2nd	12	17	+5
Pichon Lalande	588	2nd	2nd	13	16	+3
Pichon Baron	525	2nd	2nd	14	15	+1
Léoville Barton	510	2nd	2nd	15	10	-5
Lynch-Bages	502	2nd	5th	16	50	+34
Léoville Poyferré	458	3rd	2nd	17	9	-8
Pontet-Canet	423	3rd	5th	18	44	+26
Malescot St-Exupéry	394	3rd	3rd	19	26	+7
Rauzan-Ségla	386	3rd	2nd	20	6	-14
Haut-Bailly	369	3rd	new	21	new	new
Calon-Ségur	357	3rd	3rd	22	32	+10
Lascombes	348	3rd	2nd	23	13	-10
Smith Haut Lafitte	329	3rd	new	24	new	new
Beychevelle	329	3rd	4th	25	41	+16
Cantenac Brown	318	3rd	3rd	26	27	+1
Grand-Puy-Lacoste	316	3rd	5th	27	48	+21
Branaire-Ducru	311	3rd	4th	28	36	+8
Clerc Milon	311	3rd	5th	29	59	+30
Duhart-Milon	306	3rd	4th	30	37	+7
Giscours	305	3rd	3rd	31	25	-6
Lagune	305	3rd	3rd	32	30	-2
Issan	300	3rd	3rd	33	22	-11
St-Pierre	295	4th	3rd	34	20	-14
Langoa Barton	292	4th	3rd	35	24	-11
Gruaud-Larose	290	4th	2nd	36	12	-24
Brane-Cantenac	286	4th	2nd	37	14	-23
Kirwan	277	4th	3rd	38	21	-17

Wine	Average (£)	2009 Classification	1855 Classification	2009 Ranking	1855 Ranking	Move
Talbot	274	4th	4th	39	35	-4
Malartic Lagravière	266	4th	new	40	new	new
Domaine de Chevalier	265	4th	new	41	new	new
Haut-Marbuzet	254	4th	new	42	new	new
Prieuré-Lichine	250	4th	4th	43	42	-1
Lagrange	246	5th	3rd	44	23	-21
Boyd-Cantenac	239	5th	3rd	45	28	-17
Sociando-Mallet	233	5th	new	46	new	new
Ferrière	226	5th	3rd	47	33	-14
Marquis de Terme	219	5th	4th	48	43	-5
Armailhac	216	5th	5th	49	53	+4
Carbonnieux	213	5th	new	50	new	new
Haut Bages Libéral	209	5th	5th	51	47	-4
Haut-Batailley	208	5th	5th	52	46	-6
Lafon-Rochet	208	5th	4th	53	40	-13
Durfort-Vivens	206	5th	2nd	54	11	-43
Tertre	205	5th	5th	55	54	-1
Rauzan-Gassies	204	5th	2nd	56	7	-49
Dauzac	203	5th	5th	57	52	-5
Cos Labory	203	5th	5th	58	58	0
Batailley	202	5th	5th	59	45	-14
Grand-Puy Ducasse	201	5th	5th	60	49	-11

Criteria for inclusion:

Left Bank wines only (Médoc and Pessac-Léognan)

Minimum production of 2,000 cases (to remove distorting effects of "super cuvées")

First wines only

Calculation of the rankings:

Average case price calculated for every qualifying wine (lowest available wholesale price for an original wooden case in good condition, excluding duty and sales tax) for five years, 2003–2007. Prices as of December 31, 2008.

£200 taken as the minimum average case price to make the classification.

Wines classified according to price band:

1st growths: £2,000 a case and above

2nd growths: £500 to £2,000

3rd growths: £300 to £500

4th growths: £250 to £300

5th growths: £200 to £250

Year by Year 2009–1982

I have indicated the success of the vintage with a star rating (one to five stars) but urge the reader to peruse the appended commentary, since there is often considerable disparity in any given year.

2009 (potential ★ ★ ★ ★ to ★ ★ ★ ★ ★)

The wines hadn't been tasted at the time of writing, but the portents were extremely good. A hot, dry summer with rain when it was needed in September and a warm, sunny harvest had producers in exuberant mood. The wines are apparently rich, with relatively high alcohol and smooth, suave texture. Questions remain about the overall balance and tannin content. The success, if confirmed, should be across the board—for reds, dry whites, and Sauternes. The only gloomy note was from producers hit by hailstorms in May. Appellations that suffered the worst damage included Côtes de Bourg, Premières Côtes de Blaye, and Côtes de Castillon, as well as sectors of the Graves, Entre-Deux-Mers, Margaux, and St-Emilion.

2008 ★ ★ ★ ★

A wet spring and dull, damp summer (August was particularly dreary) seemed to have paved the way for a mediocre vintage. But fine weather from mid-September through to the end of October saved the day, and quality is generally far better than expected. Yields were low due to poor flowering, frost in places, and mildew, the small crop assisting ripening at the finish. The better reds have sweet fruit, smooth texture, and, rather surprisingly, a firm tannic frame. The dry whites are remarkably good (but the crop was small due to frost). Sauternes had a difficult year due to the frost and the uneven spread of botrytis, so some yields were miserably low, even by the standards of the region.

Left: The cool, dark, concrete bins such as are found at many châteaux, housing vintages that often stretch back decades

2007 ★ ★ ★

2007 and 2008 were similar in that both experienced indifferent weather in May, June, July, and August, then the threat of mildew, but both were saved by Indian summers. April 2007 was one of the hottest on record, but July 2008 was marginally warmer and drier than the same month the previous year, which may have helped with the structure. Reds in 2007 are generally charming, supple, and lightly structured— a vintage for early drinking. Dry whites are fresh and aromatic, and Sauternes (the success of the vintage) is pure and fine.

2006 ★ ★ ★ to ★ ★ ★ ★

Conditions were ideal (consistent flowering and a hot, dry June and July) until August, when cool, wet weather set in, followed by heavy bouts of rain in September. Accompanying rot meant an accelerated harvest for some. Earlier-ripening Pomerol fared best overall on the Right Bank, and Pessac-Léognan was relatively consistent, but quality was generally uneven throughout Bordeaux. The best reds (and there are some very fine wines) do have color, concentration, and an acidity that provides firmness and the potential for long aging. Dry whites were outstanding; Sauternes average.

2005 ★ ★ ★ ★ ★

Producers could not have hoped for better weather conditions than they enjoyed in 2005. The flowering was swift and consistent. June, July, and August were dry and hot (but not excessively so), and the harvest months were equally clement. Rain (a mix of storms and light showers) arrived when needed, so the vines were seldom too stressed, as they certainly had been in 2003. The wines across the board are balanced but concentrated, firm, rich, and definitely for long aging.

2004 ★★★ to ★★★★

This was a late and potentially abundant year, the wines being of a more "classic" mold. Crop-thinning and work in the vineyard was obligatory. Budding, flowering, and the harvest were late. The two redeeming features of the year were a hot, dry June, then, following a disappointing July and August, dry, sunny weather in September and early October. The reds are balanced, crisp, and fresh, if missing the concentration of a top year, while the lack of speculation makes them good value. Some can definitely age.

2003 ★★★ to ★★★★

An atypical year due to excessive heat and drought, 2003 produced some outstanding wines but also many that were cooked and are already in decline. August beat all records, with an average maximum daytime temperature for the month of 90°F (32°C), with 11 consecutive days over 95°F (35°C). Full phenolic maturity was not always possible due to vine stress, and high alcohol and low acidity are recurring themes. There's a *méridional* feel to some wines, while others have dry, pinched tannins and generally lack balance. The best wines tend to be from areas where water uptake was better regulated (the heavier soils of St-Estèphe and Pauillac, and the St-Emilion Côte and limestone plateau), and here they are rich and concentrated. Sauternes had an excellent year, the noble rot arriving swiftly and consistently in September.

2002 ★★★

A protracted budding, poor fruit-set (particularly for Merlot), and cool, dull July and August didn't augur well, and the vintage was saved only by fine, dry weather in September. It benefited the later-ripening Cabernet Sauvignon, and the better wines, in a firm, slightly austere style, come from the Médoc this year. The Right Bank was generally modest. Some decent Sauternes was produced but in a lighter, fresher style.

2001 ★★★★

The early part of the year followed a similar pattern to that of 2000, with fairly successful flowering, a cold, rainy July, and a hot August, but the difference was in September, which turned out to be cool and dry in 2001. This meant a little less power and concentration but balance, elegance, and charm. Merlot was the principal benefactor of the conditions, making this a Right Bank year, with some wines superior to 2000. The Cabernet had a harder time ripening and fell foul of rain at the end of the harvest. Sauternes had an excellent vintage.

2000 ★★★★★

As mentioned above, the early conditions were similar to those in 2001, with the exception of a severe attack of mildew in 2000. The hot, dry weather in August continued through into September, the harvest completed in generally fine conditions before the mid-October rain appeared. The wines are rich, strong, dark, and tannic, with an acidity that gives vibrancy to the fruit. They are clearly for the long haul. Rain in October dashed hopes of a successful Sauternes vintage.

1999 ★★★

Although there was a potentially abundant crop, the threat of disease and rain during the harvest made this a difficult year. The better wines come from estates that put in the work in the vineyards, making quality variable throughout the region. The best wines are solid if a little rustic and unexciting, and most were ready for drinking after ten years. In St-Emilion, a hailstorm on September 5 caused damage to 1,235 acres (500ha), including certain prominent vineyards on the limestone plateau, resulting in an early harvest to save the residue. As is often the case in an average red vintage, Sauternes had a good year.

1998 ★ ★ ★ ★
This was clearly a Right Bank year, the Merlot picked at perfect pitch, the quality at many estates exceptional. Wines from Pessac-Léognan are also very good. A generally successful flowering was followed by a drab July but hot August. The Merlot was picked in perfect conditions in mid- to late September; the Cabernet harvest was affected by rain. The wines of the Médoc are sturdy but generally less exciting.

1997 ★ ★
A prolonged flowering, cool, wet July, and tropical August with the attendant problem of rot resulted in a poor year despite the reprieve of September sunshine. The wines were light, and they matured swiftly. Only a handful of top estates still have wines of interest. Sauternes was the only true success of the vintage.

1996 ★ ★ ★ ★
Cabernet Sauvignon was the winner in 1996, producing dark, vibrant, structured wines in the Médoc that are only just beginning to open. Influencing factors were the rapid flowering, dry, hot latter part of July, and August rain, a more significant amount falling inland than in the northern Médoc. Early September sunshine with cool nights preserving acidity also set the style. The Right Bank was more varied, the best enjoyable now. Sauternes is rich but with good acidity adding balance and finesse.

1995 ★ ★ ★ ★
A heatwave and drought through June, July, and August meant that rain was needed, but the volume that fell at the harvest was a little excessive and compromised a potentially outstanding year. Still, some rich, fleshy, full-bodied wines were produced, particularly on the Right Bank and in Pauillac and St-Estèphe.

1994 ★ ★ ★
After frost in April, which hit parts of Barsac, the Graves, western Margaux, and Moulis, the weather in June, July (particularly), and August was good, providing optimism for the vintage. Rain then fell in September (less than in 1993 and 1992), meaning loss of concentration and, the hallmark of the vintage, tannins that are hard and angular. The vintage was deemed promising after the three previous years, but the best wines, though broad and robust, are austere. The Right Bank was more consistent than the Left, with wines that have more charm. Even so, they probably should have been drunk already.

1993 ★ ★
July and August were warm and dry, and the vintage looked promising. But rain fell one week into September and continued for the rest of the month (the quantity exceeded only by 1992 in the previous 30 years). Temperatures were low, which helped stave off rot, but there was inevitable dilution. At best, the wines have an easy-drinking charm but should have been drunk already.

1992 ★
The year had the distinction of having the wettest summer in 50 years, with rain for the months June to September totaling 17.5in (446mm). Rot was a problem, as was the abundant crop. Altogether this was a vintage best forgotten.

1991 ★ ★ ★
A bad frost on the night of April 20 eliminated two-thirds of the crop. Only top estates close to

the estuary in St-Julien, Pauillac, and St-Estèphe fared well and still have wines to show. Some are good, but quantities are anecdotal.

1990 ★ ★ ★ ★ ★

The flowering was earlier than in 1989 (though drawn out and uneven) and the summer months (particularly August, which experienced drought) slightly hotter, drier, and sunnier. The grapes were harvested in good conditions, and the resulting wines are dark, rich, and generous in style. There was another big crop, and this led to a lack of concentration in some wines. Overall, it was a vintage with aging potential, but with hindsight perhaps less than 1989.

1989 ★ ★ ★ ★ ★

An early flowering and harvest and, in between, a hot, dry summer were the conditions that formed the vintage. The crop was again large. Rich, powerful, structured wines were made, with a high level of alcohol (13–13.5%) and low acidity, as in 1990. But there was also length and balance. In the majority of comparisons I've been able to make between 1989 and 1990 in recent years, 1989 has come out consistently better and appears the longer-aging wine. Sauternes was successful, as it was in 1990 and 1988.

1988 ★ ★ ★ ★

This was a late-harvest year. Picking started on September 28, compared to September 3 in 1989 and September 12 in 1990. The wines lack the opulence and maturity of the two succeeding years, but tannin and acidity were high, providing a firm, "classic" Bordeaux style for aging. The better wines are drinking well now.

1987 ★ ★

Despite a heatwave in August and September, sugar levels were low when picking started in rainy conditions in October. The wines were light and accessible and should have been drunk.

1986 ★ ★ ★ ★

From mid-June until mid-September, Bordeaux experienced hot, dry conditions. The rain when it came was welcome, though by late September a little more than required had fallen. The Merlot was harvested at the beginning of October, the Cabernet soon after. It was again a large crop (bigger than 1982 and 1985). The pick of the wines came from the Médoc, where acidity and tannin levels in the Cabernet were high, making for a firm, muscular style. The best have only just softened and will be drinking for at least another ten years.

1985 ★ ★ ★ ★

The wines offered more evident fruit and charm than the tougher 1986s. Quality was fairly consistent, the wines fine and balanced. Many should have been drunk, but the best still have fragrance, fruit, and opulence.

1984 ★

Despite a clement harvest, the poor growing season accounted for wines that were lean, green, and flat. All should have been drunk long ago, so there's little interest here.

1983 ★ ★ ★ to ★ ★ ★ ★

Late July and August were hot but overcast, resulting in the threat of rot and mildew. Rain fell in early September, but the harvest was undertaken in fine conditions (September 17–October 13). The wines were sound but lacked the panache of the 1982s or the balance and charm of the 1985s. Margaux was the exception, with better wines than in 1982, perhaps due to lower yields. The better wines are for drinking now. It was a superb Sauternes year and one that helped pull the appellation out of the doldrums.

Above: The precious remaining stocks of a legendary vintage, more special for coming at the end of World War II

1982 ★ ★ ★ ★ ★

This was the year that relaunched Bordeaux. The extraordinary thing is that it was a vintage that practically made itself (technical proficiency was nowhere near what it is today), and even top estates produced a plethoric quantity of wine (70hl/ha is an average figure). It was an early-ripening year, with a hot July, a cooler August, and a particularly hot, sunny period running September 6–20. The wines were rich in sugar and tannin but low in acidity, providing a ripe, opulent, concentrated style. Many are now past their best, but the top wines are still going strong, with several delicious now.

Earlier vintages of excellence include 1970, 1966, 1964 (Right Bank), 1961, 1959, 1955, 1953, 1949, 1947, 1945, 1929, 1928, 1926, 1921, 1920, and 1900.

The Finest 100

Producers or wines appear in alphabetical order within their category.
A star (★) indicates what is, in my opinion, the finest of the fine.

Ten Outstanding Left Bank Producers
Château Cos d'Estournel
Château Ducru-Beaucaillou
Château Haut-Brion
Château Lafite Rothschild
Château Latour★
Château Léoville-Las-Cases
Château Margaux
Château La Mission Haut-Brion
Château Mouton Rothschild
Château Palmer

Ten Outstanding Right Bank Producers
Château Angélus
Château Ausone★
Château Cheval Blanc
Château L'Eglise-Clinet
Château Figeac
Château Lafleur
Château Pavie
Pétrus
Château Trotanoy
Vieux Château Certan

Ten Top Second Labels
Alter Ego (Palmer)
Carruades de Lafite
Chapelle d'Ausone
La Chapelle de la Mission Haut-Brion
Le Clarence de Haut-Brion
Clos du Marquis (Léoville-Las-Cases)
Les Forts de Latour★
Pavillon Rouge de Château Margaux
Pensées de Lafleur
Le Petit Mouton

Ten Best Dry Whites
Château Carbonnieux
Domaine de Chevalier
Clos Floridène
Château Couhins-Lurton
Château Haut-Brion
Château Laville Haut-Brion★
Château Malartic Lagravière
Château Pape Clément
Pavillon Blanc de Château Margaux
Château Smith Haut Lafitte

Ten Top Sauternes Producers
Château Climens
Clos Haut-Peyraguey
Château Coutet
Château Doisy-Daëne
Château Guiraud
Château Lafaurie-Peyraguey
Château Rieussec
Château Suduiraut
Château La Tour Blanche
Château d'Yquem★

Ten Most Improved Châteaux (2000–10)
Château Ausone★
Château Canon
Château Calon-Ségur
Château Giscours
Château La Lagune
Château Larcis Ducasse
Château Malartic Lagravière
Château Mouton Rothschild
Château Pavie
Château Pontet-Canet

Ten Best-Value Classed-Growth Reds
Château Brane-Cantenac
Château Carbonnieux
Domaine de Chevalier
Chateau Lagrange
Château Giscours
Château Grand-Puy-Lacoste
Château Gruaud-Larose
Château Léoville Barton ★
Château Léoville Poyferré
Château Malartic Lagravière

Ten Really Good-Value Wines
Château Chasse-Spleen
Château Clarke
Clos Floridène (white) ★
Clos Puy Arnaud
Château Couhins-Lurton (white)
Fiefs de Lagrange (2nd label of Château Lagrange)
Château Fontenil
Château Moulin Haut Laroque
Château Rollan de By
Ségla (2nd label of Château Rauzan-Ségla)

Ten Exciting and Unusual Wines
Domaine de l'A
Château Bel-Air La Royère
Château Coutet Cuvée Madame
Le Dôme
L'Extravagant de Doisy-Daëne ★
Château Gilette
Girolate
Haut-Carles
Château Puygueraud Cuvée George
Roc de Cambes

Ten Best Châteaux to Visit
Château Angélus
Château Figeac
Château Giscours
Château Haut-Brion
Château Léoville Barton
Château Lynch-Bages
Château Mouton Rothschild ★
Château Pichon-Longueville
Château Pontet-Canet
Château Smith Haut Lafitte

Glossary

barrique classic 225-liter Bordeaux barrel, usually made from French oak

bâtonnage stirring of the lees of white wine (and sometimes red) during maturation to increase richness and help protect against oxidation

bien national property seized by the state during the French Revolution (usually from the Church or nobility) and then sold

Botrytis cinerea/botrytis mold or rot that in favorable weather conditions can develop into the desirable form of "noble rot" (*pourriture noble*) which desiccates and concentrates the berries, a prerequisite for great Sauternes. Conversely, in humid conditions it can develop into the undesirable form of "gray rot," which spoils the grapes

boulbènes local term in the Entre-Deux-Mers for silty soils

Brettanomyces or "Brett" is a yeast genus that can produce off-aromas or flavors in wine ("animal" or "farmyard" notes) but equally can provide added complexity at a low level

cagette shallow plastic tray used by pickers to hold grapes during the harvest

calcaire à astéries starfish limestone soil

chai cellar or store room

chair tasting term meaning flesh or fleshy

chartreuse sizeable country house, usually a low-level structure

cliquage microoxygenation of the wine while it is being matured in barrel

clos/enclos walled vineyard

complant to replace individual vines that are either missing, dead, or diseased

coulure poor fruit-set resulting in tiny berries dropping from the vine

courtier third party who arbitrates and brokers transactions between the producer and the négociant for a standard 2 percent commission

crasse de fer ferruginous sand (found in the subsoil in Pomerol)

croupe mound, knoll, or hillock

cru translated as "growth" (from the verb *croître*, to grow), referring to the specific place where the vine is grown and, ultimately, to the château that owns it

cuvaison the period of time (during fermentation) when the wine macerates on the grape skins

cuvée a blended quantity/selection of wine

cuvier/cuverie fermentation or vat room

délestage method of extraction during fermentation in which the wine is pumped out of the tank then splashed back in over the grape cap; rack and return

éclaircissage removal of grape bunches to limit yield and ventilate/improve sanitary conditions for the remaining bunches on the vine

égreneur destemming device used in the winery or on machine-harvesters

élevage aging or maturing of the wine after fermentation

en primeur (or futures) system of selling wines while they are still in barrel, roughly six to eight months after the harvest (with the bottling up to a year away)

esca one of the oldest fungal diseases of the vine for which there is still no cure

eutypiose fungal disease that rots the wood. Cabernet Sauvignon and Sauvignon Blanc are particularly susceptible

garagiste term coined in the 1990s for producer of limited-edition, tailor-made wines with little or no history

grand vin the principal wine/label at a château, as distinct from the second or third wine/label

grand vin tasting term meaning "great wine"

gras tasting term meaning "fat" or rich

lieu(x)-dit(s) specific place name(s)

liquoreux sweet, concentrated wine made from noble-rotted grapes

lutte raisonnée viticultural approach that limits the use of chemical treatments

maître de chais cellar master

malolactic fermentation natural transformation of malic acid (sharp) into lactic acid (softer). Can be induced by the addition of lactic bacteria and warming the cellar

méridional southern or Mediterranean in terms of wine style

millerandange irregular fruit-set leading to uneven berry size

molasse du Fronsadais fine-textured loamy clay (the subsoil in Fronsac and parts of St-Emilion)

oidium also known as powdery mildew, a fungal disease that attacks the green tissues of the vine

ouillage topping-up (of barrels)

palus alluvial riverbank land

pigeage punching down the grape cap during fermentation, either manually or mechanically, to submerge the grape skins

prix de sortie the opening price set by producers when they release their wine(s) on to the market en primeur

profondeur depth in a wine

Quaternary last of the major geological time periods (dating from 2.6 million years ago to the present) which includes the

Bibliography

Pleistocene epoch or Ice Age
régisseur estate manager
remontage pumping over of
must/wine to aerate and drench/
break up the grape cap
rôti tasting term to describe
the roasted notes provided by
botrytized grapes
saignée bleeding or siphoning of
a proportion of the grape juice
in a tank prior to fermentation in
order to concentrate the must
sous-bois tasting term meaning
undergrowth (the notion of a
leafy forest floor)
sous marc microoxygenation of
the wine during post-(alcoholic)
fermentation maceration
soutirage racking
sucrosité sweetness
surmaturité overripeness
200% new oak the process in
which a young wine is racked
from 100% new oak barrels into
other 100% new oak barrels
taille bordelaise traditional
method of cane pruning in the
Médoc and Graves (now also
used on the Right Bank) which
resembles Guyot *double* without
the additional tiny spur or *cot*
trie sorting or selective picking
TCA short for
2,4,6-trichloroanisole, the musty-
smelling compound usually
associated with cork taint
tisane infusion
typicité typicity (i.e. a wine
showing the typical traits of its
origin or style)
vendange harvest
vigneron wine grower

Stephen Brook,
*Bordeaux: People, Power and
Politics*
(Mitchell Beazley, London; 2001)

Stephen Brook,
The Complete Bordeaux
(Mitchell Beazley, London; 2007)

Oz Clarke,
Bordeaux (2nd edition)
(Pavilion Books, London; 2008)

Charles Cocks and Edouard
Féret,
Bordeaux et Ses Vins
(18th edition)
(Editions Féret, Bordeaux; 2007)

Jean Cordeau,
"Cépages Rouges en Bordelais",
*Un Raisin de Qualité: De la Vigne
à la Cuve* (pp.67–76); *Journal
International des Sciences de la
Vigne et du Vin* (Hors Série)
(Vigne et Vin Publications
International, Bordeaux; 2001)

Hugh Johnson,
The Story of Wine
(Mitchell Beazley, London; 1989)

James Lawther,
The Heart of Bordeaux
(Stewart, Tabori & Chang, New
York; 2009)

Cornelis (Kees) van Leeuwen,
"Choix du Cépage en Fonction
du Terroir dans le Bordelais",
*Un Raisin de Qualité: De la Vigne
à la Cuve* (pp.97–102); *Journal
International des Sciences de la
Vigne et du Vin* (Hors Série)
(Vigne et Vin Publications
International, Bordeaux; 2001)

Dewey Markham Jr,
*1855: A History of the Bordeaux
Classification*
(John Wiley & Sons, New York;
1998)

Robert M Parker Jr,
Bordeaux (2nd edition)
(Simon & Schuster, New York;
1991)

David Peppercorn,
Bordeaux (2nd edition)
(Faber & Faber, London; 1991)

Jean-Philippe Roby and Cornelis
(Kees) van Leeuwen,
"Plantation de la Vigne: Aspects
Techniques et Economiques",
*Un Raisin de Qualité: De la Vigne
à la Cuve* (pp.117–28); *Journal
International des Sciences de la
Vigne et du Vin* (Hors Série)
(Vigne et Vin Publications
International, Bordeaux; 2001)

Alain Reynier,
Manuel de Viticulture
(10th edition)
(Editions Tec & Doc, Paris; 2007)

James E Wilson,
Terroir
(University of California Press,
Berkeley; 1998)

Index

Author's Acknowledgments

My thanks to Jean Cordeau, formerly in charge of the Vigne section at the Chambre d'Agriculture de la Gironde, and Kees van Leeuwen, professor of viticulture at Bordeaux University (ENITA), for their help and guidance in matters relating to viticulture, climate, and soil in Bordeaux. I would also like to extend my thanks to all the owners, managers, winemakers, and consultants who took the time to share their knowledge during my research for this book.

Photographic Credits

All photography by Jon Wyand, with the following exceptions:
Pages 6–7: Claude Joseph Vernet, *Second View of the Port of Bordeaux Taken from the Château Trompette*, Musée de la Marine, Paris; Roger-Viollet, Paris / The Bridgeman Art Library
Page 8: Effigy of Eleanor of Aquitaine and Henry II, Fontevrault Abbey, France; The Bridgeman Art Library
Page 9: Anonymous, *Arnaud III de Pontac*, Château Haut-Brion; Domaine Clarence Dillon
Page 12: Léon Joseph Florentin Bonnat, *Isaac Peréire*; Château de Versailles, France; Lauros / Giraudon / The Bridgeman Art Library
Page 24: Merlot; P Viala & V Vermorel, *Traité Général de Viticulture: Ampélographie*, with illustrations by A Kreyder & J Troncy (Masson, Paris; 1901–10); The Art Archive / Alfredo Dagli Orti
Page 25: Sauvignon Blanc; P Viala & V Vermorel, *Traité Général de Viticulture: Ampélographie*, with illustrations by A Kreyder & J Troncy (Masson, Paris; 1901–10); The Art Archive / Alfredo Dagli Orti
Page 47: Anonymous, *The Palais de l'Industrie at the Exposition Universelle of 1855*, Musée de la Ville de Paris, Musée Carnavalet, Paris; Archives Charmet / The Bridgeman Art Library
Page 90: Château Pichon Comtesse de Lalande; Château Pichon Comtesse de Lalande
Page 137: Jean Guyon; Domaines Rollan de By
Page 163: The Vat Room at Domaine de Chevalier; Domaine de Chevalier
Page 297: Château Suduiraut; Château Suduiraut / Vincent Bengold